S0-AXW-026

88   40

The WORLD Anthology

Globe Book Company, Inc.
New York / Cleveland / Toronto

The *WORLD* Anthology

RICHFIELD HIGH SCHOOL

Robert R. Potter
Roger B. Goodman

Robert R. Potter has been a teacher of English in the New York City School System, a research associate for Project English at Hunter College, and a teacher of English at the Litchfield High School in Litchfield, Connecticut. He has held professorships at the State University of New York and the University of Connecticut.

Dr. Potter received his B.S. from the Columbia University School of General Studies and his M.A. and Ed.D. from Teachers College, Columbia University. He is the author of Globe's *Myths and Folktales Around the World, The Reading Road to Writing, Making Sense, A Better Reading Workshop, Writing Sense, Writing a Research Paper, Language Workshop, Tales of Mystery and the Unknown, The Reader's Anthology, The American Anthology*, and co-author of *The Collector's Anthology.*

Robert B. Goodman has been an English teacher in the New York City School System and for 10 years was Chairman of the Department of English at Stuyvesant High School. He received his B.S.S. from the City College of New York and his M.A. from Columbia University, and is the author, also, of Globe's *World-Wide Short Stories* and *A Matter for Judgment.*

Consultants

Jonathan Swift, Director, School of Global Education, Livonia Public Schools, Livonia, Michigan, and past Chair, Secondary Section, National Council of Teachers of English

Stephanie Whitworth, Reading Consultant, Fulton County Schools, Atlanta, Georgia

Jesse Perry, Program Manager, English Language Arts, San Diego Unified School District, San Diego, California, and member of the National Council of Teachers of English Commission on the English language

Philip W. Hart, English Teacher, North High School, Phoenix, Arizona

Jeannine Atkins, English Teacher, Housatonic Valley Regional High School, Falls Village, Connecticut

Ruth D. McCubbrey, English Teacher, Tamalpais High School, Mill Valley, California

Editor: Jeanne Barrett
Photo Editor: Adelaide Garvin Ungerland
Art Director: Lee Rosenberg
Cover Design: Bass and Goldman Associates
Text Design: Celine Brandes

Acknowledgments and credits appear on pages 399–402.

ISBN: 0-87065-036-X

Copyright © 1987 by Globe Book Company, Inc., 50 West 23rd Street, New York, N.Y. 10010. All rights reserved. No part of this book may be kept in an information storage or retrieval system, transmitted or reproduced in any form or by any means without the prior written permission of the publisher. Published simultaneously in Canada by Globe/Modern Curriculum Press.

PRINTED IN THE UNITED STATES OF AMERICA   9 8 7 6 5 4 3 2 1

CONTENTS

UNIT 1: FIRST THINGS FIRST

U N I T 2: TANGLES AND TEASERS

U N I T 3: LOOKING INTO LIFE

UNIT 4: EXPLORING CONFLICTS

UNIT 5:   SOME TEARS, SOME LAUGHTER

U N I T 6:   MORE THAN MEETS THE EYE

SKILL DEVELOPMENT

INTRODUCTION

Almost all that's important in the study of literature can be summed up in a single word: React.

An author's job is to use the best words possible to express what he or she has seen, thought, and felt. A reader's job is to react to these visions, these thoughts, and these feelings in terms of previous experience. Because reading is reacting, this introduction isn't going to *say* much more about literature. Instead, it's going to ask you to *react* to a poem.

Arthur O'Shaughnessy, an Irish poet of the last century, saw the task of the writer in a special way.

> We are the music-makers,
>   And we are the dreamers of dreams,
> Wandering by lone sea-breakers,
>   And sitting by desolate streams;
> World-losers and world-forsakers,
>   On whom the pale moon gleams:
> Yet we are the movers and shakers
>   Of the world forever, it seems.

(a) How does Arthur O'Shaughnessy define poets? (b) Do you think this is an appropriate definition, or might you add something to it? Explain your response. (c) According to the poet, are writers of real importance to the world? Do you agree?

To help you react to literature, this book contains questions that encourage recall and analysis, as well as exercises that require you to express your thoughts in writting. Throughout the book literary terms are introduced in order to give you a vocabulary with which to examine and discuss the selections. You'll also find that words you may not know are defined right on the bottom of the page. Words in **bold type** are tested in the Vocabulary and Skill Reviews that occur at intervals throughout the book. For reference, the special terms are also listed in the Glossary of Terms at the back of the book.

For the writer, literature is a process of creation. For the reader, it is a process of re-creation. It is you, the reader, who make the difference.

UNIT · 1

FIRST THINGS
F I R S T

When you hear the expression "first things first," what comes to mind? The answer to this question depends on you—who you are and what you hope to achieve. The answer, you'll discover, will be as unique as your own personality.

As you consider what's first in your own life, you might think about growing up, learning to get along with others, and gaining a better understanding of yourself and the world around you. In a way, the selections in this unit will focus on these topics and will help you decide what's first and most important to you.

Anton Chekhov (1860-1904)

A scene from Chekhov's play *Three Sisters*

The life of Anton Chekhov is a study in shattered dreams. He prepared for one career, yet practiced another. He married a star, but found himself living apart in a shadow. He sought health in a place where Death stood waiting. Small wonder that many of Chekhov's masterpieces are bittersweet, tender treatments of what it means to be a human being.

The son of a merchant and the grandson of a serf, Chekhov grew up on Taganrog, in the south of Russia. He started writing to earn money while studying to be a doctor at the University of Moscow. He wrote funny stories and short jokes for magazines and newspapers. After graduation, he found himself more interested in writing than in caring for the sick. Also, poor health prevented his living the active life of a doctor. The last half of his short life was a constant battle with tuberculosis. In 1901 he married an actress in the Moscow Art Theater, but the couple lived apart much of the time because the author could not tolerate the cold Moscow climate. In 1904 he went to a health resort in Baden-weiler, Germany, where his disease finally overcame him.

Most of Chekhov's stories and plays carry a sad but tender message. As he viewed life, people want to be happy but cannot escape loneliness and defeat. Often they cannot communicate with each other. They can talk and dream endlessly, but are incapable of action. They fill their lives with unimportant things, and then wonder why they find themselves in hopeless situations. Yet at their best, people can view their lives with humor and enjoy a laugh or two. The author's usual tone is one of sympathy, not bitterness.

What single fact in Chekhov's life may have caused him to often view life as hopeless?

THE BET

by Anton Chekhov

▶ What should be the penalty for serious crimes? People have long debated this question. That's one reason this story by the Russian author Anton Chekhov has remained popular for so many years. But as you'll discover, there's another reason, too. For the tale is not about punishment, really, but about reward.

It was a dark autumn night. The old banker was pacing fretfully from corner to corner in his room, recalling to his mind the party he had given in the autumn 15 years before.

There had been many clever people at that party, and there was much good talk. They talked among other things of capital punishment. The guests for the most part disapproved of it. They found it old-fashioned and evil as a form of punishment. They thought it had no place in a country that called itself Christian. Some of them thought that capital punishment should be replaced right away with life in prison.

"I don't agree with you," said the host. "In my opinion, capital punishment is really kinder than life in prison. Execution kills instantly; prison kills by degrees. Now, which is better? To kill you in a few seconds, or to draw the life out of you for years and years?"

"One's as bad as the other," said one of the guests. "Their purpose is the same, to take away life. The government is not God. It has no right to take a human life. It should not take away what it cannot give back."

Among the company was a young lawyer, a man about 25. "Both are evil," he stated. "But if offered the choice between them, I would definitely take prison. It's better to live somehow than not to live at all."

"Nonsense!"

"It is so!"

- capital (KAP i tul) involving loss of life
- fretfully (FRET ful ee) in an anxious, worried way
- degrees (di GREEZ) small stages or steps

"No!"

"Yes!"

The banker, who was then younger and more nervous, suddenly lost his temper. He banged his fist on the table. Turning to the young lawyer, he cried out:

"It's a lie! I bet you two million you couldn't stay in a prison cell, even for five years."

"Do you mean that?" asked the lawyer.

The banker nodded eagerly, his face red.

"Then I accept your bet," the lawyer said simply. "But I'll stay not five years but 15."

"Fifteen! Fifteen!" cried the banker. He was now wild, as though he had already won the bet. "Done, then. The people here are our witnesses. I stake two million rubles. You stake 15 years of your freedom."

So this foolish, senseless bet came to pass. At the time, the banker had too many millions to count. He was beside himself with joy. All through dinner he kept talking about the bet. He said to the lawyer jokingly:

"Come to your senses, young man. It's not too late yet. Two million is nothing to me. But you stand to lose three or four of the best years of your life. I say three or four, not 15. You'll never stick the incarceration out longer than that, I can tell you. And they'll just be wasted years. Not the smallest coin do I give you if you leave earlier than 15 years. Why, just think of it! My jail will have no bars, no locks. You'll be able to walk out of it any time you want to, and that thought will be like poison to you. So you will walk out; I know that. Sooner or later, you'll walk out!"

And now the banker, pacing from corner to corner, recalled all this and asked himself:

"Why did I make this bet? What's the good? The lawyer loses 15 years of his life, and I throw away two million. That bet was a mistake. On my part, it was the foolishness of a well-fed man. On the lawyer's part, it was pure greed for gold."

He remembered further what happened after the evening party. It was decided that the "prison" would be in the garden wing of the banker's house. For 15 years the lawyer was not to pass out through its door. He was not to see living people, or even

---

- **stake** (STAYK) bet
- **ruble** (ROO bul) unit of Russian money
- **incarceration** (in KAR suh RAY shun) imprisonment; confinement

to hear a human voice. He was not to receive letters or newspapers. Musical instruments, however, were to be permitted. He could also read books and write letters, and some other things he could order. He had only to pass his order note through a special window, and a guard would bring anything allowed.

Thus, the smallest details of the bet were discussed and settled. At noon on November 14, 1870, the prison term began. It was to last until noon on November 14, 1885. The lawyer must make no attempt to break the rules agreed upon. Any attempt to escape, even for two minutes, would free the banker from having to pay the two million.

The lawyer's first year, as far as it was possible to judge from his short notes, was one of suffering. He grew lonely and bored. From his wing day and night came the sound of the piano. Short, easy novels were his only reading—love stories, crime, and comedy.

In the second year the piano was heard no more. The lawyer asked only for classics. But by the fifth year, music was heard again. Guards who peeked into his room said that he yawned often and talked angrily to himself. Books he did not read now. Sometimes at night he would sit down to write. He would write for a long time, and then tear it all up in the morning. More than once he was heard to weep.

• **classic** (KLAS ik) famous and important book

5

In the second half of the sixth year, the prisoner began zealously to study languages, philosophy, and history. He fell on these subjects with hunger. The banker hardly had time to get books enough for him. In four years' time, about 600 volumes were brought at his request. And later on, after the tenth year, the lawyer sat before his table and read only the New Testament. Then he went on to the history of religions.

During the last two years the prisoner read a huge amount, quite haphazardly. He would ask for books on science, and then it would be Shakespeare. Notes used to come from him asking at the same time for books on chemistry, theology, and medicine, as well as for a novel. He read as though he were swimming in a sea among broken pieces of wreckage. In his desire to save his life, he was eagerly grasping at one thing after another.

The banker recalled all this, and thought:

"Tomorrow at noon he receives his freedom. Under the agreement, I shall have to pay him two million. But if I pay, it's all over with me. I shall be ruined forever. . . ."

Fifteen years before he had had too much money to count. But now, he did not know which he had more of, money or debts. He had gambled on the stock market—and lost. He had made business deals that turned sour. The fearless, proud man of business had become an ordinary person, trembling with worry about money.

"That cursed bet!" murmured the old man. "Why didn't the lawyer die? He's only 40 years old. He will take all my money, and then go on and marry and enjoy life. To him, I will look like an envious beggar, and he will say, 'Look, let me help you. After all, I owe my happiness to your money.' Oh, such shame!"

"Ruin and shame," the banker went on. "No—it's too much. Too much for anyone. I must escape ruin and shame, even if he has to die—*even if he has to die!*"

The clock struck three. The banker stood listening. In the house everyone was asleep, and he could hear only the frozen trees whining outside the windows. He put on his overcoat and went out of the house, into the garden, dark and cold. It was raining, and a damp wind argued with the noisy trees. Nearing the

---

- zealously (ZEL us lee) eagerly; with enthusiasm
- **philosophy** (fi LOS uh fee) study of important ideas
- haphazardly (hap HAZ urd lee) randomly; in an unplanned way
- theology (thee OL uh jee) study of religion

garden wing, he called the guard twice. There was no answer. "Good," the banker thought. Evidently the guard had taken shelter from the bad weather. The man was probably sleeping in the kitchen or greenhouse.

"If I have the courage to kill this man," thought the old banker, "the guard will get the blame."

In the darkness he groped for the door. It opened without a sound. In the prisoner's room a candle was burning dimly. The prisoner sat by the table. Only his back, the hair on his head, and his hands were visible. Open books lay everywhere—on the table, on the two chairs, on the carpet.

Five minutes passed, and the prisoner never once stirred. "Probably asleep at last," thought the old banker, and he stepped forward. Before him, at the table, sat a man unlike an ordinary human being. It was a skeleton, with tight skin, long curly hair like a woman's, and a shaggy beard. The face was yellow, the cheeks sunken. The hands were so long and skinny that they were painful to look upon. His hair was already silvering with gray, and no one who looked at the thin aging face would have believed that he was only 40 years old. On the table, before his bent head, lay a sheet of paper covered with tiny handwriting.

"Poor devil," thought the banker. "He's asleep, and probably seeing millions in his dreams. I only have to throw this half-dead thing on the bed. Then I'll smother him a moment with the pillow. But first, let's read what he has written here."

His eyes dropped to the paper:

Tomorrow, at noon, I am to have my freedom. I shall have the right to mix with people. But before I leave this room, I want to say a few words to you. My conscience is clear, and I stand before God, who sees me. I declare to you that I despise all that most people call the blessings of the world.

For 15 years I have studied earthly life. In your books I hunted deer and sang songs. In your books I climbed Mt. Blanc. I saw from there how the sun rose in the morning. . . . In your books I worked miracles, burned cities to the ground, preached new religions, conquered whole countries. . . .

Your books gave me wisdom. I know that I am cleverer than you all. You are mad, and gone the wrong way. You worship things, not ideas. You take falsehood for truth and ugliness for beauty. So do I marvel at you, you who have

---

• **grope** (GROHP) feel about with the hands

7

traded heaven for earth. I do not want to understand you.

To show that I despise all that you live by, I give up the two million I once so desired. Can your money buy wisdom? No. I shall come out of here by my own volition five minutes before noon tomorrow. I shall thus break our agreement.

When he had read this, the banker kissed the head of the strange man. He began to weep, and soon he went out of the wing. Never, not even after his terrible losses in the stock market, had he felt such hatred for himself. Back in his own room, he lay down on the bed, but tears of guilt kept him a long time from sleeping.

The banker slept late the next morning. About noon the poor guard came running to him. The prisoner had escaped! He had walked out into the garden! He had gone to the gate and disappeared!

The banker instantly went with his servants to the wing. Yes, the prisoner was gone. To avoid rumors, he picked up the note on the table. He made two neat folds. And on his return, he locked it in his safe.

• volition (voh LISH un) choice; decision

ALL THINGS CONSIDERED ————————————

1. Early in the story, the lawyer states, "It's better to live somehow than not to live at all." By the end of the story, the lawyer has (a) proved that the statement is false. (b) shown that the statement is true for himself as an individual. (c) used the statement to change the banker's whole life.

2. During his imprisonment, the lawyer is denied (a) personal contacts and knowledge of current events. (b) the classics of literature. (c) music of any kind.

3. A note written by the prisoner (a) secures his early release. (b) causes the banker to enter his room. (c) curses the errors of the human race.

4. If the note had not been written, the banker (a) would never have gone to the prisoner's room. (b) would probably have been killed. (c) would probably have killed the prisoner.

5. If you read between the lines, it seems clear that Anton Chekhov, the author, approves of (a) the terms of the bet. (b) the lawyer's final statement about life. (c) the banker's decision to protect his money at any cost.

THINKING IT THROUGH ————————————

1. In your opinion, why did the lawyer accept the bet in the first place? To prove that he could endure the prison term? To make a fortune in rubles? Both reasons? Explain.

2. Go back and trace the lawyer's activities through the 15-year jail term. How do they reveal changes in the lawyer himself?

3. The story contrasts people who value wisdom and ideas with those who value money and things. (a) On which side of this contrast does Chekhov put the lawyer and the banker? (b) If you were a character in the story, which side of the contrast would you be on, or would it somehow be possible to be on both sides at once? (c) Do you think Chekhov's characters are at all like people you might meet today? Explain.

4. Suppose that at the age of 25, you accept such a bet. The reward is two million *dollars*, and the setting is modern America. (Add radio, TV, and magazines to the list of *no*'s.) (a) Would you stay the 15 years? If so, how do you think the experience would cause you to change? (b) If you would walk out, when would this happen, and why?

5. How might Anton Chekhov's own life (see page 2) have led him to hold ideas such as those expressed in the story?

6. A scene from an earlier time that is inserted into a story is called a *flashback*. What is the first flashback in "The Bet"?

Literary Skills

Elements of the Short Story

How can you improve your understanding of short stories? One good way is to practice thinking of the four necessary parts, or **elements, of the short story:** *setting, characters, plot,* and *theme.* Since the four elements always operate together, they are best studied together in connection with a single story.

Setting

The setting of a story, of course, is the *place* where it happens. But the setting also includes the *time,* since places may change greatly from one period to another. Furthermore, the setting includes certain *natural events.* In many stories, for instance, the weather is an important element.

1. One problem Chekhov faced in writing "The Bet" was to make the reader believe that the seemingly unlikely bet would, in fact, have been made. What setting did Chekhov create, and how does it make the action seem more believable?
2. (a) What is the weather like on the night when the story begins? (b) How does this contribute to the mood of the story?
3. Even without the background information, you might have guessed that the setting is pre-Communist Russia, not the modern USSR. What details in the story support this view?

Characters

Most people in stories can be called either *flat* or *rounded* characters. Some flat characters can be considered *stere-* otypes—one dimensional characters that most readers recognize at once: the greedy businessman, the kind old grandmother, the unreliable teenager. Rounded characters, on the other hand, are not types but real individuals. You haven't met them before in your reading, and you don't know what they will do when faced with certain problems. In many stories, the main character is rounded and the others are flat.

4. Would you call the banker in "The Bet" a stereotype or a rounded character? Why?
5. For what reasons would you consider the lawyer a rounded character?
6. Is a character who changes or learns an important lesson in a story more likely to be a rounded character or a stereotype? Explain.

Plot

The plot of a story is a series of events. As the plot unfolds, the reader not only learns *what* happens, but also notices the *way* things happen. To begin with, every story has to contain a **conflict** of some kind—a meeting of two opposing forces. Conflicts can be (a) between people, (b) within a single person (psychological conflict), (c) between people and things, and (d) between people and nature.

7. (a) What conflict in the party scene starts the action in "The Bet"? (b) Which kind of conflict is this (*a, b, c,* or *d,* above)?
8. What other kind of conflict is involved in "The Bet"?

Once a conflict is established, the story has to develop. Readers must continue to ask themselves, "What will happen next?" Early in a story, an important **plot question** is usually raised in the reader's mind. The action that follows and answers this question can either end the story or lead to still another question. Long stories often contain a number of questions. The **rising action** in such a story leads finally to an exciting **climax,** the action that answers the big plot question at or near the end.

9. What are at least two plot questions in "The Bet"? That is, what questions did the author raise in your mind to keep you reading?
10. What part of "The Bet" would you consider the climax? In other words, what action toward the end seemed to be the high point of the whole story?

Theme

The theme of a story is its message, meaning, or main idea. In many cases, the theme is what the main character learns, or at least what the reader learns.

11. Here are three possible themes for "The Bet." In your opinion, which is the main theme? Explain.
   (a) Capital punishment is wrong.
   (b) People should spend more time alone.
   (c) The truly wise person values ideas more than objects.

Composition

1. Suppose you were a teacher preparing a true-false test on "The Bet." Write five true-false questions that might be part of such a test. At least two of your statements should be true, and at least two false.

2. Write a paragraph explaining who you would rather be at the end of the story, the lawyer or the banker. First give some favorable traits of the character of your choice, then give some unfavorable traits of the other. Think about such details as physical appearance, wealth, knowledge, wisdom, occupational skills, and the ability to get along with other people.

▶ Here's a poem about brotherhood that may have a special meaning for you. It will help your understanding to know that the poet was born in South Africa in 1931.

WHERE THE RAINBOW ENDS

by Richard Rive

Where the rainbow ends
There's going to be a place, brother,
Where the world can sing all sorts of songs,
And we're going to sing together, brother,

5   You and I, though you're white and I'm not.
It's going to be a sad song, brother,
Because we don't know the tune,
And it's a difficult tune to learn.
But we can learn, brother, you and I.

10   There's no such tune as a black tune.
There's no such tune as a white tune.
There's only music, brother.
And it's music we're going to sing
Where the rainbow ends.

WAYS OF KNOWING*

1. (a) What is commonly believed to be found at the end of a rainbow? (b) How does this relate to the poem?
2. In lines 7 and 8, the poet uses the word "tune" to express a much wider meaning. Just what does he mean?
3. In a single sentence, state the *theme* (see page 11) of the poem.
4. With some poems, the **poet** (person who wrote the words) seems to be quite different from the **speaker** (the "I" voice in the poem). In this poem, do you think the poet and speaker are different, or are they really one and the same person? Explain.

---

*"A poem is a way of knowing."—John Hall Wheelock

THE NECKLACE

by Guy de Maupassant

▶ The French author Guy de Maupassant (1850–1893) wrote several hundred short stories. There is one story, however, that many readers think of whenever the author's name is mentioned. It is his famous story, "The Necklace."

She was one of those pretty and charming girls who are sometimes, as if by a mistake of fate, born into a family of quite ordinary people. She had little money and less hope. She had no way of being known in society. There was just no chance for her to meet and marry any rich and handsome man, so she let herself be married to a plebeian office worker in the Department of Education.

She dressed plainly because she could not dress well. Feeling herself born for the best that life had to offer, she suffered endlessly. She suffered from the poverty of her apartment. The walls were dirty, the chairs worn out, and the curtains ugly. All these things another young bride might not have minded at all. But not she! Her surroundings tortured her and made her angry. She dreamed often of luxuries, of candlelight dinners, of servants. She thought of huge rooms filled at five o'clock with good friends talking together. She imagined herself in conversation with famous and powerful men.

Yet her own husband was hardly a famous or a powerful man. He would come home for dinner and lift the lid on the pot. "Ah, the good soup!" he would say. "I don't know of anything better than that." And she would think of dainty dinners, of shining silverware. Rows of expensive plates would flash through her mind. On them would be the pink flesh of a trout or the wings of a quail.

She had no fine dress, no jewels, nothing. And she loved nothing but things like those. She felt that she was made for them. She would so have liked to please. She wanted to be envied, to be charming, to be a popular hostess.

She had a friend, a former schoolmate, who was rich. But she went to see this friend less and less, for she suffered so much when she came back to her own house.

But one evening, her husband came home with a smile on his face. He held a large envelope in his hand.

"Here," he said, "this is something for you."

She tore the paper quickly. In the envelope was a printed card with these words:

• plebeian (pluh BEE un) common; ordinary

THE SECRETARY OF EDUCATION AND MME
GEORGES RAMPONNEAU
REQUEST THE HONOR OF YOUR COMPANY IN
THE GRAND HALL ON
MONDAY EVENING, JANUARY 18TH.

She threw the invitation on the table with a heavy sigh. Her husband was surprised. He had expected her to be delighted.

"What do you want me to do with that?" she murmured.

"But, my dear, I thought you would be glad. You never go out, and this is a good chance. I had awful trouble getting it. Everyone wants to go, but not many of the office staff have been invited. It is a great honor for us. All the important people in Paris will be there."

She looked at him with troubled eyes. "And what do you want me to put on my back?"

He had not thought of that. "Why," he stammered, "the dress you always go out in. It looks very fine, to me." He stopped, seeing that his wife was crying. Two great tears descended slowly from the corners of her eyes to the corners of her mouth.

"What's the matter?" he asked. "What's the matter?"

She wiped one wet cheek with the back of her hand. Soon she had won the battle with her tears. "Nothing," she replied in a calm voice. "Only I have no dress. That means I can't go to this ball. Give your card to some colleague whose wife is better equipped than I."

He was in despair. "Come, let's see Mathilde," he stuttered. "How much would it cost? A suitable dress. Something very simple that you could wear on other occasions."

- Mme (mah DAHM) French term for *Mrs.*
- **colleague** (KOL eeg) professional or office associate

14

She thought for several seconds. How much could she ask for without getting a quick refusal? How much would he agree to, and how much would make him upset?

"I don't know, exactly," she finally replied. "But I think I could manage it with four hundred francs."

He grew a little pale. Four hundred francs was just what he had saved up to buy a shotgun. He had planned to do a little shooting with some friends in the spring.

But he said:

"All right. I'll give you four hundred francs. And try to have a pretty dress."

The day of the ball loomed ever nearer. Mathilde Loisel's dress was ready, but she seemed sad, uneasy, anxious. Her husband said to her one evening:

"What's the matter? Come, you've been so quiet these last few days."

"It annoys me," she said, "not to have a jewel. Not a single stone, even. Nothing to put on. I shall look so out of place. I'd almost rather not go at all."

"You might wear flowers," he suggested. "They're in style this time of year. For 10 francs you can get two or three roses."

She was not at all sure. "No," she sighed. "There's nothing worse than to look poor among other women who are rich."

"But there's your friend, Mme Forestier!" he cried. "Ask her to lend you some jewels. You're still good friends enough for her to do that."

"That's true," she said, smiling. "I never thought of that."

The next day she went to her friend and explained her problem.

Mme Forestier went to a closet with a glass door. She took out a large jewel box, opened it, and brought it back.

"Choose, my dear," Mme Forestier said.

Mathilde first of all saw some bracelets. Then a pearl necklace and a cross of gold and precious stones. She tried on the jewelry standing before the mirror. Everything looked so beautiful! It was impossible for her to make up her mind. She kept asking, "Have you any more?"

"Why, yes, take your time. I don't know what you like."

All of a sudden she discovered, in a black satin box, a superb necklace of diamonds. Her heart began to beat with desire. Her hand trembled as she took the sparkling strand. She fastened it around her throat. Her eyes would not move from the mirror.

"Can you lend me this?" she gasped finally. "Only this?"

"Why, yes, certainly."

She sprang up and kissed her friend with joy. Then she fled clutching her treasure.

The day of the ball arrived. Mathilde Loisel made a great success.

- **franc** (FRANK) unit of French money (worth about 25¢ at the time of the story)
- **loom** (LOOM) rise up threateningly
- **strand** (STRAND) string of beads or gems

She looked prettier than them all. She was brilliant, smiling, and crazy with joy. The important men looked at her, asked her name, wanted an introduction, a chance to dance. And she danced and danced, made delirious by pleasure. In the glory of success, she forgot all. She danced in a cloud of happiness, for the whole ball seemed to belong to her. She had a sense of complete victory.

She turned away from the ball at about four o'clock in the morning. Her husband had been sleeping since midnight. She found him in a little coat room, with three other gentlemen whose wives were having a very good time.

"Wait a bit," he said, wiping sleep from his eyes. "You'll catch cold outside. I'll go and call a cab."

But she did not listen. They rapidly descended the stairs. When they got to the street, there was no cab to be seen. Shivering with cold, they began to search for one. It took a long time.

Finally they arrived at their door. Feeling sad, they climbed up the stairs. All was ended for her. And as for him, he groaned that he must be at work at ten o'clock.

She removed her coat before the mirror. This would be her last chance to see herself in all her resplendent glory. But suddenly she cried out. She no longer had the necklace around her neck!

Her husband was already half undressed. "What's the matter?" he demanded.

She turned madly toward him. "I have— I have— I've lost Mme Forestier's necklace!"

"What? How? Impossible!" He stood up, alarmed.

And they looked in the folds of her dress. In the folds of her coat. In her pockets. Everywhere. They did not find it.

"You're sure you had it on when you left the ball?" he asked.

"Yes. I felt it coming down the stairs."

"But on the street we would have heard it fall. You must have lost it in the cab."

"Yes, probably. Did you notice the number?"

"No. And you?"

---

* **delirious** (di LEER ee us) wildly excited
* **resplendent** (ri SPLEN dunt) dazzling; gorgeous

"No."

They looked at one another, horrified. At last Loisel put on his clothes.

"I'll go back on foot," he said. "I'll go over the whole route. Maybe I can find it."

And he went out. She sat waiting on a chair in her ball dress, overwhelmed, without fire, without a thought. She lacked the strength to go to bed.

Her husband came back about seven o'clock. He had found nothing.

He went to Police Headquarters. He went to the newspapers, to offer a reward. He went to the cab companies.

She waited all day, in the same state of unrelieved apprehension.

Loisel returned at night with a hollow, pale face. He had discovered nothing.

"You must write to your friend," he said. "Tell her that you have broken the clasp of the necklace. You are having it fixed. That, at least, will give us some time."

She wrote at his dictation.

At the end of a week they had lost all hope. Loisel, who had aged five years, declared:

"We must find a way to replace that necklace."

The next day they took the box that had held the necklace. They went to the jeweler whose name was found inside. He examined his records.

"It was not I who sold that necklace," the jeweler finally announced. "I must simply have sold the case."

Then they went from jeweler to jeweler, searching for a necklace just like the other. Both were sick with worry and fear. At last they found a string of diamonds that seemed just right. As far as they remembered, it was exactly like the one that had been lost. The jeweler said it was worth 40,000, but they could have it for 36.

So they begged the jeweler not to sell it for three days. Then they faced the question of finding the money. Loisel had a little that his father had left him and thought he could borrow the rest.

He did borrow, asking for a thousand here, 500 there. To everyone he gave signed promises to repay, even to criminals. He risked all the rest of his life, and then signed away another life. All that mattered was to get the 36,000 together. It took time, but on the afternoon of the third day they were able to put the money down on the jeweler's counter.

Immediately, Mme Loisel left for Mme Forestier's with the necklace. She did not find her friend in a convivial mood.

"You should have returned it sooner," Mme Forestier said icily. "I might have needed it."

Mme Forestier did not open the case, as her friend had feared. If she had noticed a difference, what would she have thought? What would she have said? Would she not have taken Mme Loisel for a thief?

Mme Loisel now began to know the horrible existence of the needy. That dreadful debt must be paid. And, she declared, she would help pay it. They

---

* apprehension (ap ri HEN shun) dread of coming event
* convivial (kun VIV ee ul) very friendly; agreeable

gave up their small apartment and moved into a small attic under a roof.

She soon came to know what heavy housework meant. She learned the hated cares of the kitchen. She washed dishes, using her rosy nails on greasy pots and pans. She washed dirty clothes. She carried out garbage. She went shopping, insulting storekeepers and looking for bargains.

Each month they had to pay some debts. Others they managed to renew, gaining more time.

Her husband worked in the evening, doing anything and everything that would bring in a little money. Late at night he often copied manuscripts for a pittance per page.

And this life lasted 10 years.

At the end of 10 years they had paid back everything. They had paid back the 36,000, and almost again as much, for the high interest on the money.

Mme Loisel looked old now. She became strong and hard and rough. With messy hair and dirty skirt and red hands, she talked loudly while washing floors with great swishes of water. But sometimes, when she sat home alone, unable to find work, her thoughts went back in time. Sitting next to the window, she thought of that enthralling evening of long ago. She dreamed again of that ball where she had been so beautiful. . . .

What would have happened if she had not lost that necklace? Who knows? Who knows? Life is strange and full of changes. How little a thing can make

the difference? How little a thing is needed for us to be lost or to be saved?

One Sunday Mme Loisel wanted to refresh herself from the labors of the week. She decided to go for a walk. She soon found herself on the Champs Élysées, the finest street in Paris. In front of her she noticed a woman leading a child. It was Mme Forestier, still young, still beautiful, still charming.

Mme Loisel felt thrilled. Did she dare to speak to her? Yes, certainly. Now that she had paid for losing the necklace, she was going to tell her all about it. Why not?

She went up.

"Hello, Jeanne."

The other was astonished to hear her first name spoken by a common stranger. She did not recognize Mathilde at all, and stammered:

"But— I do not know— You must be mistaken."

"No. I am Mathilde Loisel."

Her friend cried out. "Oh! My poor Mathilde! How you have changed!"

"Yes, I have had bad days since I last saw you."

"Oh? How so?"

"Do you remember that diamond necklace you once lent me?"

"Yes. Well?"

"Well, I lost it."

"What do you mean? You brought it back."

"I brought you back another just like it. And for this we have been 10 years paying. You can understand that it was not easy for us. At last it is

- pittance (PIT uns) very small amount of money
- **interest** (IN tur est) cost of borrowed money
- enthralling (en THRAWL ing) enchanting; wonderful

ended, and I am very glad."

Mme Forestier had stopped.

"You say that you bought a diamond necklace to replace mine?"

"Yes. You never noticed it, then! We thought they were exactly alike." And

Mme. Loisel smiled with a proud joy.

Mme. Forestier, strongly moved, took her friend's hands in hers.

"Oh, my poor Mathilde! Why, my necklace was made of glass—a clever fake. It was worth at most 500 francs!"

ALL THINGS CONSIDERED

1. Mathilde Loisel has seen less and less of her friend Mme Forestier because (a) Mme Forestier has moved away. (b) Mathilde is ashamed of her own simple home. (c) Mme Forestier has slowly withdrawn her friendship.

2. The idea of borrowing jewelry from Mme Forestier first comes from (a) Mathilde. (b) Loisel. (c) Mme Forestier herself.

3. Several details in the story suggest that Loisel (a) is much more intelligent than his wife. (b) regrets ever having married. (c) is devoted to his wife.

4. The "twist" at the end of the story is that (a) Mme Forestier has stayed beautiful. (b) Mathilde finally finds the necklace. (c) the "diamonds" Mathilde borrowed were really glass.

5. Between the lines, the reader sees that at the time of the story, France was (a) a place of fixed social and economic classes. (b) a very poor country. (c) a very rich country.

THINKING IT THROUGH

1. (a) When faced with the problem of the lost necklace, what else could the Loisels have done? (b) How might this other course of action have worked out?

2. Think of the three adjectives (words that describe) that you think best suit Mathilde in the first part of the story. Give at least one detail from the story to support your choice of each adjective.

3. Although "The Necklace" is a famous story, some critics have attacked it as being too improbable to take seriously. Do you agree? Explain.

4. Perhaps the reason "The Necklace" ends so abruptly is that de Maupassant did not want to describe Mme Forestier's reaction to the news. (a) In your opinion, what would Mme Forestier have probably done if the story had continued? (b) Would this lessen the effect of the story? Why, or why not?

Literary Skills

Elements of the Short Story

Before answering the questions that follow, you may wish to review the terms in **boldface** on pages 10 and 11.

1. Some authors go into great detail when describing their *settings;* others tend to sketch the setting lightly and concentrate on **dialogue** (spoken words) and action. (a) Which kind of writer is de Maupassant? (b) Do you think his method adds to or detracts from the story?

2. Both the second and third paragraphs contrast one kind of setting with another. Why is this done?

3. What two other settings in the story contrast sharply with each other?

4. The dreaming but dissatisfied young housewife and the plodding, but adoring young husband are characters in many stories. Therefore, are such characters best called *stereotypes* or *rounded characters?*

5. Several *conflicts* occur in the story. Name at least two of them.

6. Name at least two *plot questions* that kept you interested as you read the story.

7. Where in the story does the *climax* occur?

8. Some stories forcefully suggest a very clear *theme*. Others involve two or more themes. Still others have no theme of real importance. In your opinion, what is the main theme of "The Necklace"? Can you think of other possible themes?

Composition

1. Summarize "The Necklace" in a paragraph of no more than 150 words. This assignment is not as easy as it sounds. Your job is to give all necessary information about the characters and the plot—yet make every word count so that you will be able to stay within the 150-word limit.

   You may want to start in this way. *Mme Loisel an attractive young wife who dreams of exchanging her lowly position for a life in high society, is invited to a fancy ball with her husband, a common government worker.*

2. Evaluate "The Necklace" in a short paragraph. Use this sentence as the main idea that will open your paragraph. *In my opinion, "The Necklace" is a (poor, average, or very good) story.* Then go on to support your judgment with DEFINITE REFERENCES TO THE STORY. Try to avoid the practice of supporting your opinions with other opinions you might have.

POLAR NIGHT

by Norah Burke

▶ For the polar bear, "There was pain and there was happiness. These two things drove her according to laws she couldn't understand."

The hot arctic summer drew to a close. When the sun only slid along the horizon to sink again at once, the polar bear knew that a hard time lay ahead for her.

During the months of night, 50 degrees below zero, her cubs would be born. The great task of motherhood was already begun. Soon she would bury herself deep down under the snow to give birth. From then until the day when she and her cubs burrowed up into daylight again, she would not eat. She and they must live on what she had stored in her body during the summer. Now she

must finish fattening herself up for the ordeal. There was not much time left.

At the moment she was hunting along the edge of the ice. Where there was water there were seals. There were also fish, and the chance of a porpoise or walrus. As the colder weather turned the roots and berries and seaweed of the polar islands into glass, the bears moved to the ice-edge for their food.

This was the arctic region, the area north of the limit of tree-growth. The shores of Greenland, Canada, Alaska, and Russia bordered upon this sea. It was a landscape of snow and old ice and new ice. Drifting icebergs from the glaciers were in constant motion. Lanes and pools of pure blue-green glass opened and closed all the time. Where the old ice had been pushed up together in terraces, ice-eaves burned green and lilac underneath. In summer the gulls and other birds made the air noisy with their quarrels. But now all that the bear could hear was the splash of cold water against grinding ice.

Under the dark sky, on the white land, in the loneliness of the arctic, she was part of its white power. She moved with a long swinging walk and huge flat yellow hairy footfalls. Strong and dangerous, she was the largest of bears. She could swim 40 miles out to sea if need be. She ruled her kingdom in which no natural enemy challenged her reign. Her feet, bristled underneath to give grip on the ice, carried her huge weight with a light and silent step. The low swinging head searched the ice at all times for food.

She was not clearly aware of what was happening in her body. But the instinct was there to love the unborn cubs. She would prepare for them and protect them. She did not risk her body in careless adventures as she would at other times.

But food? Food—

Already the iron of winter was in the clear cold air. She felt cold only with her eyes and black nose and lips. There the air stung her. It also stung the long pinkish-gray tongue, moving all the time to prevent freezing, in and out of her mouth among the large cruel teeth.

Suddenly, away down the ice-field, she saw a blackish dot on the ice. A seal! It was necessary to catch him. In a moment she had decided on her approach. She slipped silently into the water to cut off his line of retreat. The ice rocked as her great weight left it.

• **ordeal** (or DEEL) trial; difficult experience

The bear was as much at home in the water as on land. She swam like a dog, but on top or under the surface. The water was much warmer than the air on her face. Not wet, either. Inside the layer of fat and the shaggy oily watertight coat, she felt as dry as on land.

By a series of sly dives, and keeping under the shoulder of ice, she got near to the seal. Breathing carefully, ready to spring—to dive—to slaughter, she slid nearer—nearer—

Suddenly the seal saw her. Terror twisted his face. A moment of awful hesitation—whether to plunge into the sea, his natural line of escape, and perhaps fall straight into her jaws, or to struggle across the ice to that other hole—

He swung away from her, bobbing madly along. The bear sprung up out of the water, onto the ice, onto the terrified seal.

The water splashed off her everywhere like a huge wave. There was a flurry of snow and water and fighting seal. His quick struggling body flapped under her as she slew him. Blood spurted onto the snow.

When the seal was dead, the bear cared first for herself. She got rid of the wet from her coat before it could freeze. She shook, and the drops few off in rainbows in all directions. She rolled and nosed along in the snow. She wiped her sides, her chin, and soon all was dry. A few hairs stood up and stuck to each other with frost.

Now for the seal. She ripped up the body. She turned back the skin and blubber, letting out a cloud of steam. The hot red meat she ate greedily. Seal meat was her favorite. It was full of flavor, a hot meal, not like the white icy flakes of codfish.

Then, although the bear had no natural enemies, she stopped suddenly as she ate and lifted her head. She looked, listened, and smelled. Blood dripped from her chin onto the snow.

There was nothing.

All the same she trusted her instinct. Leaving her rest of the meal, she slipped into the water, where she could keep her cubs safe. In the water it was warmer, and easier to move.

Soon she saw upright seals coming along the shore. They were rather rare creatures, these, and dangerous even though they were so weak. The places where they lived had light and noise, and smelled full of good food. The she-bear often drew near those smells. She hunted these land-seals too, and ate them when she could. They were not like the sea-seals, though. They wore seal fur, and their skins were rubbed with seal blubber, but there was a different taste inside.

They in their turn hunted bear, as the she-bear knew well. She had sometimes found the place of the kill. She had seen the white empty skins hung up by the camps, and smelled the dark red meat cooking.

Now as she watched the approaching men, she wondered whether to kill them. No—the unborn life in her said get away. So she dived and swam and melted out of their range.

In the next few days the bear feasted on fish and seal. No longer did the summer give forth good-tasting moss or sweet berries and roots. She dived into the cold blue ocean for her food.

But now the arctic day was over. In the pink twilight a snowy owl was flying silently across the water. The bird moved south and south as life was squeezed out of the arctic desert by the polar night.

Then came the freezing of the sea. Crystals formed below the surface and rose. Needles of ice shot across from one to another, joining them together. The crystals thickened and hardened, adding more ice to the floes already many years old. The ice talked, grinding its teeth. Every now and then it sent out a singing crack. Curtains of colored flame rippled in the sky. The polar night began.

Now the real cold came. Now the food disappeared, and old male bears grew thin and savage.

Then the she-bear chose her den.

There was a great raw range of old ice that had been pushed up into mountains. Inside were hollows packed with snow. Icicles yards long hung on the south side from the summer. Behind this icicle curtain she found a great purple cave, carved in diamonds and full of snow.

This was the place.

Her body was ready now. Thick fat, gathered from seal and fish, lined her skin.

She burrowed down into the snow on the floor of the cave. It was so light that the wind blew it about like feathers. She burrowed deeper and deeper, while the snow sifted and fell silently behind her. Soon she was deep enough.

She curled up and rolled herself round and round, pushing the snow, shaping the den. All the sides of it melted with her heat, then froze again into slippery walls. And the hot breath passed up through the way she had dug. The sides of the passage also

• floe (FLOH) piece of floating ice

24

melted and froze again, leaving a tube. This would supply her with air until she came up again in the spring.

Inside the snow and ice—inside her thick oily fur and the layer of blubber, she was warm, full fed, and happy. She slept and waited.

In the fullness of time, the first familiar pain of birth trembled her stomach. The pain rose like a butterfly, and then was gone.

She stood, lifted her head, and rearranged herself.

It came again, stronger, longer.

She moved uneasily.

Then in long strong strokes it was there—hard, forcing, out of her control. Moving to a high point. She grunted, all her muscles stiff, and pressed and gasped. Another spasm, and on the smooth strong river of pain, she felt the first cub come out.

A wave of relief relaxed her.

There he lay mewing, so wet and tiny, hardly alive. She felt him with her nose, starting to clean him up.

But now another spasm—the same long final one as before, though easier. The second cub was born.

It was over now. She felt the pain fading away; her heart beat more quietly.

Now to clean them up. She licked and licked them, turning them over, rolling them. Their life strengthened in them as they dried, as they fed. She lay in bliss, feeling her own life flowing from her heart.

Meanwhile in the world above, the sun had returned. First it came as a green glow, then a rosy one; then it touched the topmost peaks, days before the first sunrise.

Deep in the snow cave, the bear knew it as the snow began to glow with the light pressing through.

One day she heard voices. The snow vibrated with footsteps. The ice ceiling cracked.

She rose, shaking herself free of the cubs. She stood ready in case one of the land-seals saw the warm yellow air hole that marked her den—in case one of them walked over her and fell in. . . .

She stood fierce, ready to defend her cubs. Her heart pounded hot and loud as fever in her thin body.

Gradually the voices and the footsteps died away.

• spasm (SPA zum) sudden tightening of muscles

Soon it was time to come out into the world again. The cubs' eyes were open. Their coats were grown. They got stronger every day. Now they must come out and face the world and swim and fight and catch seals. There was everything to teach them. And while they were still learning, still babies, they had to be kept safe and fed. All this she had to do alone. Other years she'd had a mate to help her. But this time he was gone—lost—those white skins hanging by the camps. . . . She began to tear her way out. The giant paws and black nails broke open the ice walls of the den. The ice gave; snow fell in.

They climbed out.

Clean frozen air, dazzling with sun, hit them like the stroke of an axe. Light entered the brain in needles through the eyes. Only gradually, as the pupils grew smaller, did it become possible to see.

Under a sun-halo, the arctic landscape blazed white and navy blue. Everything hit them at once—light, noise, wind—the blast of a new world.

Down there in the water—

The mother bear plunged joyfully into the wet cleanness. All the dirt and staleness of winter were washed away. It was like flight. She plunged and rose and shook and plunged again in joy. So fresh, so lean, the salt cold water running through her teeth—

Then she turned to the cubs. They were sitting on the edge, squeaking with fright. She began urging them to come in. They kept feeling forward, then scrambling back. Suddenly one came too far down the ice. He slid, shrieking, into the sea, where he bobbed up again like a cork.

His brother, seeing this, got up the courage to dive in too, in one desperate baby-jump. He landed with a painful *smack!* and blinked in the spray.

They found they could swim.

Soon she pushed them up on the ice again. They shook and dried, and the next thing was food. She left them while she killed a seal, and the three of them ate it.

After that there were lessons. How to fish. How to kill. Living was thin at first, for three hunters cannot move as silently as one. But they got along.

Until the day when land-seals approached them unseen from behind an ice ridge. The first they knew of it was an explosion. One cub gasped and doubled up as he was hit. The bears dived for the water, even the wounded little one. He managed to keep up with them. His mother and brother would die rather than desert him.

They all swam on, but slowly—slowly. Both cubs were still so small and slow, and they must hurry—

Blood ran in the blue water.

Other shots spattered around them.

Anxiety roared in the she-bear's blood. Her heart was bursting. She pushed the cubs on, and turned to meet her enemies. She reared up onto the ice and galloped toward them, a charge that nothing could stop—not even death—if they stayed to face it.

But they broke and ran.

The bear returned to her cubs.

The wounded one was sinking lower and lower in the water. He was breathing waves. She managed to push him out at last onto the ice. Then she licked him as he lay suffering in the snow. His brother licked him too, whimpering with distress as he washed.

After a while the blood stopped, and after a long time the suffering too. The cub sniffed the air. In the first real moment of recovery he was willing to take food.

Pain went away from her heart.

Before them lay all the arctic lands, the snow in retreat. The floes, soft now from the sun's heat, were being broken up by the waves. Plant life filled the water, the more open sea colored bright green by diatoms. Millions of wild flowers dotted the rocky shore. There was everything to eat at once—moss and roots and fish and seals. Salmon swam in the green water, and cod. Seaweed washed round the rocks. On the land there were rabbits and young birds.

The summer gathered to almost tropical heat. Snow water dripped into pools. Icicles, shining and wet, dropped and broke like glass.

• diatom (DY uh tum) very small plant that lives in water

And the mother bear, in the snow, with her cubs, did not know
why she behaved as she did. There was pain and there was happiness. These two things drove her according to laws she couldn't
understand. When the summer ended, and the polar night began,
she would do the same things over again, and her children after
her.

ALL THINGS CONSIDERED

1. The setting of the selection is near (a) the South Pole. (b) the
   North Pole. (c) Antarctica.
2. The creatures called "upright seals" and "land-seals" are
   (a) walruses. (b) very large seals. (c) humans.
3. The mate of the bear in the selection (a) leaves her alone every
   winter. (b) had probably been shot. (c) helps her prepare her
   den.
4. The selection states definitely that the polar bear (a) has no
   natural enemies. (b) is now an endangered species. (c) sleeps
   for months at a time without waking.
5. The word that best describes the polar bear's behavior is
   (a) *cruel.* (b) *stupid.* (c) *instinctive.*

THINKING IT THROUGH

1. Without looking back at the selection, try to list five facts
   about the polar bear that you did not know before reading
   "Polar Night."
2. The author of the selection tried hard to describe a polar bear's
   life from the bear's own viewpoint. How well did the author
   succeed? Give some details from the selection to support your
   view.
3. "Polar Night" is listed as **fiction** (a made-up story) in the table
   of contents. But sometimes the line between **fiction** and **nonfiction** (a selection based on fact) is not at all clear. Give one
   reason for calling "Polar Night" *fiction,* and another for calling
   it *nonfiction.*

Reading and Analyzing

Dramatic Irony

Do the words you use always mean exactly what you want to say? Of course they don't. Sometimes, in fact, the words used mean the very opposite of the thought behind them. For instance, if everyone knows that you're a big eater, you might jokingly say that you "eat like a bird." In the same way, a person said to "suffer from modesty" might in fact be headstrong, talkative, and overly proud. People talk like this all the time: "Yeah, I just love to do homework." "Gee, liver again—my favorite food."

The word **irony,** as commonly used, refers to the use of words that mean something quite different from what is actually meant or appears true. In literary use, however, *irony* has additional definitions. **Dramatic irony** occurs when the reader (or the viewer, in the case of a play) knows something important that a character does not know.

Dramatic irony is a source of pleasure because it's human nature to enjoy knowing something that others don't know.

In "Polar Night," the main character is, of course, a bear. Much of the pleasure in reading "Polar Night" arises from dramatic irony, from the fact that the intelligent human reader knows more than the bear knows through instinct. With this in mind, explain the following sentences in terms of dramatic irony:

1. Soon she saw the upright seals coming along the shore.
2. Other years she'd had a mate to help her. But this time he was gone—lost— those white skins hanging by the camps. . . .
3. (Find and explain another example of dramatic irony in the selection.)

Composition

1. Suppose the author, Norah Burke, were going to visit your class tomorrow. Write at least three important questions you would like to ask her.

2. Most readers are glad that "Polar Night" ends as it does, but other endings are certainly possible. Offer two other ways the story might end. You do not have to write the endings out completely; just summarize them. You can begin at any point after the men appear and there is "an explosion."

Before completing the exercises that follow, you may wish to review the **bold-faced** words on pages 4 to 22.

I. On a separate sheet of paper, write the *italicized* word that best fills the blank in each sentence.

ordeal   *philosophy*   *interest*   *grope*   *stake*
strand   *colleague*   *classic*   *franc*   *delirious*

1. What is the most famous _____ of world literature?
2. The gambler decided to _____ his last dollar on the turn of a card.
3. My last baby-sitting job was a(n) _____ that lasted till after midnight.
4. How much is a French _____ worth now in U.S. money?
5. Around her neck was a(n) _____ of pearls that looked real.
6. When Mr. Samuels was ill, a(n) _____ took over his last-period history class.
7. I woke up early and started to _____ for the light switch.
8. Banks advertise their _____ rates every day in the papers.
9. _____ with their victory, the hometown fans poured onto the field.
10. Very few high schools offer courses in _____ .

II. Read the following poem carefully before answering the questions.

THE SHEPHERD-BOY AND THE WOLF

(translated from the Greek of "Aesop's Fables")

A Shepherd-boy beside a stream
"The Wolf, the Wolf," was wont to scream,
And when the Villagers appeared,
He'd laugh and call them silly-eared.

• wont (WONT) accustomed; in the habit of

30

5   A Wolf at last came down the steep—
"The Wolf, the Wolf—my legs, my sheep!"
The creature had a jolly feast,
Quite undisturbed, on boy and beast.
For none believes the liar, forsooth,

10   Even when the liar speaks the truth.

1. If the short poem is looked at as a story, does it contain all four elements: setting, characters, plot, and theme? If *not*, explain which is (or are) missing.

2. Explain how dramatic irony might increase the good reader's enjoyment of the poem. Did *you* know what was going to happen before you reached line 7?

III. Explain how dramatic irony increases your enjoyment of the following cartoon. What do you know that the two characters don't?

• steep (STEEP) high, steep place
• forsooth (for SOOTH) in truth; in fact

THE FALCON

by Giovanni Boccaccio

▶ Love is as old as the human race, and love stories have
been around for a long, long time. Here's one of the
world's best. It was written by Giovanni Boccaccio (1313–
1375), an Italian who is still considered one of the great
storytellers of all time. Don't let the age of the story fool
you. The language of love is eternal.

Federigo Alberighi was his name, and Florence was his city.

No youth was richer. None was more handsome. And none had
more charm. He was famed above all others for courage on the
battlefield and deeds of gallantry. The citizens of Florence waited
eagerly to see which of the gentle young ladies of the city
Federigo would choose as his bride.

As for the fair and gentle young ladies, well, they held their
breath and waited. Federigo was seen dallying with one girl, then
with another. The city whispered that he was secretly engaged,
now to this girl, now to that one. But in truth, he had asked no one
to marry him. He had never seen a young woman he felt he could
love with eternal love.

Then one day, on the main street of Florence, Federigo saw
her. He stopped in his tracks as she came into view. The girl was
about a head shorter than Federigo. She neither wore nor needed
makeup. She had thick dark hair and deep-set, sparkling eyes.
Her face glowed with a beauty no artist could ever paint.

Federigo lost no time in finding out his new love's name. She
was known as Monna Giovanna, and everyone who knew her
thought her one of the most gracious women in Florence. But
Federigo also turned up a fact he didn't like. Monna Giovanna was
already married—to a very wealthy man much older than
herself.

This fact didn't stop Federigo, however. To gain Giovanna's

- **gallantry** (GAL un tree) dashing bravery; also courtesy
  to women
- dallying (DAL ee ing) playing idly
- **gracious** (GRAY shus) well mannered; courteous

attention, he sent costly gifts. He threw huge parties and he held jousts and tournaments with rich prizes for the winners. But Giovanna's virtue was a match for her beauty. She did not give a thought to all that was done for her, or to the man who did it.

Federigo still would not be stopped. He continued to spend, spend, and spend. He was so in love that money meant nothing. His banker warned him that his money would soon run out, but he paid no attention. "Without Monna Giovanna," he told himself, "I will have no need for money. There will be no happiness that money can buy."

Finally the banker's warnings came true. Federigo's riches dwindled away. He was so poor that he had left only a little farm and a falcon, rumored to be the best hunting bird in all of Italy. His only choice was to move to the farm with his falcon. He would have to earn his living by the sweat of his brow. So, still hopelessly in love, he moved to Campi, where the farm was located. There he flew his falcon and tended his gardens. He bore his poverty with patience.

Time passed slowly—until the day when Monna Giovanna's husband fell very ill. Feeling the approach of death, he made a will. A very wealthy man, he named his son, already grown to boyhood, as his heir. Giovanna, the will stated, would get the money if the son should die without children. Then he breathed his last.

Giovanna was now a widow. That summer, to escape the city heat, she went away to the country with her son. She happened to settle in a cottage she owned, near Federigo's little farm. In a short time the boy grew friendly with Federigo. Hunting with their falcons, they had great sport together.

Many a time the boy watched in amazement as Federigo's falcon outflew his own fine bird. Of course, he wanted it for his own. But he never had courage enough to ask Federigo to part with it. He knew what Federigo's falcon meant to its owner. He realized that the older man, with no wife or family to love, had given all his love to the bird. He had heard that Federigo always saw that the falcon was well fed, even if it meant that his own stomach stayed empty.

- **joust** (JOUST) combat between two opponents on horseback
- **virtue** (VUR choo) goodness; moral excellence
- **dwindle** (DWIN dul) become smaller and smaller
- **bore** (BOHR) carried; endured

33

At about this time the boy fell sick. His mother, who had no other child, loved him dearly. All day long she stayed at his bedside. She often asked him if there was anything he wanted, even pleading with him to tell her. If it could be had, she stated, she would certainly get it for him.

Over and over, the boy heard her make the offer. Finally he said, "Mother, if you can get Federigo's falcon for me, I just know I'd get well again."

The lady looked down at the new light in the boy's eyes. But still, she hesitated. She wondered how to go about it. She knew, of course, that Federigo had long been in love with her. The trouble was that she'd never given the poor man so much as a glance. "How can I ask Federigo for his wonderful falcon?" she asked herself. "It is the only thing that gives him any real pleasure in life. Can I be so selfish? The poor fellow has no other delight left in this world."

Monna Giovanna's thoughts bothered her. She knew that to get the falcon, she would only have to ask for it. The whole thing would be so easy! So at last, she allowed her love for her son to become dominant. She determined to satisfy her son, whatever the consequences. And she would not send for the falcon, but go to get it herself.

"My son," she said, "be of good cheer. Do your best to get well and strong again. I promise that the first thing in the morning I'll go for the falcon myself."

- **dominant** (DOM uh nunt) controlling; most powerful
- **consequence** (KON suh kwens) result

34

Filled with renewed motivation, the boy showed improvement that very day.

The next morning, Monna Giovanna set off for Federigo's house, taking another woman with her for company. When they arrived, they found Federigo at work in his garden. It was not the season for falconing.

Federigo looked up from his work and bowed. What had made the beautiful Monna Giovanna come to his little farm?

Giovanna greeted him with feminine grace. "Good day to you, Federigo," she said. "I have come to make up for all the harm I've caused you. I can only say I'm sorry for what you have suffered. I shall begin by dining with you in friendship, with this friend of mine."

"Madam," Federigo replied humbly. "I don't remember ever having suffered any harm through you. On the contrary, if I am worth anything today, it is due entirely to your virtues. Yes, your virtues and the love I've always had for you."

With these words, Federigo led his guests toward the house. Outside it, in the shade of a great tree, was a small bench. "Madam," he said, "since I have no one else to help me, I will have to see that a proper table is laid myself. I'm sure you can sit here in the shade, keeping each other company till I return."

Monna Giovanna smiled and sat down, as did her friend. Federigo bowed and departed. At first the two women didn't talk much. Instead, they listened to Federigo's footsteps, going from room to room in the little house. What was he doing? Setting the table? Cooking? At last all was silent, and the two began to speak to each other. They talked of inconsequential matters as time, and still more time, passed. Was Federigo *ever* going to return? And if so, when?

"Am I really doing the right thing?" Giovanna asked herself suddenly. "Oh, I should never have come! How can I ask this dear man to part with the one thing that makes his life liveable?"

But Giovanna's doubts vanished when Federigo finally reappeared, his face beaming with happiness. He led his two guests into the dining room. The tablecloth and napkins were of the whitest linen, looking new but unused for years. Federigo

- motivation (moh tuh VAY shun) purpose; reason for doing something
- **contrary** (KON trer ee) opposite side; the "other hand"
- inconsequential (in kon suh KWEN shul) unimportant; trivial

35

brought the meal and served it with devotion. The food, different kinds of vegetables and meat blended into a delicious stew, pleased everyone. A happy hour passed.

The dinner over, they lingered at the table awhile, savoring the pleasant conversation. But finally the time came when Giovanna could put off the reason for her visit no longer:

"Federigo Alberighi," she began, "you must wonder exactly what has brought me here today. The past has not been kind to you. I have not been kind to you. But please believe that it was my virtue, not a hard heart or cruelty, that made me act as I did."

Federigo nodded.

"As you know," Giovanna went on, "I am a mother. You have no children of your own, I know. But if you had, I'm sure you could half excuse what I'm going to ask of you now. You see, my son lies very ill, and my love for him has no limits. He wants, and I want, the dearest thing you have."

Giovanna's deep-set eyes were now full open on Federigo's adoring face. "It is your falcon I would have. Federigo, your falcon. My little boy must have it. If not, he will surely take a turn for the worse. I may even lose him. You really owe me nothing, I know that, Federigo. But do it for your own nobility. Let me say that I saved my son's life by your noble gift."

Federigo stared at the three empty plates on the table. He tried to get to his feet, but his legs would not support him.

"Monna Giovanna," Federigo said sadly, "there was only one meal in my poor house worthy of you. We have just eaten the falcon."

The three people sat immobile as Federigo cursed himself silently. What a fool he had been! He remembered walking madly through the house, looking everywhere for money. With just the smallest silver piece, he could have sent out for a banquet. But there had been no money. In the kitchen, he had found just the small piece of meat he had saved for his own meal. It was not enough for one person, let alone for three. Then, in another room, his eyes had fallen on the falcon in its cage. He had put his hands on it, and found it fat. It had been his last hope.

Tears welled up in Federigo's eyes. "Dear lady," he murmured, "since I first fell in love with you, I've complained of Fortune many times. Fortune has not been good to me. But all her hurts were nothing compared with what she is making me suffer now."

• **immobile** (i MOH bil) without moving

Federigo began to dry his tears. "Never more," he went on, "can Fortune and I be friends. Here, today, you have asked a little gift of me. But Fortune has made it impossible for me to grant it!"

At first the lady blamed him for killing so excellent a falcon for a mere meal. Her face turned red. She stood up, and her knuckles grew white as she gripped the back of her chair. But then she realized that all he had done had been out of love for her. For this she could not blame him. After all, she had wanted to take the falcon away from him because of her love for her son. And he had taken the bird away from himself because of his love for her.

There was little else to say. Giovanna thanked her sad host and returned to her son's bedside.

The boy died soon after.

Long did Monna Giovanna remain in tears and grieving. But as she was still a young woman, and very wealthy, her brothers urged her again and again to remarry. At first she had no wish to take another husband. Then she began to think about Federigo's fine character. Why, hadn't he killed that marvelous falcon just to honor her?

"I'd very gladly remain as I am, if you would let me," Giovanna told her brothers. "But you insist on my marrying again. All right, I'll have nobody but Federigo Alberighi."

They made fun of her. "You foolish woman! What are you saying? What do you mean by choosing him? You are a wealthy woman, and he has no money at all."

"I know very well that it's as you say," she said. "But I'd rather have a man in need of wealth, than wealth in need of a man."

Hearing her determination, the brothers bestowed her upon him as she desired. Federigo was, they declared, a man of excellence, though poor. And as for Federigo, he soon saw himself married to the woman he had so dearly loved. He found himself suddenly blessed with a vast fortune. He learned to manage his affairs more wisely, and lived with her happily to the end of his days.

- **character** (KAR ik tur) nature; inner quality of a person
- bestow (bi STOH) present as a gift

ALL THINGS CONSIDERED

1. Oddly enough, Federigo Alberighi is reduced to poverty by (a) Monna Giovanna's clever husband. (b) a hopeless love. (c) a series of foolish love affairs.

2. At one point in the story, Federigo often goes hunting with Giovanna's (a) brothers. (b) husband. (c) son.

3. Federigo decides to kill the falcon because he (a) doesn't want anyone else to own it. (b) is very hungry. (c) wants to please Giovanna regardless of the personal cost.

4. After she learns the truth, Giovanna first treats Federigo with (a) blame, then forgiveness, and finally love. (b) forgiveness, then love, and finally blame. (c) love, then blame, and finally forgiveness.

5. The story indicates that women in 14th-century Italy (a) enjoyed more freedom than modern women. (b) thought little of marriage vows. (c) were supposed to obey the men in their families.

THINKING IT THROUGH

1. Do you blame Federigo for any of his actions throughout the story? Explain why or why not.

2. The story indicates that both love and virtue were considered very important in 14th-century Italy. What about today? With some necessary changes, could events like those in the story occur in modern America? Explain your answer.

3. Did you have a hunch that the falcon had met its end before Federigo announced the fact? If so, what clues helped you foresee the climax of the story?

4. Most short stories end with the *climax* (see page 11), but some do not. These stories continue past the climax with a section called the *resolution*. A **resolution** answers any remaining questions a reader might have, ties up the loose ends, and gives the story a rounded-out, finished feeling. As the climax is preceded by *rising action*, a resolution can be considered *falling action*. (a) In your opinion, what is the climax of "The Falcon"? (b) What happens in the resolution of the story? (c) Why do you think the author thought this resolution was necessary?

Reading and Analyzing

Irony of Situation

Dramatic irony (see page 29) occurs when the reader knows something that a character in a story does not know. For instance, if you suspected that Federigo was destroying the very thing that Giovanna so desperately wanted as she sat on the bench waiting for the meal, you were treated to a moment or two of dramatic irony.

One other kind of irony is equally important in literature: *irony of situation*. **Irony of situation** occurs when there is a striking difference between what a character wants and expects to happen, and what actually does happen. The events in "The Necklace" (page 13)

provide an excellent example. After 10 long years of hard labor, Mme Loisel learns that her efforts not only failed to produce the desired result, but also that such efforts were actually needless.

Boccaccio's story "The Falcon" provides another famous example of irony of situation in literature.

1. Think about irony of situation from the viewpoint of Federigo. Give two examples of such irony from different parts of the story.
2. From Monna Giovanna's viewpoint, how is irony of situation involved?

Composition

1. Use five vocabulary words from the story in five sentences of your own. Your sentences should be about the story, but you cannot simply copy from the book. If you like, you can use the vocabulary words to present your own ideas about the story. The words are these: (1) *gallantry* (page 32); (2) *dominant* (page 34); (3) *consequence* (page 34); (4) *contrary* (page 35); and (5) *immobile* (page 36).

2. People find irony of situation fasci-

nating in literature because they find it fascinating in life. For example, a tightrope walker might trip over a stone on the sidewalk. The situation would be ironic because no one would expect it to happen. Or a minister, intending to preach a sermon against the state lottery, might buy a ticket to use as evidence against betting—and win!

Think of an ironic situation that you have experienced or heard of recently. Explain it in as interesting a way as possible.

▶ Although Solomon Bloomgarden (1870–1927) spent his mature life in the United States, he wrote in Yiddish, the language of many of the Jewish people of Eastern Europe. He used Yehoash (yee HO ash) as a pen name. This poem, written in Yiddish but about Japan, by a poet born in Lithuania but working in New York City, is certainly international in origin—as well as in meaning.

AN OLD SONG

by Yehoash (Solomon Bloomgarden)

In the blossom-land Japan
Somewhere thus an old song ran.

Said a warrior to a smith
"Hammer me a sword forthwith.
5   Make the blade
Light as wind on water laid.
Make it long
As the wheat at harvest song.
Supple, swift
10   As a snake, without rift,
Full of lightnings, thousand-eyed!
Smooth as silken cloth and thin
As the web that spiders spin.
And merciless as pain, and cold."

15   "On the hilt what shall be told?"

"On the sword's hilt, my good man,"
Said the warrior of Japan,
"Trace for me
A running lake, a flock of sheep
20   And one who sings her child to sleep."

translated by Marie Syrkin

- **smith** (SMITH) blacksmith; metal worker
- forthwith (forth WITH) at once
- supple (SUP ul) flexible; bending easily
- rift (RIFT) split; crack
- **hilt** (HILT) handle of a sword

WAYS OF KNOWING

1. At first reading, the poem seems to involve irony of situation, since the expectations aroused in lines 3–14 do not seem to be fulfilled in lines 16–20. What is the main difference between the warrior's wishes for the blade of the sword and his wishes for the hilt?

2. With some thought, however, you may be able to see how the blade and the hilt fit perfectly together in the warrior's mind. Explain how this is possible.

41

▶ Who's the detective. we remember for his huge curved pipe, magnifying glass, British accent, double-billed cap, and the saying "Elementary, my dear Watson"? Sherlock Holmes, of course. Before matching wits with the famous supersleuth, read the "Oral Interpretation" on page 61.

SHERLOCK HOLMES AND THE SECOND STAIN

Dramatized by Olive J. Morley
by Arthur Conan Doyle

CHARACTERS
SHERLOCK HOLMES, *the famous detective*
DR. WATSON, *his assistant*
THE PRIME MINISTER OF ENGLAND
THE HONORABLE TRELAWNEY HOPE, *Secretary for European Affairs*
LADY HILDA TRELAWNEY HOPE, *his wife*
BUTLER
MRS. HUDSON, *Holmes's housekeeper*
SUPERINTENDENT LESTRADE, *member of the police force*
OFFICER MACPHERSON, *member of the police force*

SCENE 1

SETTING: *Holmes's rooms.*
AT RISE: Sherlock Holmes *is seen seated in a leather chair, right, in his Baker Street rooms. A small littered sofa stands left of center, where there is a table with books and papers and a lamp on it. Left and right there are several comfortable but rather shabby leather and upholstered chairs, and a coatrack stands far right.* Dr. Watson *enters right.*

- **prime minister**—head of British government
- **secretary** (SEK ri ter ee) high government official in charge of a particular department

Dr. Watson: Well, Holmes, it looks as if some important business is coming our way. The Prime Minister and Mr. Trelawney Hope, the Secretary for European Affairs, have arrived, and they seem very troubled.

Holmes: Show them in, my dear Watson, and we'll see what's bothering them. (Dr. Watson *exits briefly and returns with the* Prime Minister *and* Trelawney Hope.)

Watson: Gentlemen, please come in. (Holmes *stands up, and the* Prime Minister *walks over to him and shakes hands.*)

Prime Minister: Mr. Holmes, you were good to see us at such short notice. This is Mr. Trelawney Hope, our Secretary for European Affairs.

Holmes (*Walking toward* Hope): I'm glad to see you both. (*They shake hands.*) Won't you please sit down? (Holmes *sits back down, and others sit right and left of him.*) You know my friend, Dr. Watson, of course? (*They nod, and* Watson *sits in chair slightly behind* Holmes.) Now, gentlemen, please tell me how I may be of service.

Prime Minister: Early this morning, Mr. Hope arrived at my home to report the loss of a very important government document. The disappearance of this paper can bring about international trouble. But I would like the European Secretary to tell you the story in detail.

Holmes: Very well. (*He leans forward and looks at* Hope.) Please proceed, Mr. Secretary.

Hope (*Fidgeting nervously with his watch chain*): When I discovered the loss of this document, which was at eight o'clock this morning, I at once informed the Prime Minister. He suggested that we come to you for help in recovering it.

Holmes: Have you informed the police?

Prime Minister (*Quickly*): No, sir, for to do so would in the long run mean informing the public. This we must avoid at all costs.

Holmes: And why, sir?

Prime Minister: Because the document in question is of such great importance. Its publication might lead to serious trouble for all of Europe. Unless this document can be recovered in secrecy, it may as well not be recovered at all!

Holmes: I understand. (*To* Hope) Can you tell me exactly how this document disappeared?

Hope: This can be done in a few words, Mr. Holmes. The letter—for the document in question is a letter—was received six days ago from a foreign ruler. After showing it to the Prime Minister, I placed it in my private dispatch box, not in my safe, and each evening I have taken it to my home in Whitehall Terrace. The box was always locked, and at night I kept it on my dressing table. The only key is in my pocket. The letter was in the dispatch box last night. Of that I am certain, for I opened it when I was dressing for dinner and saw it. This morning it was gone. I am a light sleeper and so is my wife, and we are both prepared to swear that no one could have entered the room during the night without our knowledge. Yet, the paper is missing.

Holmes: What time did you eat?

Hope: Half-past seven.

Holmes: And when did you go to bed?

Hope: My wife had gone to the theater. I waited up for her, and we went to bed at eleven-thirty.

Holmes: Then for four hours the box was unguarded?

Hope: Yes. But no one enters our room at night except my valet and my wife's maid. Both are old and trusted servants. Moreover, as I never discuss politics in the house, no one could possibly know there was anything more valuable than my ordinary papers in the box.

Holmes: Who *did* know of the existence of that letter?

Hope: No one in the house.

Holmes: Surely you have told your wife?

Hope: I said nothing to my wife till I missed it this morning.

Holmes: Who in England knew of its existence?

Hope: The Cabinet Ministers—all under a pledge of secrecy, of course—and two or three Department officers.

- **dispatch** (di SPACH) official message
- **valet** (VAL it) personal servant who takes care of a man's clothing

Holmes: Who knew of the document abroad?

Hope: Only the man who wrote it.

Holmes: What was in it, exactly?

Prime Minister: The envelope is a long, thin, pale-blue one, with a seal of red wax—

Holmes: What was *in* the *letter*?

Prime Minister (*Stiffly*): These are government secrets, Mr. Holmes.

Holmes (*Rising with a smile*): Then I regret I cannot help you.

Prime Minister (*Jumping to his feet; angrily*): I am not accustomed, sir—(*Controlling himself*) I see we must accept your terms, Mr. Holmes. (*Slight pause*) The letter, then, is from a foreign ruler who has been angered by certain actions of this country. The letter is so nasty that its publication would undoubtedly stir up strong feeling in this country. Within a week we might find ourselves close to war. (Holmes *writes something on a slip of paper he has taken from table and hands it to the* Prime Minister, *who reads it, then nods.*) Yes, that is the name of the man who wrote the letter which may well cost this country millions, and the loss of thousands of men.

Holmes: I assume, then, it is the enemies of this ruler who wish to get the letter and make it public, causing trouble between his country and ours.

Prime Minister (*Nodding*): Exactly.

Holmes: And to whom would these thieves send the letter if they are successful in stealing it?

Prime Minister: To one of the great nations of Europe. (*Bitterly*) It is probably on its way there now.

Holmes (*Sadly*): Then, sir, prepare for war.

Hope: Are you quite sure?

Holmes: Consider the facts. It could not have been taken after eleven-thirty, since, as I understand it, Mr. Hope and his wife were both in their room from that time until the loss was discovered this morning. It therefore had to be taken between seven-thirty, when they left the room to go to dinner, and eleven-thirty, when they returned—probably nearer seven-thirty, since the thief knew it was there and would want to get it as soon as possible after the Hopes left. (*Standing up and pacing back and forth*) But where can it be now? It must already be on its way to those who would want it.

Prime Minister: I feel that it is beyond our reach.

Holmes (*Thoughtfully*): Let us assume, for argument's sake, that the document was taken by a maid or the valet—

Hope (*Breaking in*): They are both tried and true servants.

Holmes (*To* Hope): Where in your house is your room located, Mr. Secretary?

Hope: On the second floor. There is no entrance from outside, and no one could go up from the inside without being seen or heard.

Holmes: It must, then, be somebody inside the house who has taken it.

Watson: To whom would the thief take the letter, Holmes?

Holmes: Elementary, my dear Watson—to one of the three chief international spies who may be said to be the best in the world. My first job is to find out if each of these is here in London as usual. If one is missing—especially if he has disappeared since last night—we shall have some clue as to where the document has gone.

Prime Minister: Why should he be missing? Would he not have taken the letter to an embassy in London?

Holmes: I think not. These agents work by themselves. They are often not on good terms with the embassies.

Prime Minister: I believe you are right, Mr. Holmes. He would deliver so valuable a prize with his own hands. (*Rising*) Hope and I must return to our other duties. If anything new happens during the day, we shall communicate with you. And you, no doubt, will let us know if you discover something important.

Holmes: Certainly.

Prime Minister: Then good morning for now, and thank you a thousand times for your help. (Watson *and* Hope *rise. The* Prime Minister *and* Hope *go off, followed by* Holmes. Watson *picks up newspaper from table, then sits down again and begins to read.* Holmes *re-enters, takes pipe from his jacket pocket and puts it into his mouth, then sits down, and is soon deep in thought.*)

Holmes (*Half to himself*): The situation is desperate, but not hopeless. If I could be sure which of them had taken the letter, it is just possible that it has not yet passed out of his hands. After all, it is a question of money with these fellows, and I have the British treasury behind me. If the letter is on the market, I'll buy it, even if it means another penny on the income tax.

Watson (*Looking up from the newspaper*): Which three agents did you have in mind?

Holmes: There are only three who would play so dangerous a game—Oberstein, La Rothiere, and Eduardo Lucas.

Watson: Is that the Eduardo Lucas of Godolphin Street?

Holmes: Yes.

Watson: You will not see him.

---

* **embassy** (EM bu see) a country's official headquarters in another country

Holmes: Why not?

Watson: According to this paper, he was murdered in his house last night.

Holmes (*Jumping up*): Good heavens! (*He seizes paper and reads eagerly.*) "A crime of a mysterious kind was committed last night at 16 Godolphin Street, the home of Mr. Eduardo Lucas, well known in society circles." (*Looks up with a smile*) They generally are! (*Scans paper quickly*) I note the household consisted only of Lucas, his housekeeper, Mrs. Pringle, and his valet, Mitton. Apparently Mrs. Pringle had gone to bed early, to her room on the top floor of the house. Mitton was visiting a friend in Hammersmith. Well, they should be able to check that alibi. (*Reading from newspaper*) "At a quarter to twelve, Police Officer Barrett, passing along Godolphin Street, saw that the door of Number 16 was open." (*Breaking off*) That points to an unexpected visitor, Watson, but *one who had a key.*

Watson: Perhaps Mitton went back and did his master in.

Holmes: Don't jump to the obvious conclusions, Watson. That would be much too neat a solution! Cases seldom run like that. (*Reading paper again*) Barrett went in and found the front room lighted, in wild disorder, with a chair overturned, and the body of Lucas beside it—"stabbed to the heart," it says here, with "a curved Indian dagger, obviously taken from a display of weapons on the wall. There was no sign of robbery." Well, Watson, what do you make of this?

Watson: It's an amazing coincidence.

Holmes: Coincidence! Here is one of the three possible actors in our drama, found murdered during the very hours when we know that drama was happening. (*Pacing about*) No, my dear Watson. This is no coincidence. The stealing of the letter and this murder are connected—*must* be connected. It is for us to find that connection.

Watson: But now the police must know all.

Holmes: Not at all. They know all they see at Godolphin Street. They know nothing of the events at Whitehall Terrace. Nor shall they. Only we know of both events, and can find the connection between them. (*Sits down*) You know, Watson, I'd have thought of Lucas, in any case. He lives only a few minutes' walk from Whitehall Terrace. The other two agents live in the West End. (Mrs. Hudson *enters, holding a tray with a card on it. She walks center to Holmes.*)

- **conclusion** (kun KLOO zhun) judgment; guess based on available facts
- **coincidence** (koh IN suh duns) two related events accidentally occurring at the same time

Mrs. Hudson (*Holding tray toward* Holmes): You have a visitor, Mr. Holmes.

Holmes (*Taking card from tray and glancing at it quickly*): Hullo! What have we here? (*He raises his eyebrows in surprise, then passes card to* Watson.) Will you please ask Lady Hilda Trelawney Hope to come up, Mrs. Hudson?

Mrs. Hudson: Right away, Mr. Holmes. (*She exits, and in a moment* Lady Hilda Trelawney Hope *enters, a dignified young woman, but obviously nervous.* Holmes *and* Watson *rise, as she walks center.*)

Lady Hilda (*Anxiously*): Has my husband been here, Mr. Holmes?

Holmes: Yes, madam.

Lady Hilda: Mr. Holmes, I beg you not to tell him I have come to see you.

Holmes: Your ladyship places me in a very delicate position. (*Motioning to chair*) Please sit down and tell me what you wish, but I fear that I cannot make any promise. (*She walks to chair farthest from* Holmes *and sits in dim light.*)

Lady Hilda: Mr. Holmes, there is complete faith between my husband and me, except on politics. On that he tells me nothing. Now I know there was a disturbing occurrence in our house last night. A paper has disappeared, and now I must understand the importance of this. I beg you, Mr. Holmes, to tell me exactly what happened and what it will lead to. (*With earnestness*) I assure you it is in my husband's best interests for me to know all. What *was* this paper?

Holmes: Madam, you ask what is impossible for me to tell you. It is your husband you must ask.

Lady Hilda: I have done so, but all in vain. Can you at least tell me one thing—is my husband's political career likely to suffer as a result of this?

Holmes: Unless it is set right, there may be very unfortunate results.

Lady Hilda (*Drawing in her breath sharply*): And I understand that terrible things may occur for the country from the loss of this document?

Holmes: You ask me more than I can answer.

Lady Hilda: Then I will take up no more of your time. (*Rises*) Please, I beg you, say nothing of my visit. (*She walks to exit, looks back at them, then goes out.*)

Holmes: Now, Watson, what was the fair lady's game? What did she really want?

Watson: Surely her statement was clear.

Holmes: Hm-m. Think of her appearance—tense, excited. And she comes from a class of people who rarely show emotion.

And what did she mean by saying that it was best for her husband that she knew all? And she sat there in the dim light where we could not read her expression.

Watson: She probably sat in the shadow because she had no powder on her nose.

Holmes: Exactly. (*Rising*) Well, good morning, Watson.

Watson: You're off?

Holmes: Just down to Godolphin Street. With Lucas lies our solution. So stand on guard, my good Watson, and receive any new visitors. I'll join you here for lunch, if I can.

Watson: Right-o, Holmes. (*Curtain*)

SCENE 2

TIME: *A few days later.*

SETTING: *The home of Eduardo Lucas. It is furnished in luxurious style, with a large table with drawer, center, and some large chairs and sofas about. At rear of stage, center, there is a fireplace over which hang Oriental weapons on the wall. There is a door, left, a loose carpet on the floor, a bookcase on right wall, and a straight-backed chair in front of table.*

AT RISE: Superintendent Lestrade *is sitting at table, reading a newspaper.* Holmes *and* Watson *enter.*

Lestrade: Ah, here you are, Holmes. Glad you got my note. Seen the Paris news?

Holmes: Yes. It's an interesting happening.

Lestrade: Our French friends seem to have touched the spot this time. Evidently this fellow Lucas lived a double life— Eduardo Lucas here, bachelor, and M. Henri Fournaye in Paris, with a wife who seems to have been very excitable. The papers say she was likely to get violent fits of jealousy.

Watson: She probably had cause!

Lestrade: No doubt, sir, no doubt. Why did he pose as a bachelor here? Probably to give himself just that bit of rope she'd never allow him over there.

Holmes: But what, I wonder, sent her dashing over here on that particular night?

Lestrade: My guess, sir, is that she had just discovered that he was living here as Eduardo Lucas. Now that, to a jealous woman, would only suggest one thing—that he had a little lady friend tucked away in London. So she comes rushing over from Paris, surprises him, they have one flaming fight, and in a wild fit she seizes one of the daggers on the wall—you can see where it was hanging—(*Points to wall*) and goes for him. Evidently, from the state of the room, he'd picked up a chair to defend himself, but too late—she got in with the dagger.

Holmes: It all fits neatly. And the paper states someone fitting her description had been seen watching this house from the other side of Godolphin Street.

Lestrade: Yes. And the fingerprints on the dagger are hers. Also, she arrived back in Paris in a state of great excitement after the murder. I should say, however, that this murder doesn't look like a planned one.

Holmes: But she seems to have chosen a very convenient night, when he was alone.

Lestrade: Oh, no doubt she would do that to pick a fight with him when the coast was clear. If she was watching, she would have seen the valet go out, and noticed the light go on in the house-keeper's room. Then in she'd pop. (*Officer* MacPherson *enters.*)

MacPherson: Excuse me, sir, but there's an officer with a message for you outside.

Lestrade: All right, I'll speak to him. (*To* Holmes *and* Watson) I'll be with you in a moment, gentlemen. (Lestrade *and* MacPherson *exit.*)

Watson: What do you make of this, Holmes?

Holmes: Make of it? Nothing.

Watson: But they seem to have cleared up Lucas's death neatly.

Holmes: My dear Watson, the man's death is only a small part of our real job—to find that letter and save Europe from war. Only one important thing has happened in the past three days— and that is, that *nothing* has happened! I get reports almost hourly, and it's certain that nowhere in Europe is there any sign of trouble. Now, where *can* this letter be? Who has it? Why was it held back? Was it a coincidence that Lucas was murdered the very night the document disappeared? Did it ever reach him? If so, why is it not among his papers? Did his jealous wife carry it off to Paris? How can I search her house there without making the French police suspicious? Stumped at every turn! (Lestrade *enters.*)

Lestrade: Yes, Mr. Holmes, we've got it all as clear as if we'd seen it.

Holmes (*Raising eyebrows*): And yet you have sent for me?

Lestrade: Ah yes, that's another matter—a small one, but strange, you know, and freakish. But it doesn't affect the main point.

Holmes: What is it, then?

Lestrade: Well, you know that after a crime we're very careful to keep things in their position. There's an officer in charge here night and day. But this morning, the investigation being over, we thought we'd tidy up a bit. You see this carpet? (*Pointing*) It's not fastened down, just laid there loose. We raised it, and we found—

Holmes (*Tensely*): Yes?

Lestrade: You see that stain on it? Well, with a man bleeding to death, a great deal of blood must have soaked through, wouldn't you say so?

Watson: A great deal.

Lestrade: Then you'll be surprised to hear there's no stain on the wood floor underneath.

Holmes and **Watson** (*Together*): No *stain?* There must be!

Lestrade: So you'd say. The fact remains there isn't! (*He takes up carpet and points. Eagerly they bend over it.*)

Watson (*Examining carpet with magnifying glass he takes from his pocket*): But the underside of the carpet is as stained as the top. It *must* have left a mark!

Lestrade (*Chuckling*): Now, I'll show you the explanation. There *is* a second stain, but it's right here. (*He lifts another portion of carpet, uncovering a stain on floor. They examine this carefully.*)

Watson: Yes, that would go with the stain over there.

Lestrade: Now, what do you make of that, Mr. Holmes?

Holmes: Elementary. The two stains did go together, but the carpet has been turned around.

Lestrade: The police don't need you, Mr. Holmes, to tell them the carpet has been turned around. What I want to know is, *who* shifted the carpet, and *why?*

Holmes (*In great excitement*): Look here, Lestrade, has that officer in the hallway been in charge all the time?

Lestrade: Yes.

Holmes: Well, take my advice. Examine him carefully, in private. You'll be more likely to get a confession out of him alone. Ask him how he dared to admit people to this room and then leave them here alone. Don't *ask* him if he has done it. Take it for granted that he has. Tell him you *know* someone has been in the room and that a full confession is his only chance.

Lestrade: By George, I'll have it out of him! (*He rushes off.*)

Holmes (*Anxiously*): Now, Watson, now! Help me with this rug! (*He bends over rug and throws back one end, as* Watson *turns back the other corner.*) Try these squares of wood and see if any of them seems loose or in any way different from the others. (*He kneels and taps on floor boards, examining them carefully.*)

Watson (*Kneeling down beside* Holmes): What are we looking for, Holmes?

Holmes (*With sudden happiness*): I think I can show you now, Watson! (*Tapping floor*) This section is hollow. (*As he lifts back lid of hinged "box"*) It should be here. (*He reaches in, but quickly draws his hand out, empty.*) Empty! It can't be! (*Voices are heard from offstage.*)

Lestrade (*From offstage*): You come in here, MacPherson.

Holmes (*Closing down lid of hinged section*): Quick, Watson, we must put this all back as it was! (*They quickly replace carpet, and* Holmes *jumps up. He takes pipe from pocket and begins puffing on it, as* Watson *sits in chair.* Lestrade *and* MacPherson *enter.*)

Lestrade: I'm sorry for the delay, Mr. Holmes. I can see that you are bored with the whole affair. Now, MacPherson, tell these gentlemen what you told me of your conduct.

MacPherson (*Uneasily*): I meant no harm, sir, I'm sure. You see, sir, this young woman came to the door last evening—

Holmes (*Sharply*): What young woman?

MacPherson: A very respectable, well-spoken young woman, sir. She mistook the house. It was lonesome, and well, we got to talking. She wanted to see where the crime was done—she'd read about it in the papers.

Holmes: And you let her in?

MacPherson: I saw no harm in letting her have a peep. But when she saw the stain, the mark on the rug, she fell down in a dead faint. I ran to the kitchen to get her some water, but couldn't bring her to. So I ran around the corner for some smelling salts. But by the time I had come back, she had recovered and was off. I guess she was too embarrassed to face me.

Holmes: Could you see if this rug (*pointing to small carpet*) had been moved while you were out?

MacPherson: Well, sir, it was a bit rumpled. You see, she fell on it when she fainted, and the floor under it is polished, with nothing to keep the rug in place. I straightened it out.

Lestrade (*To* MacPherson): It's lucky for you, my man, that nothing is missing, or you'd be in jail by now.

MacPherson: I *am* sorry, sir.

Holmes: Has this girl been here only once?

MacPherson: Yes, sir.

Holmes: Have you any idea who she was?

MacPherson: None at all, sir. She said she was answering some advertisement for typewriting and came to the wrong number. A very pleasant lady she seemed, sir.

Holmes: Tall? Good-looking?

MacPherson: She was that, sir! Some might say *very* good-looking. She had very pretty, coaxing ways.

Watson: No doubt.

Holmes: How was she dressed?

MacPherson: Quiet, sir—a long coat down to her feet.

Holmes: What time was it?

• smelling salts—powder to cure dizziness, fainting, or nausea

MacPherson: It was just dusk. They were lighting the lamps as I came back to the house.

Holmes: Very good. Come, Watson, we have more important work elsewhere. (Holmes *and* Watson *go to door, and* MacPherson *opens door to let them out.*)

Lestrade: I'm sorry to have called you out over such unimportant business, Mr. Holmes, but I thought you would find the matter of the second stain interesting.

Holmes (*Turning briefly*): It was indeed, *most* interesting! (*As* Lestrade *bends to straighten rug,* Holmes *takes something from his pocket, holds it so that* MacPherson *can see it, then puts it back into his pocket, as* MacPherson *stares in amazement.*)

MacPherson: Good Lord, sir! (Holmes *puts his finger to his lips, and exits quickly with* Watson, *as curtain falls.*)

SCENE 3

TIME: *Later that morning.*

SETTING: *Sitting room in the home of* Trelawney Hope. *A small table stands center, and a writing desk with straight chair at left. Odd chairs are placed right and left. There is a door left, with a bell rope hanging on wall next to it.*

AT RISE: Butler *enters, followed by* Holmes *and* Watson.

Butler: If you will sit down, sirs, I shall tell her ladyship that you are here. (Butler *exits, and* Holmes *and* Watson *sit down.*)

Holmes: Well, Watson, the curtain rings up on the last act. You will be relieved that our friend Trelawney Hope will suffer no setback in his brilliant career. And the Prime Minister will have no European war on his hands. In fact, with a little tact on our part, no one will be a penny the worse for what might have been very ugly.

Watson (*Amazed*): You have solved it?

Holmes: Not quite, Watson. There are still a few points to clear up. (Lady Hilda *enters, obviously nervous.* Watson *and* Holmes *rise.*)

Lady Hilda (*Angrily*): Mr. Holmes, this is most unfair of you. I begged you to keep my visit to you a secret so that my husband would not think I was snooping into his affairs. Now you come here, and he will surely know.

Holmes: Unfortunately, madam, I had no other choice. I have been asked to recover this very important paper, and I must therefore ask you to place it in my hands. (Lady Hilda *sways,*

• **tact** (TAKT) wise kindness

then grasps back of chair to steady herself, and straightens up.)

Lady Hilda (*In a controlled, angry voice*): You—you insult me, Mr. Holmes.

Holmes: Come, come, madam, it is useless. Give me the letter. (*She moves swiftly to the bell rope next to door.*)

Lady Hilda: The butler will show you out.

Holmes: Do not ring, Lady Hilda. If you do, all my efforts to prevent further trouble will be for nothing. Give up the letter and all will be set right. If you work *with* me, I can arrange everything. If you work *against* me, I must expose you.

Lady Hilda (*Proudly, with her hand still on bell rope*): You are trying to frighten me, Mr. Holmes. (*Changing her tone*) You say you know something. Just what is it?

Holmes: Pray sit down, madam. (*She walks to chair, left, and sits.*) Thank you.

Lady Hilda: Well, Mr. Holmes. I give you five minutes.

Holmes: One is enough. (*Quickly*) I know of your visit to Eduardo Lucas. I also know of your clever return to his house last evening and of the manner in which you took the letter from its hiding place under the carpet.

Lady Hilda (*Obviously upset*): You are mad, Mr. Holmes, mad! (*Holmes draws small piece of cardboard from his pocket. It has a picture of a woman's face on it.*)

Holmes (*Showing picture to Lady Hilda*): I have carried this picture with me because I thought it might be useful. The policeman on duty last night at the Lucas house recognized it! (*Lady Hilda gasps and falls back in chair.*) Come, Lady Hilda, you have the letter. My duty ends when I have returned it to your husband. Be honest with me.

Lady Hilda (*Hurt, but still trying*): I tell you again, Mr. Holmes, that you are very, very wrong.

Holmes (*Rising and walking toward bell pull*): I am sorry for you, Lady Hilda. I have done my best for you. (*He pulls bell rope.*) I can see that it is all in vain. (*Butler enters.*) Is Mr. Trelawney Hope at home?

Butler: He will be at home, sir, at a quarter to one.

Holmes (*Glancing at watch*): Still a quarter of an hour. Very good. I shall wait. (*Butler exits.*)

Lady Hilda (*Wringing her hands in great distress*): Oh, Mr. Holmes, Mr. Holmes! For heaven's sake don't tell him! I love him so much! This would break his heart!

Holmes: I am thankful, madam, you have come to your senses at last. (*Quickly*) There is not a moment to lose. Where is the letter? (*She hurries to the writing desk, unlocks it, and draws out a long, blue envelope.*)

Lady Hilda (*Handing envelope to* Holmes): Here it is.

Holmes (*Examining it briefly*): How can we return it to his dispatch box? We must think of some way! Where is the dispatch box?

Lady Hilda: Still in his bedroom.

Holmes: Good. Quickly, bring it here. (*She hurries out.*)

Watson: How did you arrive at the truth?

Holmes: Elementary, my dear Watson. (*He paces about.*) I only hope her husband doesn't arrive back too soon. (Lady Hilda *re-enters carrying a flat, red box.* Holmes *takes it and puts it onto table.*) Now, Lady Hilda, how did you open it? Of course—you have another key. Quickly—open it. (*She takes a small key from her pocket and opens box.*)

Lady Hilda: It belongs here. (*Puts her finger between papers in box.*)

Holmes: (*Pushing some papers back and slipping blue envelope between other documents*): There. (*He shuts the box quickly.*) Now lock it and return it quickly to your bedroom. (Lady Hilda *locks it and puts key back into her pocket. She picks up box and rushes out.*)

Watson: And to think she had it all the time!

Holmes: Yes. (*Resumes pacing*) But why did she take it, Watson? That's what she must tell us.

Watson: Lucas was well known in society circles—rather a lady's man. Do you think he worked up some sort of romance with her, in order to get the document out of her?

Holmes: Could be, but—no. She's not the type. I think there's something more to the whole thing. Something we haven't got as yet. (Lady Hilda *re-enters.*)

Lady Hilda: Thank heaven it's back there at last!

Holmes: Now we are ready for him. I am going far to protect you, Lady Hilda, but you must be honest with me.

Lady Hilda: Mr. Holmes, I will tell you everything. I love my husband very much and would not give him a moment of sorrow. Yet, if he knew how I have acted, how I have been forced to act, he would never forgive me. I beg you to help me. His happiness, my happiness, our very lives are at stake!

Holmes: Quickly, madam, time grows short!

Lady Hilda: It all began with a letter of mine, a love letter I wrote before I was married—the letter of a young and foolish girl to an older man who had paid me much attention. He turned my head and I was flattered, and I wrote him a note. If you were to read it now, you might think I was having an affair with him. I learned much later that he was married and had a dreadful reputation with women. It all happened years ago and I thought the whole matter was forgotten. Somehow or

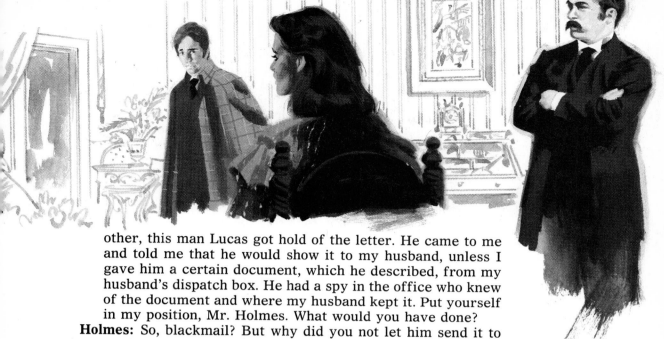

other, this man Lucas got hold of the letter. He came to me and told me that he would show it to my husband, unless I gave him a certain document, which he described, from my husband's dispatch box. He had a spy in the office who knew of the document and where my husband kept it. Put yourself in my position, Mr. Holmes. What would you have done?

Holmes: So, blackmail? But why did you not let him send it to your husband, and explain to him?

Lady Hilda: Oh, Mr. Holmes! My dear Mr. Holmes! You don't know husbands! Trelawney loves me, really. He thinks I'm perfect. He would have forgiven me, but the seed of suspicion planted in his mind when he received that letter might grow, and I couldn't risk that! Well, I got the document from my husband's dispatch box. I took an impression of the key, and this man Lucas had another one made. I opened the box, took the paper, and went with it to Godolphin Street.

Holmes: What happened when you went there?

Lady Hilda: Lucas was alone. I remember seeing a woman outside when I went in. I handed him the document. He gave me the letter. Suddenly there was a sound outside in the hallway. Lucas quickly turned back the carpet, put the envelope into some hiding place there, and pulled the rug back over it. What happened next was a nightmare. I remember a dark, angry face peering in, a woman's voice shrieking, "At last! At last! I have found you with her!" Then there was a fearful scene. The woman rushed in, and she and Lucas started talking in French. The woman sounded quite crazy. She seized a dagger from the wall, and Lucas picked up a chair—I rushed from the horrible scene. It was not till next morning in the paper that I learned the dreadful result. I realized then that I had only exchanged one trouble for another. My husband's distress at the loss of the document went to my heart. I could hardly keep

---

• **impression** (im PRESH un) copy made by pressure on some sort of mold to show shape

from telling him what I had done, but that would have meant a confession of the past. I realized that I had to get that document back. I knew it must still be where Lucas had hidden it, but how was I to get into the room? For two days I watched the house, but the door was never left open. Then I thought of pretending that I had mistaken the house for another, and asked the policeman to let me see the room.

Holmes: And we know how you managed to get the envelope from the hiding place under the rug.

Watson: Quite clever, madam.

Lady Hilda: When I brought the paper back here with me, I thought of destroying it, for I could see no way of returning it to the dispatch case without confessing my guilt. (*Sounds of footsteps and voices are heard from offstage.*) I hear my husband coming now. (Trelawney Hope *rushes into room.*)

Hope (*Excitedly*): Any news, Mr. Holmes? Any news?

Holmes: I have distinct hopes.

Hope: Thank heaven! The Prime Minister is lunching with us. May he share your hopes?

Holmes: Certainly. (Hope *goes to door and speaks to* Butler *off.*)

Hope (*To* Butler, *off*): Will you please ask the Prime Minister to join us. (*Walks back center and takes* Lady Hilda's *hands.*) How are you, my dear?

Lady Hilda: Glad that you are home and may expect good news from Mr. Holmes.

Hope: My dear, this is a matter of politics. We shall join you shortly in the dining room. (Lady Hilda *smiles and exits. In a moment, the* Prime Minister *enters.*)

Prime Minister (*Walking over to* Holmes): Have you something to report, Mr. Holmes?

Holmes: Nothing has been discovered, as yet. But I have inquired at *every point*, and I am sure there is no danger.

Prime Minister: But we cannot live forever on the edge of a volcano!

Holmes: I am—in hopes of getting the letter. The more I think, the more I am sure that it has never left the house.

Prime Minister and **Hope** (*Together*): Mr. Holmes!

Holmes: If it had been taken from here, it would have been made public by now.

Hope: But why should anyone take it and then do nothing with it?

Holmes: There is no proof that anyone did take it.

Prime Minister: Then how could it leave the dispatch box?

Holmes: There is no proof that it ever did leave the dispatch box.

Hope: You have my word that it left the box.

Holmes: Have you examined the box since Tuesday?

Hope: No, it was not necessary.

Holmes: You may have overlooked it.

Hope: Impossible! I took everything out.

Holmes: Such things have happened. It may have been mixed with the other papers there.

Hope: It was on the top.

Holmes: Someone may have shaken the box and changed the position of the letter.

Prime Minister: It is easily decided. Let us have the dispatch box brought in.

Hope: I will get it myself. But it is a waste of time. (*Exits.*)

Watson: I have known some strange cases of papers sometimes getting stuck together.

Prime Minister: Yes, but this was such an unusual envelope. Blue—and right on top. I can hardly see how anything like that could have happened—(Hope *re-enters carrying dispatch box. He puts it onto table, takes key from his pocket and unlocks box.*)

Hope (*Opening box and taking out some papers*): Now, we will make a search. (*Going through more papers*) A letter from Lord Merrow; the report from Sir Charles—

Prime Minister (*Impatiently*): But the letter—is it there?

Hope: Not yet. (*Continues going through papers, putting each on table as he identifies it*) Letter from Belgrade; a note on German grain taxes; a letter from Madrid—(*Suddenly stopping, as he picks up blue envelope*) Good heavens—Yes, this is it!

Prime Minister (*Snatching envelope and examining it*): Yes, this is the blue envelope—(*Taking letter out of envelope*) And the letter is here! Hope, I congratulate you.

Hope: What a weight from my heart! But it is impossible! Mr. Holmes, you are a wizard! How did you know it was here?

Holmes: Because I knew it was nowhere else.

Hope: I cannot believe my eyes. Oh, I must tell my wife that all is well! (*He rushes excitedly to door, calling.*) Hilda! Hilda! (*He exits.*)

Prime Minister (*Looking at* Holmes *with confusion and amusement*) Come, Holmes. There is more here than meets the eye. How came the letter back in the box? (Holmes *turns away, smiling.*)

Holmes (*As he picks up his hat and starts toward door*): We also have our diplomatic secrets. (*Turning to* Watson) Come, Watson, we must be off. (Watson *gets up. Curtain.*)

THE END

- **diplomatic** (dip luh MAT ik) concerning relationships between countries; also skillful in handling people's feelings

ALL THINGS CONSIDERED _____

1. Like many mysteries, this play involves a (a) hidden past life of one of the characters. (b) detective in disguise. (c) corpse that strangely disappears.
2. Sherlock Holmes, of course, is the hero of the play. The next most important role is that of (a) Dr. Watson. (b) the Prime Minister. (c) Lady Hilda.
3. When Holmes accuses Lady Hilda, she at first (a) confesses to the crime. (b) offers a large sum of money for Holmes's secrecy. (c) becomes angry.
4. Lady Hilda had stolen the document because (a) she wanted to blackmail her husband. (b) she was being blackmailed by Eduardo Lucas. (c) her husband, Secretary Hope, was using it as a threat in a blackmail scheme.
5. The character who is completely fooled at the end is (a) Hope. (b) the Prime Minister. (c) Dr. Watson.

THINKING IT THROUGH _____

1. Trace the course of the missing letter from the time it disappears from the dispatch box to the time it is returned. How does it create opportunities and problems for the different characters?
2. Some readers of mystery stories believe that all the clues to solve the crime should be presented to the reader before the detective figures things out. Do you think the play is fair with the reader in this regard? In answering the question, consider the (a) strange appearance of Lady Hilda right after her husband's departure in Scene 1; (b) actions of the "very respectable, well-spoken young woman" described by MacPherson in Scene 2; (c) fact that no one but trusted servants could have had access to the dispatch box, and even then a special key would have been required.
3. Some readers of mystery stories believe that everything but the mystery should be straightforward and logical. Did any detail other than the mystery itself strike you as illogical or improbable? Explain.
4. Sherlock Holmes and Dr. Watson are usually thought of as partners, yet Watson is seldom of any real help as a crime solver. What, then, is Watson's real function? What does he add to the play and other mysteries that feature Holmes?
5. Why is Hope's last speech in the play an excellent example of *dramatic irony* (see page 29)?

Oral Interpretation

Reading a Play

Oral interpretation means reading aloud with expression. Of course, there are some occasions—while reading a newspaper article or a grocery list, for instance—when good oral interpretation doesn't matter very much. A traffic accident is a traffic accident, a can of tomato soup is a can of tomato soup. But this is not usually the case when reading good literature. Stories often demand good oral interpretation, poems usually do, and plays always do.

When reading a play, try to read aloud. If this is impossible, you can do almost as well by trying to hear the words in your "mind's ear." As you begin reading a play, practice the following steps:

- Study the cast of characters until you know who the persons in the play are and understand the relationships between them. It may help to copy the list on a piece of paper for later reference. Also, skim through the first few pages to see what each character is called as the play proceeds.
- Think about how each of the characters might look and speak. To do this, read the first few pages of the play, until most of the main characters are introduced. As you become acquainted with the characters, let them develop voices of their own. Imagine them as real people, with real personalities and problems.
- When you are thoroughly familiar with the characters, go back to the beginning and start reading again. Try to take in the names and stage directions at a glance, devoting most of your attention to the speeches. As you read, the voices of the different characters will become more and more distinct. Before long, you'll discover that although your eyes are reading the words, the characters themselves dominate the play. You will continue to read effortlessly, enjoying the play as though you were seeing and hearing it on stage or screen.

Most problems with reading plays are caused by the reader's failure to follow these steps at the beginning. They may seem to take a little extra time at first, but the end result will be more enjoyment in a shorter period of reading.

Critical Thinking

Working with Analogies

An **analogy** (uh NAL uh jee) is a statement that the relationship between one pair of terms is in some way similar to the relationship between another pair. You've probably seen analogies on tests for years:

- PRESIDENT is to UNITED STATES as PRIME MINISTER is to ENGLAND.
- DOCTOR is to WATSON as DETECTIVE is to HOLMES.
- ENVELOPE is to LETTER as BRIEFCASE is to BOOK.

61

Analogies are common on tests because they test both your vocabulary and your ability to see relationships. Look, for instance, at the three analogies on page 61. The relationship in the first is HEAD OF GOVERNMENT is to COUNTRY. What are the relationships in the other two analogies?

Here are 10 incomplete analogies. For each, first state the relationship involved as precisely as you can. Then go on to supply a term that might be used to complete the analogy.

1. LONDON is to ENGLAND as WASHINGTON, D.C., is to __?__.
2. ELEMENTARY is to EASY as DIFFICULT is to __?__.
3. ELEMENTARY is to DIFFICULT as EASY is to __?__.
4. ANTON CHEKHOV (see page 2) is to RUSSIA as ARTHUR CONAN DOYLE is to __?__.
5. DETECTIVE is to SOLVE as DOCTOR is to __?__.
6. TABLECLOTH is to TABLE as RUG is to __?__.
7. COUNTRY is to WAR as PERSON is to __?__.
8. SHABBY is to CHAIR as THREADBARE is to __?__.
9. CABINET:MINISTERS::TEAM: __?__.
10. $\dfrac{\text{PARAGRAPH}}{\text{SENTENCE}} = \dfrac{\text{SENTENCE}}{\text{(?)}}$

Composition

1. In your "mind's eye," try to visualize any scene from the play. Then write a description of what you "see." Include as many specific details as you can. Be prepared to explain why you included certain things and left out others.
2. Lady Hilda's old letter in the hands of Lucas is important in the play. Reread Lady Hilda's brief description of the letter on page 56 ("It all began with a letter of mine. . . ."). Then try to write a similar letter, making up the details as you go along. For instance, what had happened that "turned my head"?

VOCABULARY AND SKILL REVIEW

Before completing the exercises that follow, you may wish to review the **bold-faced** words on pages 32 to 59.

I. On a separate sheet of paper, write the term in each line that means the same, or nearly the same, as the word in *italics*.

1. *hilt:* far side, handle, bottom, mystery
2. *consequence:* reason, accident, exercise, result
3. *dominating:* fair to all, weakening, controlling, deadly
4. *immobile:* unmoving, useless, impossible, unfeeling
5. *virtue:* goodness, warmth, joy, hospitality
6. *gracious:* honest, costly, sly, cordial
7. *dwindle:* move quickly, grow smaller, waste, relax
8. *tact:* manual skill, wise kindness, emotion, confession
9. *gallantry:* stupidity, cooperation, reasonableness, bravery and courtesy
10. *smith:* animal doctor, metal worker, potter, cobbler

II.
1. A *joust* is a (a) beam supporting a floor. (b) fight on horseback. (c) restaurant.
2. To reach a *conclusion* is to (a) arrive at a judgment. (b) get to a certain place. (c) come to a dead end.
3. It would be a *coincidence* if (a) four members of one family were born on October 12. (b) your pen ran out of ink. (c) another aircraft accident ever happened.
4. The expression "on the *contrary*" means (a) "as a result." (b) "on the level." (c) "just the opposite."
5. The *prime minister* of Great Britain is the head of the (a) official church. (b) labor unions. (c) government.
6. The word *secretary* can mean either an office worker or a (a) high government official. (b) head of government. (c) wife or husband of a minister.
7. An official charged with *diplomatic* affairs would be concerned with (a) crops and rainfall. (b) public education. (c) relations with foreign countries.
8. An *embassy* might be able to give you (a) the odds of winning a lottery. (b) information about a foreign country. (c) videotapes of popular movies.
9. A government *dispatch* is a (a) letter or other communication. (b) tax. (c) cabinet minister.
10. An *impression* might be useful in making a copy of a (a) popular song. (b) book-length manuscript. (c) key.

III. People have always enjoyed irony. Here are 10 jokes written by Hierocles, a Greek who lived in the fifth century, A.D. All concern a "scholar," the same kind of "wise fool" or "absent-minded professor" we still like to laugh at today. Note that they all involve dramatic irony or irony of situation. In your own words, explain what makes each joke funny.

JESTS OF HIEROCLES

1. A scholar, wishing his horse to eat little, gave him no food at all. The horse died. "How unlucky," said he, "as soon as I taught him to live without food, he died!"

2. A scholar, trying to sell his house, carried a stone of it with him as a sample.

3. A scholar, wanting to see if he looked good when asleep, shut both eyes and went to the mirror.

4. A scholar sealed a barrel full of wine, but his servant bored a hole in the bottom and stole half. The scholar was surprised at the loss, for the seal on the top was undisturbed. "Perhaps it was taken out of the bottom," someone suggested. "Most foolish of men," the scholar answered, "it is not the lower part but the upper that is missing."

5. A scholar, meeting a person, said to him, "I heard you were dead." "No," the other answered, "you see, I am alive." The scholar replied, "Perhaps so, but he who told me was a much more truthful person than you."

6. A scholar, hearing that crows live 200 years, bought one, saying, "I wish to make an experiment."

7. A scholar, coming to a ferry, went onto the boat on horseback. Being asked the reason, he said, "I am in great haste!"

8. A scholar, sending his son to war, heard the youth say, "I shall bring you back an enemy's head." The scholar replied, "Even if you lose your own head, I shall be happy to see you return."

9. Three men, a scholar, a bald man, and a barber were traveling together. When night came, each agreed to stay awake and stand guard for three hours, for the sake of safety. The barber's turn came first, and he shaved the scholar's head before waking him up to take his turn. The scholar scratched his head and felt it bald. "You wretch of a barber," he explained, "you have waked the bald man instead of me!"

10. A scholar, hearing one of two twins was dead, met the other on the street. "Which of you was it that died," he asked, "you or your brother?"

Even jokes that make us groan can last more than 1,500 years!

UNIT REVIEW

I. Match the terms in Column A with their definitions in Column B.

A	**B**
1. setting	**(a)** the "falling action" that follows the climax in some stories
2. rounded	
3. stereotype	**(b)** the meaning or lesson of a story
4. conflict	**(c)** the place and time of a story
5. climax	**(d)** (of a character) a real, true-to-life, complex individual
6. resolution	
7. analogy	**(e)** a statement showing that two pairs of relationships are alike in some way
8. theme	
9. dramatic irony	**(f)** a familiar, easily recognized type of character
10. irony of situation	**(g)** a case of events working out in an unexpected, often surprising, way
	(h) the meeting of two opposing forces
	(i) a case of the reader's knowing more than a character knows
	(j) the exciting high point of a story, at or near the end

II. DINNER FOR FOUR

Prove that you know the characters in Unit I well by arranging a dinner party for at least four of them. If you want, you can also include a friend of your choice. Start by choosing the characters you think might have an interesting time together. In a short sentence, explain why you chose each. Then draw a seating plan you think would lead to good conversation. Finally, in a separate paragraph, explain what might happen at your party. For instance, three of the characters might monopolize the conversation with their hard luck stories, then be silenced by Sherlock Holmes's detailed explanations of their stupidity. Be as creative as you can; it's not a real party, so almost anything can happen.

There is only one *don't* in this assignment: The polar bear is definitely not to be a guest.

SPEAKING UP

Each unit in this book is followed by an assignment that exercises your speaking voice, either through the oral interpretation of literature or through the presentation of your own thoughts and opinions. Here is the first assignment:

Jabberwocky
'Twas brillig, and the slithy toves
Did gyre and gimble in the wabe:
All mimsy were the borogoves,
And the mome raths outgrabe.

Are you confused? Of course—and so was Alice (of Wonderland fame) when she first saw the poem. She puzzled over it for some time. Then she thought, "Why, it's a looking-glass poem! And if I hold it up to the mirror, all the words will go the right way again."

This is what she saw:

JABBERWOCKY

by Lewis Carroll

     'Twas brillig, and the slithy toves
       Did gyre and gimble in the wabe:
     All mimsy were the borogoves,
       And the mome raths outgrabe.

5   "Beware the Jabberwock, my son!
       The jaws that bite, the claws that catch!
     Beware the Jubjub bird, and shun
       The frumious Bandersnatch!"

     He took his vorpal sword in hand:
10   Long time the manxome foe he sought—
     So rested he by the Tumtum tree,
       And stood awhile in thought.

And, as in uffish thought he stood,
    The Jabberwock, with eyes of flame,
15   Came whiffling through the tulgey wood,
    And burbled as it came!

One, two! One, two! And through and through
    The vorpal blade went snicker-snack!
He left it dead and with its head
20   He went galumphing back.

"And hast thou slain the Jabberwock?
    Come to my arms, my beamish boy!
O frabjous day! Callooh! Callay!"
    He chortled in his joy.

25   *'Twas brillig, and the slithy toves*
    Did gyre and gimble in the wabe:
All mimsy were the borogoves,
    And the mome raths outgrabe.

Practice reading the poem in a way that gives some sort of general meaning to all the nonsense words. In both the first stanza and the last, for instance, there are 11 nonsense words that seem to suggest certain meanings. The overall mood seems threatening, if not terrifying. Notice the other opportunities in the poem for you to convey meaning and emotion by your spoken voice alone.

WRITING A MYSTERY STORY

The perfect crime story is as rare as the perfect crime. For instance, did the Sherlock Holmes play in this unit strike you as "perfect"? Probably not. Here is a chance for you to do better.

Assignment: Write a minimystery, or a very short mystery story that can be read in a minute or so. Start like this: *Hello, my name is (some variety of your own name, like Heather Holmes or Supersleuth Hernandez), and I want to tell you about a case I call . . . ."* Then write a short paragraph retelling the events in the case—including, of course, the important clue. Finally, skip a line and write another paragraph that explains the clue and tells what happened to the criminal.

Prewriting: Most composition assignments require some research and thought before you begin to write. In this case, your research is "How I Write Minimysteries" on page 69. Read it carefully, and then think of what *you* might use as a clue. In addition to the information in the short article, you might think of what would or would not be true of a particular person. (A typist, for instance, would be unlikely to have long fingernails.) Think too of what would or would not be likely in a given situation. (A dog would probably not bark at its owner returning home, for example.)

Writing: When you have decided on your clue, go over the story in your mind several times before you start writing. Then write the story out as clearly as possible, taking care that the clue is neither too obvious nor too well-concealed. If you have first worked out all the details, this step should be the easiest one in the writing process.

Revising: It's always a good idea to let some time pass between writing and revising, so that you can view what you have written in a new light. If this isn't possible, at least try to read your mystery to several other people. Make whatever corrections are necessary to clear up confusions and be sure that you have planted your clue as skillfully as possible. Finally, review your mystery for correctness and copy it over as neatly as possible.

HOW I WRITE MINIMYSTERIES

by Julia R. Piggin

I think of a minimystery as a nuclear, or single-cell, mystery story. It consists of one situation, one crime, one clue, and a detective who observes the clue and solves the crime. It's up to the reader to guess how the detective solved it.

In real life the crime comes first, then the search for clues. But I start with a clue and then dream up a crime to go with it. I keep a notebook and jot down anything I read, hear, or experience that might serve as a clue. For example, here's a note based on a newspaper article: "Prisoners often get only a spoon to eat with, form habit." Out of that I constructed a plot in which an escaped convict was caught when he forgot himself and dug into some turkey with a spoon. Another note: "Woman pretends to be deaf when it suits her, but speaks more loudly when TV is turned up." I once knew someone like that, and around her I built a story about a woman who faked deafness to avoid telling a jury something she'd heard. She was trapped when a plane roared overhead and she raised her voice.

Clues in minimysteries are of two types: One kind requires the reader to have some special knowledge—that many prisoners have to eat everything with a spoon, for example. The other kind gives the plot away to anyone with the ability to observe: if a woman shouts to drown out noise, she must be able to hear it.

In writing a minimystery, you needn't conceal the "knowledge" type of clue too carefully. If the reader knows the crucial fact, he solves the puzzle. However, the "common-sense" type of clue has to slip past the reader's notice if it's to mystify him. Still, for the sake of fairness to the observant reader, the clue must be clearly spelled out and in plain sight. The trick in writing is to divert the reader's attention so that he'll skim over the clue, or won't grasp its importance. A favorite method is to bury the clue in a list: ". . . on his bureau lay a pair of rusty scissors, a broken tie clasp, a cracked plastic hand mirror, an engraved sterling silver comb, a watch with a frayed leather strap." Scanning all that, a reader may forget that earlier he's been told that the victim's nephew is completely bald and very poor, while she was rich and vain about her long hair. Where did that expensive, fancy comb on the nephew's dresser come from, then? See what I mean?

- crucial (KROO shul) absolutely necessary
- divert (di VURT) turn aside; distract

U N I T · 2

TANGLES
AND
TEASERS

How can one e'er be sure
If true love will endure?
   My thoughts this morning are
   As tangled as my hair.

        —Lady Horikawa
      (Japan, 13th century)

Have your thoughts and feelings ever been all tangled up? Have you ever wondered whether you could solve the problems in your own mind? If you're like most people, the answer to these questions is probably "yes." From time to time, most of us experience some "tangles and teasers."

In this unit, you'll encounter some of the best tangles and teasers in the world's literature. You'll start with a bit of magic that makes you disappear into a poem. You'll go on to meet characters who face a variety of puzzling situations—some of them terrifying, some of them comic. So turn the page, and enter the world of . . . tangles and teasers.

▶ Don't take the title too seriously. But be forewarned: This poem is a thriller. Your only escape may be to disappear!

BEWARE: DO NOT READ THIS POEM

by Ishmael Reed

tonite, thriller was
abt an ol woman, so vain she
surrounded herself w/
    many mirrors

5   it got so bad that finally she
locked herself indoors & her
whole life became the
    mirrors

one day the villagers broke
10   into her house, but she was too
swift for them. she disappeared
    into a mirror
each tenant who bought the house
after that, lost a loved one to
15   the ol woman in the mirror:
    first a little girl
    then a young woman
    then the young woman/s husband

the hunger of this poem is legendary
20   it has taken in many victims
back off from this poem
it has drawn in yr feet
back off from this poem
it has drawn in yr legs

- **vain** (VAYN) overly proud; conceited
- **legendary** (LEJ un dair ee) famous; known by a great many people

25 back off from this poem
  it is a greedy mirror
  you are into this poem from
   the waist down
  nobody can hear you can they?
30 this poem has had you up to here
   belch
  this poem aint got no manners
  you cant call out from this poem
  relax now & go w/ this poem

35 move & roll on to this poem
  do not resist this poem
  this poem has yr eyes
  this poem has his head
  this poem has his arms
40 this poem has his fingers
  this poem has his fingertips

  this poem is the reader & the
  reader this poem.

  statistic: the us bureau of missing persons reports
45   that in 1968 over 100,000 people disappeared
   leaving no solid clues
     nor trace   only
  a space   in the lives of their friends

WAYS OF KNOWING

1. In a sentence or two, describe your first reaction to the poem.
2. In your opinion, why did the poet choose to use such informal language: no capitals, words like "aint" or "yr," as well as the ampersand (&) and the slash (/)?
3. (a) Why had the woman in the first part of the poem "surrounded herself w/many mirrors"? (b) What eventually happened to her?
4. In what way is "this poem" (starting with line 19) like the mirror in the first part of the poem?
5. The poet suggests that a good poem is, in a sense, like a mirror that can "take in" the person who looks at it. Explain this comparison in your own words.

AUGUST HEAT

by W. F. Harvey

▶ In "August Heat," English author W. F. Harvey has created a minor classic. The story starts slowly, picks up speed, and ends with a double loop-the-loop that leaps right off the page and into the future. You'll have to read every sentence carefully—and you'll be glad you did!

PHENISTONE ROAD, CLAPHAM, AUGUST 20th, 19—. I have had what I believe to be the most remarkable day in my life, and while the events are still fresh in my mind, I wish to put them down on paper as clearly as possible.

Let me say at the outset that my name is James Clarence Withencroft.

I am 40 years old, in perfect health, never having known a day's illness.

By profession I am an artist, not a very successful one, but I earn enough money by my black-and-white work to satisfy my necessary wants.

My only near relative, a sister, died five years ago, so that I am independent.

I breakfasted this morning at nine, and after glancing through the morning paper I lighted my pipe and proceeded to let my mind wander in the hope that I might chance upon some subject for my pencil.

The room, though door and windows were open, was oppressively hot, and I had just made up my mind that the coolest and most comfortable place in the neighborhood would be the deep end of the public swimming pool, when the idea came.

I began to draw. So intent was I on my work that I left my lunch untouched, only stopping work when the clock of St. Jude's struck four.

The final result, for a hurried sketch, was, I felt sure, the best thing I had done.

- outset (OUT set) beginning
- oppressively (uh PRES uv lee) harshly; very uncomfortably
- **intent** (in TENT) firmly fixed; sharply focused

It showed a criminal in the courtroom immediately after the judge had pronounced sentence. The man was fat—enormously fat. The flesh hung in rolls about his chin; it creased his huge, stumpy neck. He was clean shaven (perhaps I should say a few days before he must have been clean shaven) and almost bald. He stood in the courtroom, his short, clumsy fingers clasping the rail, looking straight in front of him. The feeling that his expression conveyed was not so much one of horror as of utter, absolute collapse.

There seemed nothing in the man strong enough to sustain that mountain of flesh.

I rolled up the sketch, and without quite knowing why, placed it in my pocket. Then with the rare sense of happiness which the knowledge of a good thing well done gives, I left the house.

I believe that I set out with the idea of calling upon Trenton, for I remember walking along Lytton Street and turning to the right along Gilchrist Road at the bottom of the hill where the men were at work on the new streetcar lines.

From there onwards I have only the vaguest recollections of where I went. The one thing of which I was fully conscious was the awful heat, that came up from the dusty asphalt pavement as an almost solid wave. I longed for the thunder promised by the great banks of copper-colored cloud that hung low over the western sky.

I must have walked five or six miles, when a small boy roused me from my reverie by asking the time.

It was 20 minutes to seven.

When he left me I began to take stock of my bearings. I found myself standing before a gate that led into a yard bordered by a strip of thirsty earth, where there were flowers, purple stock and scarlet geranium. Above the entrance was a board with the inscription—

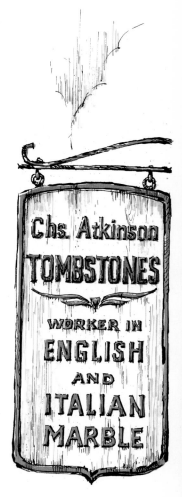

CHS. ATKINSON   TOMBSTONES

WORKER IN ENGLISH AND ITALIAN MARBLES

- **convey** (kun VAY) communicate; carry to another
- utter (UT ur) complete; total
- **sustain** (suh STAYN) keep or hold up
- reverie (REV uh ree) dreamy thoughts
- take stock—take note; record
- bearings (BAIR ingz) location; direction
- stock (STOK) kind of plant

From the yard itself came a cheery whistle, the noise of hammer blows, and the cold sound of steel meeting stone.

A sudden impulse made me enter.

A man was sitting with his back towards me, busy at work on a slab of curiously veined marble. He turned round as he heard my steps and stopped short.

It was the man I had been drawing, whose portrait lay in my pocket.

He sat there, huge and fat, the sweat pouring from his scalp, which he wiped with a red silk handkerchief. But though the face was the same, the expression was absolutely different.

He greeted me smiling, as if we were old friends, and shook my hand.

I apologized for my intrusion.

"Everything is hot and glary outside," I said. "This seems an oasis in the wilderness."

"I don't know about the oasis," he replied, "but it certainly is hot, as hot as the devil. Take a seat, sir!"

He pointed to the end of the gravestone on which he was at work, and I sat down.

"That's a beautiful piece of stone you've got hold of," I said.

- **veined** (VAYND) streaked; seamed
- **intrusion** (in TROO shun) trespassing; entry without permission

He shook his head. "In a way it is," he answered; "the surface here is as fine as anything you could wish, but there's a big flaw at the back, though I don't expect you'd ever notice it. I could never make a really good job of a bit of marble like that. It would be all right in the summer like this; it wouldn't mind the blasted heat. But wait till the winter comes. There's nothing quite like frost to find out the weak points in stone."

"Then what's it for?" I asked.

The man burst out laughing.

"You'd hardly believe me if I was to tell you it's for an exhibition, but it's the truth. Artists have exhibitions: so do grocers and butchers; we have them too. All the latest little things in headstones, you know."

He went on to talk of marbles, which sort best withstood wind and rain, and which were easiest to work; then of his garden and a new sort of carnation he had bought. At the end of every other minute he would drop his tools, wipe his shining head, and curse the heat.

I said little, for I felt uneasy. There was something unnatural, uncanny, in meeting this man.

I tried at first to persuade myself that I had seen him before, that his face, unknown to me, had found a place in some out-of-the-way corner of my memory, but I knew that I was doing little more than trying to fool myself.

Mr. Atkinson finished his work, spat on the ground, and got up with a sigh of relief.

"There! what do you think of that?" he said, with an air of evident pride.

The inscription which I read for the first time was this—

SACRED TO THE MEMORY

OF

JAMES CLARENCE WITHENCROFT.

BORN JAN. 18TH, 1860.

HE PASSED AWAY VERY SUDDENLY

ON AUGUST 20TH, 19—

"In the midst of life we are in death."

● **uncanny** (un KAN ee) mysterious; supernatural

For some time I sat in silence. Then a cold shudder ran down my spine. I asked him where he had seen the name.

"Oh, I didn't see it anywhere," replied Mr. Atkinson. "I wanted some name, and I put down the first that came into my head. Why do you want to know?"

"It's a strange coincidence, but it happens to be mine."

He gave a long, low whistle.

"And the dates?"

"I can only answer for one of them, and that's correct."

"It's a strange thing!" he said.

But he knew less than I did. I told him of my morning's work. I took the sketch from my pocket and showed it to him. As he looked, the expression of his face altered until it became more and more like that of the man I had drawn.

"And it was only the day before yesterday," he said, "that I told Maria there were no such things as ghosts!"

Neither of us had seen a ghost, but I knew what he meant.

"You probably heard my name," I said.

"And you must have seen me somewhere and have forgotten it! Were you at Clacton-on-Sea last July?"

I had never been to Clacton in my life. We were silent for some time. We were both looking at the same thing, the two dates on the gravestone, and one was right.

"Come inside and have some supper," said Mr. Atkinson.

His wife is a cheerful little woman, with the flaky red cheeks of the country-bred. Her husband introduced me as a friend of his who was an artist. The result was unfortunate, for after the sardines and watercress had been removed, she brought me out a Doré Bible, and I had to sit and express my admiration for nearly half an hour.

I went outside, and found Atkinson sitting on the gravestone smoking.

We resumed the conversation at the point we had left off.

"You must excuse my asking," I said, "but do you know of anything you've done for which you could be put on trial?"

He shook his head.

"I'm not a bankrupt, the business is prosperous enough. Three years ago I gave turkeys to some of the police at Christmas, but that's all I can think of. And they were small ones, too," he added as an afterthought.

- **watercress** (WO tur kres) kind of plant, the leaves of which may be used in a salad

He got up, fetched a can from the porch, and began to water the flowers. "Twice a day regular in the hot weather," he said, "and then the heat sometimes gets the better of the delicate ones. And ferns, good Lord! they could never stand it. Where do you live?"

I told him my address. It would take an hour's quick walk to get back home.

"It's like this," he said. "We'll look at the matter straight. If you go back home tonight, you take your chances of accidents. A cart may run over you, and there's always banana skins and orange peels, to say nothing of fallen ladders."

He spoke of the improbable with a seriousness that would have been laughable six hours before. But I did not laugh.

"The best thing we can do," he continued, "is for you to stay here till 12 o'clock. We'll go upstairs and smoke; it may be cooler inside."

To my surprise I agreed.

We are sitting in a long, low room beneath the roof. Atkinson has sent his wife to bed. He himself is busy sharpening some tools at a little oilstone, smoking one of my cigars the while.

The air seems charged with thunder. I am writing this at a shaky table before the open window. The leg is cracked, and Atkinson, who seems a handy man with his tools, is going to mend it as soon as he has finished putting an edge on his chisel.

It is after 11 now. I shall be gone in less than an hour. But the heat is stifling.

It is enough to send a man mad.

- fetch (FECH) get and bring back
- oilstone (OIL stohn) small stone used for sharpening tools
- stifling (STY fling) hot and sticky; suffocating

ALL THINGS CONSIDERED ─────────────────

1. The story begins with a date because (a) the author, W. F. Harvey, started writing the story on that day. (b) most news stories begin with dates. (c) the date later turns out to be an important detail in the story.

2. The first touch of horror for Withencroft is when he sees (a) Atkinson. (b) the tombstone. (c) the tools Atkinson uses.

3. When Withencroft and Atkinson both realize the double mystery, they regard it with (a) feelings of guilt. (b) anger at one another. (c) reasonable curiosity and worry.

4. Atkinson's main reason for inviting Withencroft to stay until midnight is that (a) Withencroft may have an accident on his way home. (b) it's too hot to walk home. (c) Atkinson enjoys talking to his guest.

5. The author suggests that Withencroft's drawing shows Atkinson in the (a) past. (b) present. (c) future.

THINKING IT THROUGH ─────────────────

1. (a) When you read the last sentence of "August Heat," what was your first reaction? (b) Some critics have called the story a "masterpiece." Do you agree? Explain your answer.

2. The discussion of *setting* on page 10 mentioned the importance of the *place,* the *time,* and certain *natural events.* Explain how all three elements of setting are important in "August Heat."

3. How is *dramatic irony* (see page 29) involved as the reader nears the end of the story?

Reading and Analyzing

Inferences and Conclusions

An **inference** (IN fur ens) is an understanding of something not stated directly. When you "read between the lines," you **infer** (in FUR) certain meanings that the writer does not clearly set forth. For instance, while reading "August Heat," you may have inferred that the story takes place in 1900. How? By adding Withencroft's age ("40") to his date of birth ("Jan. 18th, 1860"). A little figuring will show that he would turn 41 on January 18, 1901, so if he is 40 on the day of the story, August 20, the year has to be 1900.

Inferences can be small or large, from your passing reaction to a single word to an expert's hunches about Shakespeare's life experiences. A more complicated inference is sometimes called a **conclusion** (kun KLOO zhun). For instance, as you finished reading "August Heat," you probably drew a conclusion about what was to happen within the next hour.

Good readers enjoy discovering things for themselves. At times, it's much more fun to make inferences and draw conclusions than it is to have an author tell us everything directly. From start to finish, it's this kind of fun that a story like "August Heat" offers:

1. As Withencroft describes his day in the first part of the story, the reader makes inferences about the kind of person he is. In your opinion, what three adjectives best describe the man?
2. What inferences did you make when you read the inscription on the tombstone?
3. (a) What important conclusion did you reach at the end of the story? (b) What details suggested this conclusion? List as many as you can.

Composition

1. Suppose you were a teacher preparing a short quiz on the story. Write the five questions you think are most important.
2. Describe an imaginary person by using specific facts. These facts will suggest certain inferences to a reader. Your paragraph should contain *only facts* about the person's appearance and actions—no opinions, no judgments, no labels like *weird*. Yet these judgments, opinions, and labels should be clearly conveyed "between the lines." For instance, you might start like this:

She came into the bus station a little before noon, a short, thin blonde in a faded housedress. Glancing up at the clock with a frown, she put down a battered suitcase and fumbled in her purse for . . . .

Edgar Allan Poe (1809-1849)

Edgar Allan Poe's home in Richmond, Virginia

For some authors, writing is a carefully studied skill. For others, writing is a refined art. But for a very few, writing seems the outpouring of genius that cannot be contained. Edgar Allan Poe was such an author. His life proves that true talent is a powerful force indeed.

Born in 1809, Edgar Poe never knew his father, an actor who left his family and simply disappeared. Death claimed Poe's mother, an actress, when the boy was two. But luckily, the child was taken into the home of John Allan, a wealthy tobacco dealer. In 1815 the Allans went to England on business, and for five years Edgar went to a private school there.

Poe's luck, however, was not to continue. He quarreled violently with John Allan. He was forced to leave the University of Virginia because of gambling debts. He joined the army for a time, and then drifted here and there, unable to settle down. He got a number of jobs as an editor, but lost them because of excessive drinking.

In midlife Poe was taken in by an aunt, Maria Clemm. She gave him the comfort he needed, and he began to write—and sell!—the fantastic stories that made him famous. He married Mrs. Clemm's daughter, Virginia, a girl of 13.

Troubles continued to follow the struggling author. He could not hold a job for long. His stories and poems brought in some money, but never enough for a comfortable life. He, Virginia, and Mrs. Clemm drifted into poverty. Virginia died in 1847. Two years later Poe himself was found near death in Baltimore, Maryland. He died four days later.

In your opinion, what were the two worst misfortunes in Poe's unhappy life? Explain.

THE PIT AND THE PENDULUM

by Edgar Allan Poe

▶ Poe did not invent the horror story, but he did as much as any other author in history to develop it to perfection. His plots are tangles of terror that pile fear upon fear, and often corpse upon corpse. In "The Pit and the Pendulum," the tangle is more of a maze, a torture chamber in which a man is cruelly teased by hopes of survival. The **narrator** (person who tells the story) is a condemned prisoner during the Spanish Inquisition, a period when many persons were tried, convicted, and even killed for their religious beliefs.

I was sick—sick unto death with that long agony; and when they at last unbound me and I was permitted to sit, I felt that my senses were leaving me. The sentence—the dreadful sentence of death—was the last clear sound that reached my ears. After that, I heard no more. Yet, for a while, I saw the lips of the black-robed judges. They appeared to me white—whiter than the paper upon which I now write—and thin, very thin. I saw that more words were still coming from those lips. I saw them pronounce the syllables of my name, and I shuddered because no sound came forth. And then my vision fell upon the seven tall candles on the table. At first they seemed like white slender angels who would save me. But then, all at once, the angel forms became meaningless specters, with heads of flame. I saw that from them there would be no help. Finally, the figures of the judges vanished, as if by magic, from before me. The tall candles sank into nothingness. The blackness settled over all. Silence, and stillness, and night were the universe.

I had swooned. But I will not say that all consciousness was lost. The shadows of my memory tell, indistinctly, of tall figures that lifted and carried me down—down—still down. Then came a sense of sudden stillness. Then all was *madness*—the madness of a memory that busied itself with forbidden thoughts. And in that memory were thoughts of the trial, of the

---

- **pendulum** (PEN juh lum) swinging weight, as in an old-fashioned clock
- **specter** (SPEK tur) ghost; phantom
- **swoon** (SWOON) faint

83

judges, of the sentence, of the sickness, of the swoon.

So far, I had not opened my eyes. I felt that I lay upon my back, unbound. I reached out my hand, and it fell heavily upon something damp and hard. I let my hand stay there for many minutes, while I tried to imagine where and *what* I could be. I wanted, yet dared not, to use my eyes. I dreaded the first glance at objects around me. But at last, with a wild desperation at heart, I quickly opened my eyes. The blackness of eternal night surrounded me. I struggled for breath. The very air around me grew thick. I still lay quietly, and made an effort to think clearly. I brought to mind the trial. From that point on, what had happened to me? The sentence had been given, and it seemed that a very long time had then passed. The sentence had de-manded my death—yet not for a moment did I suppose myself actually dead. Those condemned to die, I knew, were usually burned, many persons together. There had been such a public burning on the very day of my trial. Had I been sent back to my cell, to wait for the next great fire? No, my cell had had a dry stone floor, and light was not completely shut out.

I at once got to my feet, trembling all over. I threw my arms wildly above and around me in all directions. I felt nothing, yet I dreaded to move a step, for fear I should be stopped by the walls of a *tomb*. Perspiration stood in big cold beads on my forehead. The agony of suspense grew at last too much, and I cautiously stepped forward. My arms felt the air in front of me. My eyes strained to catch some faint ray of light. I proceeded for many

---

● **desperation** (des puh RAY shun) the state of utter hopelessness

steps, but still all was blackness, emptiness.

And now, as I continued, there came to mind a thousand vague rumors of horrors of Spanish prisons. Of some dungeons there had been strange things told—untrue things I had always thought—but yet terrifying, and too horrible to repeat, except in a whisper. Was I left to die of starvation in this underground world of darkness? Or what other torture, perhaps even worse, awaited me? That the result would be death, a cruel, bitter death, I had no doubt. I knew my judges too well to doubt that. The time and the manner of my death were the only things left in doubt now.

My hand before me at last bumped against something hard. It was a wall, seemingly of stone, very smooth, slimy, and cold. I followed it, stepping carefully. This process, however, gave me no way of knowing how large my dungeon was. I might make a complete circle and return to the point where I started without being aware of the fact. I therefore felt for the knife which had been in my pocket, when led into the inquisitorial chamber. But it was gone. My clothes had been exchanged for a robe of coarse cloth. I had thought of forcing the blade into some small crack in the wall. Instead, I tore a part of the hem from the robe. This I laid at full length on the floor, at right angles to the wall. In feeling my way around the dungeon, I could not fail to feel the heavy cloth upon completing one trip.

So, at least, I thought. But I had not counted on the large size of the dungeon, or upon my own weakness. The ground was moist and slippery. I staggered onward for some time, when I stumbled and fell. My tired body remained flat, and sleep soon overtook me as I lay there.

Upon awakening, I stretched forth an arm. There beside me were a loaf of bread and a pitcher of water. I was much too exhausted to wonder about them, but I ate and drank eagerly. Shortly afterward I continued my tour of the prison, and at last came upon the strip of cloth. Up to the time I fell, I had counted 52 steps. Upon the rest of my walk, I had counted 48 more. There were in all then, 100 steps. Counting two steps to the yard, I judged the distance around the walls to be 50 yards.

Leaving the wall, I decided to cross the area. At first I proceeded with extreme care. The floor, although seemingly of solid material, was treacherous with slime. After some time, however, I took courage. I did not hesitate to step firmly, trying to cross in as straight a line as possible. I had gone 10 or 12 steps in this manner, when the strip of cloth from my robe became tangled between my legs. I stepped on it, and fell violently on my face. In the confusion of my fall, I did not realize a somewhat strange fact. But a few seconds afterward, as I lay there, it became clear: My chin rested upon the floor, but the upper part of my face, seemingly lower, touched nothing. At

---

• inquisitorial (in kwiz i TOHR ee ul) having to do with inquiry or questioning (here the courtroom of the Spanish Inquisition)

the same time, my forehead seemed bathed in cold, stale air. The peculiar smell of decaying fungus rose to my nose. I put forward my arm—and shuddered. I had fallen at the very edge of a circular pit. Feeling around on the rough stone wall just below the edge, I succeeded in breaking off a small piece. This I let fall into the pit. For many seconds I listened to its sound as it hit against the sides of the pit below. Finally there came the sudden plunge into water. At the same moment there came a sound from overhead. A door seemed to open and close quickly. A faint gleam of light flashed suddenly through the gloom, and as rapidly faded away.

I saw clearly the doom that had been prepared for me. Another step before my fall, and the world would have seen me no more. Shaking in every limb, I found my way back to the wall, resolving to die there rather than risk the dangers of the wells, which I now imagined in many places about the dungeon.

The terrors in my mind kept me awake for many long hours; but at last I slept again. Upon waking up, I found by my side, as before, a loaf and a pitcher of water. A burning thirst made me empty the pitcher at once. Then, for some reason, I slept once more. A deep sleep fell upon me—a sleep like that of death. How long it lasted, I know not. But when I opened my eyes, the objects around me were visible. By a wild, yellowish light, I could see the size and details of my prison.

In its size I had been greatly mistaken. The whole distance around was not more than 25 yards. How had I gone so wrong in measuring it? The truth at last flashed upon me. I had counted 52 paces to the point when I fell. I must then have been within a step or two of the strip of cloth. I then slept. Upon awakening, I must have returned upon my steps. In that way I had supposed the distance around to be nearly double what it actually was. My confusion prevented me from realizing that I began my tour with the wall to the left, and ended it with the wall to the right.

The general shape of the prison was square. I examined the walls first. What I had taken for stone now seemed to be iron, in huge plates. I now noticed the floor, too, which was of stone. In the center yawned the round pit from whose jaws I had escaped. It was the only one in the dungeon.

All this I saw indistinctly and with much effort, for much had changed during my deep sleep. I now lay upon my back. Under me was some kind of low framework of wood. To this I was tied by a long rope. It passed in many convolutions around my limbs and body. My head, however, was free, as was my left arm. I could, with much effort, supply myself with food from a dish by my side on the floor. I saw, to

---

- **fungus** (FUN gus) growths like mushrooms, molds, and mildews
- **resolving** (ri ZOLV ing) determining; deciding firmly
- plate (PLAYT) large, flat sheet, as of glass
- convolution (kon vuh LOO shun) coil; twisting roll

my horror, that the pitcher had been removed. I saw to my horror—for I was wild with thirst. This thirst seemed part of the plan of my tormentors, for the food in the dish was highly seasoned.

Looking upward, I studied the ceiling of my prison. It was some 30 or 40 feet high. On one of its iron panels a very strange figure held my whole attention. It was the painted figure of Time we have all seen often. But instead of a scythe, he held what I supposed to be the painted shape of a huge pendulum. There was something about the appearance of this pendulum that made me regard it carefully. While I gazed directly upward at it, I thought that I saw it in motion. Yes! Its sweep

was short, and of course slow. I watched it for some minutes, sometimes in fear, but more in wonder.

A slight noise attracted my notice. Looking at the floor, I saw several enormous rats crossing it. They had come from the pit, just within view on my right. Even as I gazed, they came up in troops. Their hungry eyes seemed drawn by the scent of the meat. It required much effort to scare them away.

It might have been half an hour before I again looked upward. What I then saw amazed me. The sweep of the pendulum had increased by nearly a yard. Its speed was also much greater. But what mainly disturbed me was the fact that it had *descended*. I now observed it with horror. The lower edge, I saw, was

- scythe (SYTH) a long, curved blade used for cutting grass, etc.
- **sweep** (SWEEP) steady, curving motion

a curve of glistening steel. It was about a foot long, as sharp as a razor. Attached to the solid and broad part of the pendulum above, the *shining* blade hissed as it swung through the air.

I could no longer doubt the doom that waited for me. My knowledge of the pit had become known to my persecutors. Having failed to fall, I now awaited a different destruction. How can I describe the long, long hours of horror? I lay there counting the rushing swings of the steel. Inch by inch, down and down it slowly came. Days seemed to pass before it swept so close as to fan me with its horrid breath. The odor of the sharp steel seemed to force its way into my nostrils. I prayed. I prayed for its speedy descent. I grew mad. I struggled to force myself upward against the sweep of the fearful blade. And then I fell suddenly calm. I lay there smiling at the glittering death, like a child at some rare toy.

There was another period of blackness then. I swooned again—but not for long. Upon my recovery, I felt very sick and weak. Even in the agony of that period, my human nature wanted food. With painful effort I stretched out my left arm. I picked up a small piece of meat that had been spared me by the rats. As I put it between my lips, there rushed to my mind a half-formed thought of joy. Of hope, even. It was, as I say, a half-formed thought. It was not completed. I felt that it was of hope. But I felt also that it had disappeared as

it had started to form in my mind. In vain I struggled to regain it. Long suffering had affected my mind. I was an imbecile—an idiot.

The swing of the pendulum was at right angles to my body. I saw that the knife passed over the region of my heart. It would slice through the cloth of my robe. It would return and repeat its slicing—again—and again. That would be all that would happen—at first. The hissing blade would cut only the cloth. In spite of its wide sweep—some 30 feet or more—it would at first cut only the cloth. And at this thought I paused. I forced myself to think about the sound that the steel would make as it passed across the garment.

Down—steadily down it crept. I took mad pleasure in contrasting its slow descent to its whistling sidelong speed. To the right. To the left. Far and wide. It was the shriek of a damned spirit. I laughed. I howled.

Down—certainly, cruelly down! It swung within three inches of my chest. I struggled violently—furiously—to free my left arm. It was free only from the elbow to the hand. That hand could reach from the platter on the floor to my mouth. But no farther. If I could have broken the rope above the elbow, I would have seized the top part of the pendulum. I might as well have tried to stop an avalanche.

Down—down—steadily down! I gasped and struggled convulsively at each rushing swing. I shrank at its

* **persecutor** (PUR suh kyoo tur) one one persecutes, or causes others to suffer
* **imbecile** (IM buh sil) one with a very weak mind
* **convulsively** (kun VUL siv lee) with instinctive, uncontrolled muscular movements

every sweep over me. My eyes followed its outward and upward movements with despair. They closed themselves at its descent, as though death would have been a relief.

I saw that some 10 or 12 sweeps would bring the sharp steel in actual contact with my robe. And suddenly there came over me a calm, collected feeling—the calmness of despair. For the first time in many hours—or perhaps days— I *thought*. I really used my mind. It now occurred to me that the rope that held me was a strange one. I was tied by no separate cord. The first stroke of the razor-sharp knife across the band would detach it. I would then be able to unwind it from my body with my left hand. But was it likely that my persecutors had not foreseen this possibility? Was it likely that the strap crossed my chest in the path of the pendulum? Dreading to find my last hope crushed, I raised my head and struggled for a clear view of my body. The rope circled my body and limbs closely in all places—*except in the path of the destroying steel blade.*

I dropped my head back to its original position. All at once a new thought flashed upon my mind. It was the unformed half of that idea of hope I have already mentioned. The whole thought was now present—feeble, perhaps insane, but still complete. I proceeded at once, with the nervous energy of despair, to turn that thought into action.

For many hours the floor below me had been swarming with rats. They were wild with hunger. Their red eyes glared at me, as if they awaited my death to make me their meal. They had eaten, in spite of my efforts, all but a few pieces of the meat on the dish. My hand had waved above the platter almost constantly. In their hunger, the rats had frequently fastened their sharp teeth to my fingers.

I gathered up all the pieces of oily and spicy meat that remained. With them, I rubbed the rope wherever I could reach it. Then I lay breathlessly still.

At first, the starving animals were startled and terrified at the change— the cessation of all movement. They shrank back. But this was only for a moment. I had not been mistaken about their hunger. Noticing that I remained without motion, one or two of the boldest leaped upon the framework under me. They smelled at the rope. This seemed the signal for a general rush, and forth they hurried in fresh troops. They clung to the wood. They overran it. They leaped in hundreds upon my body. The regular movements of the pendulum bothered them not at all. Avoiding its strokes, they busied themselves with the rope. They pressed— They swarmed upon me in growing heaps. Their cold lips found my own. A kind of disgust for which the world has no name chilled my heart. Yet one minute more, and I felt that the struggle would be over. Clearly I felt the loosening of the rope. I knew that in more than one place it must be already chewed through. With a more than human effort I lay *still*.

- **collected** (kuh LEK tid) controlled; undisturbed
- **cessation** (se SAY shun) stopping; ceasing

I had not suffered in vain. I at last felt that I was *free*. The rope hung in ribbons from my body. But the pendulum already pressed upon my chest. It had sliced through the cloth of the robe. Twice again it swung, and a sharp pain shot through me. Now the moment of escape had arrived. At a wave of my hand the rats hurried away. With a steady movement—cautious, sidelong, shrinking, and slow—I slid to my right, beyond the reach of the pendulum. For the moment, at least, *I was free*.

Free!—and still in the hands of the Inquisition! I stood up, moving away from my wooden bed of horror. As I did so, the motion of the huge pendulum stopped. I watched it pulled up, by some hidden force, through the ceiling. This was a lesson I took to heart. My every motion, I knew, was being watched. Free!—I had escaped death in one form, then death in another. Now, I was certain, I would face death again.

Unreal! Even as I stood there, the breath of heated iron came to my nostrils. I rolled my eyes nervously around on the walls of iron that surrounded me. A choking odor filled the prison. I panted. I gasped for breath. There could be no doubt of the plan of my persecutors. Oh, demons! I shank from the metal, beginning to glow now, to the center of the cell. At the thought of the fiery death that lay ahead, the idea of the coolness of the well came over my soul like balm. I rushed to the edge of the pit. I threw my vision below. Yet, for a wild moment, my spirit refused to allow my body to jump. Oh! for a voice to speak!—oh! horror!—oh! any horror but this! With a shriek, I rushed away from the pit. I buried my face in my hands—weeping bitterly.

The heat rapidly increased. Once again I looked up, shuddering. There had been a second change in the cell—a change in *shape*. The demons of the Inquisition who held me had been angered by my second escape. Now they would play with my terrors no longer. The room had been square. In an instant it had changed its shape to that of a diamond. And the change had not stopped there. Even as I watched, the red-hot walls closed slowly inward. Could I resist the glow? Could I withstand the pressure? And now, flatter and flatter grew the diamond. Its center, and of course its greatest width, came right over the yawning jaws of the pit. I shrank back—but the closing walls pressed me onward. At last there was no longer an inch of floor to stand on. I struggled no more. I tottered upon the pit's edge with one loud, long, and final scream of despair. I tried not to look down—

There was the discordant hum of human voices! There was a loud blast of trumpets! There was a great grinding noise, as of a thousand thunders! The fiery walls rushed back! An arm stretched out and caught my own as I fell, fainting, into the pit. It was the arm of General LaSalle. The French army had entered the city. The Inquisition was in the hands of its enemies.

- balm (BAHM) comforting ointment or salve
- **discordant** (dis KOR dunt) quarreling; struggling

ALL THINGS CONSIDERED

1. The reason the prisoner is sentenced to death (a) concerns his high position in the French army. (b) is not made entirely clear. (c) is that he refused to join any church.
2. Edgar Allan Poe states that people condemned to die in the Spanish Inquisition were usually (a) tortured in underground jails. (b) burned in public. (c) worked to death.
3. The prisoner avoids death in the pit (or well) by (a) careful planning and action. (b) a lucky accident. (c) the timely arrival of the French army.
4. The prisoner avoids death by the pendulum by (a) careful planning and action. (b) a lucky accident. (c) the timely arrival of the French army.
5. We can tell from the story that Edgar Allan Poe (a) knew both France and Spain well. (b) believed in religious freedom. (c) knew how to pile horror upon horror.

THINKING IT THROUGH

1. (a) What three main terrors did the prisoner encounter in the dungeon? (b) What other horrors did the dungeon contain? Name as many as you can.
2. The prisoner feels more and more sure that he is being watched. Upon what facts does he base this opinion?
3. In spite of his condition, the prisoner does manage to plan and attempt certain courses of action that might help save him. What are three examples, and what is the result in each case?
4. How did you react to the end of the story? Some readers feel that the final rescue is just too unbelievable to accept. After all, the French army is not mentioned until the next-to-last sentence. Do you think that Poe resorted to a "cheap ending" for an otherwise thrilling tale? Explain.
5. The Spanish Inquisition was a sad event in human history in which individuals were tortured for their beliefs. In "The Pit and the Pendulum," Poe uses elements of fantasy (such as the walls of a cell closing in and becoming hotter) in describing a torture chamber. Why do you think Poe included such elements in his story? Where might you look to find information on the actual events of the Spanish Inquisition?

Reading and Analyzing

Appreciating Imagery

Like many good writers, Edgar Allan Poe uses words skillfully to paint pictures. Think, for instance, about the first paragraph of "The Pit and the Pendulum." The reader can almost *see* the black-robed judges' lips—thin, white, moving, and to the narrator at least, silent. Then come the seven tall candles on the table, candles that first become angels and finally specters.

Not only does Poe try to appeal to the reader's sense of sight, he also enables the reader to hear, feel, smell, and even taste the horrors experienced by the suffering prisoner. In other words, Poe is a master of **imagery.**

In literature, an **image** is something that appeals to one of the five senses. A **visual image,** of course, offers the reader a mental picture of what is described. Other images appeal to the senses of hearing, touch (or feeling), smell, and taste.

1. In your opinion, what is the most powerful visual image in "The Pit and the Pendulum"? That is, what is the sharpest picture in your mind right after having read the story? Look back at the story to find some words used to create that image.
2. Of the several sounds in the story, which do you remember best?
3. Several times the narrator touches objects and experiences other physical sensations. Which image of this kind do you remember best?
4. On page 86, what words does Poe use to describe the smell of the pit?
5. On page 89, what two words are used to describe the taste of the meat?
6. In your opinion, why do authors often try hard to create effective images? That is, how can good imagery make a good story even better?

Composition

1. Write a short paragraph showing how Poe uses four kinds of imagery (all except taste) to create the effect of the pendulum. Remember to put the author's own words in quotation marks.

2. After you finish reading these directions, close your eyes, try to relax, and imagine yourself where you'd most like to be right now. The choice is up to you—in a darkened movie house, on a beach, around a campfire . . . wherever. For a few minutes, take it easy as you let your senses soak up the surroundings. What do you see and hear? Feel and smell? Perhaps even taste? Finally, break the spell and write a description of the images in a way that will invite the reader to share your thoughts and experiences.

ABU THE WAG

from The Arabian Nights (traditional)

▶ The story is a strange one. In the wonderland of ancient Persia, there once lived a very rich king. He had a horrible habit. He married one wife after another, putting each to death when he grew tired of her. But one of his wives, a beauty named Scheherazade (shuh her uh ZAHD) managed to outwit him. On the night she was to die, she began telling a story that fascinated the king. He let her live one more day to finish it. The next day she teased the king with another unfinished story. That tale turned into still another story . . . and another . . . and another. Today the world knows the series of tangled tales as *The Thousand and One Nights* (or *The Arabian Nights*).

And happily, after 1,001 nights, the king let Scheherazade live.

I will tell you (said Scheherazade) about a happy Caliph who once ruled the great city of Baghdad.* Everyone agreed that he governed his people well. He loved his work, he loved his power, and he loved his riches. But most of all, he loved a good joke.

It was the Caliph's habit at times to walk among his people disguised as a merchant. In that way he could ascertain what really was going on. He could discover for himself if the people in his government were doing a good job.

One day the Caliph left the palace in disguise. With him he took a huge guard named Masrur, also dressed as a merchant. About noon they passed over a small bridge, and there they saw a sad-faced young man leaning on the rail, looking down into the water. The Caliph and Masrur went up to him.

"Excuse me," the Caliph began. "We are thinking of doing business in this city. Tell us, is Baghdad as great a city as we have

---

- wag (WAG) joker
- caliph (KAY lif) title of the political and religious leader of the old Near East
- **ascertain** (as ur TAYN) find out definitely; determine

*Baghdad (BAG dad) was the most important city in the ancient Near East. It is the capital of modern Iraq.

heard? Are its rulers good men, or do they line their pockets with the people's gold?"

The sad-eyed man replied that Baghdad was indeed the greatest city on earth. Its government, he stated, was the best. Then he continued with a strange request:

"Now, what do you say to this? It is the hour to eat. A good meal is waiting at my house, and I should like nothing better than to have you as my guests."

This was odd, the Caliph thought. Why should this unhappy man ask two strangers to eat with him?

"Allah upon thee," the Caliph exclaimed. "But it is you who should come with me. Come, be *my* guest."

The sad-faced man refused. They argued over who should go to whose house, and at last the Caliph consented. He and the huge Masrur walked to the stranger's house. Asking his guard to stay outside the door, the Caliph entered.

The host's dining room was large and well furnished. The sad man's old mother brought food, and the men sat down to eat. The food, too, was excellent. This increased the Caliph's curiosity. Why should his host invite to such a feast an unknown person he took to be a merchant?

Before long the host's face became a little less sad. In fact, it lit up at times as he entertained his guest with stories. His hospitality and good manners pleased the Caliph. More and more, the Caliph wanted to know who his new friend was.

Soon a slave girl entered with a lute. The two men listened happily as she sang a song. When she left, the impetuous Caliph burst out:

"O my young friend, tell me about yourself, so that I can repay your kindness."

The host looked up from his roast goose. "Know, my lord, that my name is Abu al-Hasan. A year ago my father died and left me some wealth. Of the money I made two parts. One part I put aside, and with the other, I enjoyed the pleasures of friendship and laughter. My life was just one long party. It was the best restaurants, the best everything. My friends always knew that if they had no money, Abu al-Hasan would pay."

Suddenly Abu al-Hasan's face grew sad again.

"Go on," said the Caliph. "Then what happened?"

- **Allah** (AL uh) term for God in the Islamic religion
- **lute** (LOOT) kind of old-fashioned stringed instrument
- **impetuous** (im PECH oo us) overly eager; quick to act

"Well," said the other, "soon I had spent all that money on friends and good cheer. When there was no wealth left, I went around to my so-called friends. Perhaps, I thought, they would be generous with me. But alas, no help for their former friend. Not one of them would offer me so much as a slice of bread."

The Caliph nodded.

"So I wept for myself," Abu continued. "I talked things over with my mother. 'Such are friends,' she told me. 'When a person has money, they eat you up with their friendship. But when a person has none, they chase you away.'

"Right then I got out the other half of my money. And I made a promise to myself, too. I promised never again to entertain anyone more than a single day. I decided to have no real friends. If I see you on the street tomorrow, I will not even say hello. I will pretend not to notice you at all."

When the Commander of the Faithful heard this, he laughed a loud laugh. "O my brother," he said, "I have made a good friend today. I wish to be your friend for life."

"Did I not just say I would not speak to you tomorrow?" asked Abu al-Hasan.

"Well," replied the Caliph, "for *today* at least let us go on feasting like brothers."

As the meal continued, the two men talked and talked. At last the Caliph thought he could speak to his host with honest concern:

"Tell me, my friend," he began, "tell me what's on your mind. Tell me what makes your face so sad at times. Tell me what would make you the happiest man on earth."

Abu al-Hasan looked thoughtful and solemn. Then his eyes gleamed. "By heaven!" he exclaimed. "I wish that I could be Caliph for just one day!"

"Why so?" asked the Commander of the Faithful.

"To get my revenge on four holy men," Abu al-Hasan shot back. "In my neighborhood there is a mosque. In it are these four men who tell lies about me. They do not like the way I entertain guests with fine food and music, so they poison other people's minds against me. They call themselves holy men, but they are villains all. If I had my way, each and every one of them would be whipped 400 times. Then I'd set them backwards on donkeys and haul them through the streets for shame. That is what I wish, and no more."

"Allah give you what you ask," said the Caliph quietly.

• mosque (MOSK) Islamic building for worship

The two went on talking, and soon Abu al-Hasan was feeling happier. He told stories that made the Caliph bend over double with laughter. And in turn, the Caliph's tales made Abu roll his eyes toward the ceiling with mirth. Abu did not notice when the Caliph slipped something into his cup.

Before long Abu was nodding, nearly asleep. The Caliph tiptoed out. "Wait a few minutes," he told his slave Masrur. "Then go into the house. You will find the young man asleep. Pick him up and bring him to me at the palace. And when you go out, shut the door."

So saying, the Commander of the Faithful hurried ahead to the royal palace. He wanted to get everyone ready for the joke he had in mind.

The next morning Abu al-Hasan slept late. He opened his eyes on a room with gold walls. Surely, this was a dream! He blinked. A slave girl began opening curtains made of silver thread.

"Allah be praised," murmured Abu. "Either I am dreaming a dream, or this is paradise itself!" Then he shut his eyes again. He would have gone back to sleep, but a manservant approached and said:

"O my lord, this is not your usual habit."

Then more of the slave girls of the palace appeared. They lifted Abu to a sitting position. He found himself upon a silk mattress, raised about a yard from the floor. The attendants propped him up with pillows, and he looked again at the huge room. From the ceiling hung stars of red gold. Servants stood in waiting everywhere.

"It's not as if I were awake," marveled Abu, "yet I am not asleep, either." He closed his eyes and bowed his head. Then he opened his eyelids slowly and stood up. Suddenly he put a finger between his teeth and bit down hard. "Ouch!" he cried. The pain, at least, was very real.

Behind a curtain that led to an adjoining room, the real Caliph laughed and laughed.

Another slave girl stepped up. "At your service, O Commander of the Faithful," she said.

"What is your name?" Abu asked.

"Shajarat al-Durr," answered the girl.

"By the protection of Allah," Abu said, "am I the Caliph? Am I the Commander of the Faithful?"

• mirth (MURTH) noisy happiness; laughter

"Yes, indeed," she replied. "By the protection of Allah, you are—"

"No!" Abu cried. "I am *not* the Caliph! You are a liar!" He motioned to one of the chief servants, who came and kissed the floor at Abu's feet.

"Yes, O Commander of the Faithful," the servant said.

"Who is Commander of the Faithful?" Abu asked him.

"You are, of course," the servant replied.

"Liar!" Abu cried. "In one night, do I become the Caliph? Yesterday I was Abu al-Hasan, and today I am the Commander of the Faithful. That does not make sense."

The servant withdrew and another stepped forward. He gave Abu a pair of sandals made of silk and gold cloth. Abu stood there admiring the sandals, holding one in each hand.

"Allah! Allah! O my lord," the servant said, "these sandals are for your feet, so you can walk to your dressing room."

Abu put on the sandals and followed the servant across the room. In the dressing room the slave girls brought him a basin of brass and a pitcher of silver. Abu washed. Then other servants dressed him in a silk and linen robe. Finally, the royal dagger was place in Abu's hand.

Suddenly an attendant entered and bowed low. "O Prince of True Believers," he said, "the Grand Vizier is outside. He wants permission to enter."

- **attendant** (uh TEN dunt) person who serves or waits on others

"Let him come in," Abu declared. He knew that the Grand Vizier was a very important man. Surely, if anyone would know that Abu was not the Caliph, it would be the Grand Vizier.

A big fellow with a smiling, fat face came into the room. He kissed the floor at Abu's feet and remained on his knees. "O Commander of the Faithful," he said, "may the whole world be yours. May fire be the home of your enemies. Never may any man say a bad thing about you, O Caliph of all cities and ruler of all countries."

Abu scratched his head. He didn't know what to say—or do. Well, he thought, if he *were* the Caliph, he would try giving an order. He would see what happened. He told the Grand Vizier to go to such a place in such a street and deliver a hundred gold pieces to the mother of Abu al-Hasan.

"And nearby you will find a mosque," Abu continued. "Take the four holy men there. Beat each of them with a thousand lashes. Then set them on donkeys, face to tail. Parade them around the city. Have someone go before them, crying, 'This is what happens to those who say bad things about the Caliph's great friend Abu al-Hasan.'"

"With obedience," the Grand Vizier said, bowing low.

Abu held his breath as the Grand Vizier left the room. Now he had given an order. And, what was more important, he had seen it obeyed.

"It is true!" Abu cried. "I *am* the Caliph!" His face was happy as he walked with a dozen attendants to the throne room.

Abu al-Hasan was nobody's fool (Scheherazade went on), even if he did let himself be tricked into thinking he was the Caliph. After all, what would you have thought? You wake up in the Caliph's bed. You are treated like the Caliph. You give orders, and you see them obeyed. You know you aren't dreaming. So—you must be the Caliph.

In the throne room Abu counted 40 doors, all covered by curtains. He didn't know, of course, that the real Caliph, laughing all the time, crouched behind one of the curtains. No, Abu was too busy giving orders to the Captains and Lords who stood in rows before the throne. He was beginning to have trouble thinking of new orders when the Grand Vizier returned.

"Ho! Ho!" Abu laughed. "You know, last night I had a very

● vizier (vi ZEER) high official in certain Islamic countries

strange dream. I dreamed that all my life I had been not the Caliph but a man named Abu al-Hasan."

The Grand Vizier laughed at this, which made Abu laugh all
the harder. He didn't know that the real Caliph, secreted behind
one of the curtains, was laughing hardest of all.

"It is time—is it not?—to go to the room of the harem," the
Grand Vizier suggested.

Abu nodded. He followed the Grand Vizier to another large
room, where he found candles lighted and lamps burning. A
group of women played instruments as they sang. Ten beautiful
slave girls led him to a raised platform covered with silk pillows.

"By Allah, I am in truth the Commander of the Faithful," Abu
told himself. The slave girls brought him a great tray covered
with the richest viands. He ate as much as he could hold. When he
was full he called one of the girls and asked, "What is your
name?"

"My name is Miskah," she replied.

"And what is your name?" Abu said to another.

"My name is Tarkah."

Then Abu asked a third, "What is your name?"

"Tohfah," came the answer.

Abu went on, till he had learned all 10 names. He invited the
girls to eat. Soon three groups of singers entered. They sang all
kinds of melodies, and the room rang with the sweetness of the
songs. The pipes cried out and the lutes wailed. It seemed to Abu
that he was in paradise, for he had never been happier.

So the day passed, as Abu talked and joked with the slave
girls. Some sat by him; others stood. Abu's happiness made others
happy, too. There was more to eat and drink. Toward evening,
after his fourth meal of the day, Abu began to feel drowsy. He
closed his eyes and lay back. It was the same kind of deep sleep
he had fallen into the day before.

Soon the real Caliph stepped out from behind a curtain.
Laughing hard, he called for his servant Masrur. "Carry this man
to his own place," he ordered. "But first, dress him in his own
clothes so he will look more like Abu al-Hasan."

Even after Abu had been carried away, the Caliph could not
stop laughing. He kept asking for handkerchiefs to mop up the

* secreted (si KREET id) hidden; concealed
* **harem** (HAR um) group of women in an Oriental or
  Near Eastern palace
* viands (VY undz) choice foods

tears in his eyes. "Ho! Jolly good!" he would shout, and would again bend over and hold his sides.

Finally the Caliph came to his senses. "This Abu is a jolly wag," he said. "I will bring him to the palace and make him my friend. We will call him *Abu the Wag*."

As for Abu, he awoke the next morning in his own house. At first he had no idea where he was. "Ho Tuffahla!" he cried out. "Ho, Miskah. Ho, Grand Vizier."

His mother heard him and came running into the room. "Ho, yourself," she said. "Ho. Ho. Ho."

"Ho!" said Abu. "Jolly good!"

"What's 'jolly good'?" asked his mother.

"Where am I?" asked Abu.

"You're home, now," she replied. "But where have you been? I didn't see you for a day. Then here you are at home."

Abu looked at his mother through narrow eyes. "Who are you?"

"Why, your mother, Abu al-Hasan."

Abu explained that he was *not* Abu—so, of course, his mother could *not* be his mother. He was, he said, the Caliph of Baghdad, and he would now be off to his palace.

"Heaven preserve us!" cried his mother. "You have lost your mind! You are mad!"

"O my mother," Abu exclaimed, "I saw myself in a dream in a palace. There were slave girls there. And Captains, and Lords, and the Grand Vizier. I gave orders, and I had them obeyed. By Allah, O my mother, that is what I saw—*and in truth it was no dream*."

"Quiet!" ordered his mother. "Suppose people hear of this silly talk and carry it to the Caliph. We will lose our wealth. We may even lose our lives."

Abu al-Hasan sat down in a chair to think. Slowly, some of his Abu-ness came back to him. Now he didn't really know *who* he was. Was it Abu who had dreamed he was the Caliph? Or was it the Caliph who had dreamed he was Abu? It was his mother who decided the question.

"A strange thing happened yesterday," she said. "While you were gone, the Grand Vizier came here himself. He gave me a hundred pieces of gold."

"Ho!" Abu jumped up. "Jolly good! Ho! You see, I sent the Grand Vizier here. I, the Commander of the Faithful."

"You are mad!"

"You are a liar, who would make me out an idiot!"

Abu screamed the words with such force that his mother grew worried. "O Muslims!" she yelled at the top of her voice. "Help! Help! Help!"

People outside the house heard her desperate entreaties and came in. Abu's mother was cringing in a corner as he paced about the floor.

"The devil has entered him!" Abu's mother croaked. "My son is insane!"

"Old woman," Abu roared, "am I not the Commander of the Faithful? You are a witch. You have bewitched me."

When the people heard Abu's words, they were quite sure he had lost his balance. "This man is mad," they said. Some jumped forward to seize him as others ran for a heavy rope. Then they stripped him of his clothes and tied him to a high beam with the rope. He was beaten and kicked.

"We'll leave you to come to your senses," the people said. "When you decide you are Abu al-Hasan again, just call out. We will release you."

The people left finally, and Abu was as confused as ever. For a long time he did not move. Then he began to stare out the window. He cried "Ho!" to neighbors in the street. But the people seemed not to hear him, as though he were not there. "This is strange," Abu said to himself. "First I was Abu. Then I was the Caliph. Now I seem to be nobody at all."

It pleased Abu to be Nobody. Of course, it wasn't like being the happy Caliph. But it was better than being the sad Abu. And if he were Nobody, he couldn't get into any trouble. So Abu was Nobody—until he began to feel hungry. Then a question popped into his mind. Would Nobody have to eat? No, Abu decided. So, after all, he must be Somebody. But who?

The day wore on, with Abu growing more hungry and stiff with each passing hour. At last he drifted into a kind of half-sleep. Then suddenly he *knew* he was asleep and dreaming, for he heard the voice of the Grand Vizier:

"Abu, we have come."

Abu opened his eyes. There in front of him were three men: the Grand Vizier, a huge giant, and a smaller man. The last was wearing the Caliph's shoes. His robe was the Caliph's, too. And in his hand he carried the Caliph's dagger.

- Muslim (MUZ lim) follower of the Islamic religion
- entreaty (en TREE tee) earnest plea; request
- cringing (KRINJ ing) crouching down in fear

"Why!" Abu said aloud. "This is surely the Caliph. And that means I must be Abu al-Hasan."

Now, the Caliph loved nothing better than a good joke. But he had no wish to play a mean trick on anyone. When news of Abu's troubles had reached him, he had lost no time in coming to help. In a minute Abu was out of his ropes. In another he was dressed. Soon after that, everything was explained. The Caliph gave his new friend a thousand gold pieces. He invited Abu to move to a house next door to the palace.

"I want you to visit me every day," the Caliph said, putting his arm around Abu's shoulder. "We shall tell stories. We shall eat. We shall laugh."

That very day, Abu received the Caliph's gold. In a week, he had moved next door to the palace. And in a month, he had married the fairest daughter of the Grand Vizier. He was never to know another day's sadness in his life. For he soon learned that there was something better than being either the sad Abu or the happy Caliph. This was being the happy Abu.

ALL THINGS CONSIDERED

1. The *narrator* (see page 83) of "Abu the Wag" is (a) the Caliph. (b) Scheherazade. (c) Abu.
2. At the time he first meets the Caliph, Abu has (a) maintained the love of many good friends. (b) promised himself a one-day limit to all friendships. (c) given all his money to his mother.
3. The Caliph's joke on Abu involves (a) only the Caliph. (b) only the Caliph and his council. (c) everyone in the palace.
4. Abu is finally rescued from his troubles by (a) his mother. (b) friendly neighbors. (c) the Caliph himself.
5. The character who most deserves to be called a *wag* is (a) the Caliph. (b) the servant Masrur. (c) Abu.

THINKING IT THROUGH

1. The story shows Abu in a constant process of change. Give examples showing Abu (a) *sad.* (b) *happy.* (c) *confused.*
2. The introduction indicates that Scheherazade interrupted each story in *The Arabian Nights* at a point of great suspense. In your opinion, where might she have interrupted the story of "Abu the Wag"? Explain your decision.
3. "Abu the Wag" offers the modern reader an inside view of life in the Near East hundreds of years ago. Name three important differences between that society and modern America.

Relationships

Two Methods of Organization

People think in certain patterns. For this reason, writers try to arrange their material in patterns that will lead to easy understanding. The two most common of these patterns are (a) **main idea and supporting details** and (b) **details in sequence.**

(a) In nonfiction, paragraphs that begin with the *main idea* are very common. The first sentence states the main idea, and the rest of the sentences develop the main idea with *supporting details.* Such details are often examples or reasons. Look, for instance, at the introduction to "Abu the Wag" on page 93. The first sentence states the main idea: "The story is a strange one." The rest of the sentences summarize the story and indicate why it is strange.

(b) In fiction, paragraphs beginning with a main idea are rare. The usual pattern for fiction is simply to arrange *details in sequence,* or time order. The paragraph that begins "Abu put on the sandals . . ." on page 97 is an excellent example. The paragraph lists six details in the order that they happened. The order of time is made clear by the use of the transitional words *then* and *finally* to start two of the sentences.

1. Look at the first two paragraphs of the story on page 93. How are they organized, (a) main idea and details or (b) details in sequence?
2. One good example of a details-in-sequence paragraph is given above. Find at least one other example in the story.

Composition

1. Write a paragraph about "Abu the Wag" that begins with a main idea and continues with supporting details. If you wish, use either of the following as your first sentence:
   (a) *The story "Abu the Wag" indicates that women usually occupied inferior roles in the old Near East;*
   (b) *"Abu the Wag" presents a society that is very different from modern America.*
2. Write a paragraph summarizing the story by mentioning the following details in sequence. Start by putting the details in their proper order. You can use slightly different words for the details if you want to, and you may want to mention other details to make your paragraph complete. When you have finished, underline the given details. The details: (a) *four holy men;* (b) *a heavy chain;* (c) *the disguise of a merchant;* (d) *10 beautiful slave girls;* (e) *the Grand Vizier;* (f) *a bitten finger;* (g) *a new house;* (h) *an unexpected invitation.*

Before completing the exercises that follow, you may wish to review the **bold-faced** words on pages 72 to 99.

I. On a separate sheet of paper, mark each item *true* or *false*. If it is false, explain what is wrong with the sentence.

1. At their best, class discussions are *discordant* and contain an argument or two.
2. A good speaker is well organized, *collected*, and enthusiastic about the subject.
3. An *imbecile* is an overly *vain* person.
4. Caliphs and other rulers who hold absolute power sometimes become *persecutors* of their own people.
5. Small children usually enjoy the *sweep* of a large swing.
6. A *fungus* is an important part of a digital watch.
7. *Resolving* to eliminate one's bad habits is an old New Year's custom.
8. Davy Crockett is widely known as a *legendary* hero of the American frontier.
9. Some women in the ancient Near East had to live in a *harem*.
10. *Watercress* can be played by up to 20 people.

II. On a separate sheet of paper, write the *italicized* word that best fills the blank in each sentence.

sustain	*desperation*	*veined*	*intrusion*	*convey*
ascertain	*attendant*	*intent*	*pendulum*	*uncanny*

1. A grandfather's clock has a tall case for the _____.
2. People who are wild with _____ often cannot think clearly.
3. Close elections sometimes require a recount to _____ the winner.
4. A valet, or manservant, is the _____ of a gentleman.
5. Time passes quickly when one is _____ on the work at hand.
6. Sometimes the same piece of music can _____ different feelings to different people.
7. Weight lifters have to _____ not only the weights but long hours of training.
8. Some people seem to have a(n) _____ ability to read other's thoughts.

9. People who crash parties hope that others will not mind their _____.

10. A perfect diamond is absolutely clear, not _____ with visible streaks.

III. Read the three poems carefully and answer the questions that follow.

(UNTITLED)

by Kiyowara Fukuyabu
(Japan, 10th century)

Because river-fog
Hiding the mountain-base
Has risen,
The autumn mountain looks as though it hung
  in the sky.

CAT

by Mary Britton Miller

The black cat yawns,
Opens her jaws,
Stretches her legs,
And shows her claws.

5   Then she gets up
And stands on four
Long stiff legs
And yawns some more.

She shows her sharp teeth,
10 And stretches her lip;
Her slice of a tongue
Turns up at the tip.

Lifting herself
On her delicate toes,
15 She arches her back
As high as it goes,

She lets herself down
With particular care,
And pads away
20 With her tail in the air.

HOW DO I LOVE THEE?

by Elizabeth Barrett Browning

How do I love thee? Let me count the ways.
I love thee to the depth and breadth and height
My soul can reach, when feeling out of sight
For the ends of Being and ideal Grace.
5   I love thee to the level of everyday's
Most quiet need, by sun and candlelight.
I love thee freely, as men strive for Right;
I love thee purely, as they turn from Praise.
I love thee with the passion put to use
10   In my old griefs, and with my childhood's faith.
I love thee with a love I seemed to lose
With my lost saints,—I love thee with the breath,
Smiles, tears of all my life!—and, if God choose,
I shall but love thee better after death.

1. (a) Which two of the poems depend mainly upon visual imagery? (b) In your opinion, which one of these two presents the sharper images? Explain.
2. One of the two longer poems begins with a main idea and then goes on to list details. (a) Which poem is this? (b) Rewrite the main idea in a single sentence.
3. Which poem is the best example of the details-in-sequence method of organization?
4. Which poem contains more than one *stanza*? If you don't know the word, ask someone what it means or look it up.
5. The poem "Cat" not only describes a cat but also suggests certain inferences about the poet's feelings. In your opinion, how does Mary Britton Miller feel about cats? Explain.

IV. How does the cartoon below differ in idea from the poem by
Elizabeth Barrett Browning?

"How do I love thee?"

"Let me count the ways."

V. List at least three important details in the cartoon below.
What inference or conclusion do these details support?

▶ The plot question in this story is a real teaser: How do you get a hippopotamus out of a small fishpond? What would be your solution? Brainstorm the question awhile before reading the hilarious . . .

MY FATHER AND THE HIPPOPOTAMUS

by Leon Hugo

My father's farm was in South Africa about 30 miles from the Kruger National Park. Wild animals from the park were common in our daily lives. They were nearly all, in their own ways, destructive. Jackals stole my mother's chickens, koodoo broke the fencing around the farm, giraffes got their necks caught in telephone wires, and every now and then a lion made off with a cow. Sometimes they were dangerous. A lion once ate a boy, and I still remember with a shudder the time I picked up a green stick that hissed, twisted, and bit my thumb.

My father had to keep fighting a war against these wild beasts. On the whole we won—except against the hippos. The Letaba River ran through one end of our farm and then ran on down through the Kruger National Park. Sometimes, during the winter, when the water level dropped downstream, hippos would move upstream from the park and settle on our farm. They sneaked in during the night, sank softly into one of the deep pools in the river, and then let us know they had come by snorting and bellowing. Then my father would get so mad he would start a dance of rage, as angry as a man can be. It used to frighten me nearly out of my wits, but never the hippos who were a mile away. I still remember thinking (when I was eight): "If you could see my Dad now, you hippos, you'd clear out before tomorrow. Gee, he's mad!"

This was the way my father seemed to me when I was eight years old, but as I grew older I began to realize he was putting on

- brainstorm (BRAYN storm) suggest quick, spontaneous answers
- koodoo (KOO doo) kind of large African antelope

an act as if he were on a stage. He knew, I grew to know, and the hippos must have known, that he could do nothing.

For one thing, there were strict laws against the shooting of hippos; and for another, when on the mornings following their arrival my father stamped down to the river, there was never a sign of one. The reeds were crushed, of course, and the riverbank looked crushed, too, but none of us ever saw a single shining rump or head above the silent, green surface of the river. My father always swore that the animals were near. He could feel them looking at him, he said. And sometimes he would hear a sniff or a snort, and that made him angrier than ever. He would walk up and down the riverbank cursing, and daring any hippo to show its face, until my mother sent a message to say that breakfast was ready.

There was really nothing my father could do except see that fires around the farm were kept going during the night. These usually protected the crops from the hippos, but during their two-month stay my father was an anxious and overworked man.

"Give me a herd of stampeding buffalo, rather," he once remarked bitterly. "At least you can see them. But these damn hippos! I wish," he added wistfully, "I could catch one—just one—with its pants down. I'd teach it who's boss. By golly I would!"

His chance came, I remember, on a Sunday.

The hippos had been making an awful lot of noise the night before. The crashing splashes, the snorts, grunts, and squeals coming up to us through the dark sounded as if all the hippos in the world were having a picnic. To add to the noise, our two dogs, which were kept chained in the backyard, started howling. My father, worrying about his crops, kept walking round his lands to see that the farm hands were keeping the fires going.

When he finally came into the house he looked as though he had had enough. "They can eat everything," he muttered. "Everything—I don't care anymore. There's enough for them, anyway. About a ton of tomatoes per belly. I hope . . ."

"Oh, John, I'm sure it will be all right," said my mother.

"I hope they bust. I do. I really do." My father spoke very low, as if to himself. "Lee," he said to me, "shut the dogs up."

My sister, as I walked out, said, "Daddy, has a hippo got a curly tail like a piggy's?" When I came in again she was crying, and my father had gone to bed.

Someone yelling woke me the next morning. I shot up in bed

• wistfully (WIST ful ee) longingly; with great desire

to hear flat feet running through the garden toward the house. I heard more yelling, and then a lot of crazy laughing and giggling. I was out in the hallway in a moment and saw Matiba, my mother's young kitchen servant, still giggling as he banged on my parents' bedroom door.

"What's the matter, Matiba?" I cried.

He only continued his giggle until my father opened the door.

"What is it?" my father growled.

Matiba pointed to the garden. We hurried outside. It was still early, but the sun had risen enough to make the garden fairly easy to see. There, in the fishpond, was a hippopotamus, fast asleep.

My mother called, "What is it, John?"

"A hippo," said my father.

"A what?"

"I said a hippo," said my father.

"Good heavens!" said my mother. After a pause she called out, "Where?"

"In your fishpond."

There was another pause from my mother, a long one. Then "The poor goldfish!" we heard her gasp.

My father laughed. "Lee," he said, "fetch my rifle."

My mother was on the porch when I got back. She looked pale. I handed my father the rifle. "You aren't going to shoot it, are you, John?" she asked.

My father opened the breech. "I jolly well am," he answered grimly.

Sunlight had swept in a flood into the garden by then, and we could see our visitor down to the last wrinkle on its hide. It was a baby calf, a small one, weighing about 800 pounds, and it fitted snugly into the pond like a round balloon in a tin can. As my father raised the rifle to his shoulder the hippo moved. Water splashed out of the pond as it snuggled in more deeply; and then it yawned, opening its jaws wide and showing a set of young but very large teeth.

I waited, holding my breath for the crack of the rifle.

"How will you get it out?" my mother asked.

A shudder ran through my father's body. Slowly he lowered the rifle. "What did you say?" he asked softly.

"How are you going to get it out?"

"Quite simple, dear," said my father patiently. "We'll pull it out."

"You couldn't."

"Couldn't?"

"You couldn't possibly drag a huge beast that weighs close to a thousand pounds out without ruining the fishpond."

I could see by the look on my father's face that my mother had put her finger on the real problem of getting the baby hippo out. "We'll chop it up first," he suggested.

"You will not," said my mother firmly. "I'm not having any hippos cut up in my front garden, and anyway I think it's horrid and cruel. He's only a baby calf."

My father said, "If you want the goldfish to have a playmate, dear, just say so and we'll leave little Jumbo in the fishpond."

"That's not a Jumbo," remarked my sister, who had joined us.

"You're quite right, darling," my mother told her. "Daddy's just being silly."

In the fishpond the hippo belched, not softly.

"No," my mother went on, "what you've got to do is get rid of it without ruining the pond or flowers. I've slaved for years in this

---

- breech (BREECH) opening in rear part of rifle barrel into which shell is inserted
- belch (BELCH) burp

garden and I'm not going to stand by and let you destroy it just because you can't get rid of a baby hippo."

"You make me sound so stupid," my father grumbled, but he was, I think, secretly glad that he could not go on with the killing. "Matiba," he cried, "call the farmhands."

The workers came running from their houses, all of them excited. Slowly we crept up to one side of the sleeping hippo. As we drew closer we could hear it breathing, slow and deep, with the faintest rumbling snore.

"Now!" yelled my father, and they started making as much noise as possible. They yelled, screamed, and shouted at the top of their voices, and my father's rifle cracked five times as he fired into the air. Altogether it was a most satisfying noise, and it seemed to electrify our hippo.

It stood up in the pond. Drops shook from it in a silver shower and a goldfish slid from its rump into the water. And it bellowed. We fell silent. We looked at the hippo, it looked at us. There's something special about a hippo, even a baby hippo, especially if it's angry. We squirmed under its angry gaze. Then, as we silently watched, it sniffed, blinked, and settled slowly back into the pond.

We started our noise again, but the more we shouted and banged the deeper into the pond did the hippo try to get. Only its eyes, ears, and snout remained above the water. We gave up after half an hour when jabs with a very long pole had produced no results except for indignant snorts and showers of spray.

"No good," my father whispered, as he and I returned to the house, and the farmhands, strangely quiet, to their houses for their day off. "We'll have to think of something else."

Breakfast was a silent meal. Even my sister, after remarking sadly that hippos' tails were straight, said nothing. Shortly afterwards my mother left for church, but before driving off she asked my father to promise not to kill the hippo. Which he did, rather wistfully.

My father spent the greater part of the morning staring at the hippo in the pond. Finally he said, "We'll have to drag it out, all the same," and went to fetch the truck. He brought it between the trees surrounding the garden to as near the pond as he could go.

"This is what we do, Lee," he said. "Tie this rope to the bumper and loop the other end around the hippo's neck. If I can't

---

- **electrify** (i LEK truh fy) excite; startle
- **indignant** (in DIG nunt) outraged; angry

manage a dead one, a live hippo's going to find itself doing a damn quick sprint out of that pond."

I was only 10 years old then, but I saw a problem at once. "Who's going to put the rope around its neck?" I asked.

"Matiba, of course, who else?" said my father, surprised. "Call him."

I did. Matiba came running from the kitchen. We told him what we wanted him to do and he started running back to the kitchen.

"Oh well," said my father, "I'll do it myself."

First we tied the rope to the rear bumper; then my father made a wide noose of the other end and advanced slowly toward the pond. The hippo watched him suspiciously, snorting softly. It was wide awake and clearly still annoyed.

I heard my father talking to it. "Steady now, boy. Don't worry, we don't want to hurt you. Just pull your head off." Carefully he inched forward to within about three yards of the pond. "Steady now. . . ." He threw the rope. It was a good shot and the noose dropped over the hippo's ears. For a second my father looked quite pleased. Then the hippo bellowed straight into his face and suddenly jerked its head upwards. My father found himself thrown into a bed of flowers where he lay cursing; but in jerking its head the hippo had helped the noose to fall further over its ears and round its neck.

It was some moments before my father realized that the noose was happily where it was around the hippo's neck. When he did, though, he cheered up considerably, and after a few pulls on the slack of the rope, the noose was reasonably tight around the hippo's neck.

"Well," my father remarked as we climbed into the truck, "that's nearly that. But one thing's got me slightly bothered."

"What?" I asked.

"Once we've got him out he'll still be attached to us—to the truck. Can't let the fellow go with 20 yards of good rope still round his neck."

The idea of a baby hippo permanently tied to the back of our truck appealed to me, but I saw with regret that it could hardly be practical.

"Anyway," my father continued happily, switching on the truck, "we'll deal with that when it comes up." He revved the

---

- **sprint** (SPRINT) short run or race at full speed
- rev (REV) speed up

engine and slowly let in the clutch. The truck moved forward.

I could not see, sitting beside my father, but could feel when the rope tightened. We could hear, too. Behind us, from the fishpond, came tremendous splashings and snorts of rage. The engine hummed, raced, roared; the wheels screamed in the earth. Then we shot away, bounded away rather, like an impala, and thundered along the car track toward the river.

"Golly!" my father yelled jubilantly. "He can run! Thirty— and not the slightest strain. . . ." A few seconds passed and then a worried look came into his face. He slowly braked.

We climbed out to look. There was no baby hippo behind us and no rope. There was no rear bumper, either.

Up to this moment my father had been exceptionally calm. But the strain began to tell on him then and I grew a little afraid. He got very red in the face and started muttering through clenched teeth. As we drove back to the farmhouse I felt glad I was not that poor baby hippopotamus.

"You going to shoot him now, Dad?" I ventured.

"No, dammit!" my father roared. "I'll get him out alive if it takes me a week!"

The hippo was in the pond, the rope was still round its neck— the torn-off bumper in a flower bed—and my little sister was sitting on her haunches beside the pond gazing earnestly into the hippo's eyes. They seemed to be getting on well together; so well, in fact, that she strongly objected when my father, swooping on her like a bird of prey, carried her into the house and locked her up.

"Untie that rope!" he yelled at me as he disappeared through the doorway. Shaking, I ran to obey, but his rage had so unnerved me that by the time he came back I had not managed a single knot. Up to then I had been enjoying myself immensely; now I began to dislike my father for spoiling the fun.

"You're an idiot," he informed me in a rough, harsh-sounding voice. He pushed me aside, tried to untie the rope himself, broke his thumb nail, cursed, and cut the rope. I felt a little better.

He passed me the cut end. "Hold this," he said, "I'm getting under the truck to tie it to the axle." He glared at the hippo. "Just let him try to pull the axle off!" he snarled. "Hand me the rope when I'm ready."

- impala (im PAL ah) large African antelope
- **jubilantly** (JOO buh lunt lee) joyfully
- unnerve (un NURV) upset; take away courage

He slid under the rear end of the truck. I was standing facing the pond. All of a sudden a gust of warm air struck the back of my neck and I swung around.

I found myself looking into the face—just 12 inches away—of a full-grown adult hippopotamus cow that had appeared from nowhere behind me. A tree was close at hand and I was up it in about one-millionth of a second. The two-and-a-half ton monster animal hardly looked at me up in the tree. The part of my father that stuck out from the back of the truck caught her eye. She bent her head to examine it.

It was horrible. There I was up in the tree, quite speechless with fright, expecting her to open her mouth and bite my father's backside off. But she merely gave a long, interested sniff. My father said, "What the devil are you doing, Lee?" and wriggled his behind. Then he said, "All right, give me the rope," and stuck his hand out. The hippopotamus sniffed at his hand.

My father, sensing that something was near and thinking it was the rope, said, "Dammit, give it to me," and grabbed. His fingers closed on the hippo's snout.

I found my voice at last. "Daddy," I shouted, "get underneath! Get all the way underneath!"

He did not. His hand seemed stuck to that snout; and some strange power, instead of sending him for safety under the truck, brought him out in the open. They stared at one another for what seemed ages, my father and that female hippopotamus, deep into one another's eyes; then my father let go and giggled. The hippo just stood there breathing long slow breaths and twitching her ears. My father rose slowly to his feet, saying in a low, soft voice, "Good girl, good old girl," and seemed about to pat her on the head. Then the hippo opened her mouth.

What happened next was too fast for me to see clearly. It was a blur of action, and there was my father just beneath me in the tree gasping, "Get higher, you fool, higher!" and I crying, "I can't, I'm stuck!" and my father somehow appearing in the fork above my head and the hippo looking quite sadly up at him as though she regretted not having tried a piece of a human while the going was good. But if that was her thought, it was only a passing one, for she turned almost immediately to the fishpond and grunted.

The calf squeaked in reply and squirmed. The mother—the new arrival must have been that—grunted again, and the young hippo slowly came out of the fishpond, leaving a trail of destruction through my mother's dahlias. As the calf reached her she bit it, not viciously but hard enough to make the calf squeal sharply, spring aside, and start off at a smart gallop for the river. Without a glance at us, the mother hippo followed.

As they reached the trees, the calf tossed its head and the noose flew free of its neck. In another moment the two animals had disappeared.

We climbed down from the tree and without a word to each other slunk into the house.

The first rain of the season fell that night and the hippos left the river pool. They never came back. But five years passed before my father (avoiding my eye) dared boast that he had taught them a lesson.

- **dahlia** (DAL yuh) kind of large flower
- **slunk** (SLUNK) sneaked; moved secretly

ALL THINGS CONSIDERED _____

1. On the whole, the narrator (a) shares his father's rage at the hippos. (b) is much more frightened of hippos than his father. (c) thinks the experience with the hippos is rather funny.

2. The father decides not to shoot the hippo because (a) his wife is against shooting any wild animals. (b) there is no good way to get the body out of the fishpond. (c) shooting hippos is against the law.

3. The father's second plan, pulling the hippo out, fails because (a) it's impossible to get a rope around a hippo's neck. (b) the truck is not powerful enough to pull a hippo. (c) the bumper comes off the truck.

4. The father's final plan fails because (a) the mother hippo appears on the scene. (b) the axle comes off the truck. (c) the narrator refuses to help him.

5. After all the father's efforts fail to get the hippo out of the fishpond, the hippo finally (a) settles into the pond for good. (b) leaves the pond of its own free will. (c) leaves the pond after the arrival of its mother.

THINKING IT THROUGH _____

1. The main conflict in the story is between the father and the hippo calf. This conflict becomes humorous because the father and the hippo are so different. Name several differences between the man and the beast.

2. Most readers of the story laugh, or at least chuckle quietly, at certain points. In your opinion, what is the funniest detail in this story?

3. Near the end, when the father and the large hippo stand facing one another, the narrator states that ". . . my father let go and giggled." In your opinion, why would the father giggle in such a situation?

4. Explain the last sentence. Why did the father let five years pass before boasting, and even then avoid his son's eyes?

Literary Skills

Figurative Language: The Metaphor

Most words in literature mean just what the dictionary says they mean. For example, turn back to page 108 and reread the first three or four sentences of "My Father and the Hippopotamus." All the words are used according to their commonly understood meanings. Another term for such "dictionary language" is **literal** (LIT ur ul) **language.**

But sometimes authors use words in different ways. For instance, continue reading the first paragraph of the story until you come to the word "stick." Does the author *literally* mean "stick" here? Of course not. The real meaning is "snake." One word has simply been substituted for another that is like it in some way. Another term for such language is **figurative** (FIG yur uh tiv) **language.** Figurative language says one thing and suggests another.

There are several kinds of figurative language. One important kind is the **metaphor** (MET uh for). In a metaphor, a figurative term is simply substituted for what the author really

means. In the last example, "stick" is a metaphor because it is substituted for "snake" or "serpent."

Some metaphors in literature are truly original; others are so common that we hardly recognize them as metaphors at all. In fact, if a common *metaphorical* (met uh FOR i cul) definition is listed in the dictionary, it's best not to even call the word a metaphor. Think for example, about the following sentences from the selection. Which words are used with meanings that suggest a metaphorical origin?

1. My father had to keep fighting a war against those wild beasts.
2. Sunlight had swept in a flood into the garden . . . .
3. . . . my mother had put her finger on the real problem of getting the baby hippo out.
4. Then we shot away . . . and thundered along the car track toward the river.

Composition

1. On your paper, define the word *metaphor*. Then list three common expressions that have a metaphorical origin, like *broken* dreams, *lying* eyes, and *golden* years.

2. How many of your own qualities can you express metaphorically? Think in terms of a car. Try to come up

with at least 10 appropriate metaphors. Consider all the parts of a car. Then think of all that a car can do. Here are three metaphors to get you started:
(1) The *air hissed* out of my hopes.
(2) I *stalled* after the third line of the poem.
(3) My plans *backfired* suddenly.

▶ The language of poetry is often the language of metaphor. As you'll discover, the title of the following poem means much more than the dictionary would tell you about the word "mirror." When you look in a mirror or a very still lake, what do you see? What will you see there in 25 years?—in 50 years? And what would the mirror or lake say if it were alive and could speak about you? Read this poem at least three times, thinking about the meaning.

MIRROR

by Sylvia Plath

1   I am silver and exact. I have no preconceptions.
Whatever I see I swallow immediately
Just as it is, unmisted by love or dislike.
I am not cruel, only truthful—
5   The eye of a little god, four-cornered.
Most of the time I meditate on the opposite wall.
It is pink, with speckles. I have looked at it so long
I think it is a part of my heart. But it flickers.
Faces and darkness separate us over and over.

- preconception (pre kun SEP shun) opinion formed beforehand
- unmisted (un MIS tid) not misted, or clouded, over
- **meditate** (MED i tayt) concentrate; think

10   Now I am a lake. A woman bends over me,
Searching my reaches for what she really is.
Then she turns to those liars, the candles or the moon.
I see her back, and reflect it faithfully.
She rewards me with tears and an agitation of hands.
15   I am important to her. She comes and goes.
Each morning it is her face that replaces the darkness.
In me she has drowned a young girl,
   and in me an old woman
Rises toward her day after day, like a terrible fish.

WAYS OF KNOWING

1. There is a special kind of metaphor called **personification** (pur son uh fuh KAY shun). In personification, a nonhuman subject is given human qualities. For example, in the first stanza, the mirror is *personified* to the extent that it can speak about its qualities and experiences. How is personification involved in the second stanza?
2. Explain the metaphors in lines 2 ("swallow") and 12 ("liars").
3. The last two lines represent the best work of one of our best modern poets. Explain the figurative language. That is, who is the "young girl" who has been "drowned"? Who is the "old woman" who now "rises," and why should she look "like a terrible fish"?

• reaches (REE chez) depths
• agitation (aj uh TAY shun) tense, worried movements

THE HITCHHIKER

by Roald Dahl

▶ *Never pick up a hitchhiker.* That's an old rule of the road for safe drivers. But every rule has its exceptions, as the brilliant English author Roald Dahl proves in the following story. Fasten your seat belt before you read this one. There's a bump at the end of the road.

I had a new car. It was an exciting toy, a big BMW 3.3 Li, which means 3.3 liter, long wheelbase, fuel injection. It had a top speed of 129 mph and terrific acceleration. The body was pale blue. The seats inside were darker blue and they were made of leather, genuine soft leather of the finest quality. The windows were electrically operated and so was the sunroof. The radio aerial popped up when I switched on the radio, and disappeared when I switched it off. The powerful engine growled and grunted impatiently at slow speeds, but at 60 miles an hour the growling stopped and the motor began to purr with pleasure.

I was driving up to London by myself. It was a lovely June day. They were haymaking in the fields and there were buttercups along both sides of the road. I was whispering along at 70 mph, leaning back comfortably in my seat, with no more than a couple of fingers resting lightly on the wheel to keep her steady. Ahead of me I saw a man thumbing a lift. I touched the brake and brought the car to a stop beside him. I always stopped for hitchhikers. I knew just how it used to feel to be standing on the side of a country road watching the cars go by. I hated the drivers for pretending they didn't see me, especially the ones in big cars with three empty seats. The large expensive cars seldom stopped. It was always the smaller ones that offered you a lift, or the old rusty ones or the ones that were already crammed full of children and the driver would say, "I think we can squeeze in one more."

- **liter** (LEE tur) metric measure of volume, a little larger than a quart—here used for the displacement of an engine
- **wheelbase** (HWEEL bays) distance from front to back wheels
- **injection** (in JEK shun) forcing a fluid or gas directly into something

The hitchhiker poked his head through the open window and said, "Going to London, guv'nor?"

"Yes," I said. "Jump in."

He got in and I drove on.

He was a small ratty-faced man with gray teeth. His eyes were dark and quick and clever, like rat's eyes, and his ears were slightly pointed at the top. He had a cloth cap on his head and he was wearing a grayish-colored jacket with enormous pockets. The gray jacket, together with the quick eyes and the pointed ears, made him look more than anything like some sort of a huge human rat.

"What part of London are you headed for?" I asked him.

"I'm goin' right through London and out the other side," he said. "I'm goin' to Epsom, for the races. It's Derby Day today."

"So it is," I said. "I wish I were going with you. I love betting on horses."

"I never bet on horses," he said. "I don't even watch 'em run. That's a stupid silly business."

"Then why do you go?" I asked.

• guv'nor (GUV nur) British for *sir* or *mister* (governor)

He didn't seem to like that question. His little ratty face went absolutely blank and he sat there staring straight ahead at the road, saying nothing.

"I expect you help to work the betting machines or something like that," I said.

"That's even sillier," he answered. "There's no fun working them lousy machines and selling tickets to mugs. Any fool could do that."

There was a long silence. I decided not to question him anymore. I remembered how irritated I used to get in my hitchhiking days when drivers kept asking *me* questions. Where are you going? Why are you going there? What's your job? Are you married? Do you have a girl friend? What's her name? How old are you? And so forth and so forth. I used to hate it.

"I'm sorry," I said. "It's none of my business what you do. The trouble is, I'm a writer, and most writers are terribly nosy."

"You write books?" he asked.

"Yes."

"Writin' books is okay," he said. "It's what I call a skilled trade. I'm in a skilled trade too. The folks I despise is them that spend all their lives doin' crummy old routine jobs with no skill in 'em at all. You see what I mean?"

"Yes."

"The secret of life," he said, "is to become very very good at somethin' that's very very 'ard to do."

"Like you," I said.

"Exactly. You and me both."

"What makes you think that *I'm* any good at my job?" I asked. "There's an awful lot of bad writers around."

"You wouldn't be drivin' about in a car like this if you weren't no good at it," he answered. "It must've cost a tidy packet, this little job."

"It wasn't cheap."

"What can she do flat out?" he asked.

"One hundred and twenty-nine miles an hour," I told him.

"I'll bet she won't do it."

"I'll bet she will."

- mug (MUG) person's face, or the whole person
- trade (TRAYD) kind of work
- tidy (TY dee) quite large
- **packet** (PAK it) bundle of something—in this case, money

"All car-makers is liars," he said. "You can buy any car you like and it'll never do what the makers say it will in the ads."

"This one will."

"Open 'er up then and prove it," he said. "Go on, guv'nor, open 'er right up and let's see what she'll do."

There is a traffic circle at Chalfont St. Peter and immediately beyond it there's a long straight section of divided highway. We came out of the circle onto the highway and I pressed my foot hard down on the accelerator. The big car leaped forward as though she'd been stung. In 10 seconds or so, we were doing 90.

"Lovely!" he cried. "Beautiful! Keep goin'!"

I had the accelerator jammed right down against the floor and I held it there.

"One hundred!" he shouted. "A hundred and five! A hundred and ten! A hundred and fifteen! Go on! Don't slack off!"

I was in the outside lane and we flashed past several cars as though they were standing still—a green Mini, a big cream-colored Citroen, a white Land Rover, a huge truck with a container on the back, an orange-colored Volkswagen Minibus. . . .

"A hundred and twenty!" my passenger shouted, jumping up and down. "Go on! Go on! Get 'er up to one-two-nine!"

At that moment, I heard the scream of a police siren. It was so loud it seemed to be right inside the car, and then a cop on a motorcycle loomed up alongside us on the inside and went past us and raised a hand for us to stop.

"Oh, my sainted aunt!" I said. "That's torn it!"

The cop must have been doing about 130 when he passed us, and he took plenty of time slowing down. Finally, he pulled to the side of the road and I pulled in behind him. "I didn't know police motorcycles could go as fast as that," I said rather lamely.

"That one can," my passenger said. "It's the same make as yours. It's a BMW R90S. Fastest bike on the road. That's what they're usin' nowadays."

The cop got off his motorcycle and leaned the machine sideways onto its prop stand. Then he took off his gloves and placed them carefully on the seat. He was in no hurry now. He had us where he wanted us and he knew it.

"This is real trouble," I said. "I don't like it one little bit."

"Don't talk to 'im more than is necessary, you understand," my companion said. "Just sit tight and keep mum."

- loom (LOOM) appear quite suddenly in great size
- **mum** (MUM) silent

Like an executioner approaching his victim, the cop came strolling slowly toward us. He was a big meaty man with a belly, and his blue breeches were skin-tight around his enormous thighs. His goggles were pulled up onto the helmet, showing a smoldering red face with wide cheeks.

We sat there like guilty schoolboys, waiting for him to arrive.

"Watch out for this man," my passenger whispered, " 'e looks mean as the devil."

The cop came around to my open window and placed one meaty hand on the sill. "What's the hurry?" he said.

"No hurry, officer," I answered.

"Perhaps there's a woman in the back having a baby and you're rushing her to hospital? Is that it?"

"No, officer."

"Or perhaps your house is on fire and you're dashing home to rescue the family from upstairs?" His voice was dangerously soft and mocking.

"My house isn't on fire, officer."

"In that case," he said, "you've got yourself into a nasty mess, haven't you? Do you know what the speed limit is in this country?"

"Seventy," I said.

"And do you mind telling me exactly what speed you were doing just now?"

I shrugged and didn't say anything.

When he spoke next, he raised his voice so loud that I jumped. *One hundred and twenty miles per hour!*" he barked. "That's *50* miles an hour over the limit!"

He turned his head and spat out a big gob of spit. It landed on the wing of my car and started sliding down over my beautiful blue paint. Then he turned back again and stared hard at my passenger. "And who are you?" he asked sharply.

"He's a hitchhiker," I said. "I'm giving him a lift."

"I didn't ask you," he said. "I asked him."

" 'Ave I done somethin' wrong?" my passenger asked. His voice was soft and oily as haircream.

"That's more than likely," the cop answered. "Anyway, you're a witness. I'll deal with you in a minute. Driver's license," he snapped, holding out his hand.

I gave him my driver's license.

- smoldering (SMOHL duh ring) burning in anger
- **mocking** (MOK ing) making fun of

He unbuttoned the left-hand breast pocket of his tunic and brought out the dreaded book of tickets. Carefully, he copied the name and address from my license. Then he gave it back to me. He strolled around to the front of the car and read the number from the license plate and wrote that down as well. He filled in the date, the time and the details of my offense. Then he tore out the top copy of the ticket. But before handing it to me, he checked that all the information had come through clearly on his own carbon copy. Finally, he replaced the book in his breast pocket and fastened the button.

"Now you," he said to my passenger, and he walked around to the other side of the car. From the other breast pocket he produced a small black notebook. "Name?" he snapped.

"Michael Fish," my passenger said.

"Address?"

"Fourteen Windsor Lane, Luton."

"Show me something to prove this is your real name and address," the policeman said.

My passenger fished in his pockets and came out with a driver's license of his own. The policeman checked the name and address and handed it back to him. "What's your job?"

"I'm an 'od carrier."

"A *what?*"

"An 'od carrier."

"Spell it."

"H-o-d-c-a—"

"That'll do. And what's a hod carrier, may I ask?"

"An 'od carrier, officer, is a person 'oo carries the cement up the ladder to the bricklayer. And the 'od is what 'ee carries it in. It's got a long 'andle, and on the top you've got bits of wood set at an angle. . . ."

"All right, all right. Who's your employer?"

"Don't 'ave one. I'm unemployed."

The cop wrote all this down in the black notebook. Then he returned the book to its pocket and did up the button.

"When I get back to the station I'm going to do a little checking up on you," he said to my passenger.

"Me? What've I done wrong?" the rat-faced man asked.

"I don't like your face, that's all," the cop said. "And we just might have a picture of it somewhere in our files." He strolled round the car and returned to my window.

• **offense** (uh FENS) act of wrongdoing; crime

"I suppose you know you're in serious trouble," he said to me.

"Yes, officer."

"You won't be driving this fancy car of yours again for a very long time, not after *we've* finished with you. You won't be driving *any* car again, come to that, for several years. And a good thing, too. I hope they lock you up for a spell into the bargain."

"You mean prison?" I asked, alarmed.

"Absolutely," he said, smacking his lips. "In the clink. Behind the bars. Along with all the other criminals who break the law. *And* a hefty fine into the bargain. Nobody will be more pleased about that than me. I'll see you in court, both of you. You'll be getting a summons to appear."

He turned away and walked over to his motorcycle. He flipped the prop stand back into position with his foot and swung his leg over the saddle. Then he kicked the starter and roared off up the road out of sight.

"Phew!" I gasped. "That's done it."

"We was caught," my passenger said. "We was caught good and proper."

"I was caught, you mean."

"That's right," he said. "What you goin' to do now, guv'nor?"

"I'm going straight up to London to talk to my solicitor," I said. I started the car and drove on.

"You mustn't believe what 'ee said to you about goin' to prison," my passenger said. "They don't put nobody in the clink just for speedin'."

"Are you sure of that?" I asked.

"I'm positive," he answered. "They can take your license away and they can give you a whoppin' big fine, but that'll be the end of it."

I felt tremendously relieved.

"By the way," I said, "why did you lie to him?"

"Who, me?" he said. "What makes you think I lied?"

"You told him you were an unemployed hod carrier. But you told *me* you were in a highly skilled trade."

"So I am," he said. "But it don't pay to tell everythin' to a copper."

"So what *do* you do?" I asked him.

"Ah," he said slyly. "That'd be tellin', wouldn't it?"

- **clink** (KLINK) prison
- **summons** (SUM unz) order to appear in court
- **solicitor** (suh LIS uh tur) British term for *lawyer*

"Is it something you're ashamed of?"

"Ashamed?" he cried. "Me, ashamed of my job? I'm about as proud of it as anybody could be in the entire world!"

"Then why won't you tell me?"

"You writers really is nosy parkers, aren't you?" he said. "And you ain't goin' to be 'appy, I don't think, until you've found out exactly what the answer is?"

"I don't really care one way or the other," I told him, lying.

He gave me a crafty little ratty look out of the sides of his eyes. "I think you do care," he said. "I can see it on your face that you think I'm in some kind of a very peculiar trade and you're just achin' to know what it is."

I didn't like the way he read my thoughts. I kept quiet and stared at the road ahead.

"You'd be right, too," he went on. "I *am* in a very peculiar trade. I'm in the queerest peculiar trade of 'em all."

I waited for him to go on.

"That's why I 'as to be extra careful 'oo' I'm talkin' to, you see. 'Ow am I to know, for instance, you're not another copper in plain clothes?"

"Do I look like a copper?"

"No," he said. "You don't. And you ain't. Any fool could tell that."

He took from his pocket a tin of tobacco and a packet of cigarette papers and started to roll a cigarette. I was watching him out of the corner of one eye, and the speed with which he performed this rather difficult operation was incredible. The cigarette was rolled and ready in about five seconds. He ran his tongue along the edge of the paper, stuck it down and popped the cigarette between his lips. Then, as if from nowhere, a lighter appeared in his hand. The lighter flamed. The cigarette was lit. The lighter disappeared. It was altogether a remarkable performance.

"I've never seen anyone roll a cigarette as fast as that," I said.

"Ah," he said, taking a deep suck of smoke. "So you noticed."

"Of course I noticed. It was quite fantastic."

He sat back and smiled. It pleased him very much that I had noticed how quickly he could roll a cigarette. "You want to know what makes me able to do it?" he asked.

"Go on then."

- **crafty** (KRAF tee) sly; cunning
- **tin** (TIN) can

"It's because I've got fantastic fingers. These fingers of mine," he said, holding up both hands high in front of him, "are quicker and cleverer than the fingers of the best piano player in the world!"

"Are you a piano player?"

"Don't be daft," he said. "Do I look like a piano player?"

I glanced at his fingers. They were so beautifully shaped, so slim and long and elegant, they didn't seem to belong to the rest of him at all. They looked more like the fingers of a brain surgeon or a watchmaker.

"My job," he went on, "is a hundred times more difficult than playin' the piano. Any twerp can learn to do that. There's titchy little kids learnin' to play the piano in almost any 'ouse you go into these days. That's right, ain't it?"

"More or less," I said.

"Of course it's right. But there's not one person in ten million can learn to do what I do. Not one in ten million! 'Ow about that?"

"Amazing," I said.

"You're darn right it's amazin'," he said.

"I think I know what you do," I said. "You do conjuring tricks. You're a conjuror."

"Me?" he snorted. "A conjuror? Can you picture me goin' round crummy kid's parties makin' rabbits come out of top 'ats?"

"Then you're a card player. You get people into card games and you deal yourself marvelous hands."

"Me! A rotten cardsharper!" he cried. "That's a miserable racket if ever there was one."

"All right. I give up."

I was taking the car along slowly now, at no more than 40 miles an hour, to make quite sure I wasn't stopped again. We had come onto the main London-Oxford road and were running down the hill toward Denham.

Suddenly, my passenger was holding up a black leather belt in his hand. "Ever seen this before?" he asked. The belt had a brass buckle of unusual design.

"Hey!" I said. "That's mine, isn't it? It *is* mine! Where did you get it?"

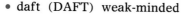

- daft (DAFT) weak-minded
- twerp (TWURP) unimportant person; a nobody (slang)
- conjuring (KON jur ing) making magic
- conjuror (KON jur er) magician; sorcerer

TANGLES AND TEASERS

He grinned and waved the belt gently from side to side. "Where d'you think I got it?" he said. "Off the top of your trousers, of course."

I reached down and felt for my belt. It was gone.

"You mean you took it off me while we've been driving along?" I asked, flabbergasted.

He nodded, watching me all the time with those little black ratty eyes.

"That's impossible," I said. "You'd have had to undo the buckle and slide the whole thing out through the loops all the way round. I'd have seen you doing it. And even if I hadn't seen you, I'd have felt it."

"Ah, but you didn't, did you?" he said, triumphant. He dropped the belt on his lap, and now all at once there was a brown shoelace dangling from his fingers. "And what about this, then?" he exclaimed, waving the shoelace.

"What about it?" I said.

"Anyone around 'ere missin' a shoelace?" he asked, grinning.

I glanced down at my shoes. The lace of one of them was missing. "Good grief!" I said. "How did you do that? I never saw you bending down."

"You never saw nothin'," he said proudly. "You never even saw me move an inch. And you know why?"

"Yes," I said. "Because you've got fantastic fingers."

"Exactly right!" he cried. "You catch on pretty quick, don't you?" He sat back and sucked away at his homemade cigarette, blowing the smoke out in a thin stream against the windshield. He knew he had impressed me greatly with those two tricks, and this made him very happy. "I don't want to be late," he said. "What time is it?"

"There's a clock in front of you," I told him.

"I don't trust car clocks," he said. "What does your watch say?"

I hitched up my sleeve to look at the watch on my wrist. It wasn't there. I looked at the man. He looked back at me, grinning.

"You've taken that, too," I said.

He held out his hand and there was my watch lying in his palm. "Nice bit of stuff, this," he said. "Superior quality. Eighteen-carat gold. Easy to sell, too. It's never any trouble gettin' rid of quality goods."

"I'd like it back, if you don't mind," I said rather huffily.

• huffily (HUF fuh lee) in an offended manner

130

He placed the watch carefully on the leather tray in front of him. "I wouldn't nick anything from you, guv'nor," he said. "You're my pal. You're givin' me a lift."

"I'm glad to hear it," I said.

"All I'm doin' is answerin' your question," he went on. "You asked me what I did for a livin' and I'm showin' you."

"What else have you got of mine?"

He smiled again, and now he started to take from the pocket of his jacket one thing after another that belonged to me—my driver's license, a key ring with four keys on it, some pound notes, a few coins, a letter from my publishers, my diary, a stubby old pencil, a cigarette lighter, and last of all, a beautiful old sapphire ring with pearls around it belonging to my wife. I was taking the ring up to a jeweler in London because one of the pearls was missing.

"Now *there's* another lovely piece of goods," he said, turning the ring over in his fingers. "That's 18th century, if I'm not mistaken, from the reign of King George the Third."

"You're right," I said, impressed. "You're absolutely right."

He put the ring on the leather tray with the other items.

"So you're a pickpocket," I said.

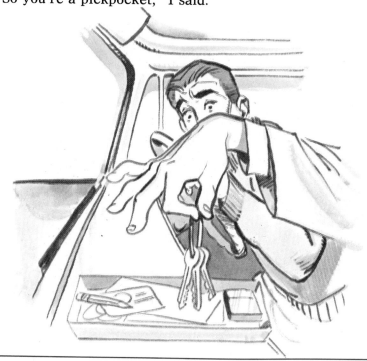

• **pound note**—main unit of British paper money

"I don't like that word," he answered. "It's a coarse and vulgar word. Pickpockets is coarse and vulgar people who only do easy little amateur jobs. They lift money from blind old ladies."

"What do you call yourself, then?"

"Me? I'm a fingersmith. I'm a professional fingersmith." He spoke the words solemnly and proudly, as though he were telling me he was the President of the Royal College of Surgeons or the Archbishop of Canterbury.

"I've never heard that word before," I said. "Did you invent it?"

"Of course I didn't invent it," he replied. "It's the name given to them who's risen to the very top of the profession. You've 'eard of a goldsmith and a silversmith, for instance. They're experts with gold and silver. I'm an expert with my fingers, so I'm a fingersmith."

"It must be an interesting job."

"It's a marvelous job," he answered. "It's lovely."

"And that's why you go to the races?"

"Race meetings is easy meat," he said. "You just stand around after the race, watchin' for the lucky ones to queue up and draw their money. And when you see someone collectin' a big bundle of notes, you simply follows after 'im and 'elps yourself. But don't get me wrong, guv'nor. I never takes nothin' from a loser. Nor from poor people neither. I only go after them as can afford it, the winners and the rich."

"That's very thoughtful of you," I said. "How often do you get caught?"

"Caught?" he cried, disgusted. "*Me* get caught! It's only pickpockets get caught. Fingersmiths never. Listen, I could take the false teeth out of your mouth if I wanted to and you wouldn't even catch me!"

"I don't have false teeth," I said.

"I know you don't," he answered. "Otherwise I'd 'ave 'ad 'em out long ago!"

I believed him. Those long slim fingers of his seemed able to do anything.

We drove on for a while without talking.

"That policeman's going to check up on you pretty thoroughly," I said. "Doesn't that worry you a bit?"

"Nobody's checkin' up on me," he said.

- **coarse** (KORS) nasty; impolite
- queue (KYOO) line

"Of course they are. He's got your name and address written down most carefully in his black book."

The man gave me another of his sly ratty little smiles. "Ah," he said. "So 'ee 'as. But I'll bet 'ee ain't got it all written down in 'is memory as well. I've never known a copper yet with a decent memory. Some of 'em can't even remember their own names."

"What's memory got to do with it?" I asked. "It's written down in his book, isn't it?"

"Yes, guv'nor, it is. But the trouble is, 'ee's lost the book. 'Ee's lost both books, the one with my name in it *and* the one with yours."

In the long delicate fingers of his right hand, the man was holding up in triumph the two books he had taken from the policeman's pockets. "Easiest job I ever done," he announced proudly.

I nearly swerved the car into a milk truck, I was so excited.

"That copper's got nothin' on either of us now," he said.

"You're a genius!" I cried.

"'Ee's got no names, no addresses, no car number, no nothin'," he said.

"You're brilliant!"

"I think you'd better pull in off this main road as soon as possible," he said. "Then we'd better build a little bonfire and burn these books."

"You're a fantastic fellow!" I exclaimed.

"Thank you, guv'nor," he said. "It's always nice to be appreciated."

ALL THINGS CONSIDERED

1. The narrator of the story starts speeding because (a) he is late for an appointment. (b) the hitchhiker dares him to prove the car's top speed. (c) he wants to outrun the police.
2. The chance that the hitchhiker's name is really "Michael Fish" is (a) very good. (b) about 50-50. (c) very poor.
3. The character described in the *least* favorable way is (a) the hitchhiker. (b) the narrator. (c) the police officer.
4. The "twist" at the end of the story is that the hitchhiker (a) has taken the police officer's two notebooks. (b) steals the car. (c) really likes to bet on the horses.
5. The story would probably be easier to believe if (a) it had happened in Germany or France. (b) the hitchhiker had gotten out of the car and stood next to the police officer. (c) the narrator had given his name.

THINKING IT THROUGH

1. In your opinion, why did the hitchhiker wait so long before telling the narrator his real occupation?
2. The whole story, of course, is make-believe. But is there anything that seemed really *impossible* to you? Explain.
3. The well-known author, Roald Dahl, is excellent at *visual imagery* (see page 92). Without looking back, what details can you recall about the appearance of the hitchhiker and the police officer?
4. The author tried hard to reproduce the hitchhiker's **dialect,** or manner of speaking. But with all the apostrophes for missing letters, some of the hitchhiker's speeches are a little hard to read. Which would you prefer, the dialogue as written or the dialogue rewritten as standard English? Why?

Literary Skills

Figurative Language: The Simile

Any example of figurative language is called a **figure of speech.** One kind of figure of speech is the *metaphor.* (See page 118.) Another is the **simile** (SIM uh lee).

A metaphor is simple and direct. One term is simply substituted for another. No extra words are used to show that a comparison is being made. A simile, however, does use a special word to show that a comparison is being made. The most common of these words are *like* and *as.* For instance, if you were to say, "Reading 'The Hitchhiker' was fun, like riding a roller coaster with a double loop-the-loop at the end," you would be using a simile. The word *like* is used to make the comparison.

Here are six sentences from the selection. First copy each sentence on a separate sheet of paper. Then explain which two things are being compared. How does this comparison help you understand the author's meaning?

1. His eyes were dark and quick and clever, like rat's eyes, and his ears were slightly pointed at the top.
2. The gray jacket . . . made him look more than anything like some sort of a huge human rat.
3. The big car leaped forward as though she'd been stung.
4. I was in the outside lane and we flashed past several cars as though they were standing still. . . .
5. We sat there like guilty schoolboys, waiting for him to arrive.
6. His voice was soft and oily as haircream.

Composition

1. All expressions starting with *like* or *as* cannot be called similes. For instance, suppose you saw some object on the distant sea and said truthfully, "That looks *like a battleship.*" If, in fact, the object really resembled a battleship to you, you would be using literal language, not a simile. But suppose you said, "She barged into the room *like a battleship ready for action.*" That's clearly figurative language, and therefore a good example of a simile.

   Write three sentences that use *like* or *as* to introduce literal expressions. Then write three more sentences that use *like* or *as* to introduce similes.

2. Follow the directions for the exercise just above, but this time the key words in the literal sentences have to be the same as the key words in the figurative sentences. The use of *battleship* in both literal and figurative sentences is a good example.

Before completing the exercises that follow, you may wish to review the **bold-faced** words on pages 111 to 132.

I. On a separate sheet of paper, write the term in each line that means the same, or nearly the same, as the word in *italics*.
   1. *crafty:* sticky, sly, artificial, impolite
   2. *clink:* carpenter's tool, defect, success, prison
   3. *packet:* type of cloud, ski pole, effort, bundle
   4. *jubilantly:* joyfully, gracefully, unfairly, easily
   5. *slunk:* marsh or bog, vegetable, waste, sneaked
   6. *mum:* face cream, silent, cooking oil, lie
   7. *indignant:* late, pleased, outraged, surprised
   8. *meditate:* cast out, sleep, think, look over
   9. *electrify:* kill, scare, excite, make visible
   10. *coarse:* nasty and vulgar, track, subject, class

II. On a separate sheet of paper, write the letter of the word or group of words that best completes each sentence.
   1. A *tin* might contain (a) prisoners. (b) tools. (c) sardines.
   2. A *pound note* is a kind of (a) accurate scale. (b) British money. (c) writing paper.
   3. A *summons* is a(n) (a) invitation to a party. (b) proposal of marriage. (c) order to appear in court.
   4. A *dahlia* is a kind of (a) tropical tree. (b) African antelope. (c) large flower.
   5. A good example of a *sprint* is the (a) 50-meter dash. (b) mile run. (c) 1,000-meter run.
   6. *Agitation* of the body is a sign of (a) a poor diet. (b) a troubled mind. (c) a regular exercise program.
   7. A *liter* is (a) the same as a quart. (b) smaller than a quart. (c) larger than a quart.
   8. The word *injection* is often accompanied by the word (a) fuel. (b) food. (c) financial.
   9. The word *offense*, with the accent on the second syllable, is (a) a point-scoring team in football. (b) an act of wrong-doing. (c) any thoughtful act.
   10. If someone were *mocking* you, you would probably feel (a) very proud. (b) thankful. (c) hurt and angry.

III. Most proverbs are expressed in figurative language. That is, their meanings go far beyond the dictionary definitions of the words. For instance, if you told someone, "Don't count your chickens before they're hatched," would you *really* be talking about birds? Almost certainly not.

Here are 10 proverbs from the Talmud, a famous collection of ancient Jewish teachings. All are written in figurative language. On a separate sheet of paper, write a sentence that explains in your own words what you think each really means.

Proverbs from the Talmud

1. Too many captains sink the ship.
2. Birds of a feather flock together.
3. Attend no auctions if you have no money.
4. Poverty comes from God, but not dirt.
5. Ignorance and pride go hand in hand.
6. If your friends agree in calling you a donkey, go and put a halter on your head.
7. He who hardens his heart with pride softens his brain with the same.
8. Keep shut the doors of your mouth, even from the wife of your side.
9. Use your best vase today, for tomorrow it may be broken.
10. The world is saved only by the breath of schoolchildren.

IV. Explain the cartoon in terms of the relationship between literal and figurative language.

"When it comes to Florida, Hersholt goes ape."

V. An **aphorism** (A for i zum) is a memorable proverb or saying that contains some general truth. Some aphorisms are very well known. "Look before you leap" and "Time heals all wounds" are good examples. Others strike readers as fresh and new.

Aphorisms occur in both figurative and literal language. In *figurative language*, they do not really mean what they seem to say. In nonfigurative, *literal language*, they mean just what they say. Think, for instance, about the Haitian proverb, "It's the frog's own tongue that betrays him." That is an example of figurative language. The real meaning of the aphorism concerns people. In literal language, one might simply say, "People's talk often reveals what they don't want known."

Think about the difference between *literal* and *figurative* language as you read the following aphorisms. Then answer the two questions that follow.

1. Wait till you cross the river before you call the alligator names. (Haitian aphorism)
2. Nobody can make you feel inferior without your consent. (Eleanor Roosevelt)
3. It is looking downward which makes one dizzy. (Robert Browning)
4. Beauty is in the eye of the beholder. (Margaret Wolfe Hungerford)
5. Forget injuries; never forget kindnesses. (Confucius)
6. Light tomorrow with today! (Elizabeth Barrett Browning)
7. If you want your eggs hatched, sit on them yourself. (Haitian aphorism)
8. Pleasure is often spoiled by describing it. (Stendahl)
9. My creed is low: Be sincere and don't fuss. (Jane Addams)
10. Time wounds all heels. (Jane Ace)

   A. Five of the aphorisms can be called *figurative*, and five *literal*. Which are which?
   B. It's not too unusual for people to copy an aphorism on a card and carry it in a wallet or purse. If you had to make one of the 10 aphorisms yours, which would it be? Be prepared to explain why you find it meaningful. If you already have your own "private aphorism," write it out and explain why you like it.

UNIT REVIEW

I. Match the terms in Column A with their meanings in Column B.

A	B
1. literal language	**(a)** a figurative comparison made directly
2. metaphor	**(b)** language that appeals to the five senses
3. simile	**(c)** words used according to their usual or "dictionary" meanings
4. imagery	**(d)** giving human qualities to nonhuman subjects
5. personification	**(e)** a figurative comparison made with a special word such as *like* or *as*

II. AWARDS ASSEMBLY

Imagine that all the authors and characters represented in this unit were now assembled before you. Most are tense and agitated, for they have been nominated for some sort of award. Imagine also that you hold the power of decision. You are both judge and jury. You are about to present and explain the 8 awards listed below.

Start this assignment by reviewing the selections. Thumb through the unit or turn back to the table of contents. Write down the authors, titles, and characters you remember best. Then take out a fresh sheet of paper on which to name your choices.

For each award, first write a sentence naming the winner. Try to make this sentence sound like what you might actually read from the stage. ("And now, it gives me GREAT pleasure to give the Best Title award to . . .") Then write another sentence explaining the reason for your choice. Make your explanations as detailed and meaningful as possible.

1. Best Title (Think about titles that made you curious about the selection.)
2. Most Imaginative Selection
3. Most Unforgettable Character
4. Funniest Selection (or Character)
5. Good Figure of Speech (Think about use of figurative language.)
6. Best Plot
7. Real Bummer Award (What selection would you refuse to read again, even if paid to do so?)
8. Best in Show (What is the single best selection?)

SPEAKING UP

Acting out scenes from stories is an old classroom tradition. This assignment is a little harder. It asks you to imagine and act out what might have happened *after* the events in a selection are over. Moreover, the actual presentation will be a "happening"; it will not be rehearsed in advance.

Start by choosing one of the three situations below. Then decide which of the two characters you will play. Note that all situations involve (or at least start with) both an interviewer and an interviewee (person who is interviewed).

1. After finishing "Abu the Wag" (page 93), Scheherazade is surprised to find that the king is a little bored. He asks her why she thought the story a good one, what the next will be about, if she really thinks she can avoid death by storytelling, and many other questions. Scheherazade must be clever and enchanting in her answers.

2. The author of "How Do I Love Thee?" (page 106) has sent her new poem to her fiancé, an unpoetic lump of a man. He now asks her why she wrote it, what certain lines mean, what some examples would be, whether he has to endure such poems in the future, and other questions.

3. The police officer in "The Hitchhiker" (page 121) has memorized the license number of the narrator's car. Now he arrives at the narrator's house to find out what has been going on.

The part of the interviewer is probably the easier of the two. Prepare about 10 questions in advance, and decide how you will react if the interviewee becomes hostile, tells lies, tries to change the subject . . . whatever. Also, bring whatever props are required, such as the poem or an arrest warrant. If you are the interviewee, you will have to decide not only what questions might be asked but also how you will react. Study the role well so that you can really *become* the character. Don't be afraid of a little drama, such as tearing up the poem to bring the poor fellow to his knees in apologetic tears. When you present your "happenings" in class, try pairing the same interviewer with different interviewees (and vice versa). Be creative and *make something happen.*

WRITING A "TRUE" STORY

Some writing assignments give you a main idea or topic sentence and ask you to develop the idea with your own words. This assignment reverses the process. It gives you the last sentence—which is also the last paragraph—and asks you to write everything that leads up to it.

Assignment: Imagine one of the following sentences as the last paragraph of a true story. What would that story be about? Use an event from your own life as the basis for an interesting story that ends with one of the following:

- It was love at first sight.
- I had never been more surprised in my life!
- "Well," I said, "this looks like the start of a promising friendship."
- I felt angry, but I just walked away.
- "Well," I said to myself, "that's the way life is."
- Oh well, another A, another day.

Prewriting: At least one of the sentences above should remind you of a good story. If two or more stories suggest themselves, ask yourself which one would be most interesting to other people. Then decide how you can tell it in the most interesting way. Go through the story in your mind, step by step. Then go through it again, sentence by sentence. Notice that the heading on this page has quotation marks around "true." The basis of the story should be true, but you can change the details to add interest.

Writing: When you can really hear the story in your "mind's ear," start putting it down on paper. The story itself should provide the pattern you will use. Some stories are best told in a single long paragraph. Others require many short paragraphs of dialogue, since each new speaker requires a new paragraph. If you do use dialogue, remember to use quotation marks correctly. When in doubt, look at any of the selections in this book for good examples to follow.

Revising: Try to read through your first draft *as though someone else had written it*. What is your overall reaction? Where can you add some powerful *imagery* (see page 92) or some good *figurative language* (see page 118)? How else can the story be improved? Make the necessary changes before neatly preparing the final copy.

U N I T · 3

LOOKING

INTO

LIFE

The inner half of every cloud
  Is bright and shining;
I therefore turn my clouds about,
And always wear them inside out
  To show the lining.

—Ellen T. Fowler
(England, 19th century)

Do you believe that every cloud has a silver lining? Or do you sometimes think that every silver lining has a dark, dark cloud? At different times in your life, both statements may seem true. It all depends on your point of view. It all depends on the way you look at life.

As you read the selections in this unit, you'll be encouraged to ponder some basic questions as you look into life. More important, you'll be encouraged to find the "bright and shining inner half of every cloud."

THE TIGER

by S. Rajaratnam

▶ *There was only one question in Fatima's mind—why hadn't the tiger killed her? It had certainly had the chance. . . .* This story by S. Rajaratnam, a citizen of Singapore in Southeast Asia, answers Fatima's question in a sad but heartwarming way.

Fatima felt the cool yellow water of the river, a sheet of polished gold in the sunglow. The water flowed slowly around her as she clung to the bank. Then she moved further along until she stood waist deep. The wet sarong clung to her brown figure, the plump body of a pregnant woman. Her face was round, with the high cheekbones of the Malays.* A delicate sadness in the black eyes gave her the expression of one brooding over some private vision within her.

With a quick toss of her head, she unloosed her black, glossy hair. She let the wind whisper gently through it. From where she stood she could neither see nor hear the village. In front of her stretched an unbroken expanse of lalang grass and tall trees. The stillness of the evening was disturbed at times by the cry of a lonely water bird. Now and then a rat dived with a gentle splash into the river. Other timid, nervous animals could be heard in the tall grass. The air was full of the scent of wild flowers and mud and grass. A feeling of loneliness and wonder came over Fatima. It was as though she had stumbled into a world still in the dawn of creation. The earth seemed a huge swamp in which wandered ancient and ugly monsters.

So, when she heard the low, rumbling growl of the tiger, it only added to her dream world. But suddenly came a dull angry roar. Fatima knew that it was not a creature of her imagination but the real thing.

- **sarong** (suh RONG) simple wraparound dress or skirt, commonly worn in Southeast Asia
- **brooding** (BROOD ing) worrying about something for a long time
- **expanse** (ik SPANS) wide, unbroken space
- lalang (LAY lan) kind of very tall, thick grass

*People of the Malay Peninsula in Southeast Asia, north of Singapore.

The tiger was framed by the lalang and low to the ground. Fatima stared at its huge head and shoulders. It was not more than 20 yards from her. The sun gave a wicked glint to its watchful yellow eyes. Its ears were drawn back warningly. It turned its head and snarled. Around its red tongue, the yellow teeth looked like tree stumps.

Fatima was frozen into helpless fear by the glaring eyes of the tiger. The sudden stillness that fell around her made her mind numb. She dared not move. She dared not take her eyes from the watching animal. Yet the tiger, too, was still, as though it had been made motionless by the unexpected meeting with a human being.

Fatima and the animal watched one another. She was frightened; it was suspicious. Its growls continued, but they became less angry each time. It showed no signs of really wanting to attack her. Instead, after a while the animal took less of an interest in her. Its huge paws stretched out in front. Now and then the claws dug into the damp grass. Except when she moved, the animal's attention seemed to be nowhere in particular. The glare in its eyes had changed into a sullen and sometimes bored expression. Fatima noticed the surprising changes of mood in the animal's eyes.

By now the dusk had crept in from over the hills. Gone was the colorful scene of a short time before. Gray shadows drifted off into darkness. A faint mist from the river had spread itself over the land. The distant hoot of an owl marked the movement of day into night.

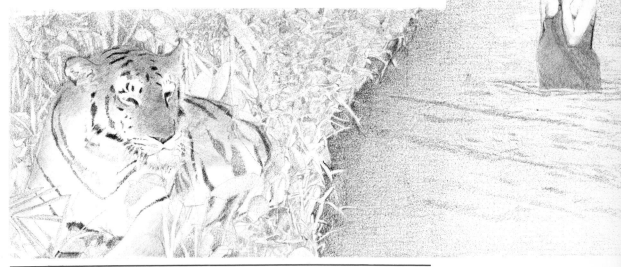

- **glint** (GLINT) bright gleam; flash

Now Fatima had only a quiet fear of the tiger. She felt tiredness creep over her. She shivered with the cold. She grew desperate, as the tiger showed no signs of going away. Her hands wandered over her stomach. She was a being of two lives, she realized. She *had* to escape. She just *had* to! Her eyes could still make out the shadowy form of the tiger in the falling light.

Fatima had studied the animal very carefully. She could tell when it was going to turn its eyes away from her. She waited, her body tense in the water with a fearful strength. Then with a desperate movement she dived underwater. She scraped the bottom of the river as she swam toward the opposite bank, in the direction of the village. She came to the surface only when she felt that her lungs would burst for air. She felt lost in the middle of the river. When she heard the faraway growl, a fear that she had not felt even close to the tiger seized her.

She swam wildly toward the shore. Finally she saw the twinkling oil lamps of the village.

The village was in a panic by the time Fatima's mother had spread an exaggerated version of the story her daughter had told her. The women gathered the children into their arms. They called out to the men to do something about the tiger. The men rushed around, worried about their cattle and goats. The old men chewed betel nuts and demanded to know what the fuss was all about.

More tired than she had ever been, Fatima lay on a straw mat. The village headman and a crowd came to question her as to the location of the tiger. Fatima's mother started to give an exciting, noisy tale of her daughter's meeting with the "hairy one." The headman grew impatient. He commanded the old lady to hold her peace for a while. Then he turned to question Fatima. She was impatient as she answered his questions. For some reason, unlike the people around her, she didn't want the tiger hunted and killed. The headman noted the reluctance in her voice. He frowned.

"Allah!" exclaimed the old lady, wishing to be the center of interest once more. "It was Allah who snatched my daughter away from the jaws of the 'hairy one.'"

She threw up her skinny brown hands, as though to thank Allah. The headman shrugged his shoulders.

- betel nut (BEET ul NUT) nut that comes from one kind of palm tree
- **Allah** (AL uh) term for God in the Islamic religion

"Perhaps it was," he said. "But the next time, Allah will not be as kind. The tiger is perhaps by now drunk with the scent of human flesh. It is not a pleasant thing to have near our village. The beast must be hunted down and destroyed without delay."

He looked at the faces of the men, silent and nervous. They knew the dangers of tracking down the tiger in the night. The thick, shadowy lalang grass gave the beast protection. It could strike quickly and silently.

"Well?" said the headman.

The men gazed at the floor in silence. The headman's face twitched. He was about to call them cowards when Mamood, a younger man, came in.

"What is this I hear?" Mamood asked eagerly. His face was on fire with excitement. He carried a gun on his shoulder. "The women told me that a tiger attacked our Fatima. Is it true?"

The headman told him the facts. Mamood listened, fingering his new double-barreled gun. He was all for hunting the tiger at once. He loved hunting. And the fact that it was a tiger made him all the more eager.

"Now," Mamood said when the headman had finished, "who will come and help kill the tiger? I shall drag home the body of that beast before sunrise. But only if you help me."

The men hesitated, but before long a dozen offered to help. They knew Mamood was a good shot.

"Good!" exclaimed Mamood, running his fingers along the gun barrel. "I knew I could count on you."

Then he and the men left.

"Believe me, daughter," said Fatima's mother, "Mamood is a wild tiger himself." She locked the door after the men.

Fatima rose up from her mat. She looked out of the narrow window. The moon cast a gentle light over everything it touched. She could see the moon through the tall coconut trees. Men moved about in the moonlight, preparing for the hunt. They called out to one another. Fatima stared at them sadly.

Then the men left. Now there were only the gray trees and the whisper of the worried wind. Straining her ears, she heard the far-off sound of the river.

Somewhere out there, she thought, was the tiger. She had wondered about the animal the whole evening. She hoped that it was far out of the men's reach.

"O Allah!" cried her mother, pounding some nuts in a wooden bowl. "Tonight is the night for death. Think of those men out there. A tiger is as clever as a hundred foxes."

147

"They should have left the tiger alone," said Fatima. She still looked out the window.

"That's a crazy thing to say," said the woman. "Somebody has to kill the tiger before it kills us. That's sense."

"Perhaps it would have just gone away."

"A tiger that comes near a village does not just go away," snapped the old woman. "It stays around till it gets what it wants. They are usually killers that come near a village."

"But this one didn't look like a killer," argued Fatima.

The old woman snorted, but said nothing.

"The tiger was not more than 20 yards away from me," said Fatima. "It could have jumped on me easily. But it didn't. Why? Can you explain that? It kept watching me, it's true. But then I was watching it too. At first its eyes glared at me, but later they were gentle and bored. There was nothing really fierce about it. . . ."

"Now you are talking crazy," said her mother, fiercely pounding the nuts. "The way your father used to. Heaven forgive me that I should talk so of your dead father, but he was a crazy man sometimes."

Fatima scowled out of the window and listened. There was a silence over the village. Her hands, swollen and red, were knotted tightly together as she strained to hear some sound. The pound, pound of her heart echoed the noise her mother made with the wooden bowl. Then a sharp pain shot through her. Her hands went to her stomach.

"What is it, Fatima?" said her mother, looking up.

"Nothing," answered Fatima between pressed lips.

"Come away from that draft and lie down," said her mother.

Fatima went on standing by the window. She felt the pain rise and fall. She closed her eyes and pictured the tiger. It crouched in the lalang, its eyes now red and glaring, now bored and gentle.

Then she heard the distant crack of a rifle. Another shot followed. Fatima quivered as if the shots had been aimed at her. Then came the roar of the tiger—not the growl she had heard that evening, but full of pain and anger. For a few seconds the cry of the animal seemed to fill up her heart and ears. Her face was tight with pain. Her body glistened with sweat. A moan broke between her shut lips.

"Allah! Allah!" cried out the old woman. "You look ill. What is it? Come and lie down. Is it . . . ?"

• **scowl** (SKOUL) frown

"I've got the pains, mother," gasped Fatima.

The old woman led the girl toward the mat. She made her lie down.

"Oi, oi, it's a fine time to have a baby!" cried her mother, a little frightened. "You lie down here while I get some hot water to drink. I'll have to wait till the men return before I go for the midwife."

Fatima lay on the mat, her eyes shut tight. Her mother boiled the water and muttered.

"Listen," said the old woman. "The men are returning. I can hear their voices."

The air suddenly was filled with the excited voices of men and women outside.

The old lady opened the door cautiously. She called out to someone.

"Hurrah for Mamood, auntie!" called a youth rushing in. "He's shot the tiger. It's a big animal. No wonder it put up a good fight. And then what do you think happened?"

Fatima looked at the youth with interest. The old lady turned her tiny wrinkled head impatiently toward the boy.

"Well, what happened?"

"They said," explained the youth, "that after they had killed the animal they heard noises. Then by the light of their lamps they saw three of the tiniest tiger cubs. Their eyes were hardly open. Mamood says that they would not be more than a few hours old. No wonder the beast fought so hard."

Fatima moaned in pain. The sweat glistened like yellow pearls on her forehead.

"Mother!" she cried.

The old woman pushed the astonished youth toward the door.

"Get the midwife, boy," she shouted. "Quick! Go! The midwife."

The youth stared, gasped, and then ran for the midwife.

• midwife (MID wyf) woman who assists at childbirth

ALL THINGS CONSIDERED ──────────────────

1. When Fatima first sees the tiger, she (a) runs off a short distance. (b) senses it is friendly. (c) is frozen with fear.
2. After a time, the tiger (a) lets go of Fatima. (b) looks bored and less fierce than earlier. (c) loses interest and goes away.
3. Fatima decides to escape when she realizes that (a) she is pregnant, and therefore responsible for two lives. (b) she must get help to kill the tiger. (c) the tiger is growing hungrier every minute.
4. Later, when Fatima hears the two shots, she (a) feels as though they had been aimed at her. (b) shouts with joy. (c) hopes the tiger has escaped.
5. Fatima and the tiger are alike in that they (a) both face death at the end. (b) are about the same age. (c) are, or are about to become, new mothers.

THINKING IT THROUGH ──────────────────

1. (a) What reason or reasons does the author suggest for the tiger's not attacking Fatima? (b) What is your own opinion? Explain in detail.
2. Why doesn't Fatima want the tiger hunted and killed?
3. Time relationships in the story are not made exact. In your opinion, how much time passes (a) from Fatima's seeing the tiger to her escape, and (b) from Fatima's escape to the shooting of the tiger? Explain your answers.
4. The *imagery* (see page 92), on the other hand, is exact and detailed. Discuss the imagery from the paragraph that begins "Fatima scowled . . ." on page 148 to the end of the story.

Literary Skills

Characterization

Although Fatima lives in another culture and half a world away from the American reader, the author succeeds in bringing her to life as a real human being. How does he do this? What literary skills are involved?

The term **characterization** (kar ik tur i ZAY shun) refers to the ways an author brings characters to life. The four main methods of characterization can be illustrated by studying the character of the young hunter Mamood.

A. *Direct statements by the author.* For instance, the sentence "He loved hunting" tells you something directly.
B. *Thoughts and spoken words of the character.* A good example is Mamood's speech, "I shall drag home the body of that beast before sunrise." It indicates he is eager for the hunt.
C. *Actions of the character.* For example, as Mamood listens to the head-man, he is "fingering his new double-barreled gun." This is another indication of his determination to shoot the tiger.
D. *Reactions of other characters to the character.* Before long, a dozen men volunteer to help Mamood kill the tiger. Their reaction to his plea further points up his strength of mind and will. And after they leave, the mother refers to Mamood as "a wild tiger himself."

The examples above all use Mamood, a minor character, to help you understand the methods of characterization. Now use Fatima, the major character, to illustrate the four methods of characterization. First write the four methods on a sheet of paper, labeling them A, B, C, and D, and skipping three or four lines between each. Then look back through the story to find a good example of each method. Note the examples on your paper and explain each.

Composition

1. Suppose you were writing a true story about the last big argument you had. To make your opponent really come to life in the reader's mind, you would want to use all four methods of characterization. Write a one-sentence example of each method—A, B, C, and D.

2. Write a character sketch of someone you like very much. Put all four methods of characterization to work. Remember, the easiest method (A—direct statement) is usually the least effective. Follow the old rule of writing: *Show, don't just tell. Show* through examples how your character speaks, thinks, and acts. Include at least one example showing how others react to him or her.

▶ Someone once said that "alone" is the saddest word in the English language. Not only is the meaning gloomy, the very sound of the word is sad, as it rhymes with "moan," "groan," and "stone." Here's a look into life by the gifted American poet Maya Angelou.

ALONE

by Maya Angelou

Lying, thinking
Last night
How to find my soul a home
Where water is not thirsty
5   And bread loaf is not stone
I came up with one thing
And I don't believe I'm wrong
That nobody,
But nobody
10   Can make it out here alone.

Alone, all alone
Nobody, but nobody
Can make it out here alone.

There are some millionaires
15   With money they can't use
Their wives run round like banshees
Their children sing the blues
They've got expensive doctors
To cure their hearts of stone.
20   But nobody
No nobody
Can make it out here alone.

Alone, all alone
Nobody, but nobody
25   Can make it out here alone.

● banshee (BAN shee) in Irish folklore, a female ghost whose wails and moans are supposed to mean that someone is about to die

Now if you listen closely
I'll tell you what I know
Storm clouds are gathering
The wind is gonna blow
30 The race of man is suffering
And I can hear the moan,
Cause nobody,
But nobody
Can make it out here alone.

35 Alone, all alone
Nobody, but nobody
Can make it out here alone.

WAYS OF KNOWING

1. (a) What two lines best express the main idea of the poem? (b) How many times are these lines repeated, exactly or with small variations?

2. (a) In the poet's opinion, which is more important, a lot of money or good friends? (b) Read the lines in the poem that express this opinion.

3. In your own words, state the theme of the poem. To what degree do you agree with this theme? Completely? Mostly? Somewhat? Very little? In answering this question, ask yourself if an equally good poem could be written on the *advantages* of being alone.

▶ Do you believe that every event in life has a natural explanation? Or do you think that some events involve mysterious forces, powers we can never fully understand? This selection raises these very questions. Some people consider *The Monkey's Paw* a story of the supernatural. Others believe it involves no magic at all. See if you can discover how this difference of opinion is possible.

THE MONKEY'S PAW

by W. W. Jacobs
(Dramatized for TV by Nancy Burroughs)

CHARACTERS

MR. WHITE: *A middle-class Englishman. About 60, he looks older than his years.*
MRS. WHITE: *His wife. Her hair is nearly white.*
HERBERT: *Their son, about 25. A clever and able youth.*
SERGEANT-MAJOR MORRIS: *A tall, red-faced retired army man.*
LAWYER: *A formal but shy person. Very dressed up.*

ACT I

Fade in: Close shot of a monkey's paw attached to a short brass chain in the manner of a rabbit's foot. It swings slowly on a man's index finger, pointed directly at the camera. Dark background. Title and credits over.

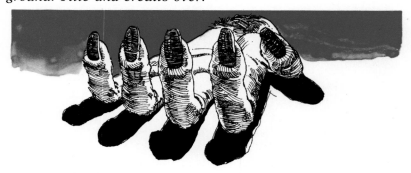

- **supernatural** (soo pur NACH ur ul) beyond what is natural; mysterious and ghostly
- **fade in**—appear gradually on a blank screen
- **credits** (KRED its) here, a TV show's writers, actors, director, etc.

Dissolve to: The living (and dining) room of an English country house, about 1900. The furniture is adequate but a little on the worn side. On the right are two windows, with a fireplace between them. On the rear wall is a door to the outside, right; a window, center; and a staircase leading up, left. On the left are a door leading to the kitchen and a piano against the wall. In the left side of the room is a large, round, general-purpose table with four straight chairs around it. Above it swings a lamp. On the right are a sofa and some chairs. It is a dark winter night, and the room has a shadowy, mysterious quality. The curtains are drawn. At the table sit Mr. White *and his son* Herbert *playing chess. It is clear that* Mr. White *has just made a mistake. He looks alarmed and angry with himself for an instant. Then, hoping* Herbert *has not seen his face, he forces himself to look calm and casual. A gust of wind is heard.*

Mr. White (*Trying to take the other's mind off the game*): Listen to that wind!

Herbert (*Studying the board*): I'm listening. (*A pause before he moves a piece*) Check.

Mr. White: Aw! (*His hand hangs above the board*) My guess is that he isn't going to come on a night like this.

Herbert: Who?

Mr. White: Morris. Sergeant-Major Morris.

Herbert: I didn't know—

Mr. White: I guess you were still at work when I got back from town. I just bumped into him by accident, and it was like old times. (*Finally moves*)

Herbert (*Moves quickly*): Checkmate.

Mr. White (*Standing and trying to ignore his loss*): You do want to meet him, don't you?

Herbert: I don't know. I never have.

Mr. White (*Remembering his afternoon*): All those years in India . . . the stories that man can tell! (*Pulls aside drape at window*) What a place this is! That's the worst of living so far out. Of all the slushy, out-of-the-way places to live, this is the worst. The road out there is a mud hole. Who looks after it? I suppose because only two houses on this road are rented, they think it doesn't matter. (*Turns back*)

- **dissolve** (di ZOLV) here, to fade out one picture as another fades in
- **adequate** (AD uh kwit) good enough; satisfactory
- **check** (CHEK) term used in chess meaning "warning"
- **checkmate** (CHEK mayt) term used in chess meaning "I've won the game"

Mrs. White (*Entering from kitchen, smiling at her husband*): You lost the game, didn't you?

Mr. White *shrugs.*

Mrs. White: Well, never mind, dear. Maybe you'll win the next one. (*Exchanging a knowing glance with* Herbert) That Morris man will cheer you up.

Mr. White: If he comes.

Mrs. White: You think not? (*Beginning to tidy up the room*) Well, I hope not.

Herbert *looks up, interested.*

Mrs. White: Even long ago, I never liked that man. There's something shady about him, something—

Mr. White: Shh! There he is.

Footsteps sound outside as Mr. White *goes to the door. He opens it and* Morris *enters.*

Mr. White: Morris!

Morris: White, old fellow! (*They shake hands*).

Mr. White (*Gesturing*): My wife—you remember. And my son, Herbert. Sergeant-Major Morris.

All mumble greetings and shake hands.

Mrs. White: A spot of coffee for our guest?

Morris: On a night like this—delightful! (*Hands her his coat and hat*).

Mrs. White *goes to kitchen as the others settle themselves around the fireplace.*

Mr. White: Morris, you wouldn't mind repeating that story about the tiger for Herbert, would you?

Morris (*Who would like nothing better*): The tiger, yes! (*His eyes light up; he tells a story well*) Not a tiger, actually. A tiger cub. We'd shot the mother, and this cub ran off into their den. Two days we waited. Put food outside and everything. Then finally I decided to crawl in after it. It was just a tunnel in the rock, really. Just big enough for a tiger or a large man like me to squeeze through. So into the cave I go, a knife between my teeth to have it out with the beast. A real scramble. But that cub must have heard me coming. It decided to get out. How? The way I was coming in. I saw it in front of me in the dim light. Then it was on my back, scratching like mad to get between me and the top of the tunnel. So finally it got past, leaving my back a clawed-up mess. I'd just got turned around to go back out, when what do I hear? A shot. The lads outside had shot at it. Hit it right in the haunch and spun it around. So right then that cub wanted nothing better than to get back *into* the cave. Again, there was that cub in front of me. And then it

---

• **haunch** (HAWNCH) back part of an animal

was clawing away at my back once more. (*Laughs loudly*) A bloody mess, a bloody mess.

Fade out.

Fade in: They are sitting around the table drinking coffee. It is an hour or so later. Morris *is laughing at another of his tales.* Mrs. White *has joined the group. All look interested.*

Mr. White: Twenty-one years of it! (*Nods at wife and son*) When he went away he was a little bit of a thing at the factory. Now look at him.

Mrs. White: He hasn't come to much harm, that's for sure.

Mr. White: I'd like to go to India myself. Just to look around a bit, you know.

Morris: Better where you are. (*He shakes head and sighs*)

Mr. White: I'd like to see those old temples. And the fakirs and jugglers, too. What was that you started telling me about a monkey's paw or something, Morris?

Morris: Oh, this afternoon. That was nothing, really.

Mrs. White: A monkey's paw?

Morris: Nothing. (*Shakes head*) Anyhow, nothing worth hearing.

Herbert: Go ahead.

Morris: (*Lightly*): Well, it's just a bit of what you might call magic. (*He raises the coffee cup to his lips, realizes it's empty, and accepts more from* Mrs. White's *pot*) To look at it (*fumbling in pocket*), it's just an ordinary little paw, dried to a mummy.

Mrs. White *draws back when he offers it to her, but* Herbert *examines it with interest.*

• fakir (fuh KEER) Indian holy man, often supposed to have magic powers

Mr. White: And what's so special about it? (*He takes it, examines it, and puts it on the table.*)

Morris: It had a spell put on it by an old fakir, a very holy man. He put a spell on it so that three separate people could each have three wishes from it.
The others laugh uncomfortably.

Mr. White: Well, why don't you have your three, then?

Morris (*Quietly*): I have. (*He looks worried*)

Mrs. White: And did you really have the three wishes granted?

Morris: I did. (*His cup taps against his teeth as his hand shakes*)

Mrs. White: And has anybody else wished?

Morris (*Sadly*): The first man had his three wishes, yes. . . . I don't know what the first two were. But the third was for death. That's how I got the paw.
During a long pause the listeners realize that the story may be true.

Mr. White: Well, Morris, if you've had your three wishes, the paw's no good to you now. Right? What do you keep it for?

Morris: Interest, I suppose. I did have some idea of selling it. But I don't think I will. It has caused enough trouble already. Besides, people don't want to pay. They aren't that sure that the spell really works.

Mr. White: Suppose you could have another three wishes. What would they be?

Morris (*Slowly*): I don't know. I don't know. (*He rises in sudden anger, picks the paw up from the table, and throws it across the room into the fire*)

Mr. White (*Dashing across the room*): Oh, no! (*He brushes the paw out of the flames*)

Morris (*Very seriously*): Better let it burn.

Mr. White (*Holding the paw*): If you don't want it, Morris, give it to me.

Morris: I won't! Throw it on the fire.
Mr. White *appeals with his eyes.*

Morris: Well, if you keep it, don't blame me for what happens. Be sensible, man. Throw it on the fire.

Mr. White: How do you do it? Make the spell work, I mean.

Morris: Hold it up in your right hand and wish aloud. But I warn you of the consequences.

Mrs. White (*Starting to doubt and rising; she has trouble picking up and holding at once the four cups and saucers*): Sounds like magic nonsense to me. Do you think it could get me another pair of hands?
Mr. White *raises the paw in his right fist.*

Morris (*Grabbing* Mr. White's *arm*): No! You'd make her a freak.

Fade out.

Fade in: Some time later. Morris, *dressed again for the weather, is just leaving. All murmur "good-bye," etc.*

Morris (*Departing*): Remember, if you must wish, wish for something sensible (*Closes door as he leaves*).

Herbert: I just can't believe that any of those stories were true. *Including* the one about the monkey's paw!

Mrs. White: Then we're not going to make much out of it, are we? (*To* Mr. White) Did you give him anything for it?

Mr. White (*A little embarrassed*): Not much. He didn't want it, but I made him accept something.

Mrs. White *looks disturbed.*

Mr. White: Well, I couldn't just take the paw, could I? And he asked me again to throw it away.

Herbert (*Kidding*): Why, we're going to be rich, and famous, and happy. Wish to be an emperor, Dad. Then you can't be henpecked.

Mrs. White *raises her arm sportively to hit* Herbert *for his joke. He runs around the table laughing, pursued by his mother.*

Mr. White (*Taking the paw from his pocket and studying it*): I don't really know what to wish for. And that's a fact.

Mrs. White: When you think about it, it seems that we have all we want.

Mr. White (*Looking around, then at his wife*): If you only had all new furniture, you'd be quite happy, wouldn't you?

Herbert: Well, wish for 200 pounds, then. Have a furniture splurge.

Mr. White, *feeling silly and embarrassed, holds the paw up in his right hand.* Herbert *and his mother exchange winks.* Herbert *sits down at the piano and strikes a few chords, as if introducing a great stage act.*

Mr. White: I wish for 200 pounds.

A loud crash comes from the piano; Herbert's *hands are on it.* Mr. White *cries out and shudders. The others rush toward him.*

Mr. White (*Looking at the paw on the floor*): It moved! Just as I wished! It twisted in my hand like a snake!

Herbert: Well, I don't see the money. (*Putting the paw back on the table*) And I'll bet I never will.

Mrs. White: It must have been your imagination.

Mr. White (*Shaking head*): Never mind, though. There's no harm done. But it gave me a shock, all the same.

- **pound**—main unit of British money
- **splurge** (SPLURJ) spending spree; spell of wild spending

Herbert (*Looking at watch*): Well, I'm going to bed. Now, *that's* where you'll find the money. The cash will all be in a big bag right in the middle of your bed. (*Moving up the stairs*) And there'll be something horrible squatting on top of your dresser. Something horrible just watching you pocket the money (*Exits up, laughing*). Mr. White *sits down in front of the fire. We see a long close-up of his confused, thoughtful face.*

Dissolve to: The fire, as Mr. White *sees it.*

Dissolve to: The fire as before, but superimposed over the huge face of a leering monkey.

Fade out.

ACT II

Fade in: The room of the evening before, but now bright with a cheerful midday sun. The curtains are open. Mr. *and* Mrs. White *are just finishing lunch.*

Mr. White (*Pushing back from the table*): That was a good lunch. We ought to eat fish more often.
Mrs. White: And you're not embarrassed about the money you gave Morris anymore?
Mr. White: Not too.
Mrs. White: The idea of our even listening to such nonsense! I suppose all old soldiers are the same.
Mr. White: And why was Morris so worried about that thing? How could anything I wished for hurt me?
Mrs. White (*Laughing*): Remember what Herbert said as he went off to work?
Mr. White: That it would be a 200-pound bag of pennies, dropped on my head from the sky. (*Shakes head and smiles*)
Mrs. White: That's a laugh.
Mr. White (*More seriously*): Morris said the wishes are granted so naturally. They don't seem like magic when they come. They just appear to be, well, things that might have happened anyhow. Nothing to make one leery.
Mrs. White (*Standing*): And that *proves* it was all a story. How could *you* ever get 200 pounds naturally?
Mr. White: You're right. But for all that, the thing moved in my hand. That I'll swear to.
Mrs. White: You just thought it did.
Mr. White: I say it did. There was no thought about it. I had just— What's the matter?

- superimposed (SOO pur im POHZD) (of a picture) put on top of another, so that both are seen
- **leery** (LEER ee) suspicious

Mrs. White (*Peering out from behind curtains*): There's someone out there.

Mr. White: The postman?

Mrs. White: No, someone I don't know. He's studying the house. And he's all dressed up formal.

Mr. White: So?

Mrs. White: Well, what's a man dressed up like that doing out here? There, there he's moving on, toward town.
Mrs. White clears the dishes off the table and enters the kitchen. There is a firm knock on the door. Mr. White jumps, then goes to answer it. The Lawyer, unsure of himself and very tense, enters as Mrs. White comes from the kitchen.

Lawyer: You are . . . Mr. and Mrs. Matthew White? (*There is a long pause after the two nod*) I—I have been asked to call. (*Picking a speck of dirt from pants*) I come from the law firm, Maw and Muggins?

Mr. White: Oh, yes.

Mrs. White: Is anything the matter?

Lawyer: Maw and Muggins, you see—I represent Booth Paper Company, your son Herbert's employer.

Mrs. White: Has anything happened to Herbert? What is it? What is it?

Mr. White (*to Mrs. White*): There, there. Sit down and stop imagining things. (*To Lawyer*) You've not brought bad news, I'm sure, sir.

Lawyer: I'm sorry—

Mrs. White: Is he hurt?

Lawyer (*Nodding and going on quietly*): Badly hurt . . . but he is not in any pain.

Mrs. White (*Clasping hands*): Oh, thank God. Thank God for that. Thank— (*Suddenly she sees the Lawyer's real meaning. She catches her breath and looks horrified. Reaching out, she takes her husband's hand.*)

Lawyer (*Distinctly, after a pause*): He was caught in the machinery.

Mr. White (*In a daze*): Caught in the machinery. (*He looks at his wife, then back at the Lawyer*) He was the only one left to us. It is hard.

Mrs. White rises, still holding her husband's hand. They look at each other, not at the Lawyer, during the following speech.

Lawyer (*Formally, with pauses*): Booth Paper Company wishes me to express their sincere sympathy. This is a great loss. . . . I beg you to understand that I am only their servant. I am only obeying orders. . . . I was to say also that Booth Paper Company was in no way responsible for the accident. They admit no legal error or oversight . . . but, because of your son's ser-vices—because of your son's services, they wish to present you with a certain sum of money for your loss.

The couple drop hands and stare with horror at their visitor.

Mr. White (*Barely able to speak*): How much?

Lawyer: Two hundred pounds.

Mrs. White *shrieks.* Mr. White *puts out his hands for support and falls in a heap to the floor.*

ACT III

Fade in: The same setting, but even darker than Act I. The fire has nearly died out. During the whole act, powerful gusts of wind make the old house produce creaking and knocking noises. Mrs. White *stands peering between the drawn curtains of a window.* Mr. White, *dressed in pajamas and robe and carrying a candle, descends the stairs.*

Mr. White: Aren't you coming upstairs, dear? (*Getting no answer*) It's cold down here.

Mrs. White (*On the edge of tears*): It is colder where my son is.

Mr. White: Don't cry, please. Or at least come up and cry in bed. (*Not really believing his words*) The dead are dead, and the living must carry on. (*Pauses*) Come on, it's been two weeks.

Mrs. White: Sixteen days.

Mr. White *puts the candle down. They stand there looking at each other for a long time.*

Mrs. White (*Excited*): The *paw!* The monkey's paw!

Mr. White: The paw? What's the matter?

Mrs. White (*Stumbling toward him*): I want it! I want it! You've not destroyed it?

Mr. White: No. It's upstairs. With my things.

Mrs. White (*Crying and laughing both, kissing him*): I only just thought of it. Why didn't I think of it before? Why didn't *you* think of it?

Mr. White: Think of what?

Mrs. White: The other two wishes! We only had one.

Mr. White: Wasn't that enough?

Mrs. White: No! We'll have one more. Go up and get it quickly, and wish our boy back with us.

Mr. White (*Horrified at the idea*): The paw? Again? You must be mad!

Mrs. White (*Kissing him*): Get it! Get it quickly. Oh, my boy, my boy.

Mr. White: You don't know what you're saying.

• **oversight** (OH vur syt) failure to notice something; careless error

Mrs. White: We got the first wish, didn't we? Why not the second?

Mr. White: The first time it was just luck—bad luck. Something that happened, that's all.

Mrs. White: No! (*Wild with excitement*) Go and get it and wish.

Mr. White: Look, sit down a moment. (*Helps her*) He has been dead 16 days. And besides, he—I didn't tell you this before. There was no need to. He was very badly mangled in the machinery. I could recognize him only by his clothing. If he was too terrible for you to see then, why now?

Mrs. White (*Hardly knowing what he's said*): Oh, bring him back! (*Rising to drag him to the stairs*) Get the paw! Bring him back! Do you think I can fear the sight of my very own son?

Mr. White (*Resignedly*): As you wish.

Mr. White, *his shoulders bowed, plods upstairs. While he is gone,* Mrs. White *becomes overcome with happiness. She clasps her hands as in prayer, looks up, and walks slowly around the room. Her behavior is most unnatural.* Mr. White *returns unchanged.*

Mrs. White (*Strongly*): *Wish!*

Mr. White: It is foolish and wicked.

Mrs. White: *Wish!*

Mr. White (*Raising his right fist, hating to say the words*): I wish my son alive again.

The monkey's paw falls to the floor. Mr. White *looks at it with horror. Both people sit down, in separate chairs.*

Mr. White (*Hoping what he says is true*): There's nothing to it. He won't come.

Mrs. White: He will! He will!

Fade out.

Fade in: As before, some time later.

Mr. White (*Looking at watch*): It's been over a half hour. (*Standing up*) You see? He won't come.

Mrs. White *ignores him. He strolls to a window slowly and stands looking out through the closed curtain. Suddenly he coughs.*

Mrs. White (*Leaping up*): Is it—

Mr. White (*Barring the window*): No! (*He grabs her*)

Mrs. White: What did you see?

Mr. White: Nothing! I saw nothing!

- **mangled** (MANG guld) badly damaged or torn
- **resignedly** (ri ZY nid lee) without opposition; in a passive manner
- **plod** (PLOD) walk slowly and heavily

During a short silence a soft knock is heard.

Mrs. White (*Screaming*): It's Herbert! It's Herbert!

Mr. White: What are you going to do?

Mrs. White: It's my boy. It's Herbert. (*Struggling to get away*) What are you holding me for?

There is another knock, louder this time. The loud knocks continue during the following. They are not regular, however, and might be noises the house is making in the wind, which increases with the knocking.

Mr. White: No!

Mrs. White: I must open the door! I forgot, it's three miles to the cemetery.

Mr. White: For God's sake, don't let it in!

Mrs. White: You're afraid of your own son! Let me go! I'm coming, Herbert! I'm coming!

With a mighty effort, Mrs. White *breaks free. She rushes for the door. As she reaches it, her husband catches up with her, seizes one hand, and whirls her around, sending her staggering across the room. Then he falls to his knees and reaches around for the monkey's paw on the floor. She makes another try for the door. Just as it starts to open, her husband raises his right fist desperately.*

Mr. White: I WISH IT WERE BACK IN THE GRAVE!

The knocking stops suddenly. The camera pans from Mr. White's *desperate face to* Mrs. White, *open-mouthed and shocked. The camera then rolls toward the door, which is slowly swinging open on a rural scene bathed in soft moonlight. It is deserted and lonely.*

Fade out.

• pan (PAN) move sideways from one view to another

ALL THINGS CONSIDERED ─────────────

1. The monkey's paw is said to give three wishes to (a) three different people. (b) only one person. (c) anyone.

2. Sergeant-Major Morris (a) wants Mr. White to have the monkey's paw. (b) wants Mrs. White to have the monkey's paw. (c) tries to destroy the monkey's paw.

3. The person who believes *least* in the powers of the monkey's paw is (a) Mr. White. (b) Mrs. White. (c) Herbert.

4. The first wish (a) seems to come true. (b) seems not to come true. (c) results in Mrs. White's death.

5. Mr. White's third wish is (a) for 200 pounds. (b) for his son's life. (c) the opposite of his second wish.

THINKING IT THROUGH ─────────────

1. The questions in this exercise and the one that follows will enable you to develop a better understanding of *The Monkey's Paw*. The first question is this: In Act I, why does Sergeant-Major Morris seem reluctant to let the Whites have the monkey's paw?

2. Immediately after the first wish is made, "a loud crash seems to come from the piano." In your opinion, does Herbert produce the crash, or does the piano sound for some other reason?

3. Do you think the monkey's paw really twists in Mr. White's hand, or does he only imagine the movement?

4. (a) What is the second wish, exactly? (Look back to the selection.) (b) What other—and better—words might Mr. White have used to get his wish?

5. Toward the end of Act III, what do you think Mr. White actually sees as he stands looking out through the closed curtain? Explain your opinion.

Critical Thinking

Cause and Effect

A **cause** is an event or idea that leads to a certain result, called an **effect**. For instance, regular exercise every day (cause) will usually lead to a sound body (effect). You have probably done many cause-effect exercises in books like this one. They're quite easy: All you have to do is match the causes in one column with the effects in another.

If you put on your critical thinking cap, however, you will see that in truth, the relationship between *cause* and *effect* is often not at all easy to understand. First, a cause almost always has several effects, and nearly all effects require several causes. Secondly, the effects of causes themselves become causes for still other effects. For instance, if hunger *causes* overeating, the overeating may in turn *cause* a stomachache. And finally, in real life it's often very difficult to match certain causes with certain effects. If this were not true, the mysteries of life would vanish and boredom would set in at once.

Good literature often leads to questions in the reader's mind. It often makes the reader wonder about complicated cause-effect relationships. *The Monkey's Paw* is a good example:

1. Considered as a cause, the monkey's paw is said to lead to the effect of three wishes coming true. This seems quite simple. But what *bad* effects does the paw seem to have had in the past?
2. Now consider the bad effects you gave in answer to question 1 as causes for still other effects. How has the past history of the paw caused Sergeant-Major Morris to think about it?
3. Explain the three wishes made by Mr. White as a chain of causes and effects. In cause-effect terms, how is the first wish related to the second, and the second to the third?

Composition

1. Go back and reread the second sentence on this page (about exercise and a sound body). Then write a paragraph explaining how this is an overly simplified cause-effect relationship. You will have to include both the *other* results of regular exercise and the *other* causes of a sound body.

2. The introduction stated that the events in *The Monkey's Paw* can be explained in two different ways. It comes down to this: Either there were supernatural causes for the events in this selection, or there were not. In your opinion, which explanation is the better one? Explain your thinking.

VOCABULARY AND SKILL REVIEW

Before completing the exercises that follow, you may wish to review the **bold-faced** words on pages 144 to 163.

I. On a separate sheet of paper, mark each item *true* or *false*. If it is false, explain what is wrong with the sentence.

1. *Sarong* is a kind of thick, tall grass.
2. Ghosts and phantoms are *supernatural* beings.
3. *Brooding* too much about bad luck can make one feel even worse.
4. To *fade in* means to appear rather gradually on a TV or movie screen.
5. The words *resignedly* and *hopefully* have nearly the same meaning.
6. A *checkmate* is a blocked goal in an ice hockey game.
7. The *credits* in this book come just before the table of contents.
8. *Allah* is the word for God in the Islamic religion.
9. Good news is often received with a *scowl* of joy.
10. In the language of TV, to *dissolve* means to fade one picture into another.

II. On a separate sheet of paper, write the *italicized* word that best fills the blank in each sentence.

adequate	*oversight*	*pound*	*glint*	*expanse*
leery	*mangled*	*haunch*	*plod*	*splurge*

1. From the top of the mountain, the explorers gazed at the endless _____ of prairie below.
2. After a day's hard work, Ramon had to _____ home through the rain.
3. Sally turned on the flashlight and saw the _____ of a cat's eyes.
4. Eight hours of sleep is _____ for most adults.
5. Packages sometimes get badly _____ in the mail.
6. The Millers' cat has a white star on its _____.
7. The British _____ was worth about $1.40 in 1985.
8. Mr. Barrett collected his lottery winnings and went on a big _____ in a department store.
9. As a result of a clerk's _____, Sara's name was not printed in the graduation program.
10. Men in uniforms nearly always make our dog _____.

III. Here are five very short poems. All are anonymous (of unknown authorship). At first glance they may seem merely
amusing and not too important. Each of them, however, is
based on some serious statement about life that can be expressed in cause-and-effect terms—that is, in a sentence, containing a word like *cause, because,* or *result.*

Number a separate sheet of paper from 1 to 6, and match
each of the poems with one of the statements that follow.

1.
Centipede

A centipede was happy quite,
    Until a frog in fun
Said, "Pray, which leg comes after which?"
This raised her mind to such a pitch,
She lay distracted in the ditch
    Considering how to run.

2.
The Rain

The rain it falls down every day,
    Upon the just and unjust fella,
But more upon the just, because
    The unjust has the just's umbrella.

3.
Epitaph

This is the grave of Mike O'Day
Who died maintaining his right of way.
His right was clear, his will was strong,
But he's just as dead as if he'd been wrong.

4.
For Want of a Nail

For want of a nail, the shoe was lost,
For want of a shoe, the horse was lost,
For want of a horse, the rider was lost,
For want of a rider, the battle was lost,
For want of a battle, the kingdom was lost.
And all for the want of a horseshoe nail.

• distracted (dis TRAK tud) mentally troubled
• maintaining (mayn TAYN ing) protecting; insisting on

168

5.

The Cats of Kilkenny

There were once two cats of Kilkenny,
Each thought there was one cat too many;
So they fought and they fit,
And they scratched and they bit,
Till, except for their nails
And the tips of their tails,
Instead of two cats, there weren't any.

(a) Some people's unfairness causes other people to suffer.
(b) Hatred of others can cause destruction of the self.
(c) Thinking too much about *how* we do certain things can cause us to do them badly, or not at all.
(d) Very small causes can have truly terrible results.
(e) Being in the right will not always cause us to be successful.

IV. On a separate sheet of paper, write a sentence explaining why each cartoon is funny. Try to use words like *logical*, *cause*, and *effect* in your explanations.

"Want to know something, Dad?"

Drawing by Alain; © 1953, 1983 The New Yorker Magazine, Inc.

Leo Tolstoy (1828-1910)

Few authors have written as much as **Leo Tolstoy.** Few have been as popular. Few have lived as interesting a life. And perhaps no author has had as much influence on the course of human thought and history. There is, in fact, a direct link between Russia's Leo Tolstoy and America's Martin Luther King, Jr.

Born into a noble family in 1828, Tolstoy had a happy childhood. He received a good education, but dropped out of college to manage the family estate. In his 20's he served for several years in the army and wrote the first of the many books that made him famous.

When he was about 30, Tolstoy turned much of his attention to improving the life of the peasants, or serfs. At the time, the serfs were nearly slaves. Attached to the land by law, they lived in poverty, at the mercy of their masters. Most could neither read nor write. Concerned with the serfs' condition, Tolstoy returned to the family estate and began a project to make them free people. In 1859 he opened a school for the serfs on his lands. He even traveled to other countries to study educational methods. During this period he was also married and wrote his best-known novels.

Another big change in Tolstoy's life came when he was about 50. He studied religion. He became convinced that the messages in the Bible should be *lived*, not simply talked about. He preached forgiveness and the love of all humanity. Believing in nonviolence, he urged that war for any reason was evil. He wanted all armies broken up. For Tolstoy, "blessed are the meek" meant dressing in peasant clothes and living a simple life. He even began to make his own shoes. He continued to set a living example of his beliefs until his death in 1910.

As a young man, Martin Luther King, Jr., read and studied the works of Tolstoy. What is the "direct link" between the two men?

WHERE LOVE IS, THERE GOD IS ALSO

by Leo Tolstoy

▶ The Russian author Leo Tolstoy is one of the few true giants in world literature. He created a small library of masterpieces, from the huge, complicated novel *War and Peace* to the short, sincere tale that follows. Before reading it, ask yourself: *How can a person be both humble and great at the same time?* You'll find out soon.

In a little town in Russia there lived a cobbler, Martin Avedeitch by name. He had a small room in a basement, the window of which looked out on the street. Through this window could be seen only the feet of the people who passed by, but Martin could recognize nearly everyone. He knew people by their boots and shoes.

There was hardly a pair of boots or shoes that had not passed through Martin's hands at least once. Some he had resoled. Others he had patched, and still others he had stitched up. He had plenty of work, for he used good material, did not charge too much, and could be counted on. If he could do a job by the day required, he took it. If not, he told the truth and turned it down.

Martin had always been a good man, and in his old age he began to think more about his soul and draw nearer to God. His life became peaceful and happy. When he finished his day's travail, he got his Bible from the shelf and sat down to read. And the more he read, the better he understood. His mind grew clear, his eyes full of hope and trust.

One morning Martin rose before daylight, and after saying his prayers, he lit a fire and prepared his cabbage soup and wheat cereal. Then he lit the samovar, put on his apron, and sat down by the window to work. He often glanced out into the street. When-

- resole (ree SOHL) put new soles on shoes or boots
- travail (truh VAYL) hard work
- samovar (SAM uh var) metal vessel for heating tea water

ever anyone passed in unfamiliar boots, he would stop work and look up. In that way he could see not only the feet but also the face of the passer-by. A janitor passed in new felt boots. Then came a water carrier. By and by an old soldier of Czar Nicholas's army came near, shovel in hand. Martin knew him by his boots— shabby, old, and cracked. The old man was called Stepanitch. A nearby businessman kept him in his house, more for charity than for the little work he could do.

Now Stepanitch began to clear away the snow in front of Martin's window. The cobbler glanced at him and then went on with his work. After a dozen stitches, he looked out the window again, to see that Stepanitch had leaned his shovel against the wall to rest. His feet were wet, and he looked cold. The man was old and broken down, with not enough strength even to clear away the snow.

"What if I were to call him in and give him some tea?" Martin asked himself. "The samovar has just come to the boil."

He stuck his awl in place and stood up. Putting the samovar on the table, he made tea. Then he tapped the window with his fingers. Stepanitch turned and saw Martin's gesture to come in.

"Enter, my friend," Martin said, opening his door. "Warm yourself a bit. I'm sure you must be shivering."

"May God bless you!" Stepanitch replied. "My old bones do ache this morning." He started in, shaking the snow off his boots. Then, so as not to leave marks on the floor, he began slapping at his feet with his hands. As he did so, he tottered and nearly fell.

"Don't bother about your feet," Martin said. "I'll wipe up the floor. It's all in a day's work. Come now, sit down and have some tea."

• awl (AWL) hand tool for making holes

Filling two cups, he passed one to his visitor. He poured his own tea out into the saucer and began to blow on it.

Stepanitch emptied his cup quickly. Turning it upside down, he put what was left of his piece of sugar on the top.

"Thank you, Martin Avedeitch," he said. "You have given me comfort for both soul and body."

"You are most welcome," Martin answered. "Come in again. I like your company."

Stepanitch went away, and Martin poured out the last of the tea and drank it up. Then he put away the tea things and sat back down to his work. As he stitched the back seam of a boot, he kept thinking about what he had read in the Bible. And his head was full of words from the Bible.

Later that day, Martin saw a woman selling apples come up the street. She carried not only her basket of apples but also, on her back, a sack of wood chips. No doubt she had picked them up at some place where building was going on.

The sack evidently hurt the old woman, for she stopped right in front of Martin's window. She put the sack down and, setting the basket on a post, began to shake down the chips in the sack. While she was doing this, a boy in a tattered cap ran up. He snatched an apple out of the basket and tried to slip away. But the old woman was too quick for him. She turned and caught him by the sleeve, her hand a steel trap on his elbow. He began to struggle, trying to free himself from the old woman's hands. She knocked his cap off and seized hold of his hair. The boy screamed as the woman scolded.

Martin let go of his awl and ran to the door. Stumbling up the steps, he dropped his spectacles in his hurry. He ran out into the street. The old woman was pulling the boy's hair and screaming at him. She threatened to take him to the police.

"I didn't take it!" cried the boy. "I didn't take it. Why are you beating me?"

Martin approached them. Taking the boy by the hand, he said to the woman, "Let him go, can't you? Forgive him."

"I'll have his hide!" she yelled. "He won't forget it for a year! I'll take the rascal to the police."

Martin tried to pacify the old woman.

"Let him go, please. He won't do it again."

The old woman finally let go. The boy wished to run away, but Martin stopped him.

• **pacify** (PAS uh fy) make peaceful; calm down

"Ask the woman's forgiveness," he said. "And don't do it another time. I saw you take that apple."

The boy began to cry and beg for pardon.

"That's right," Martin said. "And now, here's an apple for you." He took an apple from the basket and gave it to the boy, saying, "I will pay for it."

"You'll spoil them that way," the woman declared. "The young rascals. He ought to be whipped. That way, he'd remember for a week."

"No, no," said Martin patiently. "That's our way—but it's not God's way. If he should be whipped for stealing an apple, what should be done to us for our sins?"

The old woman was silent.

And Martin told her a parable. The story told of a lord who forgave his servant a large debt—only to have the servant go out and seize one of his own debtors by the throat. The old woman listened to it all. The boy, too, stood by and listened.

"God bids us forgive," said Martin, "or else we shall not be forgiven. Forgive all people, and a thoughtless boy most of all."

The old woman shook her head and sighed.

"But they are getting terribly spoiled these days."

"Then we old ones must show them better ways," Martin replied.

"That's just what I say," said the old woman. "I have had seven of them myself, and only one daughter is left." And the old woman began to talk of several things. How and where she was living with her daughter. How many grandchildren she had.

"There, now," the woman went on. "I have but little strength left. Yet I work hard for the sake of my grandchildren. And nice children they are, too. When I get home, who comes out to meet me? Only the children. Little Ann, now, won't leave me for anyone. All the time its 'Grandmother. Grandmother. Grandmother.'" And the old woman's eyes brightened as she softened at the thought.

"Of course, it was only his childishness," she said, looking at the boy.

The old woman turned, reached for her sack, and began to hoist it to her shoulders. Seeing her, the boy sprang forward.

"Let me carry it for you, please. I'm going that way."

- parable (PAR uh bul) very short story with a moral lesson
- bid (BID) command

The old woman nodded her head. She put the sack on the boy's back, and they went down the street together. The old woman had quite forgotten to ask Martin to pay for the apple. Martin stood and watched them as they went along talking to each other.

Soon they were out of sight. Martin went back to the shop. Luckily, he found his spectacles unbroken on the steps. He picked up his awl and sat down again to work. He worked a little, but before long the light started to fade. He could not see to pass the thread through the holes in the leather. He looked out at the darkening street and saw a lamplighter passing, lighting the first street lamps.

"Well, it's time to light up," thought Martin. So he filled his lamp, hung it up, and sat down again to work. He finished one boot, and turning it about, examined it. It was all right. Then he gathered his tools together and swept up the cuttings. Taking down the lamp, he placed it on the table. Then he took the Bible from the shelf. He meant to open it at the place he had marked, but if fell open somewhere else.

As Martin opened the Bible, he seemed to hear footsteps. It was as though someone were moving behind him. Martin turned around. It seemed to him now that people were standing in the dark corner, although he could not make out who they were. And a voice whispered in his ear:

"Martin, Martin, don't you know me?"

"Who is it?" muttered the old cobbler.

"It is I," said the voice. And out of the dark corner stepped Stepanitch. The old soldier smiled, and then, vanishing like a cloud, was seen no more.

"It is I," said a voice once more. And the old woman and the boy with the apple stepped out. They both smiled, and then they too vanished.

And Martin's soul grew joyful. He put on his spectacles. He began reading the Bible, just where it had opened. At the top of the page he read:

"I was hungry, and ye gave me meat. I was thirsty, and ye gave me drink. I was a stranger, and ye took me in."

And at the bottom of the page he read the words of the Lord:

"Inasmuch as ye did it unto these my brethren, even these least, ye did it unto me." (*Matthew*, XXV)

- cuttings (KUT ingz) small pieces cut off
- inasmuch as (in az MUCH az) because; since
- **brethren** (BRETH rin) old-fashioned term for *brothers*

ALL THINGS CONSIDERED ————————————————

1. By the second page of the story, it is clear that the author (a) has great respect for old Martin. (b) thinks old Martin a fool. (c) has no personal interest in his main character.
2. Martin's acts of kindness affect (a) only one person. (b) only two people. (c) three people.
3. Martin's acts of kindness seem to really change the lives of (a) one person. (b) two people. (c) three people.
4. The character who is taught to forgive is (a) the old soldier. (b) the old woman. (c) the boy.
5. The quotation that concludes the story means (a) all sins should be forgiven. (b) God helps those who help themselves. (c) people who serve others also serve God.

THINKING IT THROUGH ————————————————

1. (a) What does Stepanitch, the old soldier, do immediately after finishing his tea? (b) What meaning do you infer from this act?
2. In your opinion, are the old soldier, the old woman, and the boy *really* in Martin's room at the conclusion of the story? Explain your answer.
3. Even without knowing that Tolstoy died in 1910, you should be able to tell that the story is set in pre-communist Russia. How can you tell?
4. Of the four characters in the story, which you think is most like Tolstoy? Explain your answer. (See the profile of Tolstoy on page 170.)
5. In your own words, what is the full meaning of the title?

Reading and Analyzing

Understanding Symbols

A **symbol** is something in a literary selection that stands for something else.

Go back and read that definition again. Notice two parts of it carefully:

(a) A symbol must actually be *in* a story or poem, not just referred to in a figurative expression. For instance, toward the end of the story Tolstoy writes that Stepanitch vanished "like a cloud." But is there any real cloud *in* the story? No. The word "cloud" is not a symbol but part of a simile (page 135).

(b) A symbol must stand for or suggest something else. Although that "something else" can be a real "thing," it is usually a feeling or idea. For instance, the Bible in the story can be said to be a symbol for Martin's religious feelings and ideas about God.

1. Stepanitch's boots are described as being "shabby, old, and cracked." What do they symbolize about the man himself?
2. Martin gives Stepanitch a cup of tea. What does this cup of tea symbolize about Martin?
3. When the old woman seizes the boy, we read that her hand is "a steel trap on his elbow." (a) Is it correct to call the "steel trap" a symbol? (b) If not, what is the correct term for this kind of literary device?

Composition

1. Look again at the third paragraph from the end of the story (the quotation beginning "'I was hungry . . .'"). (a) Which actions in this quotation are illustrated in the story, and which are not? (b) If Tolstoy had chosen to illustrate the whole paragraph, what changes or additions might he have made?
2. To many people, symbols of achievement and wealth are very important. For instance, a person who buys an expensive new car may enjoy its "comfort," "safety," and "superior engineering," but such an individual is also aware of the car's symbolic value. An expensive car is a symbol of the wealth of its owner. *In the modern world, people more and more live by symbols.*

Write a paragraph using the italicized sentence above as the topic (main idea) sentence. Think about the symbolic value of things like clothing, hairstyles, and houses. Include definite examples if you can.

INTRODUCING HAIKU

▶ The **haiku** (HY koo) has been a popular poetic form in Japan for over 300 years. The first line of the haiku has five syllables. The second has seven syllables, and the third five syllables. (In English versions, this syllable count is not always exact because of problems in translation.) The haiku is like a tiny telegram that paints a picture in the fewest words possible. Here is a good example:

OVER THE MOUNTAIN
  BRIGHT THE FULL WHITE MOON NOW SMILES . . .
ON THE FLOWER-THIEF

—Issa

For the Japanese reader, most of the things mentioned in the haiku have symbolic value. We people of the Western world are unfamiliar with the elaborate system of symbols developed by Basho (1644–1694), Issa (1763–1827), and other great haiku poets. But that need not stop us from guessing at the symbolic meanings. What, for instance, does the above poem *mean*? One possible meaning is that the beauty of nature is available to, and includes, persons we think of as "evil," that there is no "good" and "bad" in nature.

Think carefully about the following poems before answering the questions.

178

FIVE HAIKU

1. HERE, WHERE A THOUSAND
   CAPTAINS SWORE GREAT CONQUEST . . . TALL
   GRASS THEIR MONUMENT

   —Basho

2. CAREFUL, CHAMPION FLEA
   AND LOOK BEFORE YOU LEAP . . .
   HERE'S RIVER SUMIDA

   —Issa

3. SUNNY FIELDS AND WARM . . .
   SEE THE MONK'S FACE PEEPING OUT
   FROM THE TEMPLE FENCE

   —Issa

4. STUBBORN WOODPECKER . . .
   STILL HAMMERING AT TWILIGHT
   AT THAT SINGLE SPOT

   —Issa

5. BY ABANDONED ROADS
   THIS LONELY POET MARCHES
   INTO AUTUMN DUSK

   —Basho

WAYS OF KNOWING

1. A classical haiku is supposed to mention something in nature. What examples do you find in the five poems?
2. Only one of the above haiku breaks the five-seven-five rule for syllables. Which one is it?
3. Think about the possible symbolic meaning of each poem. Then write a sentence about the meaning of at least three of the five.

Nathaniel Hawthorne (1804-1864)

The birthplace of Nathaniel Hawthorne in Salem, Massachusetts

The life of the American writer **Nathaniel Hawthorne** is living proof that "practice makes perfect." Upon graduation from Bowdoin College in 1825, he made up his mind to be a writer. This was a courageous decision, for at the time the number of Americans who earned a living writing fiction could be counted on the fingers of one hand. Hawthorne knew what his decision would mean—practice, practice, and more practice. He returned to his mother's house in Salem, Massachusetts, and sat down to write. A year passed and he was still at it. Another year went by, and then more years. After five years of effort, he has sold only one of his stories. Then still more time passed. Hawthorne just wouldn't give up. Finally, after "twelve dark years" as he later called them, he published his first book, *Twice-Told Tales*.

But Hawthorne's practice paid off in perfection. Today he's recognized as one of the few giants in American literature. Behind his polished sentences, the reader senses a kind, thoughtful man. Hawthorne wrote about the people of his time, of course, but first of all he wrote about ideas. What really makes a person a "criminal"? Is any person completely "good"? Which are more important to the individual, the dreams of youth or the rewards of age? Questions such as these will never die, and neither will the best of Hawthorne's stories.

What did the mature Hawthorne mean when he said there had been "twelve dark years" in his life?

DR. HEIDEGGER'S EXPERIMENT

by Nathaniel Hawthorne

▶ Ponce de Leon, as you may remember, was the Spanish explorer who conquered Puerto Rico and then went on to Florida, where he searched for the legendary Fountain of Youth. In the following story, Nathaniel Hawthorne supposes that someone really did find the Fountain of Youth. The author asks himself—and the reader—an important question: What would happen if older people really could be given that "second chance in life" so many of them say they want. Would their lives really turn out any differently? Read to find out.

That very singular man, old Dr. Heidegger, once invited four aging friends to meet him in his study. Three were white-bearded gentlemen, a Mr. Medbourne, a Colonel Killigrew, and a Mr. Gascoigne. The fourth was a withered old lady, whose name was the Widow Wycherly.

The doctor's four guests were all melancholy old people who had been unfortunate in life. Mr. Medbourne, at one time, had been a rich merchant, but had lost everything through his greed. Now he was little better than a beggar. Colonel Killigrew had wasted his best years, and his health and money, in running after sinful pleasures. Now he lived amid torments to both soul and body. Mr. Gascoigne was a ruined politician, a man of evil fame. Now time was kindly burying his name.

As for the Widow Wycherly, she had been a great beauty in her day. But for a long time now, she had lived alone, on account of certain scandalous stories which had prejudiced the people of the town against her. It is worth mentioning that all of these three old gentlemen, Mr. Medbourne, Colonel Killigrew, and Mr. Gascoigne, were once in love with the Widow Wycherly. In fact, years before they had been on the point of cutting each other's throats for her sake.

- **legendary** (LEJ un dair ee) famous; known about far and wide
- singular (SING gyuh lur) one of a kind; unlike any others
- melancholy (MEL un kol ee) gloomy; very sad
- **amid** (uh MID) among
- scandalous (SKAN duh lus) shocking; disgraceful

"My dear old friends," said Dr. Heidegger, motioning them to be seated. "I want you to help me with one of those little experiments with which I amuse myself here in my study."

If all stories were true, Dr. Heidegger's study must have been a very curious place. It was a dim, old-fashioned chamber, hung with cobwebs and sprinkled with antique dust. Around the walls stood several bookcases. In the farthest corner was a closet with its door ajar, within which appeared a skeleton. Between two of the bookcases hung a huge mirror in a dirty old frame, the subject of many wonderful stories. It was said that the spirits of all the doctor's dead patients lived within its frame, spirits that were said to stare the doctor in the face whenever he looked into it.

The opposite side of the room was decorated with a painting of a young lady, dressed in the faded loveliness of silk and satin. More than 50 years before, Dr. Heidegger had been about to marry this young lady, but she had been taken with some slight illness. She had swallowed one of her lover's prescriptions, and died on the bridal evening.

The greatest curiosity of the study remains to be mentioned. This was a huge black book, held together with large silver clasps. There were no letters on the back, and nobody could tell the title, but it was well known to be a book of magic. And once, when a maid had lifted it to brush away the dust, the skeleton had rattled in its closet, the

picture of the young lady had leaned forward from its frame, and several ghostly faces had peeped out from the mirror.

Such was Dr. Heidegger's study. On the summer afternoon of our tale, a small round table stood in the center of the room. On it was a cut-glass vase of beautiful form. The sunshine came through the window, between the heavy faded curtains, and fell directly across this vase. A mild glow was reflected from the vase on the gray faces of the five old people who sat around. Four small glasses were also on the table.

"My dear old friends," repeated Dr. Heidegger, "may I count on your aid in making a very curious experiment?"

Now Dr. Heidegger was a very strange old gentleman. When the doctor's four guests heard him talk of his experiment, they thought of nothing especially wonderful—perhaps the murder of a mouse in an air pump or some similar nonsense, with which he was always bothering his friends. But without waiting for a reply, Dr. Heidegger walked across the room to the black book which all supposed to be a book of magic. He undid the silver clasps; then he opened it and took from its pages a rose, or what was once a rose. Now the green leaves and red petals had become brown. The ancient flower seemed ready to crumble to dust in the doctor's hands.

"This rose," said Dr. Heidegger, with a sigh, "this same withered and crumbling flower, blossomed five and

---

- **curious** (KYOOR ee us) strange; odd
- **clasp** (KLASP) clip; fastener

fifty years ago. It was given to me by Sylvia Ward, whose picture hangs there on the wall. I once meant to wear it at our wedding. Five and fifty years it has been treasured between the pages of this old volume. Now, would you think it possible that this rose could ever bloom again?"

"Nonsense!" said the Widow Wycherly, with a toss of her head. "You might as well ask whether an old woman's wrinkled face could every bloom again"

"See!" answered Dr. Heidegger.

He uncovered the vase. Then he threw the faded rose into the water which it held. At first, it lay lightly on the surface. Soon, however, a singular change began. The crushed and dried petals stirred. They began to take on a deepening red color, as if the flower were waking from a deathlike sleep. The slender stalk and leaves became green. And there, finally, was the rose of 55 years! It looked as fresh as when Sylvia Ward had first given it to her lover!

"That is certainly a very pretty trick," said the doctor's friends. "Tell us, how was it done?"

"Did you never hear of the Fountain of Youth?" asked Dr. Heidegger. "Ponce de Leon, the Spanish explorer, went in search of it two or three centuries ago."

"But did Ponce de Leon ever find it?" said the Widow Wycherly.

"No," answered Dr. Heidegger. "But he never looked in the right place. The famous Fountain of Youth, if I have been told correctly, is in the southern part of Florida, not far from Lake

Macaco. It is covered only by several giant magnolias, hundreds of years old, but still as fresh as violets. That is the power of this wonderful water. A friend of mine, knowing my curiosity in such matters, has sent me the water you see in the vase."

"Ahem!" said Colonel Killigrew. He clearly believed not a word of the doctor's story. "And what is the effect of this fluid on a human being?"

"You shall judge for yourself, my dear colonel," replied Dr. Heidegger. "All of you, my friends, are welcome to as much of this fluid as may give you back the bloom of youth. For my own part, having had much trouble in growing old, I am in no hurry to grow young again. With your permission, therefore, I will only watch the experiment."

While he spoke, Dr. Heidegger had been filling the four small glasses with the water of the Fountain of Youth. Little bubbles were continually rising from the bottoms of the glasses. Bursts of silvery spray covered the surface.

"Before you drink, my old friends," said Dr. Heidegger, "I have a good idea. With the experience of a lifetime to direct you, you might draw up a few general rules for your guidance. The rules will be helpful in passing a second time through the dangers of youth. Think what a sin and shame it would be to waste a second chance! Having lived one life, you should become models of goodness and wisdom to all the young people of the age!"

The doctor's four old friends made no answer. So very ridiculous was the idea that they should ever go wrong again!

"Drink, then," said the doctor, bowing. "I rejoice that I have chosen so well the people for my experiment."

With shaking hands, the four raised the glasses to their lips. The fluid, if it was all the doctor said it was, could not have been given to four human beings who needed it more. They looked as if they had never known what youth or pleasure was, as if they had always been the gray, miserable people who now sat around the doctor's table. They drank the water, and placed their glasses back on the table.

There was an almost immediate improvement in the old people. It was as if a sudden glow of cheerful sunshine had brightened all their faces at once. There was a healthful glow on their cheeks. Gone was the ashen color that had made them look so corpse-like. The Widow Wycherly adjusted her cap, for she felt almost like a woman again.

"Give us more of this wonderful water!" cried they, eagerly. "We are younger—but we are still too old! Quick—give us more!"

"Patience, patience!" said Dr. Heidegger, who sat watching the experiment with coolness. "You have been a long time growing old. Surely, you might be content to grow young in half an hour! But the water is at your service."

Again he filled their glasses with the fluid of youth, enough of which still

---

- **magnolia** (mag NOH lee uh) kind of small flowering tree
- **ashen** (ASH un) pale gray, like the color of ashes

remained to turn half the old people in the city young again. While the bubbles were still sparkling on the surface, the doctor's four guests snatched their glasses from the table. They swallowed the water at a single gulp. Was it a trick? Why, even while the drink was passing down their throats, their eyes grew clear and bright, and a dark shade deepened on their silver heads. They sat around the table, three gentlemen and a woman of middle age.

"My dear widow, you are charming!" cried Colonel Killigrew. His eyes had been fixed upon her face as the shadows of age left it, like darkness from the rosy daybreak.

The widow knew, of old, that Colonel Killigrew's compliments were not always the truth. She stood up and ran to the mirror, still dreading that the wrinkled face of an old woman would meet her eyes. Meanwhile, the three gentlemen behaved as they had many years before. The water of the Fountain of Youth had removed the weight of years. Mr. Gascoigne's mind seemed to run on political topics. He spoke long sentences about patriotism, national glory, and the people's rights. Colonel Killigrew sang a drinking song, and his eyes wandered toward the figure of the Widow Wycherly. On the other side of the table, Mr. Medbourne was figuring in dollars and cents. He was calculating the cost of supplying the East Indies with ice. He spoke of harnessing a team of whales to polar icebergs.

As for the Widow Wycherly, she stood before the mirror smiling at her own reflection. She greeted it as the friend whom she loved better than all the world. She put her face close to the

glass, to see whether some long-remembered wrinkle had really disappeared. She examined whether the snow had entirely melted from her hair. At last, turning away, she came with a sort of dancing step to the table.

"My dear old doctor," cried she, "pray give me another glass!"

"Certainly, my dear madam, certainly!" replied the doctor. "See! I have already filled the glasses."

There, in fact, stood the four glasses, full of this wonderful water. The four guests took their third drink of the Fountain of Youth. The next moment, the exhilarating gush of young life shot through their veins. They were now in the happy prime of youth. Age, with its miserable cares and sorrows and diseases, was remembered only as the trouble of a dream. Now they had joyfully awakened. They felt like new-created people in a new-created world.

"We are young! We are young!" they cried happily.

Youth had now captured them all. They were a group of joyful youngsters. The strongest effect of their happiness was an urge to joke about the sickness and sadness that had so lately been theirs. They laughed loudly at their old-fashioned clothes. One limped across the floor like an old, old grandfather. One seated himself in an armchair and tried to imitate the stern and unyouthful dignity of Dr. Heidegger. Then all shouted joyfully and leaped about the room. The Widow Wycherly—if so fresh a girl could be called a widow—ran up to the doctor's chair, with a look of mischief in her rosy face.

"Doctor, you dear old soul!" cried she. "Get up and dance with me!" And then the four young people laughed louder than ever.

"Pray excuse me," answered the doctor quietly. "I am old and rheumatic. My dancing days were over long ago. But any of these young gentlemen will be glad for so pretty a partner."

"Dance with me, Clara!" cried Colonel Killigrew.

"No, no, I will be her partner!" shouted Mr. Gascoigne.

"She promised me her hand, 50 years ago!" exclaimed Mr. Melbourne.

They all gathered around her. One caught both her hands in his, another threw his arm about her waist, and the third buried his head among her shining curls. She blushed, panted, struggled, and laughed, her warm breath fanning each of their faces in turn. She tried to free herself, yet still remained in their hold.

The three men were now excited to madness by the coquetry of the girl-widow. They began to exchange threatening looks. Still keeping hold of their fair prize, they reached fiercely for one another's throats. As they struggled back and forth, the table was overturned, and the vase was dashed into a thousand pieces. The precious Water of Youth flowed in a bright stream across the floor, touching the wings of a dying butterfly. The insect fluttered lightly through the room, and at last it settled on the snowy head of Dr. Heidegger.

"Come, come, gentlemen! Come, Madam Wycherly," exclaimed the doctor. "I really must ask for an end to this riot."

They stood still and shivered; for it seemed as if Father Time were calling them back from their sunny youth.

- exhilarating (ig ZIL uh rayt ing) gladdening; charging with new energy
- **prime** (PRYM) best part
- **dignity** (DIG nuh tee) formal and serious manner
- **rheumatic** (roo MAT ik) having rheumatism, or pain and stiffness of the joints
- coquetry (KOH ki tree) flirting

They looked at old Dr. Heidegger, who sat holding the rose he had rescued from among the pieces of the broken vase. At the motion of his hand, the four rioters took their seats. Their exercise had tired them, youthful though they were.

"My poor Sylvia's rose!" exclaimed Dr. Heidegger, holding it up in the light of the sunset clouds. "It appears to be fading again."

And so it was. Even while the guests were looking at it, the flower continued to dry up. Soon it became as old and brown as when the doctor had first thrown it into the vase. He shook off the few drops which clung to its petals.

"I love it as well this way as in its youthful freshness," he said, pressing the withered rose to his withered lips. While he spoke, the butterfly fluttered down from the doctor's snowy head, and fell upon the floor.

His guests shivered again. A strange cold feeling was creeping slowly over them all. They gazed at one another. Now they saw that each mo-ment left a deepening wrinkle where none had been before. Had it been a trick? Had the changes of a lifetime been crowded into so brief a space? Were they now four old people again, sitting with their old friend, Dr. Heidegger?

"Are we grown old again, so soon?" cried they, sorrowfully.

In truth they had. The Water of Youth had had but a brief effect. The delirium it had created had bubbled away. Yes! they were old again. The widow put her skinny hands before her face. She wished that the coffin lid were over it, since it could be no longer beautiful.

"Yes, friends, you are old again," said Dr. Heidegger. "And the Water of Youth is all spilled on the ground. Well— I regret it not. For if the fountain were at my very doorstep, I would not lean over to touch my lips to it. No I wouldn't, even if its effect were for years instead of moments. This is the lesson you have taught me!"

But the doctor's four friends had taught no such lesson to themselves. They decided right away to make a journey to Florida. There they declared, they would drink morning, noon, and night from the Fountain of Youth.

• **delirium** (di LEER ee um) great excitement and enthusiasm

ALL THINGS CONSIDERED ────────────────

1. The three old men invited to Dr. Heidegger's study are alike in that they all (a) have been in politics. (b) once loved sinful pleasures. (c) were once in love with the Widow Wycherly.

2. All four of the guests in Dr. Heidegger's study are (a) unfortunate but happy. (b) unfortunate and melancholy. (c) fortunate but melancholy for some reason.

3. Before his guests drink the water, Dr. Heidegger suggests that they (a) draw up some rules based on experience. (b) change into more youthful clothes. (c) have their pictures taken.

4. It is *ironic* (see page 29) that (a) the guests' youthful behavior is the very thing that causes them to break the vase that has given them youth. (b) one of the guests is a woman. (c) Dr. Heidegger's lost love is named Sylvia.

5. The "lesson" Dr. Heidegger says he has learned near the end of the story is that (a) experience is the best teacher. (b) old people really do not want to be young again. (c) if given a second chance in life, people are likely to repeat the mistakes of their youth.

THINKING IT THROUGH ────────────────

1. What is the guests' first reaction when they learn what Dr. Heidegger's experiment will be?

2. (a) What reason does Dr. Heidegger give for not drinking the magic water himself? (b) What might be another reason?

3. After the rose has once again become old and brown, Dr. Heidegger says, "I love it as well this way as in its youthful freshness." Why do you think he says this?

4. How does the short final paragraph reinforce the theme of the whole story?

5. In your opinion, would the "lesson" learned by Dr. Heidegger be true for most people today? In other words, do you think most people would repeat mistakes they had made earlier in life if they were given a second chance? Explain your thinking.

Reading and Analyzing

Interpreting Symbols

To review briefly, a **symbol** is something in a work of literature that stands for something else. A symbol must *really be in* the literary work, not just referred to as part of a figure of speech. The "something else" it stands for or suggests is usually a feeling, quality, or idea, not the kind of "thing" that can be seen.

Some symbols in literature are obvious. Good readers agree that they can be called symbols, and also agree on their meaning. Other possible symbols, however, do not produce such agreement. Symbols must contain meaning, but the meaning is sometimes different for different readers.

Here are 10 items from "Dr. Heidegger's Experiment." Think about the words in quotation marks. For each term, first decide if it can properly be called a symbol. If so, explain its meaning in your own words.

1. the "skeleton" in the study closet
2. the "painting" of Sylvia Ward
3. the "huge black book" said to contain magic
4. the withered and crumbling "rose"
5. the "Fountain of Youth"
6. the "fluid of youth" in the vase
7. the "bubbles" in the magic water
8. the "snow" that "melted" from the widow's hair
9. the "wrinkles" the widow hated to see on her face
10. the "light of the sunset clouds" near the end of the story

Composition

1. Which one of your possessions do you think most clearly symbolizes *you*? Think of something that would make others say, "Yes, that, somehow, IS (your name)." It can be anything—from an old baseball glove to last year's report card to a new stereo box. Write a short paragraph describing the possession and explaining its value to you.

2. Magazine advertisements provide a fascinating field for symbol searches. Ads for luxury products are particularly productive. Symbols are sold by association with other symbols. Colors and shapes have symbolic value. Whether an ad is a photograph or a drawing, or a description, all details have been carefully planned in terms of the symbols that will sell the product.

Choose a magazine ad and write a complete analysis of it, discussing both art and text and paying particular attention to symbols. Your first job is to find an ad about which you can say a great deal. Just keep asking yourself *why* each particular detail in the ad has been included. Look only in old magazines you can tear up, for you will have to hand in the ad with the composition.

Before completing the exercises that follow, you may wish to review the **bold-faced** words on pages 173 to 187.

I. 1. A *curious clasp* might be the same thing as a(n) (a) inquiring student. (b) odd fastener. (c) questioning meddler.

2. A *legendary* hero would probably (a) be found boring in real life. (b) have many bad qualities. (c) be known by a wide variety of people.

3. The title *Life Amid the Savages* would probably refer to (a) living among uncivilized people. (b) life after all fierce and cruel people had disappeared. (c) the literature of wild, untamed people.

4. The *prime* of life is the (a) earliest part. (b) best part. (c) most dangerous part.

5. To act with *dignity* is to behave (a) in a lawless fashion. (b) always as a follower, never a leader. (c) in a self-respecting way.

6. A *rheumatic* condition might cause a person to (a) be especially helpful to others. (b) complain about pain. (c) tell interesting stories.

7. A state of *delirium* might be observed (a) at the end of a Super Bowl game. (b) during the funeral of a former U. S. President. (c) among chess players.

8. CARROT is to VEGETABLE as *MAGNOLIA* is to (a) FURNITURE. (b) FRUIT. (c) TREE.

9. FEED is to STARVE as *PACIFY* is to (a) ASSIST. (b) ANGER. (c) DROWN.

10. CHILDREN is to CHILD as *BRETHREN* is to (a) BREATH. (b) NEWBORN. (c) BROTHER.

II. This short poem was first published in 1915, when some small children had to work long hours in factories. It refers to "links" (golf course), a "mill," "children," and "men." But the poem is much more than a simple picture; its symbolic meaning concerns some idea or opinion the poet chooses not to say directly. What is this idea or opinion?

THE GOLF LINKS LIE SO NEAR THE MILL

by Sarah N. Cleghorn

The golf links lie so near the mill
  That almost every day
The laboring children can look
    out
  And see the men at play.

▶ Late in 1797, the English poet Samuel Taylor Coleridge set out to write a poem that would deal with the supernatural yet reveal important truths about human life. The result was "The Rime of the Ancient Mariner," a dream-picture that contains some of the best-known lines and perhaps the most famous symbol in all of literature. This tale of evil and its results, a phantom ship, a crew of dead men, and an overhanging curse will never be forgotten. The comments to the left of the stanzas (called a *gloss*) were intended by Coleridge to be printed just where they appear. Read them as you go through the poem.

Note: Coleridge deliberately chose to use word forms that were archaic (ar KAY ik), or old and unusual, even when the poem was written. You should have no trouble with most of them, such as *stoppeth, may'st,* and *hath.*

from THE RIME OF THE ANCIENT MARINER

by Samuel Taylor Coleridge (1772–1834)

PART THE FIRST

An ancient Mariner meets three men going to a wedding feast and stops one of them.

It is an ancient Mariner
And he stoppeth one of three.
"By thy long grey beard and glittering
   eye,
Now wherefore stopp'st thou me?

The Bridegroom's doors are opened   5
   wide,
And I am next of kin;
The guests are met, the feast is set:
May'st hear the merry din."

He holds him with his skinny hand,
"There was a ship, quoth he.   10
"Hold off! unhand me, grey-beard loon!"
Eftsoons his hand dropt he.

The Wedding-Guest is spellbound by the eye of the old man, and feels forced to hear his tale.

He holds him with his glittering eye—
The Wedding-Guest stood still,
And listens like a three years' child: 15
The Mariner hath his will.

The Wedding-Guest sat on a stone:
He cannot choose but hear;
And thus spake on that ancient man,
The bright-eyed Mariner.   20

The ship was cheered, the harbor cleared,
Merrily did we drop
Below the kirk, below the hill,
Below the lighthouse top.

The Mariner tells how the ship sailed south with a good wind and fair weather, till it reached the equator.

The Sun came up upon the left,   25
Out of the sea came he!
And he shone bright, and on the right
Went down into the sea.

- eftsoons (eft SOONZ) soon after (archaic)
- kirk (KURK) church

Higher and higher every day,
Till over the mast at noon—   30
The Wedding-Guest here beat his breast,
For he heard the loud bassoon.

The Wedding-Guest hears the
bridal music; but the Mariner
continues his tale.

The Wedding-Guest he beat his breast,
Yet he cannot choose but hear;
And thus spake on that ancient man,   35
The bright-eyed Mariner.

The ship is driven by a storm
toward the south pole.

And now the storm-blast came, and he
Was tyrannous and strong:
He struck with his o'ertaking wings,
And chased us south along.   40

It enters a land of ice, and of
fearful sounds, where no liv-
ing thing is to be seen.

And now there came both mist and snow,
And it grew wondrous cold:
And ice, mast-high, came floating by,
As green as emerald.

The ice was here, the ice was there,   45
The ice was all around:
It cracked and growled, and roared and
   howled,
Like noises in a swound!

A great seabird, called the
Albatross, comes through the
snow-fog, and is received
with great joy and hospitality.

At length did cross an Albatross:
Through the fog it came;   50
It ate the food it ne'er had eat,
And round and round it flew.
The ice did split with a thunder-fit;
The helmsman steered us through!

The Albatross proves to be a
bird of good luck, and follows
the ship as it returns north-
ward through fog and floating
ice.

And a good south wind sprung up   55
   behind;
The Albatross did follow,
And every day, for food or play,
Came to the mariners' hollo!

- tyrannous (TIR uh nus) harsh; cruel
- swound (SWOUND) swoon; fainting spell (archaic)
- albatross (AL buh traws) kind of huge sea bird. The
  albatross has the largest wingspan of any bird (12 feet),
  and can stay in the air and at sea for amazing lengths
  of time.

In mist or cloud, on mast or shroud,
It perched for vespers nine;   60
Whiles all the night, through fog-smoke
   white,
Glimmered the white Moon-shine.

*The ancient Mariner brutally
and sinfully kills the bird of
good luck.*

"God save thee, ancient Mariner!
From the fiends, that plague thee thus!—
Why look'st thou so?"—With my   65
   crossbow
I shot the Albatross.

CHECKPOINT

1. What strange power does the mariner seem to have over the wedding guest?
2. (a) After line 10, what is the next line spoken by the mariner? (b) How can you tell?
3. (a) How can the ship "drop below" the kirk, hill, and lighthouse top (lines 22–24)? (b) Why are the three objects given in this order?
4. Even without the gloss, how can you tell the ship headed south (lines 25–29)?
5. (a) Which kind of luck does the albatross seem to bring—good or bad? (b) Therefore, which kind of luck seems in store for the ancient mariner after he has killed the albatross?

PART THE SECOND

The Sun now rose upon the right:
Out of the sea came he,
Still hid in mist, and on the left
Went down into the sea.

And the good south wind still blew   5
   behind,
But no sweet bird did follow,
Nor any day for food or play
Came to the mariners' hollo!

• shroud (SHROUD) rope that steadies a ship's mast
• vespers (VES purz) church bell rung at evening

His shipmates cry out against the ancient Mariner, for killing the bird of good luck.

And I had done a hellish thing,
And it would work 'em woe: 10
For all averred, I had killed the bird
That made the breeze to blow.

But when the fog cleared off, they approve of the killing, and thus make themselves partners in the crime.

"Ah, wretch!" said they, "the bird to slay,
That made the breeze to blow!"
Then all averred, I had killed the bird   15
That brought the fog and mist.
"'Twas right," said they, "such birds to
    slay,
That bring the fog and mist."

The fair breeze continues; the ship enters the Pacific Ocean, and sails northward till it reaches the equator.

The fair breeze blew, the white foam flew,
The furrow followed free;   20
We were the first that ever burst
Into that silent sea.

The ship is forced to stop and drift for lack of wind.

Down dropt the breeze, the sails dropt
    down,
'Twas sad as sad could be;
And we did speak only to break   25
The silence of the sea!

All in a hot and copper sky,
The bloody Sun, at noon,
Right up above the mast did stand,
No bigger than the Moon.   30

Day after day, day after day,
We stuck, nor breath nor motion;
As idle as a painted ship
Upon a painted ocean.

The killing of the Albatross begins to be avenged.

Water, water, everywhere,   35
And all the boards did shrink;
Water, water, everywhere,
Nor any drop to drink.

● aver (uh VER) declare; state

Yea, slimy things did crawl with legs
Upon the slimy sea.   40
About, about, in reel and rout
The death-fires danced at night;
The water, like a witch's oils,
Burnt green, and blue, and white.

And every tongue, through utter   45
   drought,
Was withered at the root;
We could not speak, no more than if
We had been choked with soot.

The shipmates, in their dis-
tress, want to throw the
whole guilt on the ancient
Mariner, and so hang the
dead bird round his neck.

Ah! well-a-day! what evil looks
Had I from old and young!   50
Instead of the cross, the Albatross
About my neck was hung.

CHECKPOINT

1. What are the crew's changing reactions to the mariner's deed?
2. What does the sun's being *directly* overhead at noon (lines 28–29) indicate about the ship's location?
3. How can lines 37–38 be explained?
4. (a) Why does the crew hang the dead albatross around the mariner's neck? (b) Of what is the albatross now a symbol?

PART THE THIRD

The ancient Mariner sees
something coming in the dis-
tance.

There passed a weary time. Each throat
Was parched, and glazed each eye.
A weary time! a weary time!
How glazed each weary eye,
When looking westward, I beheld   5
A something in the sky.

At first it seemed a little speck,
And then it seemed a mist;
It moved and moved, and took at last
A certain shape, I wist.   10

- reel (REEL) whirling or swaying motion
- rout (ROUT) disorderly flight
- utter (UT ur) complete

As it approaches nearer, it seems to be a ship.

With throats unslaked, with black lips
   baked,
We could nor laugh nor wail;
Through utter drought all dumb we stood!
I bit my arm, I sucked the blood,
And cried, A sail! a sail!   15

At great cost, the Mariner and the crew free their speech from the bonds of thirst.

With throats unslaked, with black lips
baked,
Agape they heard me call:
Gramercy! they for joy did grin,
And all at once their breath drew in,
As they were drinking all.   20

And horror follows. For can it be a ship that comes onward without wind or tide?

See! see! (I cried) she tacks no more!
Hither to work us weal;
Without a breeze, without a tide,
She steadies with upright keel!

The strange ship comes between the Mariner and the setting sun.

The western wave was all a-flame.   25
The day was well-nigh done!
Almost upon the western wave
Rested the broad bright Sun;
When that strange shape drove suddenly
Betwixt us and the Sun.   30

A skeleton ship, its ribs look like bars. A strange woman and Death seem the only crew.

Are those *her* ribs through which the Sun
Did peer, as through a grate?
And is that Woman all her crew?
Is that a Death? and are there two?
Is Death that woman's mate?   35

The strange woman now proves to be Life-in-Death.

Her lips were red, *her* looks were free,
Her locks were yellow as gold:
Her skin was as white as leprosy,
The Night-mare Life-in-Death was she,
Who thicks man's blood with cold.   40

• unslaked (un SLAYKT) not refreshed; unwatered
• agape (uh GAYP) with mouth open in wonder
• tack (TAK) change direction at sea
• weal (WEEL) well-being; good fortune (archaic)

Death and Life-in-Death throw dice for the ship's crew, and Life-in-Death wins the ancient Mariner.

The naked hulk alongside came,
And the twain were casting dice;
"The game is done! I've won! I've won!"
Quoth she, and whistles thrice.

The sun sets, and the strange ship rushes off.

The Sun's rim dips; the stars rush out: 45
At one stride comes the dark;
With far-heard whisper, o'er the sea,
Off shot the spectre-bark.

At the rising of the Moon, the crew curses the Mariner silently.

One after one, by the star-dogged Moon,
Too quick for groan or sigh,   50
Each turned his face with a ghastly pang,
And cursed me with his eye.

His shipmates drop down dead.

Four times fifty living men,
(And I heard nor sigh nor groan)
With heavy thump, a lifeless lump,   55
They dropped down one by one.

But Life-in-Death begins her work on the ancient Mariner.

The souls did from their bodies fly,—
They fled to bliss or woe!
And every soul, it passed me by,
Like the whizz of my cross-bow!   60

CHECKPOINT

1. What might the "ribs" (text and gloss) on the skeleton ship really be?
2. (a) Who are the two spectres on the ghostly ship? (b) What are they doing? (c) Who "won" (line 43), and exactly *what* was won?
3. What does each member of the crew do just before he dies?
4. Think about what's coming next: Why might life-in-death be worse than death?

- hulk (HULK) old ship
- twain (TWAYN) two
- spectre-bark (SPEK tur BARK) ghost ship
- star-dogged (STAR dawgd) pursued by stars
- pang (PANG) distress; pain

199

PART THE FOURTH

*The Wedding-Guest fears that
a Spirit is talking to him.*

"I fear thee, ancient Mariner!
I fear thy skinny hand!
And thou art long, and lank, and brown,
As is the ribbed sea-sand.

*But the ancient Mariner as-
sures him of his bodily life.*

I fear thee and thy glittering eye,   5
And thy skinny hand, so brown."—
Fear not, fear not, thou Wedding-Guest!
This body dropt not down.

*The Mariner goes on with his
horrible story of sin and penance.*

Alone, alone, all, all alone,
Alone on a wide wide sea!   10
And never a saint took pity on
My soul in agony.

*He regrets the death of the
crew.*

The many men, so beautiful!
And they all dead did lie:
And a thousand thousand slimy things   15
Lived on; and so did I.

*Everything now appears
slimy and rotten.*

I looked upon the rotting sea,
And drew my eyes away;
I looked upon the rotting deck,
And there the dead men lay.   20

I looked to heaven, and tried to pray;
But or ever a prayer had gusht,
A wicked whisper came, and made
My heart as dry as dust.

*The curse lives for him in the
eyes of the dead men.*

The cold sweat melted from their,   25
   limbs,
Nor rot nor reek did they:
The look with which they looked on me
Had never passed away.

An orphan's curse would drag to hell
A spirit from on high;   30
But oh! more horrible than that
Is the curse in a dead man's eye!
Seven days, seven nights, I saw that curse,
And yet I could not die.

By the light of the Moon he watches the creatures of the sea.

Beyond the shadow of the ship,   35
I watched the water-snakes:
Within the shadow of the ship
I watched their rich attire:
Blue, glossy green, and velvet black,
They coiled and swam; and every track   40
Was a flash of golden fire.

He now sees their beauty and their happiness, and he blesses them in his heart.

O happy living things! no tongue
Their beauty might declare:
A spring of love gushed from my heart,
And I blessed them unaware: 45
Sure my kind saint took pity on me,
And I blessed them unaware.

The spell begins to break.

The self-same moment I could pray;
And from my neck so free
The Albatross fell off, and sank   50
Like lead into the sea.

CHECKPOINT

1. In your own words, why is the narrator unable to pray (lines 21–24)?
2. In what ways do the bodies of the crew differ from normal corpses?
3. How has the narrator's opinion of the water creatures (lines 35–43) changed (from lines 39–44, Part the Second)?
4. How might the blessing of the water snakes be related to the albatross' falling off the neck of the ancient mariner into the sea?

PART THE FIFTH

The ancient Mariner is refreshed with rain.

O sleep! it is a gentle thing,
Beloved from pole to pole!
The silly buckets on the deck,
That had so long remained,
I dreamt that they were filled with dew; 5
And when I awoke, it rained.

• attire (uh TYR) adornment; dress

My lips were wet, my throat was cold,
My garments all were dank;
Sure I had drunken in my dreams,
And still my body drank.   10

I moved, and could not feel my limbs:
I was so light—almost
I thought that I had died in sleep,
And was a blessèd ghost.

He hears sounds and sees
strange sights on the ship.

And soon I heard a roaring wind: 15
It did not come anear;
But with its sound it shook the sails,
That were so thin and sere.

The bodies of the crew move,
and then the ship moves mys-
teriously on.

The loud wind never reached the ship,
Yet now the ship moved on!   20
Beneath the lightning and the Moon
The dead men gave a groan.

They groaned, they stirred, they all uprose,
Nor spake, nor moved their eyes;
It had been strange, even in a dream,   25
To have seen those dead men rise.

The helmsman steered, the ship moved on;
Yet never a breeze up-blew;
The mariners all 'gan work the ropes,
Where they were wont to do;   30
They raised their limbs like lifeless
    tools—
We were a ghastly crew.

The ancient Mariner again
calms the Wedding-Guest.

"I fear thee, ancient Mariner!"
Be calm, thou Wedding-Guest!
'Twas not those souls that fled in pain,   35
Which to their corses came again,
But a troop of spirits blest:

- dank (DANK) disagreeably damp
- sere (SEER) withered by heat
- wont (WOHNT) accustomed; used

202

For when it dawned—they dropped their
arms,
And clustered round the mast;
Sweet sounds rose slowly through their   40
mouths
And from their bodies passed.

Till noon we quietly sailed on,
Yet never a breeze did breathe:
Slowly and smoothly went the ship,
Moved onward from beneath.   45

*A sudden motion of the ship
drives the Mariner uncon-
scious.*

Then like a pawing horse let go,
She made a sudden bound:
It flung the blood into my head,
And I fell down in a swound.

*In his senseless fit, the Mari-
ner hears two voices discussing his sin and penance.*

How long in that same fit I lay,   50
I have not to declare;
But ere my living life returned,
I heard and in my soul discerned
Two voices in the air.

"Is it he?" quoth one, "Is this the man? 55
With his cruel bow he laid full low
The harmless Albatross.
The other was a softer voice,
As soft as honey-dew:
Quoth he, "The man hath penance done,   60
And penance more will do."

CHECKPOINT

1. What dream of the narrator seems to come true?
2. What is supernatural about the wind?
3. How is the dead crew's manning the ship explained?
4. What does the narrator learn from the two voices heard during his senseless fit?

- discern (di SURN) recognize; discover
- penance (PEN uns) punishment undergone for an evil
  act

PART THE SIXTH

The Mariner awakens and his penance begins again.

I woke, and we were sailing on
As in a gentle weather:
'Twas night, calm night, the Moon was
  high;
The dead men stood together.

The pang, the curse, with which they   5
  died,
Had never passed away:
I could not draw my eyes from theirs,
Nor turn them up to pray.

The curse is finally lifted.

And now this spell was snapt: once more
I viewed the ocean green,   10
And looked far forth, yet little saw
Of what had else been seen—

Like one, that on a lonesome road
Doth walk in fear and dread,
And having once turned round walks on 15
And turns no more his head;
Because he knows, a frightful fiend
Doth close behind him tread.

But soon there breathed a wind on me,
Nor sound nor motion made: 20
Its path was not upon the sea,
In ripple or in shade.

Swiftly, swiftly flew the ship,
Yet she sailed softly too:
Sweetly, sweetly blew the breeze—   25
On me alone it blew.

The ancient Mariner sees his native country once again.

Oh! dream of joy! is this indeed
The light-house top I see?
Is this the hill? is this the kirk?
Is this mine own countree?   30

The harbor-bay was clear as glass,
So smoothly it was strewn!
And on the bay the moonlight lay,
And the shadow of the Moon.

And the bay was white with silent light, 35
Till rising from the same,
Full many shapes, that shadows were,
In crimson colors came.

But soon I heard the dash of oars,
I heard the Pilot's cheer; 40
My head was turned perforce away,
And I saw a boat appear.

The Pilot, and the Pilot's boy.
I heard them coming fast:
I saw a third—I heard his voice: 45
It is the Hermit good!
He singeth loud his godly hymns
That he makes in the wood.
He'll shrieve my soul, he'll wash away
The Albatross's blood. 50

CHECKPOINT

1. What makes the narrator feel uncomfortable in stanza 2?
2. What comment can you make on the order of the things mentioned in lines 28–29?
3. (a) What three people row out to meet the narrator? (b) Why is the narrator so glad to see the last?

PART THE SEVENTH

The Hermit and the others draw near.

This Hermit good lives in that wood
Which slopes down to the sea.
How loudly his sweet voice he rears!
He loves to talk with marineres
That come from a far countree. 5

The boat came closer to the ship,
But I nor spake nor stirred;
The boat came close beneath the ship,
And straight a sound was heard.

- pilot—harbor guide
- shrieve (SHREEV) hear a confession and give penance (archaic for *shrive*)

The ship suddenly sinks.

Under the water it rumbled on,   10
Still louder and more dread:
It reached the ship, it split the bay;
The ship went down like lead.

*The ancient Mariner is saved
in the Pilot's boat.*

Stunned by that loud and dreadful sound,
Which sky and ocean smote,   15
Like one that hath been seven days
    drowned
My body lay afloat;
But swift as dreams, myself I found
Within the Pilot's boat.

Upon the whirl, where sank the ship,   20
The boat spun round and round;
And all was still, save that the hill
Was telling of the sound.

I moved my lips—the Pilot shrieked
And fell down in a fit;   25
The holy Hermit raised his eyes,
And prayed where he did sit.

I took the oars: the Pilot's boy,
Who now doth crazy go,
Laughed loud and long, and all the   30
    while
His eyes went to and fro.
"Ha! ha!" quoth he, "full plain I see,
The Devil knows how to row."

And now, all in my own countree,
I stood on the firm land!   35
The Hermit stepped forth from the boat,
And scarcely he could stand.

*The ancient Mariner begs the
Hermit to shrieve him.*

"O shrieve me, shrieve me, holy man!"
The Hermit crossed his brow.
"Say quick," quoth he, "I bid thee say— 40
What manner of man art thou?"

• smote (SMOHT) deliver or deal, as a blow

The Mariner experiences his life-long penance for the first time.

Forthwith this frame of mine was
  wrenched
With a woeful agony,
Which forced me to begin my tale;
And then it left me free.   45

Since then, at an uncertain hour,
That agony returns:
And till my ghastly tale is told,
This heart within me burns.

He is fated to pass from land to land, telling his story.

I pass, like night, from land to land;   50
I have strange power of speech;
That moment that his face I see,
I know the man that must hear me:
To him my tale I teach.

O Wedding-Guest! this soul hath been   55
Alone on a wide wide sea:
So lonely 'twas, that God himself
Scarce seemèd there to be.

Farewell, farewell! but this I tell
To thee, thou Wedding-Guest!   60
He prayeth well, who loveth well
Both man and bird and beast.

He is to teach, by his own example, love and reverence for all things in the created world.

He prayeth best, who loveth best
All things both great and small;
For the dear God who loveth us,   65
He made and loveth all.

The Mariner, whose eye is bright,
Whose beard with age is hoar,
Is gone: and now the Wedding-Guest
Turned from the bridegroom's door.   70

He went like one that hath been stunned,
And is of sense forlorn:
A sadder and a wiser man,
He rose the morrow morn.

- forthwith (forth WITH) at once
- hoar (HOHR) white with age

ALL THINGS CONSIDERED —————————————————

1. The ship is sunk by (a) some mysterious force from below. (b) the ghostly crew. (c) shells from the shore.

2. When the ancient mariner first speaks, the pilot and the hermit (a) listen eagerly. (b) have no interest. (c) seem terrified.

3. The mariner finds that his "woeful agony" can be lifted only by (a) prayer. (b) telling his ghastly tale. (c) visiting the families of the crew.

4. After hearing the mariner's story, the wedding guest (a) finally attends the feast. (b) refuses to pay the mariner. (c) wanders off in a daze.

5. Coleridge probably intended his poem to be (a) believed in every detail. (b) amusing to most intelligent readers. (c) entertaining and useful.

THINKING IT THROUGH —————————————————

1. The "life-long penance" given by the hermit to the ancient mariner is not too clearly explained. What is it?

2. The stopping of the wedding guest in Part the First is explained in lines 50–54. Why was he stopped?

3. The narrator states the moral, or message, of his story in lines 61–66 on page 207. Explain the moral of this poem in your own words.

4. You have not read the poem as it was first printed. More than 15 years after the first version, Coleridge replaced some archaic words he had used and added the gloss. (a) Why might he have made these changes? (b) In your opinion, were they helpful or not? Explain.

5. Most readers think that Coleridge succeeded in his attempt to write a *supernatural* poem that contained *important truths*. (a) For instance, have you ever known a person who seemed forced to tell and retell some life-troubling event? If so, explain the reasons for and results of the retelling as you see them. (b) Some individual stanzas also have the ring of truth. Look at lines 13–18 on page 204, for example. Hasn't much the same thing happened to you—even on a city street? Explain.

UNIT REVIEW

I. Match the terms in Column A with their definitions in Column B.

A

1. haiku
2. characterization
3. symbol
4. cause
5. effect

B

(a) something that stands for some-thing else
(b) the result of a cause
(c) kind of three-line poem
(d) the reason something happens
(e) ways in which authors bring peo-ple in works of literature to life

II. In this unit, you have had to think about life in a serious way. Now think about each of the six statements below. Try to illus-trate five of the statements by referring to a selection in the unit. First copy the statement on your paper. Then write the words *For example*, and go on to explain how a particular se-lection supports the statement. If you wish, you can use a se-lection more than once.

Example: *A simple life is often the happiest life. For example, the old cobbler in Tolstoy's "Where Love Is, There God Is Also" leads a simple, religious life that makes him feel good about himself and other people.*

1. A happy life for an individual requires the company of other people.

2. Unfortunately, many people fail to learn from experience and can only follow their desires of the moment.

3. A good life requires one to accept and love all created things.

4. At times, people seem capable of unspoken communica-tion with animals.

5. In being of service to other people, one is of service to God.

6. So-called supernatural forces in life can, in fact, be en-tirely natural.

SPEAKING UP

This activity is a version of the old TV program *To Tell the Truth*. You may remember the show or have seen reruns of it. Three people announced that they were, in fact, the same person (really one of the three). For instance, each claimed in turn, "I am Joe Wilkins." Then they answered questions. The object of the questioners was to guess which of three people was telling the truth about his or her own life.

Prepare for the game in this way. Your teacher, in secret, will arrange to be interviewed by one student. After the interview, the student should have a lot of knowledge and notes that the teacher has supplied—*information that must be memorized*. Then, in class one day, the teacher will appear to choose three students at random. (One, of course, will be the person who really "is" the teacher.) The three students stand in front of the class and each states, "Hello, I am (teacher's name)." Then the rest of the class asks questions. The student who "is" the teacher answers as "truthfully" as possible, making up answers only when necessary. The other two students, except when they know the answers, will have to make up fast and reasonable responses on the spot. If these two students are prepared for obvious questions like "When did you graduate from college?" and do a good job with the rest, the game can go on a long time before the truth finally comes out. (If your teacher prefers, the interview can be held with another teacher or someone like the principal.)

Next, your teacher will pass out small pieces of paper, each bearing the name of an author you have read. In addition, the paper will say either "book only" or "do research." If you get a "book only" paper, your job is to know everything that this book says about the author—*and no more*. But if you get a "do research" paper, you are to go to a library or other source and learn everything you can about the author. In either case, show the paper to no one and keep your assignment a secret. The teacher will give you at least a week to prepare for a "To Tell the Truth" session concerning the authors.

On the assigned day, groups of three students will declare that each is so-and-so, author of such-and-such. The rest of the class will try to determine which one really "is" the author. All three students are to answer truthfully to the best of their ability. The rest of the answers should *sound* true, but in fact be elaborate and detailed bits of invention.

WRITING A LETTER

Assignment: Write a letter to yourself that you will receive in the mail about the time of your graduation. How will this be possible? You are to put the letter in a stamped, self-addressed, but unsealed envelope. Your teacher will (a) read, and perhaps grade, the letter now, (2) make no comment on its contents, either to you or to others, and (3) either mail it to you at the assigned time or have you give it to an older relative or friend for future mailing.

Prewriting: The purpose of the letter is to get you to do some "looking into life"—both as it is now and as it might be in the future. Start your thinking with some questions: What are your favorite activities, TV shows, and so forth? Do you think your interests will have changed by the time you actually receive the letter? What are your strong points? How can you build on them? What about your weaknesses? Do you really intend to do anything about them between now and graduation? You can go on to think about concerns such as career plans and your social and family life. You might even make yourself some promises. Don't start writing until you have made some notes that will lead to at least three paragraphs on different aspects of your life.

Writing: Start your letter with the inside address, the date, "Dear _____," and a cheerful greeting. Then write the first of your main paragraphs. Make it as clear and as honest as possible. Try to include some details that you will enjoy remembering. When the paragraph seems like a complete, self-contained package, go on to the others. You may want to close with a personal comment, such as "Karen, PLEASE be sensible and take my advice."

Revising: The old rule of writing, DON'T INSULT YOUR READER, should be easy to follow in this case. Go through your first draft carefully, imagining yourself as having just opened an envelope you'd completely forgotten about. What do you want your reaction to be? Poor handwriting, careless errors, and vague, fuzzy writing are not going to help. When you have made the necessary changes between the lines, compliment yourself with a neat final copy.

U N I T · 4

EXPLORING
CONFLICTS

If there is right in the soul,
There will be beauty in the person;
If there is beauty in the person,
There will be love in the home;
If there is love in the home,
There will be order in the nation;
If there is order in the nation,
There will be peace in the world.

Isabelle C. Chang
(from the traditional Chinese)

Conflict is a part of life. Getting along with others, standing up for what we believe, and finding our place in the world all involves conflict. But the way we handle conflict determines whether we will be happy or unhappy, successful or unsuccessful. The way we handle conflict determines whether we will find "right in the soul . . . peace in the world."

In this unit, you will read about conflicts that have led to ugliness, hate, disorder, and war. As you read each selection, think about ways that each of these conflicts instead might have been settled in beauty, love, order, and peace.

THE HISTORY OF A CAMPAIGN THAT FAILED

by Mark Twain

▶ Most students know that the famous American writer Mark Twain (1835–1910) had several careers—printer, steamboat pilot, newspaper writer, and finally popular author and lecturer. But you probably don't know that Twain had still another career—that of a soldier. This career was a short one, and the following selection from Twain's **autobiography** (story of a person's own life) explains why.

This true-life account is based on Twain's personal experience during the Civil War, when he and several teenage friends decided to form a company called *Marion's Rangers* and join the Confederate Army.

Our scares were frequent. Every few days rumors would come that the enemy were approaching. The rumors always turned out to be false. But one night we heard that the enemy was truly in our neighborhood. Up to now we had been having a very jolly time. We were filled with horse-play and schoolboy fun. But that cooled down now. Our company became silent. Silent and nervous. And soon uneasy—worried.

An almost noiseless movement presently began in the dark of our barn headquarters. We all crept to the front wall. And there we were with our hearts in our throats. We stared out toward where the forest footpath came through.

It was late, and there was a deep woodsy stillness everywhere. There was a veiled moonlight, which was only just strong enough to enable us to mark the general shape of objects.

Presently a muffled sound caught our ears. We recognized it as the hoof-beats of a horse or horses. And right away a figure appeared in the forest path. It could have been made of smoke, its

---

- **campaign** (kam PAYN) war operation; series of battles
- **mark** (MARK) take note of

mass had so little sharpness of outline. It was a man on horseback, and it seemed to me that there were others behind him.

I got hold of a gun in the dark, and pushed it through a crack between the logs, hardly knowing what I was doing. I was dazed with fright. Somebody said, "Fire!" I pulled the trigger. I seemed to see a hundred flashes and hear a hundred reports. Then I saw the man fall down out of the saddle.

My first feeling was of surprised gratification. My first impulse was a sportsman's impulse to run and pick up his game. Somebody said, hardly audibly, "Good—we've got him!—wait for the rest."

But the rest did not come. We waited—listened—still no more came. There was not a sound, not the whisper of a leaf. Just perfect stillness. It was an uncanny kind of stillness, which was all

- report (ri PORT) loud noise
- **gratification** (grat uh fuh KAY shun) satisfaction; pleasure
- **audibly** (AW dub lee) in a way that is loud and clear enough to be heard
- **uncanny** (un KAN ee) very strange

the more uncanny on account of the damp, earthy, late-night smells now rising. Then, wondering, we crept stealthily out and approached the man.

When we got to him, the moon revealed him distinctly. He was lying on his back, with his arms abroad. His mouth was open, and his chest heaved with long gasps. The thought shot through me that I was a murderer. That I had killed a man—a man who had never done me any harm.

That was the coldest sensation that ever went through my marrow. I was down next to him in a moment, helplessly stroking his forehead. I would have given anything then—my own life freely—to make him again what he had been five minutes before.

And all the boys seemed to be feeling the same way. They hung over him, full of pitying interest, and tried all they could to help him, and said all sorts of regretful things. They had forgotten all about the enemy. They thought only of this one forlorn unit of the foe.

Once my imagination persuaded me that the dying man gave me a reproachful look out of his shadowy eyes. It seemed to me that I would rather he had stabbed me than done that. He muttered and mumbled like a dreamer in his sleep about his wife and his child. I thought with a new despair, "This thing that I have done does not end with him. It falls upon *them* too, and they never did me any harm, any more than he."

In a little while the man was dead. He was killed in a war; killed in fair and legitimate war. Killed in battle, as you may say. Yet he was as sincerely mourned by the opposing force as if he had been their brother. The boys stood there a half-hour sorrowing over him and recalling the details of the tragedy. Wondering who he might be, and if he was a spy. They all said that if it were to do over again they would not hurt him unless he attacked them first.

It soon came out that mine was not the only shot fired. There were five others. This division of guilt was a great relief, since it in some degree lightened and diminished the burden I was carrying. There were six shots fired at once. But I was not in my right mind at the time, and my heated imagination had magnified my one shot into a volley.

- stealthily (STELTH uh lee) slyly; carefully
- **marrow** (MAR oh) soft tissue inside bones
- reproachful (ri PROHCH ful) blaming; accusing
- **legitimate** (luh JIT uh mut) lawful; legal

The man was not in uniform, and was not armed. He was a stranger in the country. That was all we ever found out about him. The thought of him got to preying upon me every night. I could not get rid of it. I could not drive it away. The taking of that unoffending life seemed such a wanton thing. And it seemed an epitome of war. All war must be just that—the killing of strangers against whom you feel no personal animosity. Strangers whom, in other circumstances, you would help if you found them in trouble, and who would help you if you needed it.

My campaign was spoiled.

ALL THINGS CONSIDERED

1. It seems clear that the boys (a) were very well trained and led. (b) had little real understanding of the horrors of war when they became soldiers. (c) had little real sympathy for the dying man.

2. Toward the end of the experience, the author felt less guilty because he discovered that (a) five other shots had been fired. (b) his shot had missed the man. (c) the stranger was a spy after all.

3. For many nights following the incident, the author (a) tried to escape from camp. (b) prayed for forgiveness. (c) found himself unable to stop thinking about the shooting.

4. "My campaign was spoiled" because (a) the Confederate side was outnumbered. (b) a single killing cannot be called a "campaign." (c) war involves the killing of individual human beings whom one has no personal reason to hate.

5. It seems reasonable to assume that (a) the stranger was a spy. (b) Mark Twain's career as a soldier was just about over. (c) the feelings expressed in the selection would soon fade.

- wanton (WONT un) purposely evil and vicious
- epitome (uh PIT uh mee) summary; typical example
- animosity (an i MOS i tee) violent hatred

THINKING IT THROUGH

1. Suppose you had been in Mark Twain's place throughout the experience. Do you think your thoughts and actions would have been different from his at any point? Explain.

2. Although the selection you have just read is nonfiction, it has many of the qualities of an exciting short story. In fact, good nonfiction selections can often be analyzed in terms of the short-story elements discussed on pages 10–11: (a) *Setting*. What makes the setting just right for the main event in Twain's true story? Don't forget the time of day and certain natural events. (b) *Characters*. In the beginning, are the characters stereotyped or rounded? How do they change as the true story unfolds? (c) *Plot*. What plot questions held your interest as you read? What is the basic conflict, and how does it change as the story unfolds? What parts of the story would you call the climax and resolution (page 11)? (d) *Theme*. What is the very important theme of the selection?

3. Twain's home state of Missouri was considered a "border state" as the Civil War broke out (the time of the selection). Some people favored the North, others the South. Suppose Twain's small company had decided to fight for the Union, not the Confederacy. (a) Would even one word in the selection have to be changed? (b) Would the theme of the selection remain the same? Explain your answer.

4. No army is worse than an amateur army, which Twain's group clearly was. How might a modern professional army unit have handled the situation differently, with better results?

Critical Thinking

Stereotyped Thinking

stereotype (STER ee uh typ) — **n. 1.** the process of making printing plates by pouring hot liquid type metal into a prepared mold. **2.** a simplified idea, or false set of ideas, formed by assuming as true a definition prepared by others: *The cowboy and the Indian are common stereotypes in the minds of the American people.*

A **stereotype** is the "picture in our heads" that comes to mind when we hear or see a certain word. The words "cowboy" and "Indian" are good examples. So are "teenager" and "teacher." "Northerners" often have a stereotyped idea about "Southerners," and vice versa. What pictures pop into your brain when you hear the words "rock star," "dropout" and "businessman"?

By now the truth of the matter should have emerged in your mind: *No stereotype really exists.* We get our stereotyped "cowboy" and "Indian" from movies and TV. You yourself are probably annoyed when adults consider you a typical "teenager," just as your "teacher" may resent being thought of as a type, not as an individual. A "dropout" can go on to become a success. And a "businessman," in modern America, is just as likely to be a "business*woman*."

Stereotyped thinking causes misunderstandings that often lead to trouble. As Mark Twain pointed out, it can even lead to the death of innocent people:

1. (a) What stereotype did the word "war" probably bring to the minds of Twain and his friends when they formed the *Marion's Rangers*? How was this stereotype shown to be false?
2. What about the word "enemy"? What is the difference between "*the* enemy" and "*an* enemy soldier"?
3. What about the word "battle"? How does the stereotyped "battle" differ from the "campaign that failed"?

Composition

1. Reread the dictionary definition of *stereotype* at the top of this page. Explain which definition (1 or 2) probably developed first, and which started as *figurative language* (see page 118). Then explain how these two definitions are related.

2. Explain how racial prejudice is often the result of careless, stereotyped thinking. Support your points by using specific examples.

▶ "All war must be just that—the killing of strangers against whom you feel no personal animosity. Strangers whom, in other circumstances, you would help . . . ."

Sound familiar? It should, for you read these words on page 217. Now read a poetic treatment of the same theme by the British author Thomas Hardy (1840–1928).

THE MAN HE KILLED

by Thomas Hardy

"Had he and I but met
At some old ancient inn,
We should have sat us down to wet
Right many a nipperkin!

5   "But put as infantry,
And staring face to face,
I shot at him as he at me,
And killed him in his place.

"I shot him dead because—
10   Because he was my foe,
Just so; my foe, of course, he was;
That's clear enough; although

"He thought he would sign up, perhaps
Off-hand like—just as I;
15   Was out of work, had sold his traps—
No other reason why.

"Yes; quaint and curious war is!
You shoot a fellow down
You'd treat if met where any bar is,
20   Or help to half-a-crown."

- nipperkin (NIP ur kin) liquid measure, about a pint and a half
- traps (TRAPS) tools used in a certain craft
- crown (KROUN) British coin (a "half crown" is about "two bits")

WAYS OF KNOWING

1. What can you tell about the speaker in the poem? Include in your answer a comment on his attitude toward war.

2. (a) In your opinion, why is the word "because" repeated in lines 9 and 10? (b) What does the speaker understand as the *cause* of his killing the man?

3. What **comparisons** (similarities) and **contrasts** (differences) can you find between the poem and Mark Twain's "The History of a Campaign That Failed" (page 214)?

Ann Petry (Born 1912)

The careers of most people take strange twists and turns, and writers are no exception to this general rule. In fact, the life of Ann Petry seems to prove the rule. Until she was well over 30, there was little in her life to indicate that she would become a major American author.

Ann Petry was born and raised in Old Saybrook, Connecticut, a relaxed town of graceful elm trees and neat white houses. Although she was interested in writing in high school, she decided that the practical choice in life was to go into pharmacy, the career of her father, an uncle, and an aunt. She graduated from the University of Connecticut School of Pharmacy in 1931, and then worked in the family drug store in Old Saybrook.

In 1938, she married George D. Petry and moved to the Harlem section of New York City. Work on a couple of Harlem newspapers put her in close touch with the people she would eventually write about—"Not just black people," a critic later wrote, "but *all* people who are weakened and disillusioned by poverty and by racial and sexual stereotypes." Soon she was taking courses at Columbia University and seriously trying to write fiction. In 1946 she published her first novel, *The Street*. The book received wide praise and sold more than a million copies.

The Street is a brutally honest book about big-city life. It was followed by *Country Place* (1947), a novel showing that prejudice, violence, and ugliness can be found in a small town as well as in a big city. Moving back to Old Saybrook, Ann Petry continued her writing career with two outstanding books for young people: *Harriet Tubman: Conductor on the Underground Railroad;* and *Tituba of Salem Village*, the true story of a young black woman caught up in the famous witchcraft trials.

Ann Petry once wrote that her "aim is to show how simply and easily the environment can change the course of a person's life." How does this statement apply to Ann Petry?

GO FREE OR DIE

(from *Harriet Tubman: Conductor of the Underground Railroad**)
by Ann Petry

▶ The last two selections have shown that people can get caught up in conflicts without much thought, or without really knowing what they are getting into. Sometimes, however, people choose to risk their lives for a cause they know is "right in the soul." Such a person was the remarkable American Harriet Tubman.

Not only did Harriet Tubman escape from slavery, but she then returned to the South, at great personal risk, to help others reach freedom. Nicknamed "Moses" by friends and followers, she spent the years between 1850 and 1856 leading close to 300 southern black slaves to safety in the North and in Canada. In all, she made 19 separate trips!

The selection you are about to read describes part of the difficult and very dangerous journey from the state of Maryland to Canada.

Along the Eastern Shore of Maryland, in Dorchester County, in Caroline County, the masters kept hearing whispers about the man named Moses, who was running off slaves. At first they did not believe in his existence. The stories about him were fantastic, unbelievable. Yet they watched for him. They offered rewards for his capture.

They never saw him. Now and then they heard whispered rumors to the effect that he was in the neighborhood. The woods were searched. The roads were watched. There was never anything to indicate his whereabouts. But a few days afterward, a goodly number of slaves would be gone from the plantation. Neither the master nor the overseer had heard or seen anything unusual in the quarter. Sometimes one or the other would vaguely remember having heard a whippoorwill call somewhere in the woods, close by, late at night. Though it was the wrong season for whippoorwills.

- quarter (KWAR tur) region
- **whippoorwill** (HWIP ur wil) kind of bird, known for singing at night

*The Underground Railroad was the name given to the system for helping slaves to escape.

222

Sometimes the masters thought they had heard the cry of a hoot owl, repeated, and would remember having thought that the intervals between the low moaning cry were wrong, that it had been repeated four times in succession instead of three. There was never anything more than that to suggest that all was not well in the quarter. Yet when morning came, they invariably discovered that a group of the finest slaves had taken to their heels.

Unfortunately, the discovery was almost always made on a Sunday. Thus a whole day was lost before the machinery of pursuit could be set in motion. The posters offering rewards for the fugitives could not be printed until Monday. The men who made a living hunting for runaway slaves were out of reach, off in the woods with their dogs and their guns, in pursuit of four-footed game, or they were in camp meetings saying their prayers with their wives and families beside them.

Harriet Tubman could have told them that there was far more involved in this matter of running off slaves than signaling the would-be runaways by imitating the call of a whippoorwill, or a hoot owl, far more involved than a matter of waiting for a clear night when the North Star* was visible.

In December, 1851, when she started out with the band of fugitives that she planned to take to Canada, she had been in the vicinity of the plantation for days, planning the trip, carefully selecting the slaves that she would take with her.

She had announced her arrival in the quarter by singing the forbidden spiritual—"Go down, Moses, way down to Egypt Land"—singing it softly outside the door of a slave cabin, late at night. The husky voice was beautiful even when it was barely more than a murmur borne on the wind.

Once she had made her presence known, word of her coming spread from cabin to cabin. The slaves whispered to each other, ear to mouth, mouth to ear, "Moses is here." "Moses has come." "Get ready. Moses is back again." The ones who had agreed to go North with her put ashcake and salt herring in an old bandanna,

---

- invariably (in VAIR ee uh blee) without change; regularly
- **fugitive** (FYOO juh tiv) runaway
- **spiritual** (SPIR i choo ul) religious song
- **borne** (BORN) carried
- ashcake (ASH kayk) kind of flat bread
- **bandanna** (ban DAN uh) large colored handkerchief, often worn on the neck or head

*Star used by sailors and land travelers for navigation.

hastily tied it into a bundle, and then waited patiently for the signal that meant it was time to start.

There were 11 in this party, including one of her brothers and his wife. It was the largest group that she had ever conducted, but she was determined that more and more slaves should know what freedom was like.

She had to take them all the way to Canada. The Fugitive Slave Law* was no longer a great many incomprehensible words written down on the country's lawbooks. The new law had become a reality. It was Thomas Sims, a boy, picked up on the streets of Boston at night and shipped back to Georgia. It was Jerry and Shadrach, arrested and jailed with no warning.

She had never been in Canada. The route beyond Philadelphia was strange to her. But she could not let the runaways who accompanied her know this. As they walked along she told them stories of her own first flight; she kept painting vivid word pictures of what it would be like to be free.

But there were so many of them this time. She knew moments of doubt when she was half afraid, and kept looking back over her shoulder, imagining that she heard the sound of pursuit. They

- **incomprehensible** (in kom pruh HEN suh bul) impossible to understand
- **vivid** (VIV ud) sharp and lifelike; convincing

*Law passed in 1850 that made it a crime to help a runaway slave.

would certainly be pursued. Eleven of them. Eleven thousand dollars' worth of flesh and bone and muscle that belonged to Maryland planters. If they were caught, the 11 runaways would be whipped and sold South, but she—she would probably be hanged.

They tried to sleep during the day but they never could wholly relax into sleep. She could tell by the positions they assumed, by their restless movements. And they walked at night. Their progress was slow. It took them three nights of walking to reach the first stop. She had told them about the place where they would stay, promising warmth and good food, holding these things out to them as an incentive to keep going.

When she knocked on the door of a farmhouse, a place where she and her parties of runaways had always been welcome, always been given shelter and plenty to eat, there was no answer. She knocked again, softly. A voice from within said, "Who is it?" There was fear in the voice.

She knew instantly from the sound of the voice that there was something wrong. She said, "A friend with friends," the password on the Underground Railroad.

The door opened, slowly. The man who stood in the doorway looked at her coldly, looked with unconcealed astonishment and fear at the 11 disheveled runaways who were standing near her. Then he shouted, "Too many, too many. It's not safe. My place was searched last week. It's not safe!" and slammed the door in her face.

She turned away from the house, frowning. She had promised her passengers food and rest and warmth, and instead of that there would be hunger and cold and more walking over the frozen ground. Somehow she would have to instill courage into these 11 people, most of them strangers, would have to feed them on hope and bright dreams of freedom instead of the fried pork and corn bread and milk she had promised them.

They stumbled along behind her, half dead for sleep, and she urged them on, though she was as tired and as discouraged as they were. She had never been in Canada, but she kept painting wondrous word pictures of what it would be like. She managed to dispel their fear of pursuit, so that they would not become

---

- incentive (in SEN tiv) encouragement; reason for action
- **disheveled** (dih SHEV uld) untidy; messy-looking
- instill (in STIL) cause to enter the mind gradually
- dispel (di SPEL) drive away

hysterical, panic-stricken. Then she had to bring some of the fear back, so that they would stay awake and keep walking though they drooped with sleep.

Yet during the day, when they lay down deep in a thicket, they never really slept, because if a twig snapped or the wind sighed in the branches of a pine tree, they jumped to their feet, afraid of their own shadows, shivering and shaking. It was very cold, but they dared not make fires because someone would see the smoke and wonder about it.

She kept thinking, 11 of them. Eleven thousand dollars' worth of slaves. And she had to take them all the way to Canada. Sometimes she told them about Thomas Garrett, in Wilmington.* She said he was their friend even though he did not know them. He was the friend of all fugitives. He called them God's poor. He was a Quaker** and his speech was a little different from that of other people. His clothing was different, too. He wore the wide-brimmed hat that the Quakers wear.

She said that he had thick white hair, soft, almost like a baby's, and the kindest eyes she had ever seen. He was a big man and strong, but he had never used his strength to harm anyone, always to help people. He would give all of them a new pair of shoes. Everybody. He always did. Once they reached his house in Wilmington, they would be safe. He would see to it that they were.

She described the house where he lived, told them about the store where he sold shoes. She said he kept a pail of milk and a loaf of bread in the drawer of his desk so that he would have food ready at hand for any of God's poor who should suddenly appear before him, fainting with hunger. There was a hidden room in the store. A whole wall swung open, and behind it was a room where he could hide fugitives. On the wall there were shelves filled with small boxes—boxes of shoes—so that you would never guess that the wall actually opened.

While she talked, she kept watching them. They did not believe her. She could tell by their expressions. They were thinking, new shoes, Thomas Garrett, Quaker, Wilmington—what foolishness was this? Who knew if she told the truth? Where was she taking them, anyway?

That night they reached the next stop—a farm that belonged to a German. She made the runaways take shelter behind trees at the edge of the fields before she knocked at the door. She

---

* City in Delaware.
** A religious group that stresses peace for all people.

hesitated before she approached the door, thinking, suppose that he, too, should refuse shelter, suppose—Then she thought, Lord, I'm going to hold steady on to You and You've got to see me through—and knocked softly.

She heard the familiar guttural voice say, "Who's there?"

She answered quickly, "A friend with friends."

He opened the door and greeted her warmly. "How many this time?" he asked.

"Eleven," she said and waited, doubting, wondering.

He said, "Good. Bring them in."

He and his wife fed them in the lamplit kitchen, their faces glowing, as they offered food and more food, urging them to eat, saying there was plenty for everybody, have more milk, have more bread, have more meat.

They spent the night in the warm kitchen. They really slept, all that night and until dusk the next day. When they left, it was with reluctance. They had all been warm and safe and well-fed. It was hard to exchange the security offered by that clean, warm kitchen for the darkness and the cold of a December night.

Two nights later she was aware that the feet behind her were moving slower and slower. She heard the irritability in their voices, knew that soon someone would refuse to go on. . . .

She told them about Frederick Douglass, the most famous of the escaped slaves, of his eloquence, of his magnificent appearance. Then she told them of her own first vain effort at running away, evoking the memory of that miserable life she had led as a child, reliving it for a moment in the telling.

But they had been tired too long, hungry too long, afraid too long, footsore too long. One of them suddenly cried out in despair, "Let me go back. It is better to be a slave than to suffer like this in order to be free."

She carried a gun with her on these trips. She had never used it—except as a threat. Now as she aimed it, she experienced a feeling of guilt, remembering that time, years ago, when she had prayed for the death of Edward Brodas, the Master, and then not too long afterwards had heard that great wailing cry that came

---

- guttural (GUT ur ul) formed in the throat
- **reluctance** (ri LUK tuns) unwillingness
- **eloquence** (EL uh kwens) fine or graceful speech
- **vain** (VAYN) useless
- evoking (i VOHK ing) calling forth

from the throats of the field hands, and knew from the sound that the Master was dead.

One of the runaways said, again, "Let me go back. Let me go back," and stood still, and then turned around and said, over his shoulder, "I am going back."

She lifted the gun, aimed it at the despairing slave. She said, "Go on with us or die." The husky low-pitched voice was grim.

He hesitated for a moment and then he joined the others. They started walking again. She tried to explain to them why none of them could go back to the plantation. If a runaway returned, he would turn traitor, the master and the overseer would force him to turn traitor. The returned slave would disclose the stopping places, the hiding places, the cornstacks they had used with the full knowledge of the owner of the farm, the name of the German farmer who had fed them and sheltered them. These people who had risked their own security to help runaways would be ruined, fined, imprisoned.

She said, "We got to go free or die. And freedom's not bought with dust. . . ."

Thus she forced them to go on. Sometimes she thought she had become nothing but a voice speaking in the darkness, cajoling, urging, threatening. Sometimes she told them things to make them laugh, sometimes she sang to them, and heard the 11 voices behind her blending softly with hers, and then she knew that for the moment all was well with them.

She gave the impression of being a short, muscular, indomitable woman who could never be defeated. Yet at any moment she was liable to be seized by one of those curious fits of sleep, which might last for a few minutes or for hours.

Even on this trip, she suddenly fell asleep in the woods. The runaways, ragged, dirty, hungry, cold, did not steal the gun, as they might have, and set off by themselves, or turn back. They sat on the ground near her and waited patiently until she awakened. They had come to trust her implicitly, totally. They, too, had come to believe her repeated statement, "We got to go free or die." She was leading them into freedom, and so they waited until she was ready to go on.

- **disclose** (dis KLOHZ) make known
- cajoling (kuh JOHL ing) persuading by coaxing
- indomitable (in DOM i tuh bul) hard to defeat
- **curious** (KYOOR ee us) odd; strange
- implicitly (im PLIS it lee) without question

Finally, they reached Thomas Garrett's house in Wilmington, Delaware. Just as Harriet had promised, Garrett gave them all new shoes, and provided carriages to take them on to the next stop.

ALL THINGS CONSIDERED

1. The reason the masters were rarely able to pursue escaped slaves after a visit from "Moses" was that (a) they had great respect for the man of religion. (b) the discovery of the escape was usually made on Sunday. (c) the runaway slaves would turn the masters' horses loose.

2. Harriet figured that if she were caught, she would (a) be pardoned by the Canadian government. (b) never see "Moses" again. (c) be hanged.

3. The phrase "A friend with friends" was used to (a) alert masters to how many slaves had escaped. (b) keep up the spirits of the fugitives. (c) gain shelter and food for those on the Underground Railroad.

4. Harriet, we are told, carried a gun on her trips to (a) threaten the runaways if they wanted to turn back. (b) warn away any masters they might encounter. (c) shoot small animals for food.

5. By the time they reached Wilmington, the runaways had begun to (a) wonder if they would ever see their loved ones again. (b) doubt that there was such a person as "Moses." (c) trust Harriet.

THINKING IT THROUGH

1. What tricks or sly methods did Harriet Tubman use to contact slaves and lead them to freedom? Try to name at least five.

2. (a) Were Harriet's activities not only dangerous but also illegal? (b) What famous law was involved?

3. (a) How did the people led by Harriet respond to her at first? (b) How did their attitudes change, and then change again?

4. Sometimes one hears the odd expression *cruel kindness*. Which actions of Harriet illustrate this expression?

5. Like many heroes in history, Harriet Tubman could not have acted alone. (a) Who helped her, and at what risk? (b) What was probably the *incentive* (defined on page 225) for these helpers?

Critical Thinking

More Kinds of Analogies

On page 61, an *analogy* was defined as "a statement that the relationship between a pair of terms is in some way similar to the relationship between another pair." Examples included ENVELOPE is to LETTER as BRIEFCASE is to BOOK. You were shown 10 kinds of analogies and asked to explain the relationship in each case.

There are, of course, many more than 10 kinds of analogies. Here is a more complete list. Each is followed by an example from the selection. Complete each by providing a similar example from outside the selection. The first is done as an example.

1. City is to state: WILMINGTON is to DELAWARE as CHICAGO is to ILLINOIS.
2. Classification is to kind: BIRD is to OWL as . . . .
3. Like is to like: FUGITIVE is to RUNAWAY as . . . .
4. Like is to opposite: SLAVERY is to FREEDOM as . . . .
5. Singular is to plural: SHOE is to SHOES as . . . .
6. Object is to function: GUN is to SHOOT as . . . .
7. Function is to object: OPEN is to DOOR as . . . .
8. Adjective is to noun: STRANGE is to ROUTE as . . . .
9. Object is to composition: TREE is to WOOD as . . . .
10. Part is to whole: TREE is to FOREST as . . . .
11. Worker is to job: FARMER is to FARM as . . . .
12. Grammatical form is to grammatical form: BEAR is to BORNE as . . . .
13. Smaller is to larger: HANDKERCHIEF is to BANDANNA as . . . .
14. Masculine is to feminine: WIFE is to HUSBAND as . . . .
15. Number is to number: ELEVEN is to TWENTY-TWO as . . . .

Composition

1. Words that are spelled and pronounced the same but have different meanings are called **homonyms** (HOM uh nimz). Make up a sentence using each *italicized* homonym below with a different meaning. Use a dictionary if you need to.
   (1) . . . anything unusual in the *quarter*.
   (2) singing the forbidden *spiritual*.
   (3) . . . she [Harriet] told them stories of her own first *flight*.
   (4) . . . her own first *vain* effort at running away.
   (5) . . . one of these *curious* fits of sleep.

2. Imagine you are Harriet Tubman and that you are keeping a diary on your first "trip" north on the Underground Railroad in 1850. In a page from your diary, describe your thoughts and actions on a typical day.

VOCABULARY AND SKILL REVIEW

Before completing the exercises that follow, you may wish to review the **bold-faced** words on pages 214 to 228.

I. On a separate sheet of paper, write the term in each line that means the same, or nearly the same, as the word in *italics*.

1. *disheveled:* uncovered, untidy, thoroughly searched, disgraced
2. *legitimate:* greedy, reasonable, dangerous, lawful
3. *gratification:* firm proof, greeting, satisfaction, kind of rock
4. *uncanny:* very strange, useless, clever, humorous
5. *borne:* crown, birth, carried, plumber's tool
6. *vain:* blood vessel, wind indicator, useless, empty
7. *fugitive:* cooling liquid, thoughtful, legal, runaway
8. *reluctance:* pleasure, unwillingness, great praise, cooperation
9. *mark:* English coin, take note of, metric measure, single
10. *disclose:* undress, hide, keep secret, make known

II. On a separate sheet of paper, mark each item *true* or *false*. If it is false, explain what is wrong with the sentence.

1. The adjective *curious* can be used to describe both people and things.
2. Intelligence and *eloquence* are both good qualities.
3. A *spiritual* is a kind of religious song.
4. Monkeys are known to love *bandannas*.
5. The writer checked her work to make sure it was both grammatical and *incomprehensible*.
6. George Washington led several *campaigns* during the Revolutionary War.
7. *Marrow* is the hard part of bone.
8. *VIVID* is to VAGUE as CLEAR is to UNCLEAR.
9. HEAR is to CLEARLY as SPEAK is to *AUDIBLY*.
10. SHARK is to FISH as *WHIPPOORWILL* is to PLANT.

III. "Daffy-nitions" are fun because they upset our stereotyped responses to words and force us to think of words in new ways. The American writer Ambrose Bierce was perhaps a master of the art. In his bitter *Devil's Dictionary*, he defined *year* as "a period of 365 disappointments" and *dentist* as "a magician who, putting metal into your mouth, pulls coins out of your pocket."

Bierce may have started the craze, but "daffy-nitions" are now common. Some newspapers and magazines feature them regularly. Those listed below are *anonymous* (of unknown authorship) except where the source is given in parentheses. After you have read them, write on your paper the numbers of the five that you liked best.

1. **arithmetic:** being able to count up to 20 without taking off your shoes (*Mickey Mouse*)
2. **autobiography:** the life story of an automobile
3. **bowling:** marbles for grown-ups
4. **disk jockey:** somebody who's paid a fortune to sit before a mike, separate good records from bad records, and then play the bad ones
5. **ginger ale:** a drink that tastes the way your foot feels when it's asleep
6. **grandma:** an older lady who keeps your mother from spanking you
7. **index finger:** that which can't be pointed at someone without the other three fingers pointing back at you
8. **mealtime:** when the children sit down to continue eating
9. **myth:** a female moth
10. **once:** enough (*Ambrose Bierce*)
11. **people:** the plural of *me*
12. **skunk:** a community scenter
13. **sleeping bag:** a napsack
14. **snacks:** weight lifters
15. **snore:** to sleep out loud
16. **synonym:** a word you use when you can't spell the other one (*Grit*)
17. **tears:** the juice of the emotions
18. **thief:** one who just has a habit of finding things before people lose them (*Joe E. Lewis*)
19. **whistle:** wind having a narrow escape
20. **zebra:** a horse with stripes

Now it's your turn. Make up a "daffy-nition" for at least five of the 10 words listed below:

1. banana
2. camel
3. cow
4. doughnut
5. football
6. grammar
7. hypnotist
8. moose
9. tapioca
10. TV set

KONG AT THE SEASIDE

by Arnold Zweig

▶ Conflicts sometimes arrive from out of nowhere, unannounced and unwanted. Arnold Zweig (1887–1968), a German writer, illustrates this in the following story—and adds an unusual twist. On one side of the conflict is a small boy named Willie Groll. In the middle is a dog named Kong. And on the other side are three of the strangest strangers you will ever meet in any story.

Kong got his first glimpse of the sea as he ran on the beach. He barked furiously with extravagant enthusiasm. He raced at top speed across the firm sand, still damp from the ebbing waters. Mr. Groll, strolling after, noticed that the dog and Willie, his tanned, light-haired, eight-year-old master, were attracting considerable attention. He also noticed that some controversy seemed to be in progress. Willie was standing there, slim and defiant, holding his dog by the collar. Groll hurried over. People in bathing suits looked pretty much alike, social castes and classes intermingled. Heads showed more character and expression. A stoutish man was sitting in the shade of a striped orange tent. He was bending slightly forward, holding a cigar.

"Is that your dog?" he asked quietly.

A little miss, about 10 years old, was with him. She was biting her underlip. A look of hatred for the boy and the dog flashed between her tear-filled narrow lids.

"No," said Groll with a pleasant voice, which seemed to rumble deep down in his chest, "the dog belongs to the boy, who, to be sure, is mine."

"You know dogs aren't allowed off the leash," the quiet voice continued. "He frightened my daughter a bit, has trampled her canals, and is standing on her spade."

"Pull him back, Willie," laughed Groll. "You're quite right, sir, but the dog broke away and, after all, nothing serious has happened."

- **ebbing** (EB ing) withdrawing, going out (of tides)
- **defiant** (duh FY unt) challenging; firm in opposition
- **caste** (KAST) class in society; social group

Willie pushed Kong aside, picked up the spade and, bowing slightly, held it out to the group. Its third member was a slender, remarkably pretty young lady, sitting in the rear of the tent; Groll decided she was too young to be the mother of the girl and too attractive to be her governess. Well gotten up, he reflected; she looks Irish with those auburn eyebrows.

No one took the spade from the boy, and Willie, with a frown, stuck the toy into the sand in front of the girl.

"I think that squares it, especially on such a beautiful day." Groll smiled and lay down. His legs behind him, his elbows on the sand, his face resting on his hands, he looked over at the hostile three. Willie had behaved nicely and politely. The dog, evidently not as ready to make peace, growled softly, his fur bristling at the neck; then he sat down.

- **reflect** (ri FLEKT) think
- **bristling** (BRIS ling) standing on end

"I want to shoot his dog, Father," the girl suddenly remarked in a determined voice; "he frightened me so." Groll noticed a gold bracelet about her wrist—three strands braided into the semblance of a snake. . . . "These people need a lesson. I shall give it to them."

Groll nodded reassuringly at his boy, who was indignantly drawing his dog closer to him. The man seemed to know that the girl had the right to give orders. So he quietly waited for the sequel of this charming conversation. After all, he was still there to reprimand the brat if the gentleman with the fine cigar lacked the courage to do so because the sweet darling was not accustomed to proper discipline.

"No one is going to shoot my dog," threatened Willie, clenching his fists. Without bothering to look at him, the girl continued, "Buy him from the people, Father. Here is my checkbook." She actually took the thin booklet and a fountain pen with a gold clasp from a zipper-bag inside the tent.

"If you won't buy him for me, I'll throw a soup plate right off the table at dinner; you know I will, Father." She spoke almost in a whisper and was as white as chalk under her tan; her blue eyes flashed threateningly.

The gentleman said, "Ten pounds for the dog."

Groll sat up on the sand and crossed his legs. He was awaiting developments with curiosity. "The dog is not mine; you must deal with my boy. He's trained him."

"I don't deal with boys. I offer 15 pounds, a pretty neat sum for the cur."

Groll realized that this was an opportunity of really getting to know his eldest son. "Willie," he began, "this gentleman offers you 15 pounds for Kong so he may shoot him. For the money, you could buy the bicycle you have been wanting since last year. I won't be able to give it to you for a long time; we're not rich enough for that."

Willie looked at his father, wondering whether he could be in earnest. But the familiar face showed no sign of jesting. In answer, he put an arm about Kong's neck, smiled up at Groll, and said, "I won't sell him to you, Father."

- semblance (SEM bluns) likeness; similar appearance
- **indignantly** (in DIG nunt lee) in an outraged manner
- sequel (SEE kwil) that which follows
- reprimand (REP ruh mand) scold; correct
- cur (KUR) mutt; mongrel dog

The gentleman in the bathing suit with his still untanned, pale skin turned to Groll. Apparently the argument began to interest him. "Persuade him; I offer 20 pounds."

"Twenty pounds," Groll remarked to Willie. "That would buy you the bicycle and the canoe, which you admired so much this morning, Willie. A green canoe with double paddles for the water. And for the land, a fine nickel-plated bicycle with a headlight, storage battery, and new tires. There might even be money left over for a watch. You only have to give up this old dog by handing the leash to the gentleman."

Willie said scornfully, "If I went 10 steps away, Kong would pull him over and be with me again."

The beautiful and unusual young lady spoke for the first time. "He would hardly be able to do that," she said in a clear, sweet, mocking voice—a charming little person, thought Groll—and took a small Browning, gleaming with silver filigree work, out of her handbag. "This would prevent him from running very far."

Foolish of her, thought Groll. "You see, sir, the dog is a thoroughbred, pedigreed, and splendidly trained."

"We've noticed that!"

"Offer 50 pounds, Father, and settle it."

"Fifty pounds," repeated Groll, and his voice shook slightly. That would pay for this trip, and if I handled the money for him, his mother could at least regain her strength. The sanitorium is too expensive, we can't afford it. "Fifty pounds, Willie! The bicycle, the watch, the tent—you remember the brown tent—and you would have money left to help me send mother to a sanitorium. Imagine, all that for a dog! Later on, we can go to the animal welfare society, pay three shillings, and get another Kong."

Willie said softly, "There is only one Kong. I will not sell him."

"Offer 100 pounds, Father. I want to shoot that dog. I shouldn't have to stand such boorishness."

The stoutish gentleman hesitated a moment, then made the offer. "A hundred pounds, sir," he said huskily. "You don't look as though you could afford to reject a small fortune."

- Browning (BROU ning) kind of firearm
- filigree (FIL uh gree) fine decoration; delicate ornamentation
- **pedigreed** (PED uh greed) purebred; having an unmixed blood line
- **sanitorium** (san uh TOR ee um) health resort
- boorishness (BOOR ish nus) rudeness

"Indeed, sir, I can't," said Groll, and turned to Willie. "My boy," he continued earnestly, "100 pounds safely invested will within 10 years assure you of a university education. Or, if you prefer, you can buy a small car to ride to school in. You could drive mother to market. That's a great deal of money, 100 pounds for nothing but a dog."

Willie, frightened by the earnestness of the words, puckered up his face as though to cry. After all, he was just a small boy of eight, and he was being asked to give up his beloved dog. "But I love Kong, and Kong loves me," he said, fighting down the tears in his voice. "I don't want to give him up."

"A hundred pounds—do persuade him, sir! Otherwise my daughter will make life miserable for me. You have no idea," he sighed, "what a row such a little lady can kick up."

"If she were mine," said Groll quietly, "I'd slap her little face." Then, glancing at his boy, who, with wrinkled brow, was striving to hold back his tears, he added, "And now, I think the incident is closed."

And a most astounding thing happened. The little girl began to laugh. Evidently the tall, brown man pleased her, and the idea that anyone could dare to slap her, the little lady, fascinated her by its very roughness.

"All right, Father," she cried; "he's behaved well. Now we'll put the checkbook back in the bag. Of course, Father, you knew it was all in fun."

The stoutish gentleman smiled with relief and said that, of course, he had known it and added that such a fine day was just made to have fun. Fun! Groll didn't believe it. He knew too much about people.

Willie breathed more freely and, pretending to blow his nose, wiped away two tears. He threw himself down in the sand next to Kong, happily pulling the dog on top of himself, and began to wrestle with him; the shaggy brown paws of the terrier and the slim tanned arms of the boy mingled in joyful confusion. Groll thought: Alas for the poor! If this offer had come to me two years ago . . . when we lived in a damp flat dreaming of the little house we now have, then—poor Willie!—this argument might have had a different outcome, this struggle for nothing more than a dog, the love, loyalty, courage, and generosity in the soul of an animal and a boy. Yet, speaking in terms of economics, a little financial

---

- **row** (ROW) fuss; fight
- **flat** (FLAT) apartment

237

security was necessary before one could indulge in the luxury of human decency.

The little girl with the spade put her slim bare feet into the sand outside of the tent and called to Willie: "Help me dig new ones." But her eyes invited the man Groll, for whose approval she was striving.

She pointed to the ruined canals. Then, tossing her head, she indicated Kong, who lay panting and lazy in the warm sunshine, and called merrily: "For all I care he can trample them again."

The whistle of an incoming steamboat sounded from the pier.

- **indulge** (in DULJ) take part; participate with satisfaction

ALL THINGS CONSIDERED ───────────────

1. The little girl in the story can best be described as (a) fun-loving. (b) horribly spoiled. (c) artistic.
2. Groll's speeches mentioning things like a bicycle, canoe, tent, and car are (a) really meant to persuade Willie to sell Kong. (b) made to please the little girl. (c) intended to demonstrate that Willie loves Kong more than anything money might buy.
3. Toward the end of the story, the reader learns that (a) Willie's mother is ill. (b) Kong is a cur, not a pedigreed dog. (c) Willie and the little girl are becoming good friends.
4. The character whose thoughts are revealed in the story is (a) Willie. (b) Groll. (c) the stoutish gentleman.
5. The happiest character at the end of the story is probably (a) Groll. (b) Willie. (c) the little girl.

THINKING IT THROUGH ───────────────

1. In the first paragraph, the author states that at a beach "social castes and classes" tend to disappear. Do you agree? If so, (a) why is this true? (b) In your opinion, does it make the story more believable? Explain.
2. "I want to shoot his dog, Father" comes as a surprise. (a) Why? (b) What does the response of the girl's father suggest about him?
3. In your opinion, does Groll handle the conflict in the best possible way? Explain your answer.
4. (a) How does the little girl's attitude toward Groll change when he suggests slapping her? (b) What accounts for this change?
5. Near the end, the little girl states that "it was all in fun," and her father agrees. But "Groll didn't believe it. He knew too much about people." In your opinion, who is right? Provide reasons for your answer.
6. Groll then reflects that "a little financial security was necessary before one could indulge in the luxury of human decency." (a) Explain this statement in your own words. (b) In your opinion, is the statement generally correct? Why, or why not?

Literary Skills

Using Foreshadowing to Make Predictions

Like most stories, "Kong at the Seaside" contains details in **chronological** (kron uh LOJ i kul) **order,** the natural time order of events in real life. At any given point in the story, the reader is uncertain about what is going to happen. But as in real life, the reader can use the past and the present to make **predictions** about the future. The author's *foreshadowing* helps the reader do this.

Foreshadowing is the providing of hints or clues as to what might happen in a story. Good foreshadowing lets the reader make predictions that either do or do not come true. Good reading, therefore, is often a kind of game: *Will my prediction come true, or won't it?*

1. The girl's father is first described as "a stoutish man . . . holding a cigar." What does this short description suggest about the type of person he is and the way he might behave?

2. One of the most interesting characters is mentioned only twice in the story: the beautiful young lady with the gun. In your opinion, why did the author include this character in the story?

3. Right after the little girl announces she wants the dog shot, "Groll noticed a gold bracelet about her wrist— three strands braided into the semblance of a snake." What does this description reveal about the girl and her behavior?

4. Throughout the story, most readers think that Willie will continue to refuse to sell Kong. How does the author foreshadow this view early in the story?

5. The author calls the little girl's sudden laughter toward the end "a most astounding thing." Yet most readers are willing to accept the laughter as natural. Explain why.

Composition

1. The title of the story is a strange one, since "Kong" is not the main character and "at the Seaside" doesn't give much of an idea of what the story will be about. Write three good titles that suggest something more about the story. When you finish, place a check before the title you like best.

2. Suppose your class were going to rewrite the story as a play and then give a public performance. Whom in the class would you choose for the five human roles? Before you make your final choice, carefully consider the personality of each of the actors. Explain why your chosen actors seem to fit the parts assigned.

▶ Sometimes, life seems to consist of one humdrum routine after another. We get up in the morning, get dressed, go to school or work, come home . . . etcetera, *etcetera*! Perhaps one of your parents works at a place where everyone punches a time clock.

Here is a poem by a Czech, Miloš Macourek (MEE lohsh muh KOOR ek), that has something to say about time clocks and life's less thrilling moments.

THE PUNCHING CLOCK

by Miloš Macourek

There will come a day
when the punching clock
will no longer just wait in the doorway

it will come directly to our beds
5   and will ask politely
that we punch good morning

then it will accompany us
like a courteous servant would
and punch;
10   when we start to yawn
when we bite into a sandwich . . .
when we think of old age . . .

how wonderful will it be
to have one's whole life punched by seconds
15   up to the very end . . .

WAYS OF KNOWING

1. Notice the three "examples" in lines 10 through 12 of typical times the clock might punch. Why do you think the poet chooses "when we start to yawn" as a typical example?
2. The poem has few punctuation symbols in it. Notice that line 13 might be considered either a statement or a question. Judging from the overall message of the poem, which do you think the poet intended? Explain.

241

Rabindranath Tagore (1861-1941)

Rabindranath Tagore with his daughter in 1926

If there is one thing that cannot be said of **Rabindranath Tagore,** it is that he was a man of few words. He turned out 50 plays, more than 100 books of poetry, and dozens of novels.

Tagore was born in Calcutta, India, to a wealthy family. After studying law briefly in England, he returned home to India to manage his father's estates. At one time, the Tagore family had 100,000 tenants on the land and farms they owned.

Because he traveled a great deal, Tagore became known to the Western world as well as the Eastern. In 1913 he received the Nobel Prize for Literature—the first Asian to be so honored. And in 1915 he was knighted at Buckingham Palace.

While Tagore admired the people of the West for their handling of practical affairs, he felt that the East better understood the spiritual nature of things. He spent his life trying, through his writings and social actions, to create a blend of the two ways of thought and life.

What goals did Tagore try to achieve through his writing?

MY LORD, THE BABY

by Rabindranath Tagore

▶ Raicharan's conflict began with what he believed to be his
duty in society. And it ended with a painful decision.

Raicharan was 12 years old when he
came as a servant to his master's
house. He belonged to the same caste
as his master, and was given his master's little son, Anukul, to take care of.
As time went on, the boy left
Raicharan's arms to go to school. From
school Anukul went on to college, and
after college he entered the judicial
service. Always, until the boy married,
Raicharan was his only caretaker.

But, when a wife came into the
house, Raicharan found two masters
instead of one. All his former influence
passed to the new wife. Then Anukul

had a son born to him, and Raicharan,
whose own wife was childless, was
given charge of the child. He used to
toss him up in his arms, and speak baby
language. He would put his face close
to the baby's and draw it away with a
grin.

Presently the child was able to
crawl and cross the doorway. When
Raicharan went to catch him, the child
would scream with mischievous laughter and make for safety. Raicharan was
amazed at the skill and exact judgment
the baby showed when pursued. He
would say to his mistress with a look of

• caste (KAST) religious and social class in India

awe and mystery, "Your son will be a judge some day."

New wonders came in their turn. When the baby began to toddle, that was to Raicharan an epoch in human history. When he called his father Ba-ba and his mother Ma-ma and Raicharan Chan-na, then Raicharan's ecstasy knew no bounds. He went out to tell the news to all the world.

After a while Raicharan was asked to show his ingenuity in other ways. He had, for instance, to play the part of a horse, holding the reins between his teeth and prancing with his feet. He had also to wrestle with the boy, and if he could not, by a wrestler's trick, fall on his back defeated at the end, a great outcry was certain.

About this time Anukul was transferred to a district on the banks of the Padma River. On his way through Calcutta he bought his son a little go-cart. He also bought him a yellow satin vest, a gold-laced cap, and some gold bracelets. Raicharan made it his custom to dress the child in the vest and bracelets whenever they went for a walk.

Then came the rainy season, and day after day the rain poured down. The hungry Padma River, like an enormous serpent, swallowed down terraces, villages, corn fields. With its flood, it covered the tall grasses and wild trees on the sand banks. From time to time there was a deep thud, as the river banks crumbled. Masses of foam, carried swiftly past, proved to the eye the swiftness of the stream.

One afternoon the rain cleared. It was cloudy, but cool and bright. Raicharan's little despot did not want to stay in on such a fine afternoon. His lordship climbed into the go-cart. Raicharan dragged him slowly along till they reached the rice fields on the banks of the river. There was no one in the fields, and no boat on the stream. In the midst of that stillness the child suddenly pointed with his finger and cried, "Chan-na. Pitty fower."

Close by on a mud flat stood a large tree in full flower. My lord, the baby, looked at it with greedy eyes, and Raicharan knew his meaning. Only a short time before, he had made, out of those very flower balls, a small go-cart; and the child had been so happy dragging it about with a string that for the whole day Raicharan was not made to put on the reins at all. He was promoted from a horse into a groom.

But Raicharan had no wish that evening to go splashing knee-deep through the mud to reach the flowers. So he quickly pointed in the opposite direction, calling out, "Oh, look, baby, look! Look at the bird." And with all sorts of strange noises he pushed the go-cart rapidly away from the tree.

But a child who is someday to be a judge cannot be put off so easily. And besides, there was at the time nothing to attract his eyes. You cannot point

- **awe** (AW) respectful wonder and fear
- epoch (EH pok) important period in time
- **ecstasy** (EKS tuh see) great joy; delight
- **ingenuity** (in juh NOO uh tee) great skill; cleverness
- despot (DES pot) tyrant; harsh ruler

forever toward an imaginary bird.

The little master's mind was made up, and Raicharan was at his wits' end. "Very well, baby," he said at last, "you sit still in the cart, and I'll go and get you the pretty flower. Only, mind you, don't go near the water."

As he said this, he made his legs bare to the knee, and waded through the oozing mud toward the tree.

The moment Raicharan had gone, his little master went off at racing speed to the forbidden water. The baby saw the river rushing by, splashing and gurgling as it went. At the sight, the heart of the child grew excited and restless. On his way he picked up a small stick, and leaned over the bank, pretending to fish.

Raicharan had plucked a handful of flowers from the tree, and was carrying them back in the end of his cloth, his face covered with smiles. But when he reached the go-cart, there was no one there. He looked everywhere but found no one.

In that first terrible moment his blood froze within him. Before his eyes the whole universe swam round like a dark mist. From the depth of his broken heart he gave one piercing cry, "Master, Master, little Master."

But no voice answered "Chan-na." No child laughed mischievously back. No scream of baby delight welcomed his return. Only the river ran on, with its splashing, gurgling noise as before— as though it knew nothing at all, and had no time to attend to such a tiny human event as the death of a child.

As the evening passed by, Raicharan's mistress became very worried. She sent men out everywhere to search. They went with lanterns in their hands, and reached at last the banks of the Padma. There they found Raicharan rushing up and down the fields, like a stormy wind, shouting the cry of despair, "Master, Master, little Master."

When they got Raicharan home at last, he fell down at his mistress's feet. They shook him, and questioned him, and asked him repeatedly where he had left the child. All he could say was that he knew nothing.

Though everyone held the opinion that the river had swallowed the child, there was a lurking doubt left in the mind. For a band of gypsies had been noticed outside the village that afternoon, and some suspicion rested on them. The mother went so far in her wild grief as to think it possible that Raicharan himself had stolen the child. She called him aside and pleaded, "Raicharan, give me back my baby. Oh! give me back my child. Take from me any money you ask, but give me back my child!"

Anukul tried to reason his wife out of this unjust suspicion. "Why on earth," he said, "would Raicharan commit such a crime as that?"

The mother replied, "The baby was wearing gold bracelets. Who knows?"

It was impossible to reason with her after that.

Raicharan went back to his own village. Up to this time he had had no son, and there was no hope that any child would now be born to him. But it came

---

• **lurking** (LURK ing) lingering in a half-hidden way

about before the end of a year that his wife gave birth to a son. Then she died.

Overwhelming resentment at first grew up in Raicharan's heart at the sight of this new baby. At the back of his mind was resentful suspicion that it had come to take the place of the little master. He also thought it would be a grave offense to be happy with a son of his own after what had happened to his master's little child. Indeed, if it had not been for a widowed sister who mothered the new baby, it would not have lived for long.

But a change gradually came over Raicharan's mind. A wonderful thing happened. This new baby in turn began to crawl about, and cross the doorway with mischief in its face. It also showed an amusing cleverness in making its escape to safety. Its voice, its sounds of laughter and tears, its gestures, were those of the little master. On some days, when Raicharan listened to its cryings, his heart began thumping wildly against his ribs. It seemed that his former little master was crying somewhere in the unknown land of death because he had lost his Chan-na.

Phailna (that was the name of the new baby) soon began to talk. It learned to say Ba-ba and Ma-ma with a baby accent. When Raicharan heard those familiar sounds the mystery suddenly became clear. The little master could not cast off the spell of his Chan-na, and therefore he had been reborn in his own house.

The arguments in favor of this were, to Raicharan, altogether beyond dispute:

(1) The new baby was born soon after his little master's death.

(2) His wife could never have accumulated such merit as to give birth to a son in middle age.

(3) The new baby walked with a toddle and called out Ba-ba and Ma-ma. There was no sign lacking which marked out the future judge.

Then suddenly Raicharan remembered that terrible accusation of the mother. "Ah," he said to himself with amazement, "the mother's heart was right. She knew I had stolen her child." When once he had come to this conclusion, he was filled with regret for his past neglect. He now gave himself over, body and soul, to the new baby, and became its devoted attendant. He began to bring it up as if it were the son of a rich man. He bought a go-cart, a yellow satin vest, and a gold-embroidered cap. He melted down the jewelry of his dead wife, and made gold bracelets. He refused to let the little child play with anyone of the neighborhood, and himself became its only companion day and night. As the baby grew to boyhood, he was so petted and spoiled that the village children would call him "Your Lordship," and jeer him; and older people regarded Raicharan as unaccountably crazy about the child.

At last the time came for the boy to go to school. Raicharan sold his small piece of land, and went to Calcutta. With great difficulty he got a job as a servant, and sent Phailna to school. He spared no expense to give him the best education, the best clothes, the best food. Meanwhile he himself lived on a

---

• **resentment** (ri ZENT munt) anger; irritation

mere handful of rice, and would say in secret, "Ah! my little master, my dear little master, you loved me so much that you came back to my house. You shall never suffer from any neglect of mine."

Twelve years went by. The boy was able to read and write well. He was bright and healthy and good-looking. He paid a great deal of attention to his personal appearance, and was especially careful in parting his hair. He behaved extravagantly and spent money freely. He could never quite look on Raicharan as a father, because, though fatherly in affection, Raicharan had the manner of a servant. A further fault was that Raicharan kept secret from everyone that he himself was the father of the child.

The students at Phailna's school were greatly amused by Raicharan's country manners, and Phailna joined in their fun. But, in the bottom of their hearts, all the students loved the innocent and tenderhearted old man, and Phailna was very fond of him also.

Raicharan grew older and older, and his employer was continually finding fault with him for his incompetent work. He had been starving himself for the boy's sake. He had grown physically weak, and was no longer able to work. He would forget things, and his mind became dull and stupid. But his employer expected a full servant's work out of him, and would not stand for excuses. The money that Raicharan had brought with him from the sale of his land was gone. The boy was continually grumbling about his clothes, and asking for more money.

Raicharan made up his mind. He gave up his job as a servant, and left some money with Phailna and said, "I have some business to do at home in my village, and shall be back soon."

He went off at once to Baraset where Anukul was a judge. Anukul's wife was still broken down with grief. She had had no other child.

One day Anukul was resting after a long and weary day in court. His wife was buying, at a high price, an herb from a quack, which was said to insure the birth of a child. A voice of greeting was heard in the courtyard. Anukul went out to see who was there. It was Raicharan. Anukul's heart was softened when he saw his old servant. He asked him many questions, and offered to take him back into service.

Raicharan smiled faintly, and said in reply, "I want to pay my respects to my mistress."

Anukul went with Raicharan into the house, where the mistress did not receive him as warmly as his old master. Raicharan took no notice of this, but folded his hands, and said, "It was not the river that stole your baby. It was I."

Anukul exclaimed, "Great God! Eh! What! Where is he?"

Raicharan replied, "He is with me. I will bring him the day after tomorrow."

It was Sunday. Both husband and wife were looking expectantly along

---

- **extravagantly** (eks TRAV uh gunt lee) freely; wildly
- **incompetent** (in KOM puh tunt) careless and unskillful
- **quack** (KWAK) person who pretends to be a doctor

the road, waiting from early morning for Raicharan's appearance. At 10 o'clock he came, leading Phailna by the hand.

Anukul's wife, without question, took the boy into her lap, and was wild with excitement. Sometimes she laughed, sometimes she wept. She kissed the boy's hair and forehead and gazed into his face with hungry, eager eyes. The boy was very good-looking and dressed like a gentleman's son. The heart of Anukul brimmed over with a sudden rush of affection.

Nevertheless the judge in him asked, "Have you any proof?"

Raicharan said, "How could there be any proof of such a deed? God alone knows that I stole your boy, and no one else in the world."

When Anukul saw how eagerly his wife was clinging to the boy, he realized the futility of asking for proof. It would be wiser to believe. And then, where could an old man like Raicharan get such a boy from? And why should his faithful servant deceive him for nothing?

"But," he added severely, "Raicharan, you must not stay here."

"Where shall I go, Master?" said Raicharan in a choking voice, folding his hands. "I am old. Who will take an old man as a servant?"

The mistress said, "Let him stay. My child will be pleased. I forgive him."

But Anukul's conscience would not allow him. "No," he said, "he cannot be forgiven for what he has done."

Raicharan bowed to the ground and clasped Anukul's feet. "Master," he cried, "let me stay. It was not I who did it. It was God."

Anukul's conscience was stricken worse than ever, when Raicharan tried to put the blame on God's shoulders.

"No" he said, "I could not allow it. I cannot trust you anymore. You have done an act of treachery."

Raicharan rose to his feet and said, "It was not I who did it."

"Who was it then?" asked Anukul.

Raicharan replied, "It was my fate."

But no educated man could take this for an excuse. Anukul remained obdurate.

When Phailna saw that he was the wealthy judge's son, and not Raicharan's, he was angry at first, thinking that he had been cheated all this time of his true parents. But seeing Raicharan in distress, he generously

* **futility** (fyoo TIL uh tee) uselessness
* **treachery** (TRETCH uh ree) betrayal
* **obdurate** (OB doo rut) stubborn; not yielding

said to his father, "Father, forgive him. Even if you don't let him live with us, let him have a small monthly pension."

After hearing this, Raicharan did not utter another word. He looked for the last time on the face of his son; he paid respects to his old master and mistress. Then he went out and mingled with the numberless people of the world.

At the end of the month Anukul sent him some money to his village. But the money came back. There was no one there by the name of Raicharan.

ALL THINGS CONSIDERED

1. Raicharan loses his influence over Anukul to (a) a new master. (b) a wife. (c) a new baby in the family.
2. The baby disappears most probably because he (a) is kidnapped by gypsies. (b) falls into the river. (c) is stolen by Raicharan.
3. Later, Raicharan feels that his own son is really (a) the former little master reborn. (b) smarter than his former little master. (c) a reward for faithful service to his master.
4. Near the end of the story, Raicharan (a) is given a pension by his son. (b) regains his job with Anukul and his wife. (c) presents Phailna to Anukul and his wife as their long-lost child.
5. At the end, Raicharan seems to (a) be fully happy at last. (b) be living comfortably, though not happily. (c) have disappeared or died.

THINKING IT THROUGH

1. "My Lord, the Baby" takes place in a culture that many modern Americans find hard to understand. Do you believe that this story of love, guilt, and self-sacrifice could ever really have happened? Explain why or why not.
2. (a) What is your personal opinion of the character Raicharan— is he a foolish man, a wise man, a great man, or what? (b) Reading between the lines, what do you infer that the author, Rabindranath Tagore, thought about Raicharan?
3. The profile of Tagore on page 242 stated that he tried to blend the "practical affairs" of life with "the spiritual nature of things." How are both the practical and the spiritual reflected in the story?
4. (a) When you first saw the title, "My Lord, the Baby," what did you think it meant? (b) After having read the story, has the meaning of the title changed for you? Explain.

Reading and Analyzing

Interpreting Character Clues

The discussion of *characterization* on page 151 indicated the difference between *telling* and *showing*. Sometimes authors simply *tell* the reader directly what their characters are like. For instance, at various places in "My Lord, the Baby," we are told that Raicharan is "amazed," "innocent," "tenderhearted," "resentful," and "fatherly." More usually, however, authors try to *show* us their characters in action. From the hints an author provides, the reader infers an understanding of the characters. These hints can be called **character clues.**

Look back, for instance, at the second paragraph of the story. Does the author tell us directly that Raicharan "adores" his master's newborn son? No. Instead, he provides us with character clues: Raicharan tosses the baby into the air, speaks baby talk, and plays a simple sight game. These actions tell the reader that Raicharan loves the baby.

Think about a few more character clues in the story:

1. "He [Raicharan] had, for instance, to play the part of a horse, holding the reins between his teeth and prancing with his feet." What does this tell us about Raicharan's character?

2. When Raicharan discovers that the child is missing, we read the following: "In that first terrible moment his blood froze within him. Before his eyes the whole universe swam around like a dark mist." Suppose the author had simply chosen to use adjectives (descriptive words) to tell us how Raicharan feels. What adjectives might he have used?

3. For his own son, we read that Raicharan "bought a go-cart, a yellow satin vest, and a gold-embroidered cap." What does the purchase of these items tell us about Raicharan? What comparison is suggested?

Composition

1. The day Raicharan returns to Anukul, his former mistress buys "at a high price, an herb from a quack, which was said to insure the birth of a child." This sentence tells us at least two things about the woman. What are they? How is at least one of them related to her behavior later on? Explain in a short paragraph.

2. Look back at the scene in which Raicharan presents his own child Phailna to Anukul and his wife (pages 247–248). What are the actions of Anukul's wife? What question does Anukul ask? Does he immediately accept Anukul as his own child? How do the two parents differ in their reaction to meeting Phailna? Explain in your own words.

VOCABULARY AND SKILL REVIEW

Before completing the exercises that follow, you may wish to review the **bold-faced** words on pages 233 to 248.

I.
1. *Ebbing* waters at the beach are (a) unusually calm. (b) coming in or rising. (c) going out or withdrawing.
2. *Bristling* hair is often considered a sign of (a) surprise or alarm. (b) good grooming. (c) a free and casual lifestyle.
3. To spend money *extravagantly* is to (a) watch every penny. (b) be unusually generous to others. (c) spend it wildly.
4. An *incompetent* worker (a) is better than average. (b) doesn't know or care about the job. (c) is often absent because of illness.
5. *Awe,* the root word in *awesome,* means (a) full of wonder. (b) flaw or defect. (c) dangerous.
6. FAKE is to REAL as *QUACK* is to (a) DUCK. (b) FALSE. (c) DOCTOR.
7. PUREBRED is to HORSE as *PEDIGREED* is to (a) DOG. (b) GREED. (c) EAGLE.
8. SCHOOL is to EDUCATION as *SANITORIUM* is to (a) DISEASE. (b) HEALTH. (c) INTELLIGENCE.
9. TALE is to STORY as *FLAT* is to (a) HILLY. (b) FERTILE. (c) APARTMENT.
10. HEROISM is to HERO as *TREACHERY* is to (a) TRAITOR. (b) BETRAYAL. (c) LEADERSHIP.

II. On a separate sheet of paper, write the *italicized* word that best fills the blank in each sentence.

reflect	*resentment*	*row*	*defiant*	*ecstasy*
indulge	*indignantly*	*futility*	*lurking*	*ingenuity*

1. Nearly reeling with sudden _____, Maria stood up to receive the Citizenship Award at graduation.
2. Having expected to receive the reward himself, Scott was filled with _____.
3. A _____ suspicion is the same thing as a lingering doubt.
4. Thomas A. Edison combined scientific _____ with good business sense.
5. The Mountaineers lost all 19 games last year in the team's long season of _____.
6. Not till retirement did Mrs. Morales _____ in that great thief of sleep, a VCR.

251

7. Tossing his head _____, Tom groaned at the umpire's close call at third base.

8. Tom felt _____, but he knew it was better to hold his tongue.

9. No one really wanted a big _____ with the officials or the other team.

10. A year ago he would have lost his head, but now he found it possible to _____ rather than react.

III. Some character clues are known to almost everyone. They are so well-known, in fact, that an author can write in a kind of "character-clue language," indicating feelings by action and description. For instance, scratching the head is supposed to be a sign of puzzlement. (Is it, really?) Instead of writing "Sam was puzzled," an author can write "Sam scratched his head." To the average reader, they mean the same thing.

Here are 10 sentences that contain "character-clue language." First explain the character clue, and then tell what it is supposed to mean.

1. Max looked down at his clenched hands; the fingernails were white.

2. Dad stood quite silently, pulling at his right ear.

3. The man on the other side of the desk began to tap his foot rapidly.

4. All during the test, Helene bit the nails on her one free hand.

5. Tania's hair stood on end when she heard the news.

6. The woman in the employment office yawned as she read my short résumé.

7. "Are you sure?" Luis asked, his eyes narrowing.

8. "Your paper is really excellent," the teacher said, looking me in the eye.

9. "One more hour to work," Bob muttered through clenched teeth.

10. Little Seth stared at his shoes when his mother questioned him about the missing cookies.

THE BULLY

by Gregory Clark

▶ When does an enemy stop being an enemy? You'll find out in the following true story, set partly in the Battle of Vimy Ridge, during World War I, when four Canadian fighting divisions met to overthrow a strong German position.

Aubrey was his name. He could have been about eight or nine years of age. I was about seven.

He would lie in wait for me on my way to school. Four times every day. Being at that time a very small, measly little boy consisting largely of freckles, knuckles, knees and feet, I believed devoutly in the principle of non-resistance. Even before I started to school, I had learned I could not run fast enough to escape predators among my fellow-beings. Nor had I the weight, speed or courage to fight when overtaken.

Aubrey was a large, loose boy with sallow skin, pale eyes, a nasal voice and a frustrated character. Nobody loved him. The teachers didn't like him. He was avoided in the schoolyard. In the knots and squads of children going to and coming from school, Aubrey, large and louty for his age, was always mauling, pushing, shoving the smaller kids. The groups would either hurry to leave him behind or stop and wait for him to go on. Nobody, nobody loved him.

Then he found me. I fancy he lived two blocks closer to the school than I. He would wait for me just around a corner. He would lie in wait in side alleys, lanes, behind hedges. As Aubrey

---

- devoutly (di VOUT lee) sincerely; religiously
- non-resistance (NON ri ZIS tuns) refusal to fight or be violent, as a principle
- predator (PRED uh tur) creature that preys on others
- sallow (SAL oh) pale; sickly-looking
- nasal (NAY zul) sounding through the nose
- louty (LOUT ee) awkward; clumsy

was large for his age, I was small for mine. I found difficulty joining the right gangs of children heading to or from school. I, like Aubrey, often found myself walking alone.

Aubrey would throw me down and kneel on me, his knees on my biceps. He would glare down at me out of his pale eyes with a look of triumph. He would pretend he was going to spit on me. He would grind his fist on my nose, not too heavy, but revelling in the imagined joy of punching somebody on the nose. It was inexpressible pleasure to him to have somebody at his mercy.

I tried starting to school late; lingering at school after dismissal. I tried going new ways, around strange blocks. No use. Aubrey got me. I had no protectors. My father was a fighting man who would have laughed if I had revealed to him my terror. "Why," he would have cried gaily, "punch him in the nose!"

After about two years, Aubrey vanished. I suppose his family moved away. But as the years came and went, like ever-rising waves of the tide of life and experience, my memory kept Aubrey alive. As I grew, the memory of him grew. When I was 15, the hateful memory of Aubrey was my age too. When I was 20, there in my life still lived the large, sallow, cruel figure of Aubrey. My hatred of him matured, became adult, took on the known shape of a presence.

In the Vimy battle, by 8:30 a.m., I was the only officer left in my company. I had started, three hours earlier, the baby lieutenant. Now I was alone with 200 men.

Orders came, now that we had reached the crest and the last final wonderful objective. The R.C.R.* had been held up at a semifinal objective, and there was a gap on our left between us and the Princess Pats.**

"You will take the necessary party," orders said, "and bomb across to meet a party from the Patricias, which will start from their flank at 9 a.m. You should attempt to meet their party halfway across."

- biceps (BY seps) large muscle in the front part of the upper arm
- revelling (REV ul ing) having great fun; making merry
- presence (PREZ uns) spirit felt to be nearby
- objective (ub JEK tiv) goal
- flank (FLANGK) side (of an army)

*Royal Canadian Regiment.
**Princess Patricias was a nickname of a Canadian fighting regiment.

"Who," I said to my sergeant, Charlie Windsor, "will I take with me?"

It was a pretty dreadful time. It was sleeting. The air shook with shell fire, whistled and spat with machine-gun fire; and without shape or form, random monsters fell around us, belching up gray earth, gray smoke, gray men.

"Me," answered Sgt. Windsor, "and five others."

We got the canvas buckets and filled them with bombs. Sgt. Windsor got a Lewis gun*** and five pans for it. At 9 a.m., peering across the grisly expanse toward where the Patricias should be, we saw, sure enough, a glimpse of furtive forms, half a dozen of them, bobbing, dodging, vanishing, reappearing. They were coming toward us.

"They've already started!" said Sgt. Windsor, hoisting the Lewis.

"Let's go," I croaked.

So, bobbing, dodging, vanishing, reappearing ourselves, we seven headed out to meet the Pats half-way. Down into shell craters, up over crater lips; down into the next craters, pools, mud;

- pan (PAN) container of ammunition
- grisly (GRIZ lee) horrible
- furtive (FUR tiv) sneaking

***Machine gun.

fresh hot holes, charred and new-burned, big holes, little holes, we slithered and slid and crouched. Two or three times, we had to cringe while German stick bombs whanged close; we lobbed ours back until we got silence. Two or three times, Sgt. Windsor had to slide the nozzle of the Lewis over the lip of craters and spray half a pan of fire into brush clumps. And once into a tree, half-way up, out of which a gray sack fell, heavily.

But each time up, we saw the Pats coming to us. And their bombs rang nearer, and ours rang nearer to them. We now could hear each other's shouts of encouragement and greeting.

"One more spurt!" I assured my crew.

The Pats squad was led by a long-geared, rangy man for whom I felt sorry each time I glimpsed him coming toward us. A pity all men can't be half-pints in war!

Our next plunge would be the last. We could hear the Pats only a few yards away.

Out over the lip I crouched and hurtled, feet first. Feet first, I slid into a big crater; and over its lip skidded, feet first, the rangy, long-geared Pat.

You're right. It was Aubrey.

His pale eyes stared incredulous and triumphant down into mine. His sallow face split in a muddy grin.

"Don't I know you, sir?" he puffed.

"You sure should," I sighed, struggling erect as possible and holding out my hand.

Hate dies funny.

- charred (CHARD) blackened
- cringe (KRINJ) shrink down
- whang (HWANG) strike
- lob (LOB) toss in a wide arc
- rangy (RAYN jee) long-limbed; lanky
- hurtle (HUR tul) rush wildly
- incredulous (in KREJ uh lus) not believing

ALL THINGS CONSIDERED ─────────────────────

1. The title of the selection most clearly refers to (a) a Canadian soldier. (b) Sgt. Charlie Windsor. (c) a lanky, sallow-skinned schoolboy who once made the author's life miserable.

2. During the battle of Vimy, the author was ordered to (a) bully a couple of prisoners. (b) help fill a gap between two Canadian regiments. (c) lead his company to the rear.

3. As the approaching squad grew near, the author noticed that its leader was (a) badly wounded. (b) small and measly. (c) long-geared and rangy.

4. When the author and squad leader finally met in a crater, the author discovered that the man was (a) his best childhood friend. (b) a German. (c) Aubrey.

5. The line that best sums up the meaning of the true story is (a) "Nobody, nobody loved him." (b) "A friend is a friend." (c) "Hate dies funny."

THINKING IT THROUGH ─────────────────────

1. In the first paragraph, the author refers to the "principle of non-resistance." (a) What does this usually mean? (b) Why did the author believe in it at the time? (c) Did he always believe wholeheartedly in the principle? Explain why or why not.

2. Consider your feelings about Aubrey as you read the first six paragraphs of the selection. (a) What were your feelings— hatred of a bully, pity for an ill-looking and unloved child, or what? (b) Do you think your feelings would have been the same about a *real* Aubrey in your life? Explain.

3. Even after Aubrey moved away, the author carried around a mental image, a feared presence of Aubrey, for many years. Has something like this ever happened to you? Explain.

4. The fifth paragraph from the end begins, "You're right." But was the *author* right? Did you foresee the surprise at the end of the story? If so, explain what clues helped you.

5. The selection suggests a moral or lesson that most people should remember more of the time. In your own words, what is this moral or lesson?

UNIT REVIEW

I. Match the terms in Column A with their definitions in Column B.

A

1. stereotyped thinking
2. foreshadowing
3. chronological order
4. contrast
5. character clue

B

(a) the natural time order of events in real life

(b) difference

(c) clue provided by an author about what will happen in the future

(d) action, dialogue, and other hints that reveal what a certain character is like

(e) responding automatically to certain words with mental pictures and ideas that may or may not be true in individual cases

II. "Exploring Conflicts" is the title of this unit. As you have seen, different people handle conflicts in different ways. Here are five possible responses to conflict situations. Choose four of them, and for each, (a) name a selection that illustrates the response, and (b) tell how the response worked out in that particular case.

1. Withdraw from the conflict, only to have the memory of your opponent haunt your mind for years.

2. Submit completely, sure that the desires of others are always more important than your own happiness.

3. Use conflict situations to test others out in a nice way and perhaps to teach them lessons.

4. Rush into a conflict because shallow, stereotyped thinking tells you it's the "thing to do."

5. Get into the conflict because you are *absolutely certain* it's the right and only course of action.

III. ORDER, PLEASE!

Chronological order is just one of the many orders in which items or events can be listed. Think of all the other ways you might arrange the five prose selections in this unit (omitting "The Bully" if you did not read it):

Are all possible orders important? Of course not. The order of length may be important, but the alphabetical order of main characters' names certainly is not. Look at the list of possible orders below. Which do you think is most important— next most important—and least important?

1. *Chronological Order.* One of the nonfiction selections is set just before a war, one during that war, and one during another war. What is the order here? Now think about the fiction selections. Look back at the authors' dates and think about the stories themselves. In one case you might have to guess, but otherwise the order of the five selections should be clear.

2. *Spatial (space) Order.* Where are the selections set? Go in an easterly direction around the globe. There should be only one case where you may have to guess.

3. *Order of Importance.* Consider the themes of the selections and the importance of the factual events in history. Put the selection you consider *most* important first.

4. *Order of Interest.* Recall your reactions as you read the selections. Use the *most* interesting as the first item.

5. *Order of Difficulty.* This is another easy one. You probably breezed through some selections and had trouble with others. Put the most difficult first.

6. *Order of "Truth."* The label *nonfiction* does not guarantee that a selection will seem true to all readers. Some nonfiction selections seem more real than others. Which one of the nonfiction selections in the unit do you think really happened? List this selection first. Then list the other nonfiction selections according to their degree of truth. Start your list with the highest degree of truth.

When you have decided how the above orders should be ranked in importance, take out two sheets of paper. Fold them lengthwise. Start by writing the number and name of *your* "most-important" choice in the top left-hand column. Then list the selections vertically beneath. Use the right-hand column to explain your ordering of the selections. You do not have to account for every item, but you should indicate some of the reasons for your decisions.

When your first group is complete, skip a line and go on to the next. Complete all six lists.

SPEAKING UP

The term "three-minute speech" makes some students leap to the challenge and causes others to shrink in frozen fear. Your first job is to accept the challenge as one you can not only meet but easily master. To help you meet the challenge, start by thinking of the "speech" as a "talk." Don't worry too much about the time limit; if you do a good job, no one is going to object if you quit after two minutes or go on to four. And as for fear, forget about it. If you're well prepared, enthusiastic, and eager to speak, there will simply be no place in your act for fear. At the very least, don't be fearful as you prepare your speech. That's not "speaking-fear" but fear of fear. One of the greatest speakers of modern times, President Franklin D. Roosevelt, once told the nation, "The only thing we have to fear is fear itself." Think about that.

Your subject is largely up to you, but it must be some sort of "How to . . ." or "How Not to . . ." speech. If no specific subject comes to mind, try to think of a humorous approach. One good topic is "How to Write a Failing Paper," illustrated by examples of all the *don'ts* in good writing (which you also incorporate into your speech). Spend whatever time it takes to think of an excellent topic. The rest of your preparation will then be a breeze.

The content and organization of your speech will be discussed on the next page. It's often a good idea to write a speech out before you give it, but *do not read your speech*. No one can read from a paper and establish good eye contact with an audience at the same time. You may want to write down a few key words on a card. If you must have your paper in front of you, try circling the key words in red so you will need to look down as little as possible. Above all, *know your material well and be enthusiastic about it*. When you find just the subject that makes you eager to speak, you'll find that all the so-called problems of speaking—what to do with your hands, how to pitch your voice, and so on—will not be problems at all.

WRITING A SPEECH

Assignment: Write a speech that will take about three minutes to deliver on a "How to . . ." or "How Not to . . ." topic.

Prewriting: The key to success is finding the right subject. First, you will have to come up with an original subject. Don't be afraid to be ridiculous. For instance, you might try to follow directions (supposedly from a book) on "How to Draw a Triangle." Then, you demonstrate that although you "follow" the directions in several ways, you find it impossible to actually draw that triangle. That idea may *sound* ridiculous, but it has actually been used with great success.

Writing: As you write your speech, try to incorporate some suggestions from the experts on public speaking:

1. The beginning is the only time when you can be sure the audience is with you. Start by arousing further interest with something like a striking statement, a question, or a story.

2. Early in the speech, make sure your point, or purpose, is made very clear. You may have to repeat it in several ways.

3. Most of the speech will consist of examples of your point or explanations of steps in a process. Try to be clear, and remember to show relationships.

4. Involve the audience as much as possible. Ask for a show of hands on a questionable point. Tell your listeners to take notes. Ask a question or two. Get a few students up to do a demonstration. An involved audience is an interested audience.

5. At least once in the speech, show something. Even if what you show is not too important, the very act of reaching into your pocket, a folder, or a bag will arouse curiosity.

6. Finish the speech with a summary statement or some other conclusion that lets the audience know that the end has arrived. Don't just stop with your last example and sit down.

Revising: Read your speech several times, trying to be your own best listener. At this point, you might also want to try your speech on a friend. You and your friend should keep the following questions in mind. Is the speech the right length? Does it incorporate points 1 to 6, above? Above all, does it sound like *you*? Don't be satisfied until it becomes a speech that you would be eager to hear yourself. Finally, make a neat copy of your final draft.

UNIT · 5

SOME TEARS, SOME LAUGHTER

Laugh, and the world laughs with you;
  Weep, and you weep alone;
For the sad old earth must borrow its mirth,
  But has troubles enough of its own.

—Ella Wheeler Wilcox

Some tears, some laughter—and often both at the same time. What makes one person weep may cause others to laugh and laugh. At times, in fact, a person may experience "tears of laughter," crying and laughing at the same situation.

The selections in this unit show that life, at its very best, is a mixture of tears and laughter. In fact, in reading the selections that follow, you will discover that the most important moments in life are often made up of some tears, some laughter.

AFTER YOU, MY DEAR ALPHONSE

by Shirley Jackson

▶ "Practice what you preach," we are told. What Mrs. Wilson had apparently preached in raising her son was the importance of judging all people fairly. Johnny learned the lesson well. Whether Mrs. Wilson practiced what she preached . . . well, you decide. Shirley Jackson (1919–1965) gives you all the clues you need in this insightful story of rising anger and playful joy.

Mrs. Wilson was just taking the gingerbread out of the oven when she heard Johnny outside talking to someone.

"Johnny," she called, "you're late. Come in and get your lunch."

"Just a minute, Mother," Johnny said. "After you, my dear Alphonse."

"After *you*, my dear Alphonse," another voice said.

"No, after *you*, my dear Alphonse," Johnny said.

Mrs. Wilson opened the door. "Johnny," she said, "you come in this minute and get your lunch. You can play after you've eaten."

Johnny came in after her, slowly. "Mother," he said, "I brought Boyd home for lunch with me."

"Boyd?" Mrs. Wilson thought for a moment. "I don't believe I've met Boyd. Bring him in, dear, since you've invited him. Lunch is ready."

"Boyd!" Johnny yelled. "Hey, Boyd, come on in!"

"I'm coming. Just got to unload this stuff."

"Well, hurry, or my mother'll be sore."

"Johnny, that's not very polite to either your friend or your mother," Mrs. Wilson said. "Come sit down, Boyd."

As she turned to show Boyd where to sit, she saw he was a Negro boy, smaller than Johnny but about the same age. His arms were loaded with split kindling wood. "Where'll I put this stuff, Johnny?" he asked.

● insightful (in SYT ful) full of insight, or awareness of underlying truths or causes

Mrs. Wilson turned to Johnny. "Johnny," she said, "what did you make Boyd do? What is that wood?"

"Enemies," Johnny said mildly. "We stand them in the ground and run over them with tanks."

"How do you do, Mrs. Wilson?" Boyd said.

"How do you do, Boyd? You shouldn't let Johnny make you carry all that wood. Sit down now and eat lunch, both of you."

"Why shouldn't he carry the wood, Mother? It's his wood. We got it at his place."

"Johnny," Mrs. Wilson said, "go on and eat your lunch."

"Sure," Johnny said. He held out the dish of scrambled eggs to Boyd. "After you, my dear Alphonse."

"After *you,* my dear Alphonse," Boyd said.

"After *you,* my dear Alphonse," Johnny said. They began to giggle.

"Are you hungry, Boyd?" Mrs. Wilson asked.

"Yes, Mrs. Wilson."

"Well, don't you let Johnny stop you. He always fusses about eating, so you just see that you get a good lunch. There's plenty of food here for you to have all you want."

"Thank you, Mrs. Wilson."

"Come on, Alphonse," Johnny said. He pushed half the scrambled eggs on to Boyd's plate. Boyd watched while Mrs. Wilson put a dish of stewed tomatoes beside his plate.

"Boyd don't eat tomatoes, do you, Boyd?" Johnny said.

"*Doesn't* eat tomatoes, Johnny. And just because you don't like them, don't say that about Boyd. Boyd will eat *anything*."

"Bet he won't," Johnny said, attacking his scrambled eggs.

"Boyd wants to grow up and be a big strong man so he can work hard," Mrs. Wilson said. "I'll bet Boyd's father eats stewed tomatoes."

"My father eats anything he wants to," Boyd said.

"So does mine," Johnny said. "Sometimes he doesn't eat hardly anything. He's a little guy, though. Wouldn't hurt a flea."

"Mine's a little guy, too," Boyd said.

"I'll bet he's strong, though," Mrs. Wilson said. She hesitated. "Does he . . . work?"

"Sure," Johnny said. "Boyd's father works in a factory."

"There, you see?" Mrs. Wilson said. "And he certainly has to be strong to do that—all that lifting and carrying at a factory."

"Boyd's father doesn't have to," Johnny said. "He's a foreman."

Mrs. Wilson felt defeated. "What does your mother do, Boyd?"

"My mother?" Boyd was surprised. "She takes care of us kids."

"Oh. She doesn't work then?"

"Why should she?" Johnny said through a mouthful of eggs. "You don't work."

"You really don't want any stewed tomatoes, Boyd?"

"No, thank you, Mrs. Wilson," Boyd said.

"No, thank you, Mrs. Wilson, no, thank you, Mrs. Wilson, no, thank you, Mrs. Wilson," Johnny said. "Boyd's sister's going to work, though. She's going to be a teacher."

"That's a very fine attitude for her to have, Boyd." Mrs. Wilson restrained an impulse to pat Boyd on the head. "I imagine you're all very proud of her?"

"I guess so," Boyd said.

"What about all your other brothers and sisters? I guess all of

---

- **restrain** (ri STRAYN)   hold back
- **impulse** (IM puls)   sudden urge to do something

you want to make just as much of yourselves as you can."

"There's only me and Jean," Boyd said. "I don't know yet what I want to be when I grow up."

"We're going to be tank drivers, Boyd and me," Johnny said. "Zoom." Mrs. Wilson caught Boyd's glass of milk as Johnny's napkin ring, suddenly transformed into a tank, plowed heavily across the table.

"Look, Johnny," Boyd said. "Here's a foxhole. I'm shooting at you."

Mrs. Wilson, with the speed born of long experience, took the gingerbread off the shelf and placed it carefully between the tank and the foxhole.

"Now eat as much as you want to, Boyd," she said. "I want to see you get filled up."

"Boyd eats a lot, but not as much as I do," Johnny said. "I'm bigger than he is."

"You're not much bigger," Boyd said. "I can beat you running."

Mrs. Wilson took a deep breath. "Boyd," she said. Both boys turned to her. "Boyd, Johnny has some suits that are a little too small for him, and a winter coat. It's not new, of course, but there's lots of wear in it still. And I have a few dresses that your mother or sister could probably use. Your mother can make them over into lots of things for all of you, and I'd be very happy to give them to you. Suppose before you leave I make up a big bundle and then you and Johnny can take it over to your mother right away. . . ." Her voice trailed off as she saw Boyd's puzzled expression.

"But I have plenty of clothes, thank you," he said. "And I don't think my mother knows how to sew very well, and anyway I guess we buy about everything we need. Thank you very much, though."

"We don't have time to carry that old stuff around, Mother," Johnny said. "We got to play tanks with the kids today."

Mrs. Wilson lifted the plate of gingerbread off the table as Boyd was about to take another piece. "There are many little boys like you, Boyd, who would be very grateful for the clothes some-one was kind enough to give them."

"Boyd will take them if you want him to, Mother," Johnny said.

"I didn't mean to make you mad, Mrs. Wilson," Boyd said.

"Don't think I'm angry, Boyd. I'm just disappointed in you, that's all. Now let's not say anything more about it."

She began clearing the plates off the table, and Johnny took Boyd's hand and pulled him to the door. "Bye, Mother," Johnny said. Boyd stood for a minute, staring at Mrs. Wilson's back.

"After you, my dear Alphonse," Johnny said, holding the door open.

"Is your mother still mad?" Mrs. Wilson heard Boyd ask in a low voice.

"I don't know," Johnny said. "She's screwy sometimes."

"So's mine," Boyd said. He hesitated. "After *you*, my dear Alphonse."

ALL THINGS CONSIDERED

1. When Boyd enters the house, Mrs. Wilson discovers that he is (a) French. (b) black. (c) very handsome.
2. Mrs. Wilson tells Johnny that Boyd (a) will probably eat anything. (b) doesn't care for tomatoes. (c) looks sickly.
3. Mrs. Wilson infers that Boyd's family is (a) rich. (b) snobbish. (c) poor.
4. Between the lines, the reader can see that both Johnny and Boyd (a) have a sympathetic understanding of Mrs. Wilson. (b) really do not like Mrs. Wilson. (c) are not overly concerned with the way Mrs. Wilson is behaving.
5. At the end of the story, Mrs. Wilson (a) has gained a new understanding of herself. (b) has learned little or nothing from the events. (c) states the theme of the story in her own words.

THINKING IT THROUGH

1. In your opinion, do Johnny and Boyd have a good friendship? Support your opinion with details from the story.
2. Consider how Mrs. Wilson and Boyd interact. Then comment on the story in terms of *stereotypes* (see page 219).
3. Near the end of the story, Mrs. Wilson lifts the plate of gingerbread off the table. Does this indicate anything about her inner feelings? If so, what?
4. Near the end also, Mrs. Wilson says to Boyd, "I'm just disappointed in you, that's all." In your opinion, why does she say this? Explain fully.
5. Comment on the story in terms of *dramatic irony* (see page 29).

LITERARY SKILLS

Point of View

When Shirley Jackson sat down to write "After You, My Dear Alphonse," one of her first jobs must have been to decide from which position she would tell the story. Every story has to be written from a certain point of view. In other words, someone has to relate the events. This "someone" may or may not be involved as a character in the story. The **point of view** of a story is simply the position from which the events are related.

The two points of view commonly used to tell stories are called the *first-person* and *third-person* points of view:

- **First person:** The storyteller is involved as a character in the story. This **narrator** (person who tells the story) refers to herself or himself with the pronouns "I," "me," and "myself."
- **Third person:** The storyteller is *not* involved as a character in the story. The narrator remains outside the story and must refer to all characters with pronouns like "he" and "she."

1. "After You, My Dear Alphonse" is written in the third person. Why do you think the author chose the third person, rather than the first person, to tell the story? Before answering this question, ask yourself: (a) Why would it seem odd to have either Johnny or Boyd tell the story? (b) What would be strange in having Mrs. Wilson narrate the story (starting "I was just taking the gingerbread out . . . .")?

2. What is at least one advantage of the first-person point of view? To answer this question, first select a first-person story that you have read and liked. ("The Pit and the Pendulum," "The Hitchhiker," "August Heat," and "The Bully" are possible choices.) Then imagine that the story was written in the third person. What element would be missing?

3. Sometimes the nature of a character or the events in a plot demand that the story be told in the third person. What are two examples of such details that would prevent use of the first person? Think about stories like "Polar Night" and "My Lord, the Baby."

COMPOSITION

1. Write a short paragraph describing yourself from the third-person point of view. Include details about your appearance and your personality. *Do not mention your name.*

2. Summarize "After You, My Dear Alphonse" by telling the story from Mrs. Wilson's point of view (starting "I was just taking the gingerbread out . . . .") Your first-person summary must explain the situation as she understood it at the time. Feel free to include opinions.

▶ Here's a famous poem about the problems six blind men have when they meet an elephant. Will you laugh at the blind men, cry for them, or both? Read the poem and see.

THE BLIND MEN AND THE ELEPHANT

by John Godfrey Saxe

It was six men of Indostan*
To learning much inclined,
Who went to see the Elephant
(Though all of them were blind),
5   That each by observation
Might satisfy his mind.

The FIRST approached the Elephant,
And happening to fall
Against his broad and sturdy side,
10   At once began to bawl:
"God bless me! but the Elephant
Is very like a wall!"

The SECOND feeling of the tusk,
Cried, "Ho! what have we here
15   So very round and smooth and sharp?
To me 'tis mighty clear
This wonder of an Elephant
Is very like a spear!"

The THIRD approached the animal,
20   And happening to take
The squirming trunk within his hands,
Thus boldly up and spake:
"I see," quoth he, "the Elephant
Is very like a snake!"

• **inclined** (in KLYND) attracted to; likely to

*Old name for India.

25 The FOURTH reached out an eager hand,
And felt about the knee.
"What most this wondrous beast is like
Is mighty plain," quoth he;
"'Tis clear enough the Elephant
30 Is very like a tree!"

The FIFTH, who chanced to touch the
    ear,
Said, "Even the blindest man
Can tell what this resembles most;
Deny the fact who can,
35 This marvel of an Elephant
Is very like a fan!"

The SIXTH no sooner had begun
About the beast to grope,
Than, seizing on the swinging tail
40 That fell within his scope,
"I see," quoth he, "the Elephant
Is very like a rope!"

And so these men of Indostan
Disputed loud and long
45 Each in his own opinion
Exceeding stiff and strong,
Though each was partly in the right,
And all were in the wrong!

WAYS OF KNOWING

1. In your own words, explain the meaning of this poem.
2. Relate an incident you know of in which several people gave differing reports about the same occurrence.

- **grope** (GROHP) feel around blindly
- scope (SKOHP) reach; range
- **exceeding(ly)** (ik SEE ding lee) very; extremely

MY FINANCIAL CAREER

by Stephen Leacock

▶ Opening a bank account can be a pretty dull experience. Unless, of course, the depositor happens to be as mixed up as the individual in the following selection by Stephen Leacock, a Canadian writer.

When I go into a bank I get rattled. The clerks rattle me; the wickets rattle me; the sight of the money rattles me; everything rattles me.

The moment I cross the threshold of a bank and attempt to transact business there, I become an irresponsible idiot.

I knew this beforehand, but my salary had been raised $50 a month and I felt that the bank was the only place for it.

So I shambled in and looked timidly around at the clerks. I had an idea that a person about to open an account ought to consult the manager.

I went up to a wicket marked "Accountant." The accountant was a tall, cool devil. The very sight of him rattled me. My voice was sepulchral.

"Can I see the manager?" I said, and added solemnly, "Alone." I don't know why I said "Alone."

"Certainly," said the accountant, and fetched him.

The manager was a grave, calm man. I held my $56 clutched in a crumpled ball in my pocket.

"Are you the manager?" I said. Heaven knows I didn't doubt it.

"Yes," he said.

"Can I see you," I asked, "alone?" I didn't want to say "alone" again, but without it the thing seemed self-evident.

- wicket (WIK it) teller's window in an old-fashioned bank
- **threshold** (THRESH ohld) door sill; doorway
- **transact** (tranz AKT) carry on; engage in
- shamble (SHAM bul) walk with the feet dragging
- sepulchral   (suh PUL krul) as from out of a sepulcher, or tomb
- **self-evident** (self EV i dunt) needing no proof; "crystal clear"

272

The manager looked at me in some alarm. He felt that I had an awful secret to reveal.

"Come in here," he said, and led the way to a private room. He turned the key in the lock.

"We are safe from interruption here," he said. "Sit down."

We both sat down and looked at each other. I found no voice to speak.

"You are one of Pinkerton's men, I presume," he said.

He had gathered from my mysterious manner that I was a detective. I knew what he was thinking, and it made me worse.

"No, not from Pinkerton's," I said, seeming to imply that I came from a rival agency.

"To tell the truth," I went on, as if I had been prompted to lie about it, "I am not a detective at all. I have come to open an account. I intend to keep all my money in this bank."

The manager looked relieved but still serious: he concluded now that I was a son of Baron Rothschild or a young Gould.*

"A large account, I suppose," he said.

"Fairly large," I whispered. "I propose to deposit $56 now and $50 a month regularly.

The manager got up and opened the door. He called to the accountant.

"Mr. Montgomery," he said unkindly loud, "this gentleman is opening an account; he will deposit $56. Good morning."

I rose.

A big iron door stood open at the side of the room.

"Good morning," I said, and stepped into the safe.

"Come out," said the manager coldly, and showed me the other way.

I went up to the accountant's wicket and poked the ball of money at him with a quick convulsive gesture as if I were doing a conjuring trick.

My face was ghastly pale.

"Here," I said, "deposit it." The tone of the words seemed to mean, "Let us do this painful thing while the fit is on us."

He took the money and gave it to another clerk.

He made me write the sum on a slip and sign my name in a

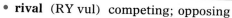

- **rival** (RY vul) competing; opposing
- convulsive (kun VUL siv) clumsy and shaky
- conjuring (KON jur ing) magic

*Rothschild and Gould were the names of millionaire families.

book. I no longer knew what I was doing. The bank swam before my eyes.

"Is it deposited?" I asked in a hollow, vibrating voice.

"It is," said the accountant.

"Then I want to write a check."

My idea was to draw out six dollars of it for present use. Someone gave me a checkbook through a wicket and someone else began telling me how to write it out. The people in the bank had the impression that I was an invalid millionaire. I wrote something on the check and thrust it in at the clerk. He looked at it.

"What! Are you drawing it all out again?" he asked in surprise. Then I realized that I had written $56 instead of six. I was too far gone to reason now. I had a feeling it was impossible to explain the thing. All the clerks had stopped writing to look at me.

Reckless with misery, I made a plunge.

"Yes, the whole thing."

"You withdraw your money from the bank?"

"Every cent of it."

"Are you not going to deposit any more?" said the clerk, astonished.

"Never."

A crazy idea struck me that they might think something had insulted me while I was writing the check and that I had changed my mind. I made a wretched attempt to look like a man with a fearfully quick temper.

The clerk prepared to pay the money.

"How will you have it?" he said.

"Oh"—I caught his meaning and answered without even trying to think—"in fifties."

He gave me a $50 bill.

"And the six?" he asked dryly.

"In sixes," I said.

He gave it to me and I rushed out.

As the big door swung behind me I caught the echo of a roar of laughter that went up to the ceiling of the bank. Since then I bank no more. I keep my money in cash in my trousers pocket and my savings in silver dollars in a sock.

274

ALL THINGS CONSIDERED _____

1. The narrator tells us that he decided to open a bank account when (a) he heard about a robbery in his apartment house. (b) the bank began offering free gifts to depositors. (c) he received a raise in salary.

2. Because of the narrator's behavior, the manager mistakes him for (a) an important bank official. (b) a Pinkerton detective. (c) a criminal.

3. Since this terrible experience, the narrator states, he keeps his money (a) in stocks and bonds. (b) in the office safe. (c) in the pocket of his trousers.

4. In writing the story, the author was trying to show that (a) banks are not to be trusted. (b) crime does not pay. (c) humor can be found anywhere you look for it.

5. The story is told from the point of view called (a) first person. (b) second person. (c) third person. (See page 269 if you have trouble.)

THINKING IT THROUGH _____

1. "My Financial Career" is the kind of selection that is hard to label either *fiction* or *nonfiction*. In your opinion, is it (a) completely true, (b) totally made up, or (c) mostly fictional, but based on a true feeling or experience? Explain the reason for your choice.

2. In your opinion, why did the author choose to use short paragraphs and many short sentences?

3. Now answer two more questions: (a) What, in your opinion, was the author's purpose? (b) How well did he succeed in achieving that purpose? Then answer another: (c) Unless you used a word like *completely* or *totally* to answer (b), explain what the author might have done to improve the selection.

CRITICAL THINKING

Fact and Opinion

A **fact** is something known to be true. If you can't check on a fact yourself, you can usually rely on the reports of reliable witnesses.

An **opinion,** on the other hand, is what a person thinks or believes about something. No matter how many people hold a particular opinion, it cannot be called a fact unless it can be proven to be true.

Think about "My Financial Career" in terms of fact and opinion:

1. What was the narrator's opinion of the events at the time they happened?
2. Reading between the lines, you should be able to see that the author, Stephen Leacock, has a different opinion of the same events. What is Leacock's opinion?

3. Which single word in each of the following sentences most clearly expresses an opinion?
   (a) The accountant was a tall, cool man.
   (b) My voice was sepulchral.
   (c) He felt that I had an awful secret to reveal.
   (d) "Come out," said the manager coldly.
4. On page 275, you were asked an *opinion:* Are the events in the selection facts, or not? If you had unlimited time and money, how might you go about answering this question? (Note: Stephen Leacock, the author, died in 1944.)
5. It has been observed that older readers tend to have a better *opinion* of "My Financial Career" than younger readers do. What *fact(s)* might account for this difference of opinion?

COMPOSITION

1. In a single complete sentence, express your opinion of the selection. Then go on to support your opinion in as factual a manner as possible. (This is not as easy as it seems. Most of the time, when people try to "prove" their opinions, they rely on other opinions, not facts.)
2. Have you ever been so rattled that you found yourself doing silly things that embarrassed you? Of course you have. Describe such a situation in as humorous a way as possible. Try to use the style of "My Financial Career": short sentences and paragraphs. You can add some fiction to your experience as long as it remains believable.

▶ Did you ever laugh yourself sick over something? In the
following poem you get a good picture of just how dangerous a joke can be. But, of course, it's all in fun.

THE HEIGHT OF THE RIDICULOUS

by Oliver Wendell Holmes

I wrote some lines, once on a time,
In wondrous merry mood,
And thought, as usual, men would say
They were exceeding good.

5   They were so queer, so very queer,
I laughed as I would die;
Albeit, in a general way,
A sober man am I.

I called my servant, and he came;
10   How kind it was of him,
To mind a slender man like me,
He of the mighty limb.

"These to the printer," I exclaimed,
And, in my humorous way,
15   I added (as a trifling jest)
"There'll be the devil to pay."*

He took the paper, and I watched,
And saw him peep within:
At the first line he read, his face
20   Was all upon the grin.

- **exceeding(ly)** (ik SEE ding lee) very; extremely
- albeit (awl BEE it) although
- **trifling** (TRYF ling) unimportant; of little worth
- **jest** (JEST) joke

*At the time the poem was written, a printer's assistant was called a *print-
er's devil;* hence the pun in "devil to pay."

He read the next; the grin grew broad,
And shot from ear to ear;
He read the third; a chuckling noise
I now began to hear.

25   The fourth; he broke into a roar;
The fifth; his waistband split;
The sixth; he burst the buttons off,
And tumbled in a fit.

Ten days and nights, with sleepless eye,
30   I watched that wretched man,
And since, I never dare to write
As funny as I can.

WAYS OF KNOWING

1. Is it really likely that a person would laugh for 10 days and nights? If not, find two other examples of exaggeration that make the title of the poem especially fitting.
2. According to the speaker, was the poem that made the servant laugh funnier than "The Height of the Ridiculous"? How do you know?
3. Oliver Wendell Holmes (1809–1894) was an American doctor whose hobby was writing poems. Many of his poems poke fun at important people of his time. Explain what is humorous in the following limerick about Henry Ward Beecher, a famous clergyman:

> The Reverend Henry Ward Beecher
> Called a hen a most elegant creature:
> The hen, pleased with that,
> Laid an egg in his hat;
> And thus did the hen reward Beecher.

Before completing the exercises that follow, you may wish to review the **bold-faced** words on pages 266 to 277.

I.   1. A *trifling jest* is a(n) (a) piece of fishing equipment. (b) unimportant joke. (c) foolish mistake.

    2. If you act on an *impulse,* you (a) thoroughly consider all the possible results. (b) obey another person. (c) do something suddenly and thoughtlessly.

    3. If you are *inclined* to do something, you (a) must do it. (b) will probably do it. (c) hate the very idea of doing it.

    4. You might *grope* for (a) a light cord. (b) the sun. (c) a rewarding career.

    5. Business to *transact* is business to (a) carry on. (b) avoid. (c) delay until a future date.

    6. TEACHER is to INSTRUCTOR as *RIVAL* is to (a) FRIEND. (b) OPPONENT. (c) EDUCATION.

    7. DAY is to NIGHT as *SELF-EVIDENT* is to (a) CLEAR. (b) EMBARRASSED. (c) DOUBTFUL.

    8. GATE is to STADIUM as *THRESHOLD* is to (a) FOOTBALL. (b) HOUSE. (c) DOOR.

    9. SHUT is to OPEN as *RESTRAIN* is to (a) HOLD BACK. (b) FORBID. (c) LET GO.

    10. TOTALLY is to COMPLETELY as *EXCEEDINGLY* is to (a) EXTREMELY. (b) PARTLY. (c) RARELY.

II. Read the box labeled "Concrete Poetry" on page 280. Then study the three "poems" that follow. When you see the point or meaning of each poem, explain it in a clear sentence of your own, leaving three or four lines between explanations. Finally, go back and state whether you would call each of your explanations a *fact* about the poem or an *opinion* of your own. Explain your thinking. You may find it useful to define the word *fact* as you are using it here, such as "a statement with enough evidence to prove it is true."

CONCRETE POETRY

One of the most popular forms of poetry in recent years has been "concrete poetry." A "concrete poem" is an arrangement of words that visually conveys the meaning of the poem. For instance, you may have seen holiday greeting cards with the message printed in the form of a star or a Christmas tree.

Look at the three examples below. The fact that two are in foreign languages should cause you no trouble. Strangely, it's the English one that may be difficult: *rendering* means "making" and *legible* means "clear enough to read."

```
silencio  silencio  silencio
silencio  silencio  silencio
silencio            silencio
silencio  silencio  silencio
silencio  silencio  silencio
```

```
rendering the legible illegible
  rendering the il legible
    rend illegible he
       re illegible
```

▶ Cyrano de Bergerac (1619–1655) was a French soldier who gained some fame at the time as the writer of novels, plays, and poems. Cyrano was also known for his swaggering personality, his quick wit, and his readiness to duel with anyone who spoke of the size or shape of his unusual nose.

The following play is a tragicomedy by the French playwright Edmond Rostand (1868–1918). The Cyrano in the play, a larger-than-life version of the 17th-century original, is one of the best-known romantic heroes in drama.

CYRANO DE BERGERAC

by Edmond Rostand
(from the English translation by Gertrude Hall)

CHARACTERS

CYRANO DE BERGERAC: *A soldier, swordsman, and poet.*
ROXANE: *The beautiful young cousin of Cyrano.*
CHRISTIAN DE NEUVILLETTE: *A young soldier. In love with Roxane.*
RAGUENEAU: *A pastry cook and poet.*
LISE: *The wife of Ragueneau.*
LE BRET: *A friend and fellow soldier of Cyrano.*
DE GUICHE: *A powerful count and military commander.*
VALVERT: *A nobleman. Friend of De Guiche.*
MONTFLEURY: *A tragic actor.*
BELLEROSE: *A theater manager.*
ALSO a hundred or so others: a doorkeeper, soldiers, servants, marquises, a flower girl, a father and son, a pickpocket and followers, pages, a counter girl, a duenna, actresses, poets, nuns, and many more.

TIME: *Acts I through IV: 1640. Act V: 1655.*

- swaggering (SWAG ur ing) boastful; bold in movement
- **tragicomedy** (traj i KOM i dee) a play that combines both tragedy and comedy

ACT I
The Theater in Paris

SETTING: *A small theater in a busy hotel. At the left is a slightly raised stage. In the center are several benches. At the right, raised, is a row of box seats, the extension of a balcony that is offstage right. Under the boxes is a refreshment counter. A poster on a stand in the rear right announces the play of the day:* La Clorise.

AT RISE: *The theater is empty and nearly dark, lit only by a row of candles. Two chandeliers holding unlit candles are slowly lowered to the floor. Noises are heard offstage as the audience and theater workers start to arrive. A Soldier enters briskly.*

Doorkeeper (*running in after him*): Hold it, there! Not so fast. You have to pay!

Soldier: I come in admission free!

Doorkeeper: And why is that?

Soldier: I am in the King's light cavalry!

Doorkeeper (*to another* Soldier *who has entered*): And you?

Second Soldier: I do not pay!

Doorkeeper: But—

Second Soldier: Musketeer!

First Soldier (*seeing the* Second): The play does not begin before two. The floor is empty. Come, to your foil!

Second soldier: On guard! (*They fence with foils they have brought.*)

A Servant (*to another who has entered*): Psst! . . . Flanquin!

Second Servant: Ah, you here!

First Servant (*taking a pack of cards from his coat*): Look, I have cards and dice. Let's have a game.

Second Servant: You rascal, willingly! I'll take your coins.

- **musketeer** (mus ki TEER) soldier who carries a musket in battle
- foil (FOIL) sword with a thin blade, used for fencing

First Servant (*sitting down with the other and taking a candle from his pocket, which he lights and puts on the floor*): I have stolen a little of my master's light.

A Marquis (*one of several people who continue to enter*): So many here!

The Flower Girl (*coming forward*): Flowers, anyone? Flowers?

Marquis (*seeing her*): How sweet of you, coming even before they light the hall! (*He puts his arm around her waist.*)

First Soldier (*to the other fencer*): A hit!

Second Servant (*to the other gambler*): A club!

Marquis (*pursuing the girl*): A kiss!

Flower Girl (*pushing him off*): But— we shall be seen!

Marquis (*pulling her into a dark corner*): No, no danger here.

A Father (*one of the crowd that continues to enter, to his* Son): This should be a good place to sit, my boy. Let's stay here.

The Son: No, too far front.

First Servant: Ace wins!

Father: Just look at this place! (*He points with his cane.*) Gamblers! Brawlers! (*He falls over a man who has lain down on the floor to wait.*) Drunkards!

(*The theater continues to fill with people. The noblemen are finely dressed, and most bear swords. The other people are dressed according to their social class, down to a few in worn and tattered clothes.*)

Marquis (*still after the* Flower Girl): A kiss!

Father (*to the* Son): And to think that in this very theater, my son, were given the plays of the great Rotrou!

Son: And those of the great Corneille!

Pages (*entering noisily as a group*): Tra la la la la!

Doorkeeper (*severely*): Look, now! You pages! None of your tricks!

First Page (*looking wounded*): Sir! Your lack of trust in us! (*He turns to a* Second Page *as the* Doorkeeper *leaves.*) You have brought the string?

Second Page: With a fish hook at the end!

First Page (*pointing to balcony*): We will sit up there and fish for wigs!

A Pickpocket (*to a group of evil-looking young fellows*): Come now, my little hopefuls, and learn the ABC's of the trade.

Second Page (*to others in the balcony*): Hey! Did you bring the peashooters?

Third Page (*from above*): Yes, and here's how! (*A round of peas showers from above.*)

Son (*to his* Father): What play are we to see today?

Father: *La Clorise.*

Son: By whom?

Father: By Balthazar Baro. Ah, what a play it is!

Pickpocket (*to his students*): Now watch. Sometimes you have to snip the coattail neatly. Like this. (*He does so to a finely dressed man.*)

Father: The actors you are about to see, my son, are among the best in—

Pickpocket (*producing one*): A handkerchief!

Father: And the greatest of all today is that actor everyone is waiting for, Montfleury.

- marquis (MAR kwis) kind of nobleman
- page (PAYJ) young male servant

A Man (*overhearing*): Yes, Montfleury! (*He shouts.*) Montfleury! Let's start the show! Montfleury!

Somebody (*shouting from the balcony*): Make haste! Light the chandeliers!

The Audience: Let's go! It's time. Why wait? (*Etc.*)

Counter Girl (*coming out from behind the refreshment stand with a tray, as if to quiet the crowd*): Oranges? . . . Milk? . . . Chocolate?

Audience (*greeting the arrival of the candle lighter as she starts work*): Ah! Ah!

A Second Marquis (*entering*): You see? They waited my arrival. (*He comes in with* Christian De Neuvillette, *a handsome young man in elegant but somewhat dated clothes.*)

First Marquis (*coming up to them*): My pleasure?

Second Marquis (*introducing them*): Marquis De Cuigy . . . Baron De Neuvillette.

First Marquis: Monsieur has lately arrived in Paris?

Christian: Yes, I have been here not over 20 days. I enter the King's Guards tomorrow. (*He walks off a few steps, looking up at the boxes.*)

First Marquis (*to the other*): A handsome one, that man. Charming.

Second Marquis: Pooh!

First Marquis (*looking toward boxes*): Ah, here come the precious ones!

Second Marquis: The beauties of the beautiful ones in Paris . . . in all of France . . . in the world! (*They watch as the young women of noble rank file into their boxes above.*)

First Marquis: There's Mademoiselle de Bois-Douphin.

Second Marquis: Whom . . . time was! . . . we loved!

First Marquis: Ah, I love their very names! (*He starts to name them all.*) Porchères . . . Cassendance . . . Félixerie—

Second Marquis: Yes! She who still plays kindly with our hearts!

First Marquis (*continuing*): Bourdon . . . Arbault—

Christian (*overhearing*): You know them all! You know their names?

First Marquis (*boasting*): *All* of them, my friend.

Christian: Then . . . you will be able to tell me for whom it is I am dying of love! She's always there, but not today. On the end, the empty box!

Counter Girl: Raspberries? . . . Lemonade? . . . Sweets?

Audience: Ah, Ragueneau! (*A merry-faced, plump man enters.*)

First Marquis (*to* Christian): That's Ragueneau, who keeps the great pastry shop.

Ragueneau (*coming forward toward the* First Marquis): Tell me, have you seen Monsieur de Bergerac?

First Marquis (*presenting him to* Christian): Here is Ragueneau, the pastry cook of poets and players.

Ragueneau (*embarrassed*): You do me too much honor.

First Marquis: In his shop, poems and pastries go together. He is expert at both, and his poems are as good as his pastries.

Ragueneau (*looking around*): Monsieur Cyrano is not here. I wonder at it.

- **monsieur** (muh SYUH) French title for a man, like *Mr.* or *Sir*
- **mademoiselle** (mad mwah ZEL) French title for *Miss*, or unmarried woman

Second Marquis: And why?

Ragueneau: Montfleury is to play today.

Second Marquis: So he is, indeed. That ton of man is soon to walk on-stage to start the play. But what is that to Cyrano?

Ragueneau: Have you not heard? Monsieur de Bergerac has forbidden Montfleury, whom he now hates, to appear for one month upon the stage.

First Marquis: But Montfleury is announced . . . to play the part today.

Second Marquis: He cannot be prevented.

Ragueneau: He cannot? Well, that is what I am here to see.

Christian (*stepping toward the others*): Cyrano? Who is this Cyrano de Bergerac?

First Marquis: "Who is this Cyrano de Bergerac?" (*He laughs.*) Well . . . well . . . for one thing, he is a soldier in the Guards. (*He points at another Guard, who has just come in and is walking about as if in search of someone.*) But there is Le Bret, his friend! Le Bret can tell you. (*He calls.*) Le Bret!

— **Le Bret** (*coming up*): Yes, Monsieur.

First Marquis: You are looking for Cyrano?

— **Le Bret:** Yes. I am uneasy.

First Marquis: (*for* Christian's *benefit*): Is it not a fact that Cyrano is a most unusual man?

— **Le Bret** (*thoughtfully*): The most unusual being that walks beneath the moon.

Ragueneau: Poet!

Second Marquis: Swordsman!

First Marquis: Musician!

— **Le Bret:** Soldier! A fellow member of the Guards!

Christian (*somewhat confused*): Yes . . . yes, I see.

Ragueneau: And such an unusual appearance he presents to the world!

— **Le Bret:** Yes, always. Ever the fighter, eager for action. The swaggering hero, his cloak behind him over his long sword. Hat with three white plumes, waving defiance to all. And to complete the picture, there, there forever, is the nose. No one can look at that nose without crying, "Oh, no, impossible! The man exaggerates!" After that, one smiles and says, "By and by, he will take if off." But Monsieur de Bergerac, he never takes it off at all.

Ragueneau (*seriously*): He wears it always, and he cuts down the man who dares to smile.

— **Le Bret:** His sword is half the shears of Fate.

First Marquis (*shrugging his shoulders*): He will not come.

Ragueneau: He will come!

Christian (*looking toward boxes*): There she is! The very one!
(*The dazzling* Roxane *has appeared in her box. She takes a seat in the front, her* Duenna *at the back. All look at her.*)

First Marquis: So fresh! The bloom of the peach!

Second Marquis: The blush of the strawberry!

- **plume** (PLOOM) very large feather
- **defiance** (di FY uns) disrespect; challenge to another person's authority
- **duenna** (doo EN uh) older woman who escorts or chaperones a young lady

Ragueneau (*to* Christian): Is she not everything a man could—

Christian: Yes! Tell me at once—her name!

Ragueneau: Magdeleine Robin, but called Roxane.

Christian (*still gazing at her*): Roxane! . . . Roxane!

Ragueneau: And unmarried, too. An orphan now, but money enough. A cousin of Cyrano's, the one we were just talking about.
(*A richly dressed nobleman, wearing a blue ribbon with medals across his chest, enters the box and smiles at* Roxane. *He stands while talking to her. The* First Marquis, Second Marquis, *and* Le Bret *wander off.*)

Christian: That man?

Ragueneau: That's the Count De Guiche. In love with her, but married himself. Wishes to arrange a marriage between Roxane and a certain sorry friend of his, a count also, Monsieur Valvert. Valvert is, well, glad to be of use—but she will have none of it. Nevertheless, De Guiche is a powerful lord who will stop at nothing. He'll find a way. . . . Hey, where are you going?

Christian (*his hand on his sword*): To find this Monsieur Valvert.

Ragueneau: No, stay! You are the one who will get killed. (*He indicates* Roxane, *above.*) Say, someone is looking at you.

Christian (*looking up*): You are right! (Christian *stands in a daze, lost in his admiration of* Roxane. De Guiche *has left the box.* Ragueneau *smiles and walks away. The* Pick-pocket, *noticing* Christian's *condition, draws near behind him. Throughout the following,* Christian *and* Roxane *remain lost in each other's eyes.*)

Le Bret (*approaching* Ragueneau): I have made a tour of the house. Cyrano is not here, thank God.

Ragueneau: That's good. We want no trouble.

Audience: Begin! Begin!

De Guiche (*entering below, followed by a group of flatterers*): Come, my lords, let us sit in our seats upon the stage.

First Marquis (*to* De Guiche): These ribbons you're wearing, Count De Guiche. Are they new? What color do you call them?

De Guiche (*proudly*): I call that shade Dying Spaniard. (*He laughs at his own joke.*) I think that I have found the right name.

Second Marquis: The right name, indeed! For soon, thanks to your troops, the Spaniard will be dying daily.*

De Guiche: Sit with us, my friends. (*The group approaches the stage, where special seats are reserved for powerful nobles.* De Guiche *turns and calls.*) Come, Valvert!

Christian (*hearing the name*): Valvert! Ah, that's the man. Now, in his face I will fling my glove! (*He puts his hand to his pocket, but finds the* Pickpocket's *hand already there.*)

Pickpocket: Oh!

Christian (*holding the other's wrist tightly*): Who are you? I was looking for a glove.

Pickpocket: And you found a hand! (*He*

---

*At the time, the Spanish were fighting the French in what is now the north of France.

shifts to a different and lower tone.) Let me go . . . and I will tell you a secret.

Christian (*still holding him*): Well? Let me hear it.

Pickpocket: This Cyrano de Bergerac? The man they were just talking of?

Christian: Yes.

Pickpocket: He has not long to live. A poem he made up annoyed a certain noble lord. So now a hundred rogues—and I am one of them—will attack this Cyrano de Bergerac tonight.

Christian: Where?

Pickpocket: At the Nesle Gate, on his way home. You can inform him?

Christian (*letting him go*): I've heard he is not here.

Audience: Begin! Begin!

A Man: My wig! (*He shakes his fist as his wig goes sailing off at the end of a string from the balcony above.*)

Others: He is bald. Well done, pages! Ha, ha, ha!

Man (*furious*): Child of the devil!
(*The audience quiets down as the curtains finally open. The noblemen are seated at the sides, their feet crossed, looking casual. Four small groups of candles light the simple stage, and a violin plays softly.*)

Ragueneau (*to* Le Bret, *nearby*): Montfleury is the first to appear?

Le Bret: So I have heard.

Ragueneau: And Cyrano is still not here.

Le Bret: Let us be thankful.
(*A bagpipe is heard, and Mont-fleury appears on the stage. He is*

an enormous man dressed in a ridiculous shepherd's costume with a flowered hat. The bagpipe looks small against his huge body.)

Audience: Montfleury!   Bravo! Montfleury!

Montfleury (*after bowing, proceeds with his lines*):
Happy the man who, freed from Fashion's cruel power
Can in some sweet woodland spot spend hour by hour,
And from the trees hear messages from winds—

A Voice (*shouting, from the back*): Rogue! Did I not forbid you for one month?

Audience: What? Who's that? What's the matter? (*Etc.*)

Le Bret: It is he!

Ragueneau: Cyrano!

Voice: King of the clowns! Ugly tub of butter! Leave the stage—at once!

Montfleury: But—

Voice: You stop to think about my order?

Audience: Hush! Be quiet, you! Proceed, Montfleury. Go on. (*Etc.*)

Montfleury (*unsteadily, starting over*):
Happy the man who, freed from Fashion's cruel p—

Voice: QUIET, I say! You loathsome bag of wind! Must my sword point pierce your hide and let the odor out?

Montfleury (*weakly*):
Happy the—

Voice: GO! GO NOW! (Cyrano *appears for the first time, leaping to the area in front of the stage, his mustache*

- **rogue** (ROHG) rascal; shifty person
- **bravo** (BRAH voh) wonderful!
- **loathsome** (LOHTH sum) disgusting

on end, the plumes in his hat quivering, his nose terrifying.) Ah! I shall lose my temper soon!

Montfleury *(to the nobles)*: Noble lords, I appeal to you!

Cyrano: Let every little lordling keep silence in his seat! *(He draws his sword.)*

Montfleury: Sir, you insult not only me. You insult these gentlemen. You insult the author of our play, Balthazar Baro.

Cyrano *(coldly polite)*: Monsieur, if Baro could be here to witness you, just as you stand there, a decorated barrel with legs trying to speak his lines . . . he would agree with me.

Montfleury: I—

Cyrano: You goose! Be off!

Montfleury: But can't—

Cyrano: You waddling goose! Hiss! Hiss!

A Man: This is terrible!

A Page: But what fun!

Cyrano *(stepping forward)*: Hiss! Hiss!

Audience: Hiss! Hiss! Bow-wow! Ba-a-a-a! Hee-haw!

Cyrano: I will—

A Page: Meeeow!

Cyrano: I order you all to hold your tongues! *(He waves his sword.)* I challenge you, one and all. I will take down your names, and give you turns. Come, who is to get the first number? You, Monsieur? You? You? Let all who wish to die hold up their hands. *(Silence.)* Not a hand? Very good. I will proceed. As I was saying, it is my wish to have the stage cured of this vile disease. *(He faces Montfleury.)* Three times will I clap my hands. And at the third, I'll turn you inside out! *(He claps.)* One!

Montfleury: Perhaps the better thing to do—

Cyrano *(clapping)*: Two!

Audience: He'll go! He'll stay. *(Etc.)*

Cyrano *(clapping)*: Three! *(Montfleury vanishes as if through a trapdoor.)*

Cyrano *(to all)*: Let him come back, if he dare.

(A sudden wave of applause comes from the boxes. Realizing that he has pleased the young ladies, Cyrano bows and sweeps his hat. The applause and cheers spread, along with a few boos and angry shouts.)

A Youth *(to Cyrano)*: But now that Montfleury has gone, Monsieur, you must tell us why. What grounds do you have for hating him?

Cyrano *(politely)*: What grounds? I have two, and each alone would be enough. First, he is a terrible actor, who bellows, and with grunts that would disgrace a hippopotamus, sends forth lines that should take off on wings. And second—but that is my secret.

A Man *(shouting)*: We want our money back! Where is the manager?

Audience: The manager! We want Bellerose! *(Etc.)*

Bellerose *(coming from behind the stage)*: Ladies and gentlemen, I beg of you. I have to pay the players, show or no show. Musicians, too. Guards. Doorkeepers. They have been hired, and they must be paid. Was it *their* fault that Monsieur here chose to stop the play? Was it—

Audience: Are we to pay for nothing? Our money! No play, no cash! *(Etc.)*

Cyrano *(loudly)*: Bellerose, what you have said is right. Far be it from

---

• vile (VYL) very bad

from me to hurt anyone but Montfleury. (*He reaches in his pocket for a leather bag.*) Here! Catch!

Bellerose (*catching bag and then weighing it in his hand*): Thank you, Monsieur. (*He smiles.*) For such a heavy price, you can come and stop the play on any day.... All right, everyone, you get your money back—but at the door. We have another play tonight, and the theater must be emptied soon.

(*The audience begins to leave, but few people actually go. Instead, they become interested in the scene that follows. The young ladies in the boxes, who were standing and putting on their wraps, stop to listen and soon are sitting back down.*)

Le Bret (*to* Cyrano): What you have done . . . is mad!

A Man (*coming up to* Cyrano): Montfleury! A famous tragic actor. And the Duke de Candale is his patron! . . . Have you a patron, you?

Cyrano: No.

Man: You have not?

Cyrano: No!

Man: What? You are not given money and protection by some great nobleman who wants his reputation—

Cyrano: No! I have told you three times now. Must I say the same thing again? No, I have no protector. (*He puts his hand on his sword.*) But this will do.

Man: Look here! You cannot threaten—

Cyrano: I can, yes.

Man: But—

Cyrano: And now, face about!

Man: But—

Cyrano: Face about, I say! . . . Or else, tell me why you stare at my nose.

Man (*confused*): I—

Cyrano (*advancing angrily*): In what way is it unusual?

Man (*backing*): Your worship is mistaken.

Cyrano: Is it flabby and long, like an elephant's?

Man: I never said—

Cyrano: Or hooked, like a hawk's beak?

Man: I—

Cyrano: You see a fly upon the tip?

Man: No, but—

Cyrano: Is it a freak of nature?

Man: But I had not given it so much as a glance.

Cyrano: And why, I pray, should you not look at it?

Man: I had—

Cyrano: Its color strikes you as unwholesome?

Man: Sir—

Cyrano: Its shape, unfortunate?

Man: But far from it!

Cyrano: Perhaps Monsieur would say it is a shade too large?

Man: Indeed not! No, I think it small. Small? I should have said tiny.

Cyrano (*threatening*): What? You dare charge me with such a defect! Small, my nose? Ha!

Man: Heavens!

Cyrano: Enormous, my nose! Magnificent, my nose! You snub-nosed, flathead, understand that I am proud, proud, proud of such a nose. Have you not heard? A great nose is a sign of a kindly, courteous man, such as I am. A nose is a measure of intelligence, of wit, of heavenly spark. And you dare to hand me the insult of a *tiny* nose! Just so you will remember. . . . (*He turns the man around, kicks him, and watches him run off.*)

Man: Help! The guards!
(*There is a long silence.*)

De Guiche (*standing with a group of nobles on the stage*): This Cyrano is becoming tiresome.

Valvert (*shrugging his shoulders*): It's all empty talk. Noise from a bragger, that's all.

De Guiche: Will no one challenge him?

Valvert: No one? (*He looks around.*) Wait! I'll have a shot at him. (*He approaches* Cyrano *with a show of silly courage.*) Your nose, Monsieur, your nose ... is ... err. . . . Your nose is . . . very large!

Cyrano (*seriously*): Very.

Valvert: Ha!

Cyrano (*politely*): Is that all?

Valvert: That's—

Cyrano: Ah, no, young man. You might have said—dear me, there are a thousand things. Have you no wit, Monsieur, no imagination? Keep changing the tone. For instance, start with yourself—AGGRESSIVE: "Monsieur, if I had such a nose, nothing would do but that I cut it off." FRIENDLY: "How do you ever drink with such a nose? You ought to have a special beaker made." DESCRIPTIVE: "It's a rock! . . . a hill! . . . a mountain! A mountain, did I say? It's a *peninsula*!" CURIOUS: "Ah, do you love the birds so much that when they come, you have a birdhouse ready?" BLUNT: "And when you smoke, my friend, don't all the neighbors say, 'That chimney is on fire!'?" TENDER: "Have a little sunshade made for it. It might get freckled or fade." CASUAL: "Say, tell me, is that sort of peg in style? Just right to hang your hat on!" POETIC: "When you blow your nose, how the hurricane roars, how the clouds darken!" DRAMATIC: "And when it bleeds—the Red Sea!" SIMPLE: "A monument! When is admission free?" BUSINESSLIKE: "What a sign for some perfume shop!" RESPECTFUL: "Sir, I recognize in you a man of prominence." COUNTRY: "Call that a nose? You don't kid me. It's a prize-size cucumber." MILITARY: "Direct it against the cavalry!"—That, Monsieur, is what you would have said to me, had you the smallest drop of wit or learning. But you lack wit, and as for learning, I doubt

---

- **defect** (DEE fekt) fault; weakness
- **beaker** (BEE kur) wide-mouthed cup or glass
- **prominence** (PROM uh nuns) importance; standing out so as to be noticed

that you could spell your name—
F-O-O-L.

De Guiche (*trying to lead the amazed* Valvert *away*): Come on. Let it be.

Valvert (*to* Cyrano, *drawing his sword*): A fool, am I? Then what are you, a donkey?

Cyrano (*drawing*): Hee-haw. (*They circle each other, swords drawn.*)

Valvert: A pig!

Cyrano (*making a face*): Oink, oink.

Valvert: A horse!

Cyrano: A horse, a horse! Of course, of course!

Valvert (*sneering*): And worst of all, a poet!

Cyrano: A poet, yes! But a poet *best* of all! So while we fence, I'll make you up a poem on the spot. And at the last line, I will hit you!

Valvert: Indeed you will not!

Cyrano (*proudly*): Poem about the famous duel in which Monsieur Cyrano de Bergerac fought with and killed a jabberface.

Valvert: And what does all that mean?

Cyrano: That is the title.

Audience: Make room! Form a circle! Down in front! (*Etc.*)

(*A ring of people rapidly forms around* Cyrano *and* Valvert. *On one side are* De Guiche *and his followers; on the other* Ragueneau, Le Bret, *and* Christian. *The common people crowd each other to get a better view. The women in the boxes are all standing.*)

Cyrano (*closing his eyes*): Wait! Let me think of my rhymes. . . . There! I have them. (*He opens his eyes, and the two men start to fence. Throughout the following, Cyrano suits his action to the word.*)

I face you, poet and fighter,
Armed with both steel and wit,
To make your body lighter,
And at the last line, I'll hit!

Ha! Ha! You missed me by a
mile!
Where would you best be slit?
At once I fight and speak and
smile,
And at the last line, I'll hit!

Monsieur, where would you best
be gored?
Tell me, and soon I'll quit.
Right here, where all that food is
stored?
For at the last line, I'll hit!

That's good!—but hardly good
enough.
I sidestep . . . wait a bit . . . .
Spin . . . and give you my best
stuff . . .
Now, at the last line—I hit!

(*Applause and cheers fill the hall as* Valvert *staggers and falls back into the arms of* De Guiche. *Flowers and handkerchiefs are thrown from the boxes.* De Guiche *and others help* Valvert *off the stage.* Le Bret *looks tearfully happy but also deeply troubled.*)

Bellerose (*rushing up to* Cyrano): I am the force of order here! My property! What have you done to this—

Cyrano: Now, now, it's nothing. A slight wound is all I tried for. A weak man faints when he is scratched.

Bellerose: Now, everyone, listen! The show is over. It's all over, I tell you. Please, please, will you now leave!

• gored (GOHRD) pierced, as with horns

(*During the following exchange, nearly everyone leaves but the* Counter Girl, *who stays to clean up her stand.*)

Le Bret (*approaching* Cyrano *with* Ragueneau *and* Christian): You fool! You went too far!

Christian (*overjoyed at* Valvert's *defeat, to* Cyrano): A marvelous performance, Monsieur! Marvelous! (*He throws his arms around* Cyrano.)

Cyrano (*pushing him off*): Who is this man?

Ragueneau: Christian De Neuvillette. Soon to join the Guards.

Cyrano (*smiling*): A comrade, then.

Christian: Monsieur, I must tell you. . . . I have certain information. . . . I—

Cyrano: Then tell me! Don't—

Christian: I have heard that many men, over a hundred armed rascals, are waiting to kill you on your way home.

Cyrano (*worried for the first time*): A hundred men?

Christian: A noble lord, they say, is angry about a poem you wrote.

Cyrano (*his old self again*): Oh, this begins to sound silly.

Le Bret: No, it does *not* sound silly!

Ragueneau (*to* Christian): Where are these men waiting?

Christian: At the Nesle Gate.

Ragueneau: Can this be true?

Le Bret (*quickly*): We have to know. Look, I'll stay here with our friend. Ragueneau and Christian, you two go to Nesle Gate. See what you can find. We'll be right here, or at the restaurant next door.

Ragueneau: Yes, a good idea. (*He and* Christian *leave.*)

Le Bret: My friend, you must take seriously the fact that—

Cyrano: —that I cannot eat with you.

Le Bret: And this, because . . . ?

Cyrano: Because . . . I have not a penny.

Le Bret: Not a penny! But we were paid just yesterday! (*He makes the motion of tossing a bag of coins.*) That bag of money you threw to—

Cyrano: My monthly pay. It lasted but a day.

Le Bret: Then, flinging that bag . . . was a child's gesture!

Cyrano: But *what* a gesture!

Counter Girl (*coughing behind the refreshment stand*): Hm! (Cyrano, *followed by* Le Bret, *approaches her as she comes out timidly.*) Monsieur, to know you have not eaten . . . makes my heart ache. Look at all I have here yet, unsold. Please, help yourself.

Cyrano (*taking off his hat*): Dear child, despite my pride, which forbids me to accept, I cannot hurt your loveliness. Therefore, I will accept. (*She offers him a bunch of grapes.*) No, a single one. My dessert. (*She gives him a macaroon; he hands half back.*) A half will do. My dinner. (*She starts pouring lemonade in a glass; he stops her.*) No, just the water there. And only half a glass. My drink.

Le Bret: Now who is sounding silly?

Counter Girl: Oh, please take something more!

Cyrano: Yes. Your hand to kiss. (*He kisses the hand she holds out to him, as if it belonged to a princess.*)

Counter Girl: Monsieur, I thank you. (*She smiles and leaves.*)

Cyrano (*arranging the grape, the half*

• **macaroon** (mak uh ROON) kind of rich cookie

macaroon, and the water on the counter): And now, my dinner. (*He eats the macaroon with a great show of enjoyment.*) To go on, you were saying?

Le Bret: You must take seriously the fact that you have many enemies.

Cyrano (*brightly*): With those I made tonight, how many in all?

Le Bret: Too many to count. De Guiche and all his people. And today you added Montfleury and his patron, the Duke de Candale. Also, there is—

Cyrano: No more! Those make me happy enough.

Le Bret (*growing more excited*): But why do you go on like this? For instance, what reason do you have for hating Montfleury?

Cyrano (*holding up the glass of water as if it were an expensive drink*): My drink. (*He drinks it.*) That Montfleury! I have hated him . . . since the night he was so daring as to feast his ugly frog's eyes on her . . . her who . . . . Oh, it was like watching a slug crawl over a flower!

Le Bret (*amazed*): What? Is it possible that—

Cyrano: —that I should love?

Le Bret: Who is it?

Cyrano: "Who is it?" Come, think a little. The dream of being loved myself, even by the beauty-less, is made an empty dream by this good nose of mine. So, whom should I love? Since I can never be loved back, in return, the answer should be clear. I love the most beautiful that breathes!

Le Bret: The most beautiful?

Cyrano: The most beauty . . . the most wit . . . the most . . . everything. I love my cousin, Magdeleine Robin.

Le Bret: Roxane!

Cyrano (*with both joy and sorrow*): Yes, Roxane.

Le Bret: But what could be better? You love her? Tell her so! You covered yourself with glory in her sight just this afternoon.

Cyrano (*popping the grape into his mouth in an effort to be cheerful*): My dessert. (*He grows serious.*) Look well at me. How much hope can I really have, with this great flab of flesh that precedes me by a quarter of an hour? You know . . . sometimes I see couples out walking together . . . holding hands . . . arms . . . . I begin to dream that I, too . . . . But then I see the shadow of my profile on a wall, and . . . .

Le Bret (*touched*): My friend . . . .

Cyrano: I have a bad half hour, sometimes, in feeling so unsightly . . . and alone.

Le Bret (*in quick sympathy*): You weep?

Cyrano: Weep! No, never! Can you imagine—tears trickling all the long way down this great nose of mine? No, tears are, in their way, both beautiful and holy. On my face they would look . . . ridiculous.

Le Bret: Is this Cyrano speaking? Does Cyrano give up? Love is a lottery, and you have to take your chances.

Cyrano (*shaking his head*): No . . . no.

Le Bret: But your courage . . . and your wit! Think of that little girl who just gave you your dinner here. Her eyes—you must have seen as much— did not exactly hate you.

• slug (SLUG) kind of slimy, wormlike creature, somewhat like a snail without a shell

Cyrano (*thoughtfully*): That is true.

Le Bret: You see? So, then! I tell you that Roxane herself, while watching your duel, went paler than—

Cyrano: Pale?

Le Bret: Yes, lily-pale. Her lips parted, and her hand went .... (*He gestures.*) I saw it! Speak to her. That's all you have to do, to make her—

Cyrano: —laugh in my face? No, not that. If there is anything I fear, it is that. (*He looks off to the right.*) What! Ragueneau!

Ragueneau (*entering with a group of Guards and other friends of Cyrano*): It's true, what Christian said. A hundred men are waiting.

Cyrano: You saw them?

Ragueneau: No, but Paris talks of little else. Christian went on ahead to .... (*He hears someone entering and turns his head.*)

Cyrano: My God! Her duenna!

Doorkeeper (*entering with the* Duenna): Monsieur, a message for you.

Duenna (*very politely*): Someone wishes to know when she may see her courageous cousin—in private.

Cyrano: See me?

Duenna (*with a bow*): See you. There are things for your ear.

Cyrano: There are ...?

Duenna (*with another bow*): Things.

Cyrano (*staggering*): Yes .... Ah ... er ....

Duenna: This someone, at the first blush of dawn tomorrow, will be having mass at Saint Roch.

Cyrano (*holding onto Le Bret for support*): Oh, my God!

Duenna: When mass is over, where might she meet you?

Cyrano (*losing his senses*): Where? ... I .... But ....

Duenna: Well, where?

Cyrano: I am thinking. . . .

Duenna: Where?

Cyrano: At ... at ... it's close ... at Ragueneau's, the pastry shop.

Duenna: We will be there. Do not fail. At seven.

Cyrano: I will be there. (*He watches the* Duenna *exit and then holds onto* Le Bret.) To me! From her! A meeting!

Le Bret: Well, so all your gloom is gone?

Cyrano: She knows that I exist!

Le Bret: And now will you be calm?

Cyrano (*excited*): Be calm? Who can be calm at such a time as this? This *news*! And now I have a hundred men to fight! That's not one too many for my mood!

Bellerose (*entering from behind the stage with a group of young actresses*): I must insist! You all be quiet and leave.

Cyrano (*shouting*): I have 10 hearts and 20 arms! Give me an army to defeat! (*He starts moving toward the exit.*)

An Actress: Now, that was well said!

Bellerose (*to* Cyrano): Please! Will you be gone?

Another Actress (*leaving the stage*): Oh, who can stay here? I'm going, too.

Other Actresses: That's right! Me, too. I'll come. (*Etc.*)

Bellerose: But the rehearsal! (*He watches helplessly as his actresses join the* Guards *and others to form a band behind* Cyrano.)

All: Let us go! Onward! To the Nesle Gate! (*Etc.*)

Cyrano (*drawing his sword for a final speech*): A hundred men against me! Tonight, a hundred are too few, too few to ruffle even one of these white plumes. And you, gentlemen, when I start to attack, whatever you suppose to be my danger, I want no help. Now to the Nesle Gate! So far in life, I have fought with none but little men—BRING ON THE GI-ANTS!

(*The others cheer as they follow* Cyrano *out.*)

CHECKPOINT

Answer the following questions before going on with the play. If you have trouble with any of the answers, go back and review the first act before you continue reading.

1. Although she has not yet been given a line to speak, Roxane can already be seen as a kind of central character, a person around whom other characters revolve. What is the relationship between Roxane and (a) De Guiche, (b) Christian, and (c) Cyrano?

2. Cyrano's long speech to Valvert about his nose (pages 290–291) is one of the most famous in dramatic literature. Go back and reread it now. Why do you think it has always appealed to audiences and readers?

3. Cyrano's white plumes, first mentioned on page 285, are clearly to be seen as *symbols* (see page 177). Of what?

4. The introduction states that *Cyrano de Bergerac* is a "tragicomedy." (a) What in the first act most struck you as tragic or sad? (b) What most struck you as comic or funny? (c) What seemed to be both tragic and comic *at the same time*? Explain.

5. Two so-called rules of writing plays are these: (1) Nothing truly important to the plot should occur during the first few pages (or minutes). (2) The main characters should be kept off the stage until the play is well underway (the "delayed entrance"). (a) Does *Cyrano de Bergerac* follow each of these rules? (b) What might be the reason for each of the rules?

6. As Act I ends two important events are about to take place. What are these events, and what do you predict might happen in each case?

ACT II
The Pastry Shop of Poets

SETTING: *A room in the pastry shop of* Ragueneau, *early the next morning. On the right, a window and a double door face the street. At the rear and to the left, two doors lead to other parts of the bakery. At the right rear is a half-filled counter at which products are sold, and here and there are tables and chairs for customers.*

AT RISE: *It is the early beginning of a workday. Outside, in the gray dawn, people are passing on their way to work.* Ragueneau, *now dressed in a white apron and in a chef's hat, is seated at a table. He is writing and counting on his fingers.*

Ragueneau (*reading his poem and counting the rhythm on his fingers*): "Spread thy wings, and fly far away. Fly newly born, into a new day." (*He frowns.*) Something is wrong.

A Baker (*entering with a tray of hot pastries*): I hope these are better.

Ragueneau (*examining one*): To perfection.

A Young Baker (*entering as the other leaves*): Master, in your honor, see what I have baked. I hope you are pleased. (*He lifts a large napkin off a platter.*)

Ragueneau (*more than pleased*): A harp!

Young Baker: Of pie crust.

Ragueneau: With candied fruit!

Young Baker: And the strings, see —of spun sugar!

Ragueneau (*giving him money*): For true creation, genius must be paid. Yes, for both pastry cooks and poets . . . . (*He sees* Lise *entering.*) Hush! My wife! Move on, and hide that money.

Lise (*approaching with an untidy stack of papers*): What is it this time?

Ragueneau: A harp. Fine, is it not?

Lise: Ridiculous!

Ragueneau: What have you there?

Lise (*showing him a paper*): We have no wrapping paper, so I brought these.

Ragueneau (*standing*): Heavens! The poems of my friends! To wrap up pastries in?

Lise: I can think of no better use for the poems of your friends.

Ragueneau (*reading*): "Phyllis, thy soft beauty is the strength of all my—"

Lise: Nonsense!

Ragueneau: Now, put all these poems over there. My poet friends will be here soon. (*He sees* Cyrano *entering from the street.*) Bravo! Bravo! I, too, was witness to the fight last—

Cyrano (*ignoring him*): What time is it?

Ragueneau: Just ten of seven. Eight ugly rogues, they say, laid open by your sword, still—

Cyrano: Talk not of that! I am expecting someone. You are to leave us alone in here.

Ragueneau: But how can I do that? My poets will be arriving.

Lise: For *breakfast*?

Cyrano: When I signal to you, you will clear the place of them. What time is it?

Ragueneau: Nine minutes to seven.

Cyrano (*seating himself nervously at* Ragueneau's *table and helping himself to paper and pen*): Remember, at my signal—out!

(*Five* Poets *enter, sorry-looking men dressed in black and splattered with mud. They exchange friendly greetings with* Ragueneau. *During the following scene they go to the counter and help themselves, then sit down at the tables.*)

First Poet: A single man, I heard, put the whole gang to flight!

Cyrano (*thinking, to himself*): Write to her . . . fold the letter . . . hand it to her . . . and make my escape. (*He throws down the pen.*) Coward! May I die on the spot if I lack the courage to speak to her! Still, why not? (*He picks the pen up.*) Let me write it, then—the love letter I have written in thought so many times. I have only to lay my soul beside the paper—and copy! (*He writes.*)

Second Poet: Oh, it was a rare sight! The ground was littered with knives and sticks and hats.

Third Poet: He must have been a madman—a giant!

Cyrano (*reading*): "I love you . . . ." (*He goes on writing furiously.*)

Fourth Poet: Who was the man? Do you know, Ragueneau?

Ragueneau (*glancing at* Cyrano): That

question is not for me to answer.

Cyrano (*reading*): "Your eyes . . . ."

Fifth Poet: They say he laughed with mad joy as he chased the ones still left all the way to Goldsmith Square.

First Poet: What have you lately written, Ragueneau?

Ragueneau: A recipe, in rhyme.

Cyrano (*reading*): "Your lips . . . ."

Second Poet (*at the counter, taking a bite out of the harp*): For once the harp will have filled me with pleasure.

Third Poet (*tasting a cream puff*): Ragueneau, all your recipes seem to rise on wings.

Cyrano (*as before*): ". . . who loves you devotedly." There! No need to sign it. I deliver it in person.

Lise (*approaching* Cyrano): Oh! What is the matter with your hand?

Cyrano: Nothing. Call it a scratch.

Lise: All right, but a scratch that needs a doctor.

Cyrano: It's nothing.

Lise (*shaking a finger at him*): I think your "nothing" is a lie.

Cyrano: From the swelling of my nose? The lie in that case must be a good-sized . . . . (*He stands as* Roxane, *her face veiled, comes in, followed by her* Duenna. *He signals to* Ragueneau). Psst!

Ragueneau (*to the* Poets, *urging them to the door on the left*): We will be much more comfortable in there. I have a spice cake that needs your special tasting. (*They leave.*)

Cyrano (*to the* Duenna): Madam, a word with you.

Duenna: A dozen, if you please. We have heard how, last night at the Nesle Gate, you took on all the—

Cyrano: No, no talk of that! (*He glances at* Roxane.) From anyone! Today we turn to matters of impor-

tance. Tell me, do you . . . like sweets?

Duenna: To the point of indigestion.

Cyrano: Good. (*He goes to the counter.*) Here are some almond drops. (*Looking for wrapping paper, he sees the pile of poems.*) I wrap them in a poem called "Heaven's Answer." And here, fruit cake. And here, cream puffs! (*He wraps everything up for the* Duenna *and guides her toward the door.*) Now, do me the favor of eating these out on the street.

Duenna: But—

Cyrano: And do not come back till you have finished. (*He pushes her out. For a long minute* Cyrano *and* Roxane *stand looking at each other. She finally removes her veil.*

Roxanne (*smiling*): Hello.

Cyrano (*the words pour out of him*): You are so beautiful! You were good to come . . . to remember that so lowly a being still draws breath . . . to tell me?

Roxane: First of all, to thank you for teaching some manners with your sword in the theater yesterday. Your pupil was a man that some great lord, who thinks he is in love with me—

Cyrano: De Guiche?

Roxane (*dropping her eyes*): —has tried to force upon me as a husband.

Cyrano (*bowing*): Then, in truth, I fought not for my nose, as I had thought, but for your beauty.

Roxane (*smiling*): Thank you. We should have talked before this. . . . Before I make the confession I want you to hear. . . . Do you remember how we used to play as children, by the lake?

Cyrano: Yes, you came every summer to the country.

Roxane (*remembering*): We were like

brother and sister then. . . . You were older, but you let me have my way. (*Her eyes light up at a sudden memory.*) Remember the time you came running to me, your hand bleeding from a fall? I pretended to scold you: "You bad, bad boy! Will you never keep out of trouble?" (*She stops, amazed.*) Oh, this is too much! You have done it again! (*She takes his injured hand, which he tries to draw back.*) We must wash this naughty blood away.

Cyrano: Really, it is nothing. (*He lets* Roxane *lead him to the counter. She dips a handkerchief from her purse in a glass of water and cleans his wound. Then they sit down, still holding hands. A silent moment passes.*) Can you tell me, now, what you called your confession?

Roxane: I think so. . . . There is someone that I love. . . . But as yet . . . he does not know it.

Cyrano: Ah!

Roxane: A certain someone who until now has loved me timidly, and from a distance.

Cyrano: Ah!

Roxane: No, let me have your hand still. It is hot, and this will cool it. . . . But I have read his heart in his face.

Cyrano (*growing very hopeful*): Ah! (*They keep their eyes on each other.*) Then you two . . . have not spoken?

Roxane: Only with our eyes.

Cyrano: But then . . . how can you know?

Roxane (*laughing*): Now I say, "Ah!" Love knows, that's all. It's an odd thing. He, like you, is in the Guards.

Cyrano: Ah!

Roxane: In your same company! Is that not strange?

Cyrano (*beside himself with joy*): Ah!

Roxane (*also joyful*): He is proud, brave, courteous, handsome.

Cyrano (*drawing back a little*): Did you say handsome?

Roxane: Why, what's the matter?

Cyrano: Nothing.

Roxane: In short, I love him.

Cyrano: In the Guards, did you say?

Roxane: In the Guards, and in your very company.

Cyrano (*hoping for the best*): His name?

Roxane: Baron Christian De Neuvillette.

Cyrano (*dropping his eyes*): How quickly, quickly, everything . . . . (*He looks up.*) My poor little girl.

Duenna (*opening the door*): Monsieur de Bergerac, I have eaten them, every one.

Cyrano: Then go back out and read the poems on the wrappings!

Roxane (*as the* Duenna *leaves*): Of

course, I thought, when I learned that he had joined your company, that I could ask . . . .

Cyrano: Very well, I will protect your little baron. I will make sure that no harm comes to him.

Roxane (*putting both of her hands on his*): For me, you will?

Cyrano: Yes, yes.

Roxane: You will be his friend? You will protect him? And he will never have to fight in a duel?

Cyrano: I swear it.

Roxane: Oh, Cyrano, I love you.

Cyrano (*near the point of tears*): Yes, yes.

Roxane: You'll tell him all that I have said? And have him write to me? (*Cyrano looks down once more.*) No, look at me again, and give me your other hand. (*He does so.*) You'll have him write to me? . . . Today? (*The street door bursts open and Christian enters. Beside him is Carbon, the captain of the company. They are followed by a dozen excited Guards who shout greetings to Cyrano. Ragueneau and the Poets, hearing the noise, enter from the other room. Cyrano and Roxane drop each other's hands and stand up.*)

Guards: Bravo! We have found him! The hero of the Nesle Gate. (*Etc.*)

Roxane (*near the door, to Cyrano*): Remember this: I love you. (*She kisses her hand to him, bids him farewell, and leaves.*)

Carbon (*to Cyrano*): My troop has gone mad as March, looking for you.

Cyrano: And who told them where I was?

Le Bret (*entering*): I did! All our comrades desire to share your triumph! (*He crosses to Cyrano and whispers.*) How did it go?

Cyrano: Be quiet!

Guards: Bravo! Tell us your story! We want to hear it! How did you do it?

Cyrano (*standing up, as if trying his legs, and realizing that he is forced to play the part he has always played*): My adventure? (*He leaps onto a table, draws his sword, and starts his story. The Guards, Bakers, Poets, and others crowd around to listen.*) Well, then . . . I was marching to meet them. The moon, at first as bright as a silver watch, went down. It was the darkest night. You could see no farther than—

Christian (*who has been standing alone in one corner, frozen with anger at his rival in love*): —no farther than your nose!

Cyrano (*starts to leap down, but then sees who it is and controls himself*): Very well, as I was saying, it was darker than dark. Yet courage was ever by me. I had gotten into this by poking my—

Christian (*louder*): —nose!

Cyrano (*stopping short to keep himself from attacking Christian, then going on*): —into the sad affairs of some great noble. I marched forward, scarcely knowing where my attackers were. Then, suddenly, I found myself—

Christian (*shouting*): —nose to nose!

Cyrano (*pale with anger now, in a stiff voice*): —with my foe. The moon came out; it was dark no longer. I leapt forward, head lowered, sword slicing the air, and—

Christian: —nose to the wind!

Cyrano (*springing toward Christian, acting out his repeated words*): I leapt forward, head lowered, sword slicing the air! (*He stops suddenly.*) Go! All of you! Let me at this man— alone!

(*Everyone runs for a door as* Cyrano *and* Christian *circle each other with drawn swords. When the room is empty and the doors shut,* Cyrano *forces* Christian *near the large double door, the only place in the room that cannot be seen from the street. Suddenly* Cyrano *takes a half-step backward, lets his sword clatter to the floor, and spreads his arms.*)

Cyrano: Embrace me!

Christian: What? . . . Monsieur!

Cyrano: Brave fellow.

Christian: But what does this—?

Cyrano: Embrace me. I am her brother.

Christian: Whose?

Cyrano: Hers! Roxane's!

Christian (*dropping his sword*): Heavens! You—her brother?

Cyrano: Or the same thing, her first cousin.

Christian: Does she love me?

Cyrano: Perhaps.

Christian (*on one knee*): Forgive me! If you but knew, Monsieur, how greatly I admire you!

Cyrano: But all those noses that you—

Christian: I take them back!

Cyrano: Roxane expects a letter from you . . . tonight.

Christian: A letter? Oh, no!

Cyrano: What is the matter?

Christian: Oh, I could kill myself for shame. When it comes to women, I find words . . . hard. I never know what to say. I do not know how to talk of love.

Cyrano: Alas! If I but had your nose, and you mine, I would not find words a problem.

Christian: But what can I do now? Anything I do . . . will only disillusion her.

Cyrano (*as if to himself but looking directly at Christian*): If I had to express my soul, an interpreter like this one . . . .

Christian (*desperately*): I ought to have eloquence!

Cyrano (*eagerly*): Eloquence I can lend you!

Christian: What? . . . What do you mean?

Cyrano: Just what I say: Eloquence I can lend you. So, eloquence I *will* lend you! . . . And you, to me, will lend the charm of your good looks.

Christian: But . . . I don't understand.

Cyrano: Between us, we will make a hero of romance!

Christian: You are suggesting . . . ?

Cyrano: Surely you can say to her, as your own words, things that I will teach you day by day.

Christian: But Cyrano . . . !

Cyrano: Roxane must not be disillusioned!

Christian: You frighten me! . . . Your eyes shine!

Cyrano: Will you do it?

Christian: But why would it please you?

Cyrano (*realizing what Christian may be thinking*): Well, not *please* me, exactly. But it would *amuse* me. I am a poet. And this is an experiment just made to tempt a poet. We

---

- disillusion (dis i LOO zhun) disappoint by taking away an illusion, or favorable mental picture
- **interpreter** (in TUR pruh tur) someone who explains or translates
- **eloquence** (EL uh kwens) fine speaking; the art of using language well

will walk side by side, you in the full light, I in your shadow. I will be wit to you, and you, to me, good looks.

Christian: I see.... Without your plan, there is no hope.... But the letter, which must be sent today!

Cyrano (*taking from his pocket the letter written early in the act*): Here it is. It needs only the address.

Christian (*puzzled*): You had the letter with you?

Cyrano: We poets do these silly things.... Write letters to the women of our dreams. Carry them around with us. You will like this letter. I was as eloquent as if I had been sincere.

Christian: But written to a dream, will it fit Roxane?

Cyrano: Like a glove!

Christian (*suddenly free of all doubt, throwing himself in Cyrano's arms*): Ah! My friend!

ACT III
Roxane's Kiss

SETTING: *Outside Roxane's house, about two weeks later. On the right is a high garden wall, above which are spreading treetops. Attached to the wall is the narrow house itself, in the center of the stage. On the first floor is a door with a bench beside it, but no windows. Over the door is a wide balcony, or deck, reached from the inside by a French door (a window that opens like a double door). Covering part of the wall and balcony rail is a heavy vine, so that the balcony can be reached from the ground by jumping onto the bench and then climbing the vine. On the extreme left is a narrow street.*

AT RISE: *The door opens and* De Guiche *steps out of the house, followed by* Roxane. *He is dressed in a military uniform with many medals. It is nearly dark.*

De Guiche: I can only tell you again: I love you with a love that will not be—

Roxane: But you must go!

De Guiche: Does this love mean all to me, and nothing to you?

Roxane (*firmly*): Hush! My duenna has heard too much already. Please, no more talk of love tonight. If you go now, I will agree to see you tomorrow.

De Guiche: Then I must tell you.

Roxane: What?

De Guiche: There will be no tomorrow.

Roxane: You are going away?

De Guiche: To war.

Roxane: Ah!

De Guiche: I have my orders. Arras* is

---
* Arras (ah RAHS) a city in northern France. At the time of the play (1640), it was occupied by Spanish troops.

under siege. We march later to-night. . . . You know that I have been made Supreme Commander?

Roxane (*uninterested*): I congratulate you.

De Guiche: Of the Guards.

Roxane (*suddenly curious*): Ah! . . . Of the Guards?

De Guiche: Among whom is your cousin Cyrano de Bergerac. Now I shall have the chance to give that rascal what he deserves!

Roxane: So, you are thinking of revenge upon my cousin?

De Guiche: The man has insulted me for the last time, I assure you.

Roxane: Do you see much of him?

De Guiche: Not much. He is just one man in one of the companies I command. Lately, I have often seen him with a recruit, a man named Christian something.

Roxane (*looking down*): I wonder . . . . Is there no way?

De Guiche: Way? What kind of way?

Roxane (*still looking down*): To spare my cousin's life.

De Guiche (*after a pause*): There may be.

Roxane (*forcing a smile*): You can?

De Guiche (*coming nearer*): You smile! Then you do love me . . . a little. (*He takes several folded papers from an inside pocket.*) I have here the marching orders for every company under me . . . except, this one! (*He takes one from the others.*) The company of Captain Carbon, in which your cousin serves. This, I will keep! (*He puts it in another pocket.*)

Roxane (*overcome with relief*): You will do this, for me?

De Guiche (*very near her*): For you, yes! Roxane, I love you madly. Listen. It is true that I must go now, but I can come back . . . soon. Listen! This very evening, not more than—

Roxane: But don't you have to march . . . tonight?

De Guiche: Bah! The siege can wait a day. You say yes?

Roxane: No!

De Guiche: Then you say no. . . .

Roxane: No. . . . I just mean . . . I don't say yes.

De Guiche: But you don't say no, either!

Roxane (*in tears*): Yes . . . no . . . who can say?

De Guiche (*seizing her hand*): Who can say? I can say! I can make up your mind for you! Look at me. (*She does.*) You have my word: The company of Captain Carbon will not march tonight. (*He kisses her hand.*) Are you satisfied with that?

Roxane (*smiling in confused relief*): My friend, I am. (*She breaks from him suddenly and dashes into the house, slamming the door.*)

De Guiche (*calling loudly*): I will send word to you later! (*He starts to leave, but then, overcome with emotion, sits down on the bench.*)

Cyrano (*entering from the street, left*): Monsieur! (*He removes his hat and bows in the grand manner.*) The Supreme Commander.

De Guiche (*standing up, icily*): Monsieur de Bergerac.

Cyrano: Is it true, Sir, that we are soon to march on Arras? I have heard rumors.

De Guiche: Don't ask me that. You

- **siege** (SEEJ) continued and often long attack
- **recruit** (ri KROOT) new soldier

know the rules of war.

Cyrano: Plans are not announced beforehand. That is war.

De Guiche (*more pleasantly*): I have been thinking, Monsieur, about another kind of war . . . the war between you and me. We both hold your cousin, the fair Roxane, in high regard. For her sake, therefore, we should consider a truce.

Cyrano: But on whose terms?

De Guiche: On both our terms, Monsieur. It is well known that you have little money. On the other hand, I have a lot. Your poetry is every day more popular in Paris. I hear you even have a play ready for the stage. I must confess that I admire your writing highly.

Cyrano: Why, you cannot mean to—

De Guiche: Just let me finish! Yes, it would be an honor to be the patron of Cyrano de Bergerac. Of course, some of your writing would have to be at my direction, for my purposes. But I assure you, Monsieur, that I am willing to pay handsomely for—

Cyrano (*insulted*): Why, who can pay me as I pay myself? By saying the best of my poems over and over! Sir, my blood runs cold at the thought of writing a single word, or even a comma, to please the Count De Guiche! No, I thank you. Every day to pat the goat of your own pride? No, I thank you. Eat every day a toad? No, I thank you. (*As Cyrano gets more and more excited, De Guiche shakes his head and starts off backward down the street. He has almost disappeared by the time Cyrano has finished.*) Push myself from lap to lap because a little great man tells me to? No, I thank you. No, I thank you. No, I thank you. . . . I want to sing, to dream, to laugh, to loaf, to be free! Be free to, if I want, journey to the moon! . . . (*He speaks more quietly.*) My friend, the moon. I think that there I could live happily.

Duenna (*opening the door*): What is all this? . . . Oh, it's you.

Cyrano: Cyrano de Bergerac, loudly rejecting money that has passed through ugly hands.

Roxane (*coming out*): Cousin!

Cyrano: Yes, cousin still—not a trained monkey.

Roxane: Why did you come?

Cyrano: As usual, to find how your romance goes on.

Roxane (*beaming*): How wonderful he is! What wit he has! How I love him!

Cyrano: Can you not find a single fault?

Roxane: Not a single fault! . . . Oh, sometimes he gets absentminded. He seems to search for words . . . and when he finds them, common words, indeed. But then, suddenly, he says the most enchanting things. His clever wit returns again.

Cyrano: And he still writes to you?

Roxane: Every day! Listen to this. (*She recites a sentence from memory.*) "The more of my heart you steal from me, the more heart I have."

Cyrano: Pooh!

Roxane: Or this. (*She gestures to the Duenna to leave and lowers her voice.*) "If kisses could be sent in writing, Love, you should read this letter with your lips."

Cyrano: Well, he tries.

Roxane: You know what, cousin? You are eaten up with jealousy! My Christian has more wit than even you.

Cyrano (*secretly delighted*): You seem to know his letters by heart.

Roxane: Yes . . . by heart. In the art of expressing love, he is a master.

Cyrano: A master?

Roxane: A master!

Cyrano: As you please, then . . . a master.

Roxane (*seeing* Christian *coming on the street*): Oh, there he is! I must get ready. (*She goes inside.*)

Christian (*coming up*): What! Cyrano, you here?

Cyrano: Where have you been all day?

Christian (*shrugging*): Here and there.

Cyrano: I came here to find you, since I knew this was one spot you would surely cross. But we cannot lose more time. Prepare your memory.

Christian: No.

Cyrano: What?

Christian: Cyrano, I am tired of borrowing my words, my sentences . . . of playing a part. It was fine at first, but now I feel that she loves me for . . . myself. I thank you, but from now on I will speak my own words.

Cyrano: Are you sure of this?

Christian: Yes, I am sure. . . . Oh, I hear her coming down the stairs. Quick, around the corner—and listen. (Cyrano *goes around the side of the house.*)

Roxane (*coming out*): You are here! . . . The night is closing around us. . . . The air is mild. . . . All is quiet in the streets. . . . Let us sit here. (*They sit on the bench.*) Talk . . . and I will listen.

Christian: Well, I love you.

Roxane (*closing her eyes*): Yes, talk to me of love!

Christian: I do love you.

Roxane: Yes. That is the theme. Now play variations upon it.

Christian: I love you very much.

Roxane: What further can you say?

Christian: Here, I can show you.

Roxane: Wait! First tell me not *that* you love me, but a little about *how* you love me.

Christian: Why . . . very, very much.

Roxane: Go on.

Christian: I want to kiss you.

Roxane: Christian! (*She starts to get up.*)

Christian (*holding her down*): All right, then! I do not love you.

Roxane: Am I lucky in that?

Christian: I adore you!

Roxane (*escaping him this time and rising*): Christian, you know the way I love to hear you speak. What has happened to your eloquence?

Christian: I—

Roxane: You love me. I have heard that. Good evening! (*She starts toward the door.*)

Christian: No, no, not yet! You must listen. I . . . . I . . . .

Roxane: You adore me, then. Yes, I know. Now, please go.

Christian: But I . . . . (*She closes the door in his face.*)

Cyrano (*appearing from the left*): No question about it—a success.

Christian: Cyrano, help me!

Cyrano: No.

Christian: *Please*, help me!

Cyrano: How can I help you now? You have no time to memorize the words.

Christian: Oh, I shall die!

Cyrano (*taking his arm*): There! . . . Look! . . . See? (*A light has appeared in the balcony window.*)

Christian: Her window!

Cyrano: Not so loud!

Christian (*whispering*): I shall die!

Cyrano: It is a dark night. There may

• **variation** (var ee AY shun) different form (as a melody, or theme, may be played in different ways)

Roxane (*opening window*): Who is calling me?

Christian: Christian, who loves you.

Roxane: Oh, you! You told me that you did not love me, remember? Besides, your conversation is too common. (*During this speech,* Cyrano *has been whispering to* Christian.)

Christian: You accuse me, dear lady, of loving you no more . . . when I *can* love you no more!

Roxane (*stops shutting the window*): Ah, that is a little better!

Christian (*again getting his words from* Cyrano's *whispers*): Roxane, your name is in my heart . . . the golden clapper in a bell. . . . Roxane, the more my heart is shaken . . . the more it rings your name.

Roxane: Much, much better. But why do you speak so slowly? Why all the pauses? Has your eloquence lost its wings?

Christian (*continuing to get the words*

be some hope. . . . There, stand there, miserable boy. In front of the balcony. I will stand under it and prompt you.

Christian: But—

Cyrano: Quick! Do as I tell you. (*They get in place.*) Now, call her.

Christian: Roxane!

Cyrano (*picking up some pebbles and handing them to* Christian): Here. These may help.

Christian (*throwing pebbles at the window*): Roxane! Roxane!

- **prompt** (PROMPT) give words to; remind what to say
- **clapper** (KLAP ur) the striking part of a bell

from Cyrano *throughout this scene*): Because of the dark.... My words have to grope to find your ear.

Roxane (*coming out onto the balcony*): But my words do not find the same difficulty.

Christian: Of course! That is because I catch them with my heart.... Take care! ... A hard word dropped from such a height ... would shatter it.

Roxane (*with a motion of leaving*): I will come down!

Christian: Do not!

Roxane: And why?

Christian: Roxane, when I feast my eyes upon your beauty, I am so filled with feeling ... that ... I find it hard to speak. Do you know how, after gazing at the sun ... one sees bright, blinding circles everywhere? ... Just so your sunshine blinds me ... makes me run in circles.... Roxane, I would give my own happiness for yours. I would destroy my own dim light ... for your sunshine. And in return, just let me hear ... sometimes ... all alone ... the far-off, ringing laughter of your joy.

Roxane: Yes, that is love!

Christian: Roxane, protected by the dark ... I dare at last to be myself.

Roxane: Go on.

Christian: Here in the dark, I am free to reach for stars.... Roxane, I choke with love.... My brain reels.... Does some little part of my soul ... make itself felt to you there in the darkness? For surely I can feel you here beside me ... trembling, like a flower on a branch.... And I have worshipped the trembling of your hand ... right here in this blissful bunch of leaves. (*He madly kisses the hanging piece of vine he has been holding.*)

Roxane: Yes, I tremble ... and weep ... and love you ... and am yours!

Christian: Then let death come! I have no more to ask. (*After a long pause, he speaks without prompting.*) Except one thing—a kiss.

Cyrano (*in a loud whisper to* Christian): No!

Christian (*whispering to* Cyrano): Why not?

Roxane (*leaning over the rail*): What are you whispering?

Cyrano (*to* Christian): Oh, all right. (*He again whispers in* Christian's *ear.*)

Christian (*to* Roxane): I was scolding myself for having gone too far.... I was saying, "Hush, Christian."

Roxane: But we were speaking of ... of ... of ... of a ....

Christian: Kiss.... The word is sweet.... If the word itself seems to burn your lips, what of the thing itself?

Roxane: Say no more!

Christian: A kiss.... What is a kiss? ... An oath of allegiance ... a promise ... a rose-red dot upon the letter i in *loving* ... a secret, but not for the ear ... an instant of eternity.

Roxane: Say no more! Come, and make that instant now!

Cyrano (*whispering to* Christian, *who hesitates*): Go! (Christian *still hangs back.*) Go! ... Go! (*He pushes* Christian.) To the balcony, you donkey!

(Christian *springs to the bench, leaps from there to the vine, and then pulls himself over the railing.*)

Christian: Ah, Roxane! (*He clasps her to him.*)

Cyrano (*to himself, looking up at the bottom of the balcony*): And not even a crumb falls to me. On Christian's lips are my words still . . . and Roxane is kissing them. (*He walks softly to the left, into the street, and stands watching* Roxane *and* Christian. *Suddenly he calls.*) Hello, there!

Roxane (*separating herself from* Christian): Who is it?

Cyrano: Cyrano. I was passing this way. Is Christian there?

Christian (*astonished*): Cyrano!

Roxane: Good evening, cousin. I will come down. (*She and* Christian *leave the balcony.*)

An Old Monk (*coming up the street*): I am looking for the house of a certain . . . (*looks at an envelope*) . . . Magdeleine Robin.

Cyrano: You have found it, then. Right here.

Monk: I carry a letter for her, from a high and noble lord I will not name. (*He sees* Roxane *and* Christian *at the door.*) Are you Mademoiselle Robin?

Roxane: I am. (*She takes the letter.*) It is from De Guiche!

Christian: He dares to . . . ?

Roxane (*while opening the letter*): He will not trouble me much longer. (*She reads to herself in a very low voice, at one side.*) "Mademoiselle: The drums are beating. I am about to leave. This letter comes to you by a trusted monk who has no suspicion of what it contains. The march to Arras should begin—yet I cannot bear to leave Paris without once more meeting you. You smiled so sweetly upon me an hour ago. I am coming to you, and when I get there . . . ." (*She stops reading and looks at the* Monk.) Father, this is what the letter tells me. Good news! (*All draw near as she pretends to read, aloud.*) "Mademoiselle: I have chosen to carry this letter a good and holy man. It is my wish that he should immediately join you and Christian in marriage. I have my reasons for wanting this done right now. May heaven bless the two of you."

Christian: Oh, who could have hoped for this?

Monk: The worthy, worthy gentleman. I had the feeling, when he handed me the envelope, that it contained happiness.

Roxane (*breathless*): How long will it take to marry us?

Monk: Not long. Not long at all.

Roxane: Then we must hurry. Gentlemen? (*She opens the door. The* Monk *and* Christian *enter, but she stops* Cyrano *to speak to him alone.*) Listen! De Guiche is coming! Stay outside and keep him here. Do not let him enter!

Cyrano: I understand. Go on. (*She goes in.*) Now I am left alone . . . alone. (Cyrano *stands still a minute, then takes off his hat and looks at the three white plumes. Smiling sadly, he puts the hat back on and walks to the edge of the balcony, where* Christian *had stood to deliver his eloquent speeches. He looks up to where* Roxane *had been and repeats one of the earlier speeches in his own voice, this time slightly rearranged as a poem.*)

Cyrano (*with feeling*):
Do you know how, after gazing
　　at the sun,
One sees bright, blinding circles
　　everywhere?
Just so your sunshine blinds me,
　　makes me run
In selfless circles of my own
　　despair.

For your happiness, I would give
my own,
And for your sunshine, my own
dim light destroy.
Just let me hear, sometimes, all
alone,
The far-off, ringing laughter of
your joy.

(*Another long moment passes be-fore the action continues. Then* De Guiche *is seen hurrying up the street. He wears a cloak to hide his uniform and medals, and on his face is a ridiculous party mask.*)

De Guiche (*stopping short*): What! You here!

Cyrano (*with a bow and sweep*): Why, it sounds like Count De Guiche! Returning from a party, Monsieur? I hope you had a merry time.

De Guiche (*angrily*): A merry time in-deed!

Cyrano: Then your happiness can only continue, Monsieur. I must tell you: They are married.

De Guiche (*tearing off the mask*): What?

Cyrano (*bowing*): They have ex-changed vows within the last few minutes.

De Guiche: Who have? (*He turns around as the door to the house opens.* Roxane *and* Christian *come out, holding hands. Behind them is the* Monk, *smiling happily. The* Duenna, *in her nightgown, and a servant complete the group with flaming torches.*) Heavens! (*He looks at* Roxane, *then at* Christian.) You? And *you?*

Monk (*pointing at the lovers*): A beau-tiful couple, Monsieur. And brought together by you!

De Guiche (*stiffly, trying to contain his anger*): My compliments to you both. (*He turns to* Roxane.) And now get ready, Madam, to take leave of your husband.

Roxane: What?

De Guiche (*to* Christian): The regi-ment is on the point of starting. You are to join it!

Roxane: To go to war?

De Guiche: Of course!

Roxane: But his company is not to go!

De Guiche: It is to go! (*He takes out the order which he had put in his pocket earlier and turns to* Chris-tian): I command you to take this order to Captain Carbon yourself.

Roxane (*throwing herself in his arms*): Christian!

Cyrano (*to* Christian): You have no choice . . . but jail or death.

Christian (*still holding* Roxane): Oh, it is hard to leave her! . . . You cannot know . . . .

Cyrano (*trying to pull him away*): I know.

(*Drums are heard in the distance; the march is starting to form.*)

De Guiche: The regiment is on its way!

Roxane (*to* Cyrano, *as she clings to* Christian, *whom he is trying to draw away*): Oh! I give him to your care!

Cyrano: I will try . . . but clearly I can-not promise—

Roxane: Promise that his life will not be placed in danger!

Cyrano: I will do my best, but—

Roxane: That you will protect him!

Cyrano: Of course, but you see—

Roxane: That he will write to me often!

Cyrano (*standing quite still*): Ah, that! . . . That I promise freely!

• **regiment** (REJ uh munt) large military unit

CHECKPOINT

Review Acts II and III by answering the following questions. If you have trouble, go back and reread before continuing with the play.

1. What happens during the important interview between Cyrano and Roxane early in Act II? Include in your answer the promises Cyrano makes to Roxane and how he feels about them.

2. In your opinion, why does Cyrano offer to help Christian court Roxane in the last part of Act II?

3. Early in Act III, De Guiche, in a desperate attempt to win Roxane's favor, makes her a promise. (a) What is this promise? (b) Is it later kept? Explain why or why not.

4. Act III contains several examples of *dramatic irony* (see page 29). Find and explain at least one of these.

5. The last two words in Act III are "promise freely." Explain (a) exactly what Cyrano promises, and (b) why he can and wants to make the promise.

ACT IV
The Siege of Arras

SETTING: *The camp of the company of* Guards *at the siege of Arras, over a month later. Toward the back, across the whole stage, is a sloping bank of earth. Beyond this, against the sky, are the far-distant walls and roofs of Arras. Here and there on the plain around the city are the ugly symbols of war: cannons, piles of earth, tents, etc. In front of the bank of earth is the camp of the* Guards. *Campfires, bedrolls, knapsacks, firearms, and drums are scattered around. An improvised desk at the left has some papers and a lantern on it. Gunfire is heard occasionally throughout the act.*

AT RISE: *It is shortly before sunrise, and the campfires are low. Most of the* Guards *are asleep on the ground. They are dirty, pale, and thin.* Christian *lies sleeping in the foreground, his face lightened by one of the fires. At the right,* Le Bret *and* Captain Carbon *sit talking quietly, propped up against some bags.*

• improvised (IM proh vyzd) quickly put together from materials at hand

Le Bret: It is dreadful!

Carbon: Yes, something has to happen soon. Look at those men.

Le Bret: They would rather die fighting than of slow starvation here.

Carbon: There was never a stranger siege than this one of Arras. We surround the city, trying to starve the Spanish into slow defeat. But then another Spanish army surrounds us! (*A few shots are heard in the distance, and some of the sleeping Guards lift their heads.*) It is nothing, men. Go back to sleep.

A Sentinel (*offstage*): Halt! Who goes there?

Cyrano's Voice: Bergerac, you donkey. (*He enters.*)

Le Bret: Are you wounded at last?

Cyrano: No, the enemy has made it a habit to miss me.

Carbon: Cyrano, why does it make sense to go on risking your life every morning, just for the sake of a letter?

Cyrano (*crossing to* Christian *and looking down*): I promised that he would write often.... He sleeps.... He has grown pale ... but handsome as ever.

Le Bret: To think ... that every day you put your life in danger for his happiness.... Hey, where are you going?

Cyrano (*stops at the desk and sits down*): I am going to write another letter.

(*There is a long silence as it slowly gets lighter. In the distance the city of Arras brightens like a jewel. Suddenly, from very near, comes a roll of drums.*)

Carbon: Who is there?

Le Bret (*standing up*): Oh, no! Monsieur De Guiche.

Carbon (*leaping up with a groan*): All right, men! Now, up! Everyone! Attention! The Supreme Commander! (*The* Guards *raise their heads, but only a few rise.*)

De Guiche (*entering, to* Carbon): Ah, good morning. (*He looks around.*) So! Here are the disloyal rascals! Gentlemen, it is reported to me on every side what you say about your Supreme Commander. I hear I am a coward. I hear I would let you starve to gain a little glory for myself. (*He nudges a* Guard *with his boot.*) You, soldier, stand up now!

The Guard: Yes, sir. (*He tries to stand, and he almost makes it before collapsing in a heap.*)

De Guiche: What's wrong with him?

Another Guard (*from the ground*): I caught him yesterday eating paper ... fried in axle grease.

De Guiche: The fool! (*He turns to* Carbon.) Captain, there is, at last, some news. We are to be relieved! Marshal Dourlens is now on the way with troops in such number that the Spanish must regroup. So, before Dourlens arrives, we are sure to be attacked.

Carbon: When will that be?

De Guiche: This very day, certainly. It could be in an hour.

A Guard (*one of the few who have been standing*): Oh! ... If there is a whole hour .... (*He yawns and lies back down.*)

De Guiche (*to* Carbon, *briskly*): The first attack is sure to come at our weakest spot ... right here ... this company. The main thing is to gain

---

- sentinel (SEN tuh nul) soldier on guard duty
- marshal (MAR shul) very high-ranking officer in the French army

time before Marshal Dourlens arrives.

Carbon: You mean, then, that we should keep the Spanish busy killing us until—

Cyrano (*leaping up and bounding toward* De Guiche): Ah! So this is your revenge!

De Guiche (*icily*): Monsieur de Bergerac, I will not pretend that I am fond of you. But as you have often boasted, your bravery is beyond that of others. Therefore, in giving you this battle, I am serving my King's interest as well as my own.

Cyrano: Allow me, Monsieur, to thank you.

De Guiche: I know that you like to fight one against a hundred. You cannot complain of lacking such a chance.

Cyrano (*kneeling down to put a hand on* Christian's *shoulder*): Christian?

Christian (*shaking his head*): Roxane!

Cyrano: No, me. (*He gives him the letter he has just written.*) I had a feeling that the end might come today. So here it is . . . your farewell letter.

Christian (*sitting up*): Let me read it!
(*From outside comes the sound of carriage bells, horses' hoofs, wheels on ground, and people shouting.*)

Carbon: What is it?

A Guard (*climbing the bank*): A coach! Driving into camp, and from the direction of the enemy! The coachman is shouting something. What does he say? Oh, yes: "Service of the King!"
(*Everyone rises as the coach comes in at a trot and stops. The curtains are drawn, and mud covers everything.*)

De Guiche: Quick! Let down the steps!
(*Two Guards do so.*)

Roxane (*stepping gracefully from the carriage*): Good morning!
(*Roxane is beautifully dressed and radiant. Everyone gathers around in amazement.*)

De Guiche: Service of the King? You?

Roxane: Say rather service of the only King . . . of Love.

Christian (*rushing to her*): You! Why are you here?

Roxane: This siege has lasted too long!

Christian: Why have you come?

Roxane: I will tell you. (*She kisses him; the* Guards *cheer.*)

De Guiche: But you cannot stay here!

Roxane: Indeed I can!

Cyrano: But how did you get through the Spanish lines?

Roxane (*laughing*): I simply drove through them, in my coach, at a trot. If some soldier seemed likely to stop us, I put my face to the window, wearing my sweetest smile, and waved, just so. . . . The Spanish are known as the most gallant men in the world . . . so I passed.

Cyrano: But didn't anyone stop the coach, order you out, and demand to see by whose orders you were passing?

Roxane: More than once. I would say, "My orders are unwritten, from the greatest commander of all . . . the god of Love." The Spanish knew what I meant, and the muskets aimed at me would be lifted. They would fall back and bow low. "Pass, señorita, pass!" (*She laughs.*) I was even cheered!

De Guiche: You must leave at once!

Cyrano: At once!

Le Bret: As fast as you can.

Roxane: But why?

Cyrano: We are to be attacked.

Roxane (*looking at* De Guiche): Well, in that case, perhaps it is time that Count De Guiche should go.

De Guiche: That is insulting! I must go

and inspect my guns, but I will be back. You still have time to leave. (*He starts off.*)

Roxane (*to his back*): Never! . . . But the fresh air makes me hungry. What have you to eat?

Christian (*sadly*): Nothing but memories of food.

Roxane: Then look in my coach.

Guards: What?

Roxane: And take a closer look at the coachman.

(*The coachman stands up for the first time and takes off a hood. It is* Ragueneau, *now smiling and waving as he opens the coach seat.*)

Ragueneau: Two hams! Roast beef! A leg of lamb! Here, catch! (*He throws them down.*)

Guards: Bravo! Ragueneau! Bravo! (*Etc.*)

Ragueneau: How could the Spaniards, when so much beauty passed, suspect a feast? (*He continues to throw down food from the tool box and other hiding places.*)

Roxane: Look inside. The cushions are stuffed with rolls!

Cyrano (*at one side, to* Christian, *as the* Guards *sit in small groups to eat*): I must tell you . . . the letters. You have written her more often than you think.

Christian: Ah! Have I?

Cyrano: Yes. I sometimes wrote . . . without telling you.

Christian: How often? Twice a week? Three times?

Cyrano: No, every day. Sometimes twice. . . . Be still. Here she is.

Roxane (*coming up*): And now, Christian . . . . (*She glances at* Cyrano, *who walks off.*)

Christian (*holding her*): But why did you come? Was it worth risking your life . . . to join me?

Roxane: Because of the letters.

Christian: What? Because of a few little love letters?

Roxane: Ah, think how many you have written to me in a month! The truth is . . . I really fell in love with you one evening, when a voice in the dark began to reveal a soul . . . a soul so tender . . . so . . . . Think, then, about your letters. To me, they were a voice heard constantly for one month. Christian, for one whole month I have heard the voice of your soul speaking to me . . . and now I am ashamed. I want to ask your pardon . . . for having done you the wrong, at first, in my shallow way, of loving you for . . . your looks.

Christian: Roxane! You mean . . . you don't love what you see? You don't love . . . me?

Roxane: Well, maybe . . . in a way. But now, you see, you are victor over yourself. I love you for your soul alone.

Christian: But who could want to be loved like that? No, I just want to be loved quite simply . . . .

Roxane: For that which other women can see in you? Oh, let yourself be loved in a better way . . . a deeper way.

Christian: No . . . I was happier before.

Roxane (*desperate*): But can't you understand? It isn't that I don't love what I see, but that it doesn't matter now. Suppose in battle you got wounded in face and form, badly disfigured . . . .

• disfigured (dis FIG yurd) damaged or spoiled in appearance

Christian: What? If I were ugly, really ugly? You would still love me?

Roxane: If you were ugly, Christian. I swear it!

De Guiche (*entering as all turn to him*): The guns are set. All preparations have been made. Captain Carbon, have . . . . (*He looks around.*) What? . . . Food?

Roxane: Yes, food for everyone. There isn't much left, but here . . . and here. (*She picks up scattered leftovers.*)

De Guiche (*looking at the* Guards): Do you imagine that I will eat your leftovers? (*He faces* Roxane.) And you still here? You refuse to leave?

Roxane: I do.

De Guiche (*after a pause*): Then, Captain, give me a musket.

Carbon: What do you mean?

De Guiche: I do not leave a woman in danger! (*He takes the musket, looks around, and slowly smiles.*) And since we all may die within the hour, let us do so on a full stomach! (*He accepts* Roxane's *food.*)

A Guard: Look! (*He points to* De Guiche.) He is now a human being!

Another Guard: Almost one of us! (*The* Guards *cheer, half in mockery.*)

Christian (*approaching* Cyrano, *to one side*): She does not love me anymore.

Cyrano: What do you mean?

Christian: She loves you.

Cyrano: No!

Christian: She loves only my soul!

Cyrano: No!

Christian: Yes! Therefore, it is you she loves. . . . And you love her.

Cyrano: I—

Christian: You do! I know it!

Cyrano (*quietly*): It is true.

Christian: You love her to madness.

Cyrano: Even more.

Christian: Tell her, then.

Cyrano: No!

Christian: Why not?

Cyrano: Just look at me.

Christian: She would love me grown ugly.

Cyrano: She told you so?

Christian: Yes, she insisted on it.

Cyrano: No, I cannot tell her. . . . The letters . . . what I have done . . . . She would never forgive me.

Christian: But how can you be sure? That is what I must discover.

Cyrano: No! No!

Christian: You must tell her everything! Let her choose between us!

Cyrano: Christian, it is a mistake to tempt me . . . and cruel.

Christian: Listen! Our marriage—if such it can be called—can easily be annulled. I'm sure if—

Cyrano: Christian, I beg of you, don't tempt me.

Christian: Yes, I will! I want to be loved for myself, or not at all. (*A few shots are heard outside.* Le Bret *and two other* Guards *seize muskets and go over the top of the bank.*)

Cyrano: But would you destroy her happiness?

Christian: I will go out there to see what's happening. You spend five minutes with her. Tell her, and let her choose between us.

Cyrano: She will choose you.

Christian: All right, then! I can only hope she will. (*He calls.*) Roxane! Roxane!

Cyrano: No! No!

Roxane (*coming up*): What is it?

• **annulled** (uh NULD) canceled; removed from legal or church records

Christian: Cyrano has something to tell you . . . something important. (*He grabs a musket and goes over the bank.*)

Roxane: Something important?

Cyrano: No, it's nothing. He sometimes . . . you must know . . . sometimes doesn't understand . . . refuses to believe . . . .

Roxane (*quickly*): Yes, he didn't believe what I told him a while ago. I saw that he didn't believe.

Cyrano (*taking her hand*): But what you told him . . . . Was it the very truth?

Roxane: Yes, yes! I told him that I would love him, even if he were . . . .

Cyrano (*smiling sadly*): You find it hard to say the word before me? Then I will say it. Even if he were ugly?

Roxane: Yes . . . ugly. (*Musket shots are heard outside.*) They are firing!

Cyrano: Dreadfully ugly?

Roxane: Dreadfully.

Cyrano: Disfigured?

Roxane: Disfigured!

Cyrano: Grotesque?

Roxane: Nothing could make him grotesque . . . to me. I would love him all the more, if that is possible.

Cyrano (*losing his head with happiness*): Roxane! What you say . . . if you mean it . . . and you do mean it . . . gives me the . . . . I . . . Roxane . . . listen carefully.

Le Bret (*having just come in, calling softly*): Cyrano!

Cyrano (*turning*): What?

Le Bret: Hush! (*He whispers a few words to* Cyrano.)

Cyrano (*letting* Roxane's *hand drop, with a cry*): Ah!

Roxane: What do you mean?

Cyrano (*almost to himself*): It is finished! (*There are more shots.*)

Roxane: I don't understand. What's happening out there? (*She goes to the back to look.*)

Cyrano: It is finished! . . . My lips are sealed forevermore.
(*A group of* Guards *come in, carrying something they try to keep from* Roxane's *view. They surround it, preventing* Roxane *from seeing it.*)

Roxane (*coming back*): What has happened? (*She runs to the group of* Guards *and pushes them aside.*)

Cyrano: It is finished!

Roxane (*seeing* Christian *stretched out on his cloak*): Christian!

Le Bret (*to* Cyrano): At the enemy's first shot.
(*Roxane throws herself down on* Christian *as more shots come from outside. Drums and a fife sound the call to battle.*)

Carbon: The attack! To your muskets! Over the top! (*The* Guards *do so.*)

Roxane: Christian! Oh, Christian!

Christian (*in a dying voice*): Roxane!
(*Ragueneau comes running in with water in a steel helmet and some cloths. He touches* Roxane's *shoulder; she stands up to dampen a cloth for* Christian's *wound.*)

Cyrano (*quick and low in* Christian's *ear, while* Roxane *is distracted*): I told her everything! . . . She made her choice. . . . You are still the one she loves. (Christian *closes his eyes.*)

Carbon (*from outside*): Fall into line!

Roxane (*at* Christian's *side*): Oh! His cheek grows cold!

Carbon: Take aim!

Roxane (*feeling something in the*

- grotesque (groh TESK) unnatural in appearance; very ugly

pocket of Christian's *shirt*): What's this? A letter! (*She starts to read it.*)

Cyrano: But Roxane! They are fighting!

Carbon: Fire! (*Muskets sound, swords clash, and the fife and drums grow louder.* Cyrano *starts to leave.*)

Roxane: No! Stay with me a little! . . . He is dead.

Cyrano (*standing bareheaded as he pulls* Roxane *up*): Yes, Roxane.

Roxane (*clinging to* Cyrano): You are the one who knew him best. Was he not a . . . marvelous being?

Cyrano: Yes, Roxane.

Roxane: A man of eloquence?

Cyrano: Yes, Roxane.

Roxane: A noble soul?

Cyrano: Yes, Roxane.

Roxane: A noble soul . . . that I must love until I die. (Roxane *starts to faint as* De Guiche *enters from the bank. His forehead is bloody, his jacket torn.*)

De Guiche: Marshal Dourlens's troops are near! You can see them, on the hill in back! We shall win the day if we can hold out a little longer!

Cyrano: Your courage no one will question now. Come and help me with Roxane.

Ragueneau (*to* De Guiche): We must take her to a safer place.

De Guiche (*to* Cyrano): Can you rally the men for me? Be the one against the hundred?

Cyrano: Fear nothing! I have two deaths to avenge: Christian's and all my hopes'!

(De Guiche, *helped by* Ragueneau, *carries* Roxane *off right as* Cyrano *leaps to the top of the bank. He delivers his last speech in the grand manner of old, slicing the air with his sword.*)

Cyrano: Steady, my men! Never give them an inch! Fall on them, boys! Crush them! Play, fifer, play! (*With a final sweep of the sword, he leaps over the top, into the battle.*)

ACT V
Cyrano's Gazette

SETTING: *The convent of the Sisters of the Cross, in Paris, 15 years later (in 1655). In the center of the stage is the trunk of a huge tree; its lower branches can be seen above. The ground is littered with autumn leaves, which keep falling. At the left is a chapel with a center door, and at the right a stone bench in the shape of a half-circle. Behind the bench is a park.*

AT RISE: *A few nuns come and go in the park. It is getting dark, and leaves from the giant tree keep falling.*

A Young Nun (*coming with an* Older Nun *from the chapel*): I must tell you . . . this morning, after putting on my cap, I went back to the mirror, to have another look.

Older Nun: That was unbecoming, my child.

Young Nun: I try so hard . . . .

Older Nun (*good-humoredly*): Hush, hush. I dare say there are worse things in the world. This evening, when Monsieur Cyrano comes, do you want me to tell him?

Young Nun: No, no! He loves to kid me. (*They sit down on the stone bench.*) Is it true that Monsieur Cyrano has come here every Saturday for the last 10 years?

Older Nun: Longer! Ever since his cousin brought her mourning coif of black to this convent, 14 years ago.

Young Nun: He's so funny! I love it when he teases us. And he alone can lift the sorrow of Madam Magdeleine. (*She looks toward the park.*) Oh, there she is right now!

Who is that walking with her? Could it be . . . the great Count De Guiche?

Older Nun: I think it is. He hasn't been to visit her in a long, long time. . . . Come, let's not get in their way. (*They go off, right.*)

De Guiche (*coming forward with* Roxane, *who is dressed in black and carries embroidery to work on.*) And so you live here, uselessly beautiful, always dressed in mourning?

Roxane: Always.

De Guiche: As faithful as of old?

Roxane: As faithful. I carry his last letter . . . here against my heart.

De Guiche (*after a pause*): Have you forgiven me?

Roxane: Since I am here. (*They sit down.*)

De Guiche (*after another pause*): Does Cyrano still come to see you?

Roxane: Yes, every Saturday. He will be here soon. I don't even have to look up from my work. I hear the tapping of a cane, and I know who it is. . . . He calls himself my gazette.

- gazette (guh ZET) newspaper
- coif (KOIF) kind of hood-shaped cap

He sits in an old armchair here, and he tells me all the news.

De Guiche: Poor Cyrano. As I once hated the man, so I love him now. But all that I foretold has come to pass. His writing makes him more enemies every day. He attacks all the frauds in Paris, and dishonesty wherever he finds it. No one can stop him.

Roxane: Even you? (*She has started work on her embroidery.*)

De Guiche: Even me. . . . And if his enemies do not catch up with him, his poverty will have him by the throat at last. I have tried to give him money, but he is too proud. He turns his back on me and walks away . . . in the only clothes he has.

A Nun (*appearing right*): Monsieur Ragueneau begs to see you, Sir.

De Guiche: Let him in. (*The Nun leaves; a moment passes.*)

Ragueneau (*rushing in, out of breath and excited, to De Guiche*): You are . . . . (*He sees Roxane and turns to her.*) Will you excuse us, Madam?

Roxane: Certainly, if you wish. (*She withdraws to the park.*)

Ragueneau (*still breathing hard*): I've run all over Paris, looking for you.

De Guiche: What's the matter?

Ragueneau: You are his only friend with money, so I come to see you first.

De Guiche (*concerned*): Is it Cyrano?

Ragueneau: About two hours ago, I was on my way to see him. I was not 30 feet from his door, when I saw him come out. I hurried to catch up with him. He was about to turn the corner, when from a window over him someone drops a block of wood—

De Guiche: The cowards!

Ragueneau: I reach the spot, and find him . . . .

De Guiche: Horrible!

Ragueneau: Our friend, our poet, stretched there on the ground, with a great hole in his head!

De Guiche: Is he dead?

Ragueneau: No. I carried him to his room. He's still unconscious.

De Guiche: Has a doctor come?

Ragueneau: Yes, a doctor came, out of good nature. But without money, there will be little done. Cyrano needs a hospital . . . a hundred doctors.

De Guiche: And he shall have them! I'll go to him now. (*They start to leave.*) You go get Le Bret. I'll meet you soon at Cyrano's. (*They leave.*)

Roxane (*coming forward and calling*): Monsieur De Guiche! Ragueneau! . . . De Guiche not turning around when I call? What can be the trouble?

(*Roxane sits down on the bench and takes up her embroidery. A clock strikes in the distance. Two Nuns come from the right with a large armchair that they place under the tree. They go off.*)

Roxane: The clock has struck . . . and his armchair is here. I wonder at this! Is it possible that for the first time he is late?

A Nun (*from the side*): Monsieur de Bergerac.

Roxane: What was I saying? . . . (*She continues to embroider.*)

(*Cyrano appears from the right, very pale. His hat, which now bears only one white plume, is drawn down over his eyes. He crosses to the armchair very slowly, having trouble keeping his feet and leaning heavily on his cane. Roxane, as is her habit, does not look up. When Cyrano is seated, a slight breeze makes the leaves fall.*)

Cyrano: The leaves!

Roxane (*still looking down*): You sound serious today.

Cyrano: In that brief fluttering from branch to ground, how they manage still to put forth beauty! Although they're doomed to turn to mold in the earth that draws them, they wish their fall to be like a free bird's flight!

Roxane: Come, never mind the falling leaves! Give me the weekly gazette, instead.

Cyrano (*growing paler, and struggling with pain*): On Sunday, at the Queen's great ball, were burned 763 wax candles. Monday: the King was taken with a fever, having filled his plate eight times with pig's-head jelly. Tuesday: four sorcerers were hanged. Wednesday: the fair Monglat said to the Count Fiesco, "No." Thursday: our troops, it is said, defeated Austrian John. Friday: the fair Monglat said to the Count Fiesco, "Yes." And Saturday, the twenty-sixth . . . . (*He closes his eyes, his chin now on his chest.*)

Roxane (*surprised at the silence, turning to him and rising to her feet in alarm*): Cyrano!

Cyrano (*opening his eyes, in a faint voice*): What is it? What's the matter?

Roxane: Did you faint?

Cyrano (*shrinking back*): No, no. I assure you. It's nothing. . . . Just the old wound I received at Arras. Sometimes, you know, even now . . . .

Roxane: Poor friend.

Cyrano: It's nothing. . . . It will pass. (*He smiles with effort.*) It has passed.

Roxane: Each of us has a wound. . . . I, too, have mine. . . . I carry it here. (*She places her hand over the letter and her heart.*)

(*The light is beginning to fade.*)

Cyrano: His letter? Ah, didn't you once say that you would let me read it . . . someday?

Roxane: Do you wish . . . his letter . . . now?

Cyrano: Yes. I think . . . the day has come.

Roxane (*handing him the little bag from her neck*): Here. Open it. . . . Read.

Cyrano (*reading*): "Good-bye, Roxane. I am going to die."

Roxane (*in astonishment*): You are reading it aloud?

Cyrano (*reading*): "My soul is heavy with love it had not time to utter. And yet my end will come tonight, my beloved, I believe. Now Time is at an end. Never again, never again, shall my eyes see—"

Roxane: But how can you see to read? In this dying light?

(*It is growing dark fast.*)

Cyrano: "—the grace in your every gesture. To even think of you tucking back a little curl, I cannot keep from crying out, 'Good-bye, my dearest—'"

Roxane: How can you go on reading? It is dark!

Cyrano: "'—my darling, my treasure, my love.' My heart never left your side for a second, and I am and shall be in the world that has no end—"

Roxane: But it is dark! (*She lays a hand on his shoulder. The echoes of his voice seem to continue into a long silence.*) And you, for 14 years, have played the part of a comical old friend who came to see me!

Cyrano: Roxane!

Roxane: So it was you. . . .

Cyrano: No, no, Roxane!

Roxane: I see it all now. The letters . . . every one of them . . . came from your heart. There is a teardrop stain on that letter you have just

pretended to read. That tear was yours!

Cyrano: No! Christian sent those letters! I only . . . .

Roxane: You only what?

Cyrano (*quietly*): All right. . . . I wrote the letters.

Roxane: How many things within me have now died . . . and how many have been born! Why, why have you been silent all these years, when on this letter, the tears are yours?

Cyrano (*handing her the letter*): Because . . . the blood was his. (Ragueneau, De Guiche, *and* Le Bret *enter, running.*)

Le Bret: Madness! . . . Ah, I was sure he would be here!

Cyrano (*smiling*): Where else?

Ragueneau: Madam, he is likely to have invited his death by getting out of bed.

Roxane: Merciful God. . . . A moment ago, then . . . that faintness . . . .

Cyrano: It is true. I had not finished telling you the news. And on Saturday, the twenty-sixth, at an hour after sundown, Monsieur de Bergerac died of murder at his own invitation. (*He takes off his hat, and his head is seen in bandages.*)

Roxane: What is he saying? Those bandages!

Cyrano: Fate will have his laugh at us! Here I am killed. . . . I who fought with a hundred at a time . . . killed by some vile rogue with a log from above.

De Guiche (*to* Ragueneau *and* Le Bret): Shouldn't we get him out of here? To the hospital?

Cyrano (*firmly*): No! (*He reaches up for* Roxane's *hand.*) I left her once. . . .

Roxane: I love you. . . . You shall live.

Cyrano: No, that only happens in fairy tales.

Roxane: I have hurt you! . . . I have ruined your life!

Cyrano: You? Just the opposite. Fate

never favored me . . . but thanks to you, I have had, at least, among the gentle and fair, one friend.

De Guiche (*calling his attention to the moonlight peering through the branches*): Your other friend, among the gentle and fair, is there. She comes to see you.

Cyrano (*smiling at the moon*): I see her.

Roxane: I never loved but one . . . and twice I lost him.

Le Bret (*in revolt*): No! No! You shall not die! It is too senseless, too cruel, too unfair! So true a poet! So great a heart! To die . . . like this . . . .

Cyrano: As ever, Le Bret is grumbling.

Le Bret (*bursting into tears*): My friend! My friend!

Cyrano (*seized with shivering, getting to his feet*): But begging your pardon, I must go. . . . I wish to keep no one waiting. (*He is now as delirious as he is poetic.*) See, a moonbeam, come to take me home! (*He looks at* Roxane *and gently touches her mourning veil.*) I have a wish. When I am gone, this mourning veil should have two meanings . . . and I am one of them. Can every other teardrop be for me?

Roxane: I promise. (*She sobs.*) Oh, my love!

Cyrano (*swaying, as others try to help*): No! No! Let no one help me. Nothing but this tree. (*He stands against it, breathing in heaves.*) So let him come, old Death. He shall find me waiting, sword in hand. (*He draws; the others stand in helpless confusion.*)

Le Bret Cyrano!

Roxane (*nearly fainting*): Cyrano!

Cyrano (*delirious*): Ah, there you are, old Death, looking at me! Looking at my nose! What are you saying? (*He raises his sword.*) That it is no use? . . . I know that. But one does not fight because there is hope of winning. No, one fights for what is right! Who are these with you? Ah, I see—my ancient enemies. (*He leaves the tree, striking with his sword.*) Hypocrisy? Take this! And Prejudice, that I should come to terms with you? No, never! (*He strikes hard.*) Falsehood, take this! (*He tries to swing the sword.*) Cowardice! Surrender! (*He stops, gasping for breath. When he speaks again, it is in a more normal voice.*) In spite of all you can do to me, there is one thing I can take with me to where I go. Tonight, when I march into heaven, I will carry with me something tall and proud, unbent by the world. . . . (*He starts forward with lifted sword.*) And that is . . . .

(Cyrano *staggers and his sword clatters to the ground. Then he falls backward into the arms of* Le Bret *and* Ragueneau.)

Roxane (*kissing him on the forehead*): And that is . . . ?

Cyrano (*opening his eyes and smiling at her with his last words*): My white plume!

THE END

- **delirious** (di LEER ee us) mentally disordered
- **hypocrisy** (hi POK ruh see) falseness; pretending virtue one does not possess

ALL THINGS CONSIDERED ───────────────────

1. Part of De Guiche's reason for having the Spanish attack Cyrano's company, rather than another, is that De Guiche (a) knows the company is the strongest part of his regiment. (b) wants to take revenge against Cyrano. (c) wants Captain Carbon out of the way.

2. In spite of his high rank, De Guiche seems to have the reputation for being (a) a very poor commander. (b) very kind to the common soldiers. (c) somewhat of a coward.

3. When news that Christian has been hit reaches him, Cyrano is about to (a) tell Roxane the truth. (b) end his relationship with Roxane. (c) lie to Roxane about the letters.

4. Cyrano manages to tell the dying Christian that (a) he will take care of Roxane. (b) more letters have been sent than Christian supposes. (c) Roxane still loves Christian and has chosen him over Cyrano.

5. Act V is called "Cyrano's Gazette" because (a) a newspaper is important in the plot. (b) Cyrano has been giving Roxane the weekly news in witty form. (c) the plot was taken from a 1655 newspaper.

6. Roxane learns that Cyrano had written the love letters when (a) Cyrano "reads" the farewell letter in the dark. (b) Ragueneau informs her of the fact. (c) she sees other samples of Cyrano's handwriting.

7. When Roxane accuses Cyrano of writing the letters, he (a) denies it to the end. (b) calls her a liar. (c) confesses the truth.

8. Just before he dies, Cyrano (a) duels with Death and imaginary evils. (b) says he wants to recover and marry Roxane. (c) gets even with De Guiche.

9. The whole play covers a period of about (a) five years. (b) 10 years. (c) 15 years.

10. Although the play is called a *tragicomedy*, the most important element is probably (a) the comedy. (b) the tragedy. (c) neither, since both are equally balanced throughout the play.

THINKING IT THROUGH

1. Just before Cyrano leaps into battle at the end of Act IV, he states, "I have two deaths to avenge: Christian's and all my hopes'!" Exactly what does he mean?

2. How does the setting in Act V underscore the events in the plot? Consider both the symbolism of the leaves and the time of day and year.

3. How does the cause of Cyrano's death involve *irony of situation* (see page 39)? (He states the answer himself on page 320.)

4. What is the significance of Cyrano's three dying words?

5. *Cyrano de Bergerac* shows the reader a lot about life in 17th-century France. What do you consider three important differences between that period and life in modern America?

6. *Cyrano de Bergerac* is the kind of play that is more often read than performed on a stage. Why might this be true? Starting with the horses and carriage coming on stage, list several reasons that the play would be hard to produce.

7. In your opinion, is Cyrano an admirable character or not? List some of the factors you might weigh in the balance as you answer this question.

8. *Cyrano de Bergerac* is an excellent example of *romantic* literature—highly emotional, unrestrained, somehow larger than life. Yet because the playwright accepted so few limits on what he was doing, the reader is asked to accept some things that could hardly have really happened. What about the characters or the plot do you find hard to believe?

9. In your opinion, what did the author, Edmond Rostand, intend as the play's *theme* (see page 11)?

Literary Skills

Denotation and Connotation

What do we mean when we say that words have meanings? Think about that question. In a way, spoken words are just sounds, and written words are simply marks on paper. Those sounds and marks have no "meanings" that all human beings can easily recognize. Words have "meanings" only because speakers of a certain language attach significance to them. In a sense, the "meanings" of words are to be found in people's minds, not in the words themselves.

People react to words in at least two different ways. Suppose you wanted to know the "meaning" of an unfamiliar word. You might look it up in a dictionary. There you would find the **denotation** (dee noh TAY shun), or the "dictionary meaning" of the word.

But your reactions to certain words go far beyond their denotations. You respond to some words emotionally. The word suggests feelings and ideas that no dictionary would ever mention. These "emotional meanings" of a word are its **connotation** (kon uh TAY shun), or all that a word suggests or brings to mind.

Since you have just read *Cyrano de Bergerac*, the word *love* is a good example. You could get its *denotation* from the dictionary. But is that denotation all that the word now "means" to you? Of course not. Its *connotation* is equally important. Even before you read the play, you had certain feelings and ideas about the word and now you have more.

Good writers try to involve the reader's emotions by using words that are rich in connotation. The eloquent Cyrano is a master of the art. Study the following examples. In each of them, try to explain what the *italicized* term suggests that the substitute [in brackets] does not.

1. You *goose* [fool]! Be off!
2. Monsieur, where would you best be *gored* [pierced]?
3. That Montfleury! . . . he was so daring as to *feast his ugly frog's eyes on* [stare at] her. . . .
4. . . . Roxane herself . . . went . . . *lily-pale* [pale].
5. . . . BRING ON THE *GIANTS* [BIG MEN].

Composition

1. Tragic plays are sometimes rewritten so that they have a happy ending. Explain how this might be done with *Cyrano de Bergerac*. You will probably want to change the end of Act IV and omit Act V altogether.

2. The five examples of connotation above all come from Act I. Find two other examples in the rest of the play and explain the effectiveness of each. (The balcony scene in Act III is a good place to look.) In each case ask yourself what would be lost if a more common term were used for one rich in connotation.

VOCABULARY AND SKILL REVIEW ─────────────

Before completing the exercises that follow, you may wish to review the **bold-faced** words on pages 281 to 321.

I. On a separate sheet of paper, write the term in each line that means the same, or nearly the same, as the word in *italics*.
1. *rogue:* reddish brown, rascal, kind of pastry, tired
2. *eloquence:* beauty, expense, fine speaking, false praise
3. *defect:* weakness, firearm, very high, falsehood
4. *bravo:* Spanish soldier, French soldier, small coin, wonderful
5. *plume:* small stream, large feather, pencil, cloud
6. *defiance:* disrespect, authority, intelligence, quick wit
7. *recruit:* hard biscuit, new soldier, edible root, disease
8. *siege:* kind of cloth, continued attack, smooth, anger
9. *regiment:* military unit, dessert, ruler, long sword
10. *hypocrisy:* honesty, sympathy, great skill, falseness

II. On a separate sheet of paper, mark each item *true* or *false*. If it is *false*, explain what is wrong with the sentence.
1. A *tragicomedy* combines both tragedy and comedy.
2. A *musketeer* is a kind of firearm.
3. *Monsieur* is a kind of insult in the French language.
4. A *loathsome* lie is the same as a disgusting falsehood.
5. You might be able to drink from a *beaker.*
6. A *macaroon* is a kind of pastry.
7. A person who knows two languages well might serve as an *interpreter.*
8. In music, a *variation* on a theme is a different form of the same basic melody.
9. Sometimes a person stands just offstage to *prompt* actors who forget their lines.
10. A *delirious* person is always to be believed.

III. Think about each of the following pairs of terms. In each case, which term has the more favorable connotation?
1. *bashful* or *modest*
2. *slender* or *skinny*
3. *partly cloudy* or *partly sunny*
4. *statesman* or *politician*
5. *home* or *house*

THE FACE IS FAMILIAR BUT—

by Max Shulman

▶ "The face is familiar, but the name escapes me."

Nearly all people say that—or something like that—once in a while. You recognize a face, but you can't recall the name. You get all tangled up with names to remember, hands to shake, and the right thing to say at the right time.

Few people, however, have ever had as much trouble with a name as the lovable hero in the story that follows. Meet Dobie Gillis, a college freshman during World War II.

You can never tell. Citizens, you can never tell. Take the weekend of May 18. From all indications it was going to be a dreamboat. Saturday night was the fraternity formal, and Sunday night Petey Burch was taking me to the Dr. Askit quiz broadcast. Every prospect pleased.

At 7:30 Saturday night I got into my rented tux and picked up my rented car. At 8:30 I called for my date and was told that she had come down with the measles at 7:30. So I shrugged my rented shoulders, got into my rented car, and went to the dance alone.

I had taken my place in the stag line when Petey Burch rushed up to me, his face flushed with excitement. He waved a letter at me. "I've got it!" he cried. "Here's a letter from my parents saying I can join the Navy." Petey, like me, was 17 years old and needed permission from home to enlist.

"That's swell, Petey," I said. "I've got some news, too. My date has the measles."

- fraternity (fruh TUR ni tee) men's club in a college
- formal (FOR mul) formal, "dress-up" dance
- prospect (PROS pekt) outlook for the future
- tux (TUKS) full-dress suit (tuxedo)
- stag line (STAG LYN) group of boys without dates

"Tough," he said sympathetically. Then he suddenly got more excited than ever and hollered: "No! No, that's perfect. Listen, Dobie, the recruiting station is still open. I can go right down and enlist now."

"But what about the dance? What about your date?"

"The Navy," said Petey, snapping to attention, "needs men *now*. Every minute counts. How can I think of staying at a dance when there's a war to be won? I've got to get out of here, Dobie. I owe it to the boys Over There."

"What are you going to tell your date?"

"That's where you come in, Dobie. You take my girl; I go catch a bus. I won't tell her anything. I'll just disappear and you explain it to her later."

"Won't she mind?"

"I suppose she will, but it doesn't really matter. This is the first date I've ever had with her and I'll probably never see her again." He set his jaw. "Who knows when I'll be coming back from Over There."

"I understand," I said simply.

"Thanks, old man," he said simply.

We shook hands.

"By the way," I said, "what about those two tickets you've got for the Dr. Askit broadcast tomorrow night?"

"They're yours," he said, handing them to me.

"Thanks, old man," I said simply.

"Here comes my date now," Petey said, pointing at the powder-room door. I took one look at her and knew what a patriot he must be to run out on a smooth operator like that. She was strictly on the side of the angels.

"Where'd you find her?" I drooled.

"Just met her the other night. She's new around here. Now. I'll introduce you and you dance with her while I make my getaway."

"Solid," I agreed.

She walked over to us, making pink-taffeta noises. The timing was perfect. The orchestra was tuning up for the first number just as she reached us.

"Hi," said Petey. "I want you to meet a friend of mine. Dobie Gillis, this is—"

At that instant the orchestra started to play and I didn't catch

---

• operator (OP uh ray tur) one who is attractive to the opposite sex
• taffeta (TAF i tuh) kind of crisp, shiny fabric

her name. And no wonder. The orchestra was led by a trumpeter who had a delusion that good trumpeting and loud trumpeting are the same thing. Between him and Harry James,* he figured, were only a few hundred decibels of volume. Every time he played he narrowed the gap.

"Excuse me," shouted Petey, and left.

"Dance?" I yelled.

"What?" she screamed.

I made dancing motions and she nodded. We moved out on the floor. I tried to tell her while we were dancing that I hadn't caught her name, but it was impossible. The trumpeter, feeling himself gaining on Harry James, was pursuing his advantage hard. At last there came a short trumpet break, and I made a determined stab at it.

"I don't like to seem dull," I said to the girl, "but when Petey introduced us, I didn't catch your—"

But the trumpeter was back on the job, stronger than ever after his little rest. The rest of the song made the "Anvil Chorus"** sound like a lullaby. I gave up then, and we just danced.

Came the intermission and I tried again. "I know this is going to sound silly, but when we were intro—"

"I wonder where Petey is," she interrupted. "He's been gone an awfully long time."

"Oh, not so long really. Well, as I was saying, it makes me feel foolish to ask, but I didn't—"

"It has, too, been a long time. I think that's an awfully funny way for a boy to act when he takes a girl out for the first time. Where do you suppose he is?"

"Oh, I don't know. Probably just—oh, well, I suppose I might as well tell you now." So I told her.

• decibel (DES uh bul) unit for measuring loudness

*Harry James was a well-known trumpet player at the time of the story.

**The "Anvil Chorus" is a loud, rousing vocal piece.

She bit her lip. "Dobie," she quavered, "will you please take me home?"

"Home? It's so early."

"Please, Dobie."

Seventeen years of experience have taught me not to argue with a woman whose eyes are full of tears. I went and got my Driv-Ur-Self limousine, packed her into it, and started off.

"I—live—at—2123—Fremont—Avenue," she wailed.

"There, there," I cooed. "Try to look at it this way. The Navy needs men *now*. The longer he stayed around the dance tonight, the longer the war would last. Believe me, if my parents would sign a letter for me, I'd be Over There plenty quick, believe me."

"You mean," she wept, "that you would run off and stand up a girl at a formal affair?"

"Well," I said, "maybe not that. I mean I would hardly run out on a girl like you." I took her hand. "A girl so beautiful and lovely and pretty."

She smiled through tears. "You're sweet, Dobie."

"Oh, pshaw," I pshawed. "Say, I've got a couple of tickets to the Dr. Askit quiz broadcast tomorrow night. How about it?"

"Oh, Dobie, I'd love to. Only I don't know if Daddy will let me. He wants me to stay in and study tomorrow night. But I'll see what I can do. You call me."

"All right," I said, "but first there's something you have to tell me." I turned to her. "Now, please don't think that I'm a jerk, but it wasn't my fault. When Petey introduced us, I didn't—"

At this point I ran into the rear end of a bus. There followed a period of unpleasantness with the bus driver, during which I got a pithy lecture on traffic regulations. I don't know what he had to be sore about. His bus wasn't even nicked. The radiator grille of my car, on the other hand, was a total loss.

And when I got back in the car, there was more grief. The sudden stop had thrown the girl against the windshield headfirst, and her hat, a little straw number with birds, bees, flowers, and a patch of real grass, was now a heap of rubble. She howled all the way home.

"I'm afraid this evening hasn't been much fun," I said truly as I walked her to her door.

- quaver (KWAY vur) speak in a trembling voice
- pshaw (SHAW) expression of annoyance
- pithy (PITH ee) full of meaning
- rubble (RUB ul) bits of waste or junk

"I'm sorry, Dobie," she sniffled. "I'm sorry all this had to happen to you. You've been so nice to me."

"Oh, it's nothing any young American wouldn't have done," I said.

"You've been very sweet," she repeated. "I hope we'll get to be very good friends."

"Oh, we will. We certainly will."

She was putting her key in the lock.

"Just one more thing," I said. "Before you go in, I have to know—"

"Of course," she said. "I asked you to call and didn't give you my number. It's Kenwood 6817."

"No," I said, "it's not that. I mean, yes, I wanted that too. But there's another thing."

"Certainly, Dobie," she whispered and kissed me quickly. Then the door was closed behind her.

"Nuts," I mumbled, got into the car, returned it to the Driv-Ur-Self service, where I left a month's allowance to pay for the broken grille, and went back to the fraternity house.

A few of the guys were sitting in the living room. "Hi, Dobie," called one. "How'd you come out with that smooth operator? Petey sure picked the right night to run off and join the Navy, eh?"

"Oh, she was fine," I answered. "Say, do any of you fellows know her name?

"No, you lucky dog. She's all yours. Petey just met her this week and you're the only one he introduced her to. No competition. You lucky dog."

"Yeah, sure," I said. "Lucky dog." And I went upstairs to bed.

It was a troubled night, but I had a headful of plans when I got up in the morning. After all, the problem wasn't so difficult. Finding out a girl's name should be no task for a college freshman, a crossword-puzzle expert, and the senior-class poet of the Salmon P. Chase High School, Blue Earth, Minnesota.

First I picked up the phone and dialed the operator. "Hello," I said, "I'd like to find out the name of the people who live at 2123 Fremont Avenue. The number is Kenwood 6817."

"I'm sorry. We're not allowed to give out that information."

I hung up. Then I tried plan No. 2. I dialed Kenwood 6817. A gruff male voice answered, "Hello."

"Hello," I said, "who is this?"

"Who is *this?*" he said.

"This is Dobie Gillis. Who is this?"

"Who did you wish to speak to?"

Clearly, I was getting nowhere. I hung up.

Then I went and knocked on the door of Ed Beasley's room. Ed was a new pledge of the fraternity, and he was part of my third plan. He opened the door. "Enter, master," he said in the manner required of new pledges.

"Varlet," I said, "I have a task for you. Take yon telephone book and look through it until you find the name of the people who have telephone number Kenwood 6817."

"But, master—" protested Ed.

"I have spoken," I said sharply and walked off briskly, rubbing my palms.

In 10 minutes Ed was in my room with Roger Goodhue, the president of the fraternity. "Dobie," said Roger, "you are acquainted with the university policy regarding the hazing of pledges."

"Hazing?"

"You know very well that hazing was outlawed this year by the Dean of Student Affairs. And yet you go right ahead and haze poor Ed. Do you think more of your own amusement than the good of the fraternity? Do you know that if Ed had gone to the dean instead of me we would have had our charter taken away? I am going to insist on an apology right here and now."

Ed got his apology and walked off briskly, rubbing his palms.

"We'll have no more of that," said Roger, and he left too.

I took the phone book myself and spent four blinding hours looking for Kenwood 6817. Then I remembered that Petey had said the girl was new around here. The phone book was six months old; obviously her number would not be listed until a new edition was out.

The only course left to me was to try calling the number again in the hope that she would answer the phone herself. This time I was lucky. It was her voice.

"Hello," I cried, "who is this?"

"Why, it's Dobie Gillis," she said. "Daddy said you called before. Why didn't you ask to talk to me?"

- pledge (PLEJ) new member of a club
- varlet (VAR lit) servant; one of low station
- hazing (HAYZ ing) making new club members perform difficult or embarrassing tasks
- dean (DEEN) official in a college
- edition (uh DISH un) group of copies published at one time

"We were cut off," I said

"About tonight: I can go to the broadcast with you. I told Daddy we were going to the library to study. So be sure you tell the same story when you get here. I better hang up now. I hear Daddy coming downstairs. See you at eight. 'Bye."

"Goodbye," I said.

And goodbye to some lovely ideas. But I was far from licked. When I drove up to her house at eight in a car I had borrowed from a fraternity brother (I wisely decided not to try the Driv-Ur-Self people again), I still had a few aces up my sleeve. It was now a matter of pride with me. I thought of the day I had recited the senior-class poem at Salmon P. Chase High School and I said to myself, "By George, a man who could do that can find a simple girl's name, by George." And I wasn't going to be stupid about it either. I wasn't going to just ask her. After all this trouble, I was going to be sly about it. Sly, see?

I walked up to the porch, looking carefully for some marker with the family name on it. There was nothing. Even on the mailbox there was no name.

But in the mailbox was a letter! Quickly I scooped it out of the box, just in time to be confronted by a large, hostile man framed in a suddenly open doorway.

"And what, pray, are you doing in our mailbox?" he asked with dangerous calmness.

"I'm Dobie Gillis," I squeaked. "I'm here to call on your daughter. I just saw the mail in the box and thought I'd bring it in to you." I gave him a greenish smile.

"So you're the one who hung up on me this afternoon." He placed a very firm hand on my shoulder. "Come inside, please, young man," he said.

The girl was sitting in the living room. "Do you know this fellow?" asked her father.

"Of course, Daddy. That's Dobie Gillis, the boy who is going to take me over to the library to study tonight. Dobie, this is my father."

"How do you do, Mr. Zzzzzm," I mumbled.

"What?" he said.

"Well, we better run along," I said, taking the girl's hand.

"Just a moment, young man. I'd like to ask you a few things," said her father.

"Can't wait," I chirped. "Every minute counts. Stitch in time

---

• confront (kun FRUNT) face boldly

saves nine. Starve a cold and stuff a fever. Spare the rod and spoil the child." Meanwhile I was pulling the girl closer and closer to the door. "A penny saved is a penny earned," I said and got her out on the porch.

"It's such a nice night," I cried. "Let's run to the car." I had her in the car and the car in low and picking up speed fast before she could say a word.

"Dobie, you've been acting awfully strange tonight," she said with perfect justification. "I think I want to go home."

"Oh no, no, no. Not that. I'm just excited about our first real date, that's all."

"Sometimes you're so strange, and then sometimes you're so sweet. I can't figure you out."

"I'm a complex type," I admitted. And then I went to work. "How do you spell your name?" I asked.

"Just the way it sounds. What did you think?"

"Oh, I thought so. I just was wondering." I rang up a "No Sale" and started again. "Names are my hobby," I confessed. "Just before I came to get you tonight I was looking through a dictionary of names. Do you know, for instance, that Dorothy means 'gift of God'?"

"No. Really?"

"Yes. And Beatrice means 'making happy,' and Gertrude means 'spear maiden.'"

"Wonderful. Do you know any more?"

"Thousands," I said. "Abigail means 'my father's joy,' Margaret means 'a pearl,' Phyllis means 'a green bough,' and Beulah means 'she who is to be married.'" My eyes narrowed craftily; I was about to spring a trap. "Do you know what your name means?"

"Sure," she said. "It doesn't mean anything. I looked it up once, and it just said that it was from the Hebrew and didn't mean anything."

We were in front of the broadcasting studio. "Curses," I cursed and parked the car.

We went inside and were given tickets to hold. In a moment Dr. Askit took the stage and the broadcast began. "Everyone who came in here tonight was given a ticket," said Dr. Askit. "Each ticket has a number. I will now draw numbers out of this fishbowl here and call them off. If your number is called, please come up

---

- justification (jus tuh fuh KAY shun) good reason
- craftily (KRAF ti lee) slyly

on the stage and be a contestant." He reached into the fishbowl. "The first number is 174. Will the person holding 174 please come up here?"

"That's you," said the girl excitedly.

I thought fast. If I went up on the stage, I had a chance to win $64. Not a very good chance, because I'm not very bright about these things. But if I gave the girl my ticket and had her go up, Dr. Askit would make her give him her name and I would know what it was and all this nonsense would be over. It was the answer to my problem. "You go," I told her. "Take my ticket and go."

"But, Dobie—"

"Go ahead." I pushed her out in the aisle.

"And here comes a charming young lady," said Dr. Askit. He helped her to the microphone. "A very lucky young lady, I might add. Miss, do you know what you are?"

"What?"

"You are the ten thousandth contestant that has appeared on the Dr. Askit quiz program. And do you know what I am going to do in honor of this occasion?"

"What?"

"I am going to pay you 10 times as much as I ordinarily pay contestants. Instead of a $64 maximum, you have a chance to win $640!"

I may have to pay $640 to learn this girl's name, I thought, and waves of blackness passed before my eyes.

"Now," said Dr. Askit, "what would you like to talk about? Here is a list of subjects."

Without hesitation she said, "Number Six. The meaning of names of girls."

I tore two handfuls of upholstery from my seat.

"The first one is Dorothy," said Dr. Askit.

"Gift of God," replied the girl.

"Right! You now have $10. Would you like to try for $20? All right? The next one is Beatrice."

Two real tears ran down my cheeks. The woman sitting next to me moved over one seat.

"Making happy," said the girl.

"Absolutely correct!" crowed Dr. Askit. "Now would you care to try for $40?"

"You'll be sorry!" sang someone.

"Like heck she will!" I hollered.

"I'll try," she said.

"Gertrude," said Dr. Askit.

DR. ASKIT

"Forty dollars," I mourned silently. A sports coat. A good rod and reel. A new radiator grille for a Driv-Ur-Self car.

"Spear maiden," said the girl.

"Wonderful! There's no stopping this young lady tonight. How about the $80 question? Yes? All right. Abigail. Think now. This is a toughie."

"Oh, that's easy. My father's joy."

"Easy, she said. Easy. Go ahead," I wept, as I pommeled the arm of my seat, "rub it in. Easy!"

"You certainly know your names," said Dr. Askit admiringly. "What do you say to the $160 question? All right? Let's try Margaret."

"A pearl."

The usher came over to my seat and asked if anything was wrong. I shook my head mutely. "Are you sure?" he said. I nodded. He left, but kept looking at me.

"In all my years in radio," said Dr. Askit, "I have never known such a contestant. The next question, my dear, is for $320. Will you try?"

"Shoot," she said gaily.

"Phyllis."

"A green bough."

"Right! Correct! Absolutely correct!"

Two ushers were beside me now. "I've seen those types before," one whispered to the other. "We better get him out of here."

"Go away," I croaked.

"Now," said Dr. Askit, "will you take the big chance? The $640 question?"

She gulped and nodded.

"For $640—Beulah."

"She who is to be married," she said.

The ushers were tugging at my sleeves.

"And the lady wins $640! Congratulations! And now, may I ask you your name?"

"Come quietly, bud," said the ushers to me. "Please don't make us use no force."

"Great balls of fire, don't make me go now!" I cried. "Not now! I paid $640 to hear this."

"My name," she said, "is Mary Brown."

- pommel (PUM ul) beat
- mutely (MYOOT lee) without speaking

"You were sweet," she said to me as we drove home, "to let me go up there tonight instead of you."

"Think nothing of it, Mary Brown," I said bitterly.

She threw back her head and laughed. "You're so funny, Dobie. I think I like you more than any boy I've ever met."

"Well, that's something to be thankful for, Mary Brown," I replied.

She laughed some more. Then she leaned over and kissed my cheek. "Oh, Dobie, you're marvelous."

So Mary Brown kissed me and thought I was marvelous. Well, that was just dandy.

"Marvelous," she repeated and kissed me again.

"Thank you, Mary Brown," I said.

No use being bitter about it. After all, $640 wasn't all the money in the world. Not quite, anyhow. I had Mary Brown, now. Maybe I could learn to love her after a while. She looked easy enough to love. Maybe someday we would get married. Maybe there would even be a dowry. A large dowry. About $640.

I felt a little better. But just a little.

I parked in front of her house. "I'll never forget this evening as long as I live," she said as we walked to the porch.

"Nor I, Mary Brown," I said truthfully.

She giggled. She put her key in the front door. "Would you like to come in, Dobie—dear?"

"No thanks, Mary Brown. I have a feeling your father doesn't care for me." Then it dawned on me. "Look!" I cried. "Your father. You told him you were at the library tonight. What if he was listening to the radio tonight and heard you on the Dr. Askit program?"

"Oh, don't worry. People's voices sound different over the radio."

"But the name! You gave your name!"

She looked at me curiously. "Are you kiddin'? You know very well I didn't give my right name. . . . DOBIE! WHY ARE YOU BEATING YOUR HEAD AGAINST THE WALL?"

• dowry (DOW ree) money from bride's parents

ALL THINGS CONSIDERED ———————————————————

1. When the girl learns that she's been abandoned at the formal, she (a) dances with Dobie all night. (b) runs out of the room, crying. (c) asks to go home.

2. On the first day of the story, Dobie tries several times to (a) kiss the girl. (b) learn the girl's name. (c) dance a new dance.

3. The girl's phone number isn't in the book because (a) her family are newcomers to the area. (b) her mother is famous. (c) the phone company made a mistake.

4. Luckily for the girl, on the way to the quiz show, she and Dobie discuss (a) their favorite hobbies. (b) the meanings of girls' names. (c) Dr. Askit.

5. At the end of the story, the reader (a) knows the girl's name is Mary Brown. (b) is fairly sure the girl's name is Mary Brown. (c) has no idea of the girl's name.

THINKING IT THROUGH ———————————————————

1. Why does Dobie lose control of himself near the end of the quiz show and cry, "I paid $640 to hear this"?

2. (a) In your opinion, how likely are the events in the story? Explain. (b) If you answered "not very," how does the author hold your interest in a tale that would probably never happen in fact?

3. The story was written more than 40 years ago. Just for fun, suppose that the author had rewritten it last year for modern readers. What changes would he make to update the story? Try to name at least three.

4. Why is the story an excellent example of *tragicomedy* (see page 281)? Include at least two examples in your answer.

5. Max Shulman is the kind of writer who always seems to come up with just the right words, rich with the right *connotations* (see page 324). For instance, the weekend is going to be a "dreamboat," the new girl is "strictly on the side of the angels," and the narrator gives the girl's father a "greenish smile." Find two more examples of words or phrases that you think are unusually well chosen.

UNIT REVIEW

I. Match the terms in Column A with their definitions in Column B.

A

1. tragicomedy
2. fact
3. point of view
4. opinion
5. denotation
6. connotation
7. first person
8. third person

B

(a) position from which a story is told

(b) the "dictionary meaning" of a word

(c) play that involves "some tears, some laughter"

(d) told from an outsider's viewpoint— does not include an "I/me" character

(e) what one thinks or believes about something

(f) told from the position of a character in the story

(g) something known to be true

(h) all the feelings and ideas that a word suggests

II. Who Am I?

Here are 11 statements written in the *first person.* Each of them identifies a character, event, or object in one of the selections in this unit. Identify each and then go on to state one more *fact* or *opinion* about that person, event, or object.

1. Today Johnny brought his friend Boyd home for lunch.
2. Having those six blind guys all around me was just too much!
3. "I never loved but one . . . and twice I lost him."
4. Only the health of others keeps me from writing as humorously as I can.
5. I am the last word my dying owner said.
6. I stood beneath a balcony and spoke another's words of love.
7. I laughed until I died—almost.
8. After that horrible time in the bank, I keep my money in cash in the pocket of my trousers.
9. My size and shape were a major force in the direction of my owner's life.
10. "I see," quoth I, "the Elephant is very like a rope."
11. I drove a coach of food and beauty through the Spanish lines.

SPEAKING UP

▶ What lies beyond tears and laughter? The English poet Algernon Charles Swinburne (1837–1909) deals with this question in the melodious poem that follows. The speaker in the poem, having died a natural death, imagines himself as having arrived at "The Garden of Proserpine" (proh SUR puh nee). In Greek mythology, Proserpine was the goddess of the underworld, and therefore of death.

Swinburne is known for writing poems that combine beautiful sounds with sorrowful subjects. Practice reading the poem aloud until your voice expresses both the beauty and the sorrow of the poem.

from THE GARDEN OF PROSERPINE

by Algernon Charles Swinburne

I am tired of tears and laughter,
    And men that laugh and weep;
Of what may come hereafter
    For men that sow to reap:
5 I am weary of days and hours,
    Blown buds of barren flowers,
Desires and dreams and powers
    And everything but sleep.

Here . . . the world is quiet;
10   Here . . . all trouble seems
Dead winds' and spent waves' riot
    In doubtful dream of dreams.

We are not sure of sorrow,
    And Joy was never sure;
15 Today will die tomorrow;
    Time stoops to no man's lure;
And Love, grown faint and fretful,
    With lips but half regretful
Sighs, and with eyes forgetful
20   Weeps that no loves endure.

Pale, beyond porch and portal,
    Crowned with calm leaves, she stands
Who gathers all things mortal
    With cold immortal hands.

25   From too much love of living,
    From hope and fear set free,
    We thank with brief thanksgiving
    Whatever gods may be
    That no life lives forever;
30   That dead men rise up never;
    That even the weariest river
    Winds somewhere safe to sea.

Before you practice your reading, think about these questions and try to answer them:

1. What kind of people does the phrase "men that sow to reap" (line 4) suggest?
2. "Time" (line 16) and "Love" (line 17) are both examples of *personification* (see page 120). In your own words, explain what is said about each.
3. Who is the "she" in line 22?
4. What is the *figurative* meaning (see page 118) of the last two lines?

- reap (REEP) harvest; cut and gather in
- barren (BAR un) not producing; useless
- spent (SPENT) worn out; exhausted
- lure (LOOR) attractive temptation meant to trick or trap
- fretful (FRET ful) worried; anxious
- portal (POR tul) entrance; gate or doorway
- mortal (MOR tul) living; human
- immortal (im MOR tul) beyond death; enduring forever

WRITING: ABOUT A CHARACTER

Assignment: First select a character in this unit that interested you as you read. Then write a short paper that, as much as possible, (1) *describes* the character's appearance, personality, and behavior, (2) *explains* the character's behavior, and (3) *evaluates* the character's behavior according to your own standards of opinion.

Prewriting: Choose a character about whom you can write at least a page. Then think about the three requirements given above. Either Mrs. Wilson in "After You, My Dear Alphonse" or the narrator in "My Financial Career" is a good choice (although you will have to infer most of the *appearance* in each case). Roxane in *Cyrano de Bergerac* may be an even better choice for you. You should already have a clear idea of her appearance and personality. Now think about her behavior in detail. When does she use other people for her own purposes? Why does she do this, and are her purposes good or bad? When does she lie or withhold the truth from others? What causes this behavior, and what do you think of it? Go on to other good questions that you can ask and answer. Whatever character you choose, make notes on all that you intend to say about him or her.

Writing: Studying your notes will provide the best guide for dividing the paper into paragraphs. For instance, you might decide on three paragraphs. The first would mention author, title, and character, and then go on to appearance and personality. The second would deal with the character's behavior and its probable causes. The third would present your opinions about that behavior and state why you hold these opinions. In any case, start your writing with the first sentence of every paragraph you intend to use. These sentences will keep you organized as you write; later they will let your reader know what every paragraph is to be about.

Revising: Follow the suggestions for revision given earlier in this book. Since this assignment calls for you to evaluate as well as to describe, make sure that your opinions are supported by reasons. You are entitled to your own opinions only if you can explain them to others.

U N I T · 6

MORE THAN

MEETS

THE EYE

A gift it once was from Annam—
A parrot, red as peach-tree bloom,
Painted with streaks of evening sky,
And needing naught but elbow room
To tell the truth in tongue of men.
And so it shared the common doom
Of all whose words strike near the Truth:
They put it in a small cramped cage,
A cell that soon became its tomb.

—Po Chü-i
(9th century, China)

Have you heard the expression "more than meets the eye"? It simply means "more than one notices at first." For most of us, it's easy to overlook important ideas and events when we first encounter them. That's why a second look is so important.

In this unit, you will meet people who become involved in unusual situations and events. When you read about each of them, remember that there is more to any situation than originally meets the eye.

THREE LETTERS . . .
AND A FOOTNOTE

by Horacio Quiroga

▶ Here, from the country of Uruguay in South America, is a story of boy-meets-girl-and-boy-doesn't-even-know-it! Not only is the story unusual, but it is told in an unusual manner. It takes the form of a "Letter to the Editor" plus a "Letter *From* the Editor."

Sir:

I am taking the liberty of sending you these lines, hoping you will be good enough to publish them under your own name. I do this because I have been told that no newspaper would accept these pages if I sign them myself. If you think it wiser, you may alter my impressions by giving them a few masculine touches.

My work makes it necessary for me to take the streetcar twice a day. For five years I have been making the same trip. Sometimes, on the return ride, I travel in the company of some of my girl friends. But on the way to work I always go alone. I am 20 years old, tall, not too thin, with a pleasing complexion. My mouth is somewhat large but not pale. My impression is that my eyes are not small. These features are all I need to help me form an opinion of many men. In fact, so many that I'm tempted to say all men.

You know also that you men have the habit before you board a streetcar of looking rapidly at its occupants through the windows. In that way you examine all the faces (of the women, of course, since they are the only ones that have any interest for you). After that little ceremony, you enter and sit down.

Very well, then. As soon as a man leaves the sidewalk, walks over to the car and looks inside, I know perfectly well what sort of fellow he is, and I never make a mistake. I know if he is serious, or if he merely intends to invest 10 cents of his fare to flirt a little. I quickly distinguish between those who like to ride at their ease, and those who prefer less room at the side of some girl.

When the place beside me is unoccupied, I recognize accurately which men are indifferent and will sit down anywhere. Which are only half-interested and will turn their heads in order to look us over, after they have sat down. Finally, which are the fellows who will pass by seven empty places so as to perch uncomfortably at my side, way back in the rear of the streetcar.

These fellows are the most interesting. Quite contrary to the regular habit of girls who travel alone, instead of getting up and offering the inside place to the newcomer, I simply move over toward the window to leave plenty of room.

Plenty of room! That's a meaningless phrase. Never will three-quarters of a bench left by a girl to her neighbor be sufficient. After moving and shifting at will, he seems suddenly overcome by a surprising restlessness. But that is mere appearance. If anyone watches this lack of movement, he will note that the body of the gentleman is slipping little by little down an imaginary plane toward the window, where the girl happens to be. Of course, the man isn't looking at her and apparently has no interest in her at all.

That's the way such men are. One could swear that they're thinking about the moon. However, all this time, the right foot (or the left) continues slipping delicately to the side.

- **distinguish** (di STING gwish) tell apart; recognize as different
- indifferent (in DIF ur unt) not caring; without interest
- **contrary** (KON trer ee) opposite
- **plane** (PLAYN) flat surface, which may be tilted

I'll admit that while this is going on, I'm very far from being bored. With a mere glance as I shift toward the window, I have taken the measure of the fellow. I know whether he is spirited, and yields to his first impulse, or whether he is really a brazen lad. I know whether he is a courteous young man or just a rude one.

The tactics of the man never vary. First of all the sudden rigidity and the look of thinking about the moon. The next step is a fleeting glimpse at our person, which seems to linger slightly over our face. Really the purpose is to see the distance between his foot and ours.

I think there are few things funnier than the way you men look, when you move your foot along in gradual shifts of toe and heel. Obviously you men can't see the joke. This pretty cat-and-mouse game played with a size 11 shoe at one end, and at the other, a silly face, bears no comparison with any other silly things you men do.

I said before that I was not bored with these performances. From the moment the charmer has figured the exact distance he has to cover with his foot, he rarely lets his gaze wander down again. He is certain of his measurement, and he has no desire to put us on our guard by repeated glances.

Very well, then. When he has gone about halfway, I start the same maneuver that he is executing. I do it with equal slyness. And I have the same kind of absentminded way of thinking, let us say, about the stars. Only, the movement of my foot is away from his. Not much. A few inches are enough.

It's a treat to see, presently, my neighbor's surprise when, upon arriving finally at the calculated spot, he contacts absolutely nothing. Nothing! His size 11 shoe is entirely alone. This is too much for him. First he takes a look at the floor. Then at my face. My mind is still wandering a thousand miles away, up in the stars. But the fellow begins to understand.

- brazen (BRAY zun) bold; shameless
- **tactics** (TAK tiks) methods
- rigidity (ri JID i tee) stiffness
- **maneuver** (muh NOO vur) skillfully planned movement
- **executing** (EK suh kyoot ing) carrying out; putting into action
- **calculated** (KAL kyuh lay tid) planned; carefully thought out

Fifteen out of 17 times (I mention these figures out of long experience) the annoying gentleman gives up. In the two remaining cases I am forced to give a warning look. Actually, it is enough to make a movement of the head in his direction, toward him but without looking straight at him. In these cases it is better always to avoid crossing glances with a man who by chance has been really and deeply attracted to us. This fact is well known to young women, not thin, not dark, with mouths not little and eyes not small, as is the case with yours truly.

M. R.

Dear Miss:

Deeply grateful for your kindness. I'll sign my name with much pleasure to the article on your impressions, as you request. Nevertheless, it would interest me very much to know your answer to the following questions. Aside from the 17 cases you mention, haven't you ever felt the slightest attraction toward some neighbor, tall or short, blond or dark, stout or lean? Haven't you felt the temptation to yield, ever so slightly, which made the withdrawing of your own foot disagreeable and troublesome?

H. Q.

Sir:

To be frank, yes, once in my life. I did feel that temptation to yield to someone, or more accurately, that lack of energy in my foot to which you refer. That person was *you*. But you didn't have the sense to take advantage of it.

M. R.

ALL THINGS CONSIDERED ———————————————

1. Reading between the lines, one can tell that the young woman considers herself (a) very shy. (b) quite good-looking. (c) very serious.

2. The young woman joins in the "cat-and-mouse game" by (a) leaving the streetcar. (b) glancing directly at the man. (c) moving her foot.

3. The young woman states that men have behaved as she describes (a) one or two times. (b) nine out of 10 times. (c) 15 out of 17 times.

4. The writer of the second letter is (a) the editor to whom the first letter is addressed. (b) a young woman. (c) an unknown man.

5. It is clear that the young woman (a) dislikes the editor. (b) knows the editor by sight. (c) is in for the biggest surprise of her life.

THINKING IT THROUGH ———————————————

1. The "Three Letters" in the title are included in the story—but what is the "Footnote"?

2. In your opinion, approximately when was the story written? Give at least one reason for your answer.

3. Do you think events such as those described in the selection could happen on a bus in an American city today? Explain your answer.

4. Suppose that the third letter is not "the end of the story" but just one step in a growing romance. What might be the next communication between M.R. and H.Q.?

5. The character of M.R. is revealed through a series of letters. Reread M.R.'s first letter to H.Q. From her letter, what kind of person do you suppose H.Q. is? Think of at least five adjectives to describe her.

Relationships: Review

If you wish to review the meaning of any term in *italics* in this exercise, refer to the Glossary of Terms.

1. Here are seven details from the selection. Arrange them on your paper so that they form a *details-in-sequence* pattern:
   a) He takes a fleeting glimpse at the distance between his foot and hers.
   b) A slight warning look makes him stop.
   c) She moves her foot.
   d) He looks over the occupants of the streetcar before boarding.
   e) Surprised, he takes a look at the floor, then at her face.
   f) He sits down next to her, in the back of the streetcar.
   g) He starts moving his foot.
2. Here are three statements about "M.R." Which do you consider a *main idea*, and which are *supporting details*?
   a) "M.R." writes playful "letters to the editor."
   b) "M.R." plays a "cat-and-mouse game" with men on streetcars.
   c) "M.R." is a fun-loving young woman.
3. In the fifth paragraph, the writer distinguishes three categories of men who enter streetcars. (a) What are the three categories? (b) With which group is she most concerned? Why?
4. In the sixth paragraph, the young woman contrasts her behavior with "the regular habit of girls who travel alone." What is this *contrast*?
5. Another contrast is involved in what the writer calls a "cat-and-mouse game." (a) What do the words "cat" and "mouse" refer to? (b) What is the *contrast*?
6. The story contains *comparisons* as well as contrasts. In what way is M.R.'s behavior like that of her seatmate?

Composition

1. Write five sentences that *contrast* "Three Letters . . . and a Footnote" with any other story in this book. In contrasting the two stories, you may focus on such details as setting, characterization, and theme. It may help you to refer to the Glossary of Terms for definitions of specific literary terms.
2. In the story, the young lady, "M.R.," has the last word. Suppose that "H.Q." wrote to "M.R." a second time in an effort to continue the relationship. Try to imagine what he would say, keeping in mind the personalities and interests of both people. Then write the letter yourself and sign it "H.Q."

YOU CAN'T TAKE IT WITH YOU

by Eva-Lis Wuorio

▶ Now travel from Uruguay to Canada for another very short story with a surprising twist. Have you ever heard the expression "You can't take it with you"? If not, find out what it means before reading the story.

There was no denying two facts. Uncle Basil was rich. Uncle Basil was a miser.

The family were unanimous about that. They had used up all the words as their temper and their need of ready money dictated. Gentle Aunt Clotilda, who wanted a new string of pearls because the one she had was getting old, had merely called him Scrooge* Basil. Percival, having again smashed his Aston Martin** for which he had not paid, had declared Uncle Basil a skinflint, a miser, tightwad, churl, and usurer with colorful adjectives added. The rest had used up all the other words in the dictionary.

"He doesn't have to be so parsimonious, that's true, with all he has," said Percival's mother. "But you shouldn't use rude words, Percival. They might get back to him."

"He can't take it with him," said Percival's sister Letitia, combing her golden hair. "I need a new fur but he said, 'Why? It's summer.' Well! He's mingy, that's what he is."

"He can't take it with him" was a phrase the family used so often it began to slip out in front of Uncle Basil as well.

"You can't take it with you, Uncle Basil," they said. "Why don't you buy a sensible house out in the country, and we could all come and visit you? Horses. A swimming pool. The lot. Think

---

- churl (CHURL) rude and insensitive person
- usurer (YOO zhur ur) one who lends money at very high rates of interest
- parsimonious (par suh MOH nee us) stingy; miserly
- mingy (MIN jee) mean and stingy

*Ebenezer Scrooge is a mean-spirited miser in *A Christmas Carol* by Charles Dickens.
**An Aston Martin is a kind of British sports car.

what fun you'd have, and you can certainly afford it. You can't take it with you, you know."

Uncle Basil had heard all the words they called him because he wasn't as deaf as he made out. He knew he was a mingy, stingy, penny-pinching screw, scrimp, scraper, pinchfist, hoarder, and curmudgeon (just to start with). There were other words, less gentle, he'd also heard himself called. He didn't mind. What galled him was the oft repeated warning, "You can't take it with you." After all, it was all his.

He'd gone to the Transvaal* when there was still gold to be found if one knew where to look. He'd found it. They said he'd come back too old to enjoy his fortune. What did they know? He enjoyed simply having a fortune. He enjoyed also saying no to them all. They were like circus animals, he often thought, behind the bars of their thousand demands of something for nothing.

Only once had he said yes. That was when his sister asked him to take on Verner, her somewhat slow-witted eldest son. "He'll do as your secretary," his sister Maud had said. Verner didn't do at all as a secretary, but since all he wanted to be happy was to be told what to do, Uncle Basil let him stick around as an all-around handyman.

Uncle Basil lived neatly in a house very much too small for his money, the family said, in an unfashionable suburb. It was precisely like the house where he had been born. Verner looked after the small garden, fetched the papers from the corner tobacconist, and filed his nails when he had time. He had nice nails. He never said to Uncle Basil, "You can't take it with you," because it didn't occur to him.

Uncle Basil also used Verner to run messages to his man of affairs, the bank, and such, since he didn't believe either in the mails or the telephone. Verner got used to carrying thick envelopes back and forth without ever bothering to question what was in them. Uncle Basil's lawyers, accountants, and bank managers also got used to his somewhat unorthodox business methods. He did have a fortune, and he continued making money with his in-

- curmudgeon (kur MUJ un) bad-tempered person
- gall (GAWL) annoy; irritate
- **precisely** (pri SYS lee) exactly
- tobacconist (tuh BAK uh nist) seller of tobacco products
- unorthodox (un OR thuh doks) unusual

*The Transvaal is a region in the mineral-rich country of South Africa.

vestments. Rich men have always been allowed their foibles.

Another foible of Uncle Basil's was that while he still was in excellent health he had Verner drive him out to an old-fashioned carpenter shop where he had himself measured for a coffin. He wanted it roomy, he said.

The master carpenter was a dour countryman of the same generation as Uncle Basil, and he accepted the order matter-of-factly. They consulted about woods and prices, and settled on a medium-price, unlined coffin. A lined one would have cost double.

"I'll line it myself," Uncle Basil said. "Or Verner can. There's plenty of time. I don't intend to pop off tomorrow. It would give the family too much satisfaction. I like enjoying my fortune."

Then one morning, while in good humor and sound mind, he sent Verner for his lawyer. The family got to hear about this, and there were in-fights, out-fights, and general quarreling while they tried to find out to whom Uncle Basil had decided to leave his money. To put them out of their misery, he said, he'd tell them the truth. He didn't like scattering money about. He liked it in a lump sum. Quit bothering him about it.

That happened a good decade before the morning his housekeeper, taking him his tea, found him peacefully asleep forever. It had been a good decade for him. The family hadn't dared to worry him, and his investments had risen steadily.

Only Percival, always pressed for money, had threatened to put arsenic in his tea, but when the usual proceedings were gone through Uncle Basil was found to have died a natural death. "A happy death," said the family. "He hadn't suffered."

They began to remember loudly how nice they'd been to him and argued about who had been the nicest. It was true too. They had been attentive, the way families tend to be to rich and stubborn elderly relatives. They didn't know he'd heard all they'd said out of his hearing, as well as the flattering drivel they'd spread like soft butter on hot toast in his hearing. Everyone, recalling his own efforts to be thoroughly nice, was certain that he and only he would be the heir to the Lump Sum.

- foible (FOI bul) strange habit or fault
- dour (DOOR) gloomy; unfriendly
- lump sum—in one piece; all together
- **decade** (DEK ayd) ten-year period
- arsenic (AR suh nik) poisonous substance
- drivel (DRIV ul) foolish talk

They rushed to consult the lawyer. He said that he had been instructed by Uncle Basil in sane and precise terms. The cremation was to take place immediately after the death, and they would find the coffin ready in the garden shed. Verner would know where it was.

"Nothing else?"

"Well," said the lawyer in the way lawyers have, "he left instructions for a funeral repast to be sent in from Fortnum and Mason. Everything of the best. Goose and turkey, venison and beef, oysters and lobsters, and wines of good vintage plus plenty of whisky. He liked to think of a good send-off, curmudgeon though he was, he'd said."

The family was a little shaken by the use of the word "curmudgeon." How did Uncle Basil know about that? But they were relieved to hear that the lawyer also had an envelope, the contents of which he did not know, to read to them at the feast after the cremation.

- **repast** (ri PAST) meal
- vintage (VIN tij) particular year or harvest

They all bought expensive black clothes, since black was the color of that season anyway, and whoever inherited would share the wealth. That was only fair.

Only Verner said that couldn't they buy Uncle Basil a smarter coffin? The one in the garden shed was pretty tatty, since the roof leaked. But the family hardly listened to him. After all, it would only be burned, so what did it matter?

So, duly and with proper sorrow, Uncle Basil was cremated.

The family returned to the little house as the housekeeper was leaving. Uncle Basil had given her a generous amount of cash, telling her how to place it so as to have a fair income for life. In gratitude she'd spread out the Fortnum and Mason goodies, but she wasn't prepared to stay to do the dishes.

They were a little surprised, but not dismayed, to hear from Verner that the house was now in his name. Uncle Basil had also given him a small sum of cash and told him how to invest it. The family taxed him about it, but the amount was so nominal they were relieved to know Verner would be off their hands. Verner himself, though mildly missing the old man because he was used to him, was quite content with his lot. He wasn't used to much, so he didn't need much.

The storm broke when the lawyer finally opened the envelope.

There was only one line in Uncle Basil's scrawl.

"I did take it with me."

Of course there was a great to-do. What about the fortune? The millions and millions!

Yes, said the men of affairs, the accountants, and even the bank managers, who finally admitted yes, there had been a very considerable fortune. Uncle Basil, however, had drawn large sums in cash, steadily and regularly, over the past decade. What had he done with it? That the men of affairs, the accountants, and the bank managers did not know. After all, it had been Uncle Basil's money, ergo, his affair.

Not a trace of the vast fortune ever came to light.

No one thought to ask Verner, and it didn't occur to Verner to volunteer that for quite a long time he had been lining the coffin,

---

- tatty (TAT ee) crude; cheap
- **tax** (TAKS) make demands of; put strain on
- nominal (NOM uh nul) small; unimportant
- scrawl (SKRAWL) poor handwriting
- ergo (UR goh) therefore

at Uncle Basil's behest, with thick envelopes he brought back from the banks. First he'd done a thick layer of these envelopes all around the sides and bottom of the coffin. Then, as Uncle Basil wanted, he'd tacked on blue sailcloth.

He might not be so bright in his head but he was smart with his hands.

He'd done a neat job.

ALL THINGS CONSIDERED ────────────

1. The family is quite mistaken about Uncle Basil's (a) deafness. (b) miserly nature. (c) generally bad temper.
2. Uncle Basil enjoys (a) the things that money can buy. (b) planning ways for his money to be spent after his death. (c) simply having a lot of money.
3. Uncle Basil leaves money only to (a) Percival. (b) his pets. (c) two servants.
4. The written message Uncle Basil leaves for his family contains (a) the names of his heirs. (b) a single sentence. (c) a list of investments.
5. At the end of the story, most of Uncle Basil's money is (a) in investments. (b) in ashes. (c) being spent foolishly.

THINKING IT THROUGH ────────────

1. "You Can't Take It with You." (a) What does the expression usually mean? (b) In what sense does Uncle Basil disprove the expression?
2. (a) Did you foresee the ending before you read it? (b) What clues helped you (or might have helped you)?
3. In your opinion, who is worse: Uncle Basil or his relatives? Explain.

- behest (bi HEST) command; request
- sailcloth (SAYL cloth) canvas

Reading and Analyzing: Review

If you wish to review the meaning of any term in *italics* in this exercise, refer to the Glossary of Terms.

1. In what way is the ending of the story a good example of *irony of situation*?
2. Explain this sentence: If you foresaw the surprise ending of the story, you enjoyed a moment of *dramatic irony*.
3. What *inference* does the family make when they learn that Uncle Basil has seen a lawyer and hear about the "lump sum"? On what evidence is this inference based?
4. Uncle Basil does leave some money to some people. (a) Who are they? (b) What *conclusion* can you draw from this fact?
5. Many readers finish the story with a certain *visual image* in their minds. What image was in your mind as you completed the story?
6. The story is full of *character clues* about Uncle Basil and members of his family. (a) What is one character clue concerning Uncle Basil, and what does it indicate? (b) What is one character clue about one of Basil's relatives (or the whole family), and what does it mean?

Composition

1. The story contains more than 10 words relating to Uncle Basil's stinginess. Go back and find at least five such words. If possible, choose words that are new to you (like "parsimonious"). Use the five words in five different sentences of your own. Use a good dictionary if you need additional help.
2. Suppose you were given the job of turning the story into a script for a half-hour TV show. Your first task would be to decide on the number of scenes. (Whenever there is a change in setting or a leap in time, you would need to begin a new scene.) On a piece of paper, list the scenes you would need. Start with "Scene 1: Uncle Basil is introduced, along with Aunt Clotilda, who wants pearls, and Percival, who wants to have his car repaired."

▶ A **narrative poem**—as the words indicate—is a poem that tells a story. One of the world's best examples of narrative poetry is "The Highwayman" by the British poet Alfred Noyes. If you wish, read the poem aloud, or at least try to capture the sounds in your "mind's ear." Notice how the rhyme and rhythm seem to heighten the action.

THE HIGHWAYMAN

by Alfred Noyes

Part One

I

The wind was a torrent of darkness among the gusty trees,
The moon was a ghostly galleon tossed upon cloudy seas,
The road was a ribbon of moonlight over the purple moor,
And the highwayman came riding—
5   Riding—riding—
The highwayman came riding, up to the old inn door.

II

He'd a French cocked hat on his forehead, a bunch of lace at
  his chin,
A coat of the claret velvet, and breeches of brown doeskin;
They fitted with never a wrinkle: his boots were up to the thigh!
10   And he rode with a jewelled twinkle,
His pistol butts a-twinkle,
His rapier hilt a-twinkle, under the jewelled sky.

- highwayman (HY way man) robber who holds up travelers
- **torrent** (TOR unt) flood; rushing flow
- **galleon** (GAL yun) large sailing ship
- moor (MOOR) open wasteland
- claret (KLAR ut) shade of red
- **butt** (BUT) rear end of a gun
- rapier (RAYP yur) thin sword
- **hilt** (HILT) handle of sword

III

Over the cobbles he clattered and clashed in the dark innyard,
And he tapped with his whip on the shutters, but all was locked
    and barred;
15   He whistled a tune at the window, and who should be waiting
    there
But the landlord's black-eyed daughter,
Bess the landlord's daughter,
Plaiting a dark red love knot into her long black hair.

IV

And dark in the dark old innyard a stable wicket creaked
20   Where Tim the ostler listened; his face was white and peaked;
His eyes were hollows of madness, his hair like moldy hay,
But he loved the landlord's daughter,
The landlord's red-lipped daughter,
Dumb as a dog he listened, and he heard the robber say—

- **cobbles** (KOB ulz) stones once used for paving roads
- **plaiting** (PLAYT ing) pleating; braiding
- **wicket** (WIK it) small gate or door
- **ostler** (OS lur) one who takes care of horses
- **peaked** (PEEKT) sickly-looking

V

25 "One kiss, my bonny sweetheart, I'm after a prize tonight,
But I shall be back with the yellow gold before the morning
    light;
Yet, if they press me sharply, and harry me through the day,
Then look for me by moonlight,
Watch for me by moonlight,
30 I'll come to thee by moonlight, though hell should bar the
    way."

VI

He rose upright in the stirrups; he scarce could reach her hand,
But she loosened her hair in the casement! His face burned like
    a brand
As the black cascade of perfume came tumbling over his
    breast;
And he kissed its waves in the moonlight,
35 (Oh, sweet black waves in the moonlight!)
Then he tugged at his rein in the moonlight, and galloped away
    to the West.

Part Two
I

He did not come in the dawning; he did not come at noon;
And out of the tawny sunset, before the rise of the moon,
When the road was a gypsy's ribbon, looping the purple moor,
40 A redcoat troop came marching—
Marching—marching
King George's men came marching, up to the old inn door.

II

They said no word to the landlord, they drank his ale instead,
But they gagged his daughter and bound her to the foot of her
    narrow bed;

- harry (HAR ee) continue to trouble; bother
- casement (KAYS munt) window
- **cascade** (kas KAYD) waterfall
- tawny (TAW nee) brownish yellow

45   Two of them knelt at her casement, with muskets by their side!
There was death at every window,
And hell at one dark window;
For Bess could see, through her casement, the road that *he*
    would ride.

III

They had tied her up to attention, with many a sniggering jest;
50   They had bound a musket beside her, with the barrel beneath
    her breast!
"Now keep good watch!" they warned her. She heard the dead
    man say—
Look for me by moonlight;
Watch for me by moonlight;
I'll come to thee by moonlight, though hell should bar the way!

IV

55   She twisted her hands behind her; but all the knots held good!
She writhed her hands till her fingers were wet with sweat or
    blood!
They stretched and strained in the darkness, and the hours
    crawled by like years,
Till, now, on the stroke of midnight,
Cold, on the stroke of midnight,
60   The tip of one finger touched it! The trigger at least was hers!

V

The tip of one finger touched it; she strove no more for the rest!
Up, she stood up to attention, with the barrel beneath her
    breast,
She would not risk their hearing; she would not strive again;
For the road lay bare in the moonlight;
65   Blank and bare in the moonlight;
And the blood of her veins in the moonlight throbbed to her
    love's refrain.

- **sniggering** (SNIG ur ing) half-smothered laughter
- **jest** (JEST) joke
- **strove** (STROHV) tried hard
- **refrain** (ri FRAYN) repeated verse or melody

VI

Tlot-tlot; tlot-tlot! Had they heard it? The horse hoofs ringing
    clear?
Tlot-tlot; tlot-tlot, in the distance? Were they deaf that they did
    not hear?
Down the ribbon of moonlight, over the brow of the hill,
70   The highwayman came riding,
    Riding, riding!
The redcoats looked to their priming! She stood up, straight and
    still!

VII

Tlot-tlot, in the frosty silence! *Tlot-tlot,* in the echoing night!
Nearer he came and nearer! Her face was like a light!
75   Her eyes grew wide for a moment; she drew one last deep
    breath,
Then her finger moved in the moonlight,
Her musket shattered the moonlight,
Shattered her breast in the moonlight and warned him—with
    her death.

• priming (PRYM ing) getting guns primed, or ready

VIII

He turned; he spurred to the West; he did not know who stood
80 Bowed, with her head o'er the musket, drenched with her own
     red blood!
Not till the dawn he heard it; his face grew gray to hear
How Bess, the landlord's daughter,
The landlord's black-eyed daughter,
Had watched for her love in the moonlight, and died in the
     darkness there.

IX

85 Back he spurred like a madman, shrieking a curse to the sky,
With the white road smoking behind him, and his rapier
     brandished high!
Blood-red were his spurs in the golden noon; wine red was his
     velvet coat,
When they shot him down on the highway,
Down like a dog on the highway,
90 And he lay in his blood on the highway, with the bunch of lace
     at his throat.

X

And still of a winter's night, they say, when the moon is in the
     trees,
When the moon is a ghostly galleon tossed upon cloudy seas,
When the road is a ribbon of moonlight over the purple moor,
A highwayman comes riding—
95 Riding—riding,
A highwayman comes riding up to the old inn door.

- **spur** (SPUR) urge on (especially a horse)
- **brandished** (BRAN disht) waved threateningly

XI

Over the cobbles he clatters and clangs in the dark innyard;
He taps with his whip on the shutters, but all is locked and
    barred;
He whistles a tune at the window, and who should be waiting
    there
100 But the landlord's black-eyed daughter,
    Bess, the landlord's daughter,
Plaiting a dark red love knot into her long black hair.

WAYS OF KNOWING

1. Summarize the poem by retelling it in your own words.
2. Do you think there is a relationship between the presence of Tim the ostler in the innyard and the arrival of the redcoat troops? If so, what might the relationship be?
3. In what way do night and darkness heighten the mood of the poem?
4. What is the best evidence that Bess truly loves the highwayman?
5. How does the poet use repetition effectively? Give examples.
6. When do you think the events in the poem took place? Give reasons for your inferences.
7. More than any other poem in this book, "The Highwayman" is full of SOUNDS. First discuss the use of sounds in lines 13 and 67. Then discuss how the poem could be divided up for **choral reading** (oral interpretation, usually by small groups). What lines or complete stanzas would you give to different groups, or in some cases, to individuals?

Before completing the exercises that follow, you may wish to review the **bold-faced** words on pages 345 to 362.

I. On a separate sheet of paper, write the *italicized* word that best fills the blank in each sentence.

tactics	*precisely*	*refrain*	*torrent*	*plane*
repast	*executing*	*galleon*	*contrary*	*strove*

1. Scott's plan to increase his wages had just the _____ effect.
2. His basic idea was a good one, but the _____ he used were all wrong.
3. Besides, he never really finished _____ his plan.
4. An inclined _____ is a flat surface that is tilted.
5. When the dam broke, a _____ of water roared down the valley.
6. The people _____ vainly to protect their houses and farms.
7. Some poems have a _____ that is repeated several times.
8. A _____ is a large ship with sails.
9. What foods are associated with the Thanksgiving _____?
10. Milagros leaves the house at _____ 8:05 every morning.

II. 1. A *calculated maneuver* is the same thing as a (a) correct answer. (b) foolish plan of attack. (c) carefully planned movement or plan of action.
2. A person who seems *peaked* would do well to (a) celebrate his or her triumph. (b) rest. (c) think more about the desires of others.
3. It would be hard to *tax* a person's (a) income. (b) strength. (c) dreams.
4. A *sniggering jest* is the same thing as a(n) (a) mean joke made with half-smothered laughter. (b) lazy or rude servant. (c) argumentative opponent.
5. The word *spur* (a) refers only to a part of a horse. (b) literally concerns a horse but is often used with wider meanings. (c) is always a noun.
6. To *distinguish* an identical twin boy would be to (a) mistake him for his brother. (b) dress him like his brother. (c) tell him apart from his brother.
7. CENTURY is to 100 as *DECADE* is to (a) 1. (b) 10. (c) 50.

8. *BUTT* is to GUN as *HILT* is to (a) CANNON. (b) MUSKET. (c) SWORD.
9. BRICKS are to HOUSE as *COBBLES* are to (a) CHIMNEY. (b) FENCE. (c) ROAD.
10. CAR is to AUTO as *CASCADE* is to (a) PLANE. (b) WATERFALL. (c) VIEW.

III. The cartoon below shows two unicorns and the departing ark. Answer the questions that follow.

Drawing by Chas. Addams © 1956 The New Yorker Magazine, Inc.

1. What *inference(s)* can you draw from the cartoon?
2. From your viewpoint, how does the drawing involve *dramatic irony*?
3. (a) State the *main idea* of the drawing in a sentence. (b) What are two *details* that support this idea?

365

▶ This short poem has been published many times—and for good reason. The poet is a native of Liberia, a small nation on the west coast of Africa. The poem is not only "Africa's Plea" but a kind of universal request. Read it thoughtfully.

AFRICA'S PLEA

by Roland Tombekai Dempster

I am not you—
but you will not
give me a chance,
will not let me be *me*.

"If I were you"—
but you know
I am not you,
yet you will not
let me be *me*.

You meddle, interfere
in my affairs
as if they were yours
and you were me.

You are unfair, unwise,
foolish to think
that I can be you,
talk, act
and think like you.

God made me *me*.
He made you *you*.
For God's sake
Let me be *me*.

WAYS OF KNOWING

1. The title indicates that the speaker in the poem—the "I"—is the continent of Africa. In your own words, just what is "Africa" asking for?

2. Who (or what) else might the speaker in the poem be? Try to think of at least two answers and explain your reason for each.

3. How does the title of this unit, "More than Meets the Eye," apply to the poem?

O. Henry (1862-1910)

If having a wide variety of experiences is an aid to a successful writing career, then it stands to reason that **O. Henry** turned out 250 works of fiction in his lifetime. From the time he left school at the age of 15 till he settled down in New York as a writer 22 years later, he held jobs in a drugstore, on a ranch, in a bank, and on a newspaper.

O. Henry was born William Sydney Porter, in Greensboro, North Carolina. He spent his early years in the Southwest, mainly in Texas. When, in 1896, he was charged with stealing a thousand dollars from a bank he had worked in, he ran away to Central America. He returned to Texas upon learning that his wife was seriously ill. He was arrested and sent to prison for three years.

It was in prison that Porter began to write short stories. It was also there that he took on the pen name "O. Henry"—based supposedly on the name of one of the guards, Orrin Henry.

O. Henry's best-known stories are city tales, most of them based on characters and scenes from New York City and Chicago. But whether he wrote about city or country, about rich people or poor, there is one thing you will find in nearly all of his stories—a surprise twist at the end.

What supposedly was the source of William Sydney Porter's pen name?

AFTER TWENTY YEARS

by O. Henry

▶ The man in the doorway was convinced his old friend would meet him. But sure enough, there was "more than meets the eye. . . ."

The policeman on the beat moved up the avenue slowly. The time was barely 10 o'clock at night, but chilly gusts of wind with a taste of rain in them had well-nigh emptied the streets.

Trying doors as he went, he twirled his club with many intricate and artful movements. Turning now and then to cast his watchful eye down the street, the officer, with his stalwart form and slight swagger, made a fine picture of a guardian of the peace. The vicinity was one that kept early hours. Now and then you might see the lights of a cigar store or of an all-night lunch counter. But the majority of the doors belonged to business places that had long since been closed.

When about midway of a certain block, the policeman suddenly slowed his walk. In the doorway of a darkened hardware store a man leaned, with an unlighted cigar in his mouth. As the policeman walked up to him the man spoke up quickly.

"It's all right, officer," he said calmly. "I'm just waiting for a friend. It's an appointment made 20 years ago. Sounds a little funny to you, doesn't it? Well, I'll explain if you'd like to make certain it's all straight. About that long ago there used to be a restaurant where this store stands—'Big Joe' Brady's restaurant."

"Until five years ago," said the policeman. "It was torn down then."

The man in the doorway struck a match and lit his cigar. The light showed a pale, square-jawed face with keen eyes, and a little white scar near his right eyebrow. His scarfpin was a large diamond, oddly set.

- **well-nigh** (WEL NY) almost; very nearly
- **intricate** (IN truh kut) complicated
- **artful** (ART ful) clever; tricky
- **stalwart** (STAWL wart) strong
- **swagger** (SWAG ur) strut; bold walk

"Twenty years ago tonight," said the man, "I dined here at 'Big Joe' Brady's with Jimmy Wells, my best chum, and the finest chap in the world. He and I were raised here in New York, just like two brothers, together. I was 18 and Jimmy was 20. The next morning I was to start for the West to make my fortune. You couldn't have dragged Jimmy out of New York. He thought it was the only place on earth. Well, we agreed that night that we would meet here again exactly 20 years from that date and time, no matter what our conditions might be or from what distance we might have to come. We figured that in 20 years each of us ought to have our destiny worked out and our fortunes made, whatever they were going to be."

"It sounds pretty interesting," said the policeman. "Rather a long time between meets, though, it seems to me. Haven't you heard from your friend since you left?"

"Well, yes, for a time we corresponded," said the other. "But after a year or two we lost track of each other. You see, the West is a pretty big proposition, and I kept hustling around over it pretty lively. But I know Jimmy will meet me here if he's alive, for he always was the truest, staunchest old chap in the world. He'll never forget. I came a thousand miles to stand in this door tonight, and it's worth it if my old partner turns up."

The waiting man pulled out a handsome watch, the lids of it set with small diamonds.

"Three minutes to 10," he announced. "It was exactly 10 o'clock when we parted here at the restaurant door."

"Did pretty well out West, didn't you?" asked the policeman.

"You bet! I hope Jimmy has done half as well. He was a kind of a plodder, though, good fellow as he was. I've had to compete with some of the sharpest wits going to get my pile. A man gets in a groove in New York. It takes the West to put a razor-edge on him."

The policeman twirled his club and took a step or two.

"I'll be on my way. Hope your friend comes around all right. Going to call time on him sharp?"

"I should say not!" said the other. "I'll give him half an hour at

---

- **destiny** (DES tun ee) fate; what will happen to a person
- **correspond** (kor uh SPOND) exchange letters
- **proposition** (prop uh ZISH un) plan; undertaking
- staunchest (STAWNCH ust) most loyal or steadfast
- plodder (PLOD ur) steady, unimaginative worker

least. If Jimmy is alive on earth he'll be here by that time. So long, officer."

"Good-night, sir," said the policeman, passing on along his beat, trying doors as he went.

There was now a fine, cold drizzle falling, and the wind had risen from its uncertain puffs into a steady blow. The few foot passengers in that quarter hurried dismally and silently along with coat collars turned high and pocketed hands. And in the door of the hardware store the man who had come a thousand miles to fill an appointment with the friend of his youth, smoked his cigar and waited.

About 20 minutes he waited, and then a tall man in a long overcoat, with collar turned up to his ears, hurried across from the opposite side of the street. He went directly to the waiting man.

"Is that you, Bob?" he asked, doubtfully.

"Is that you, Jimmy Wells?" cried the man in the door.

"Bless your heart!" exclaimed the new arrival, grasping both the other's hands with his own. "It's Bob, sure as fate. I was certain I'd find you here if you were still in existence. Well, well, well!—20 years is a long time. The old restaurant's gone, Bob; I wish it had lasted, so we could have had another dinner there. How has the West treated you, old man?"

"Bully; it has given me everything I asked it for. You've changed lots, Jimmy. I never thought you were so tall by two or three inches."

"Oh, I grew a bit after I was 20."

"Doing well in New York, Jimmy?"

"Moderately. I have a position in one of the city departments. Come on, Bob; we'll go around to a place I know of, and have a good long talk about old times."

The two started up the street, arm in arm. The man from the West was beginning to outline the history of his career. The other listened with interest.

At the corner stood a drugstore, brilliant with electric lights. When they came into this glare each of them turned to gaze upon the other's face.

The man from the West stopped suddenly and released his arm.

- quarter (KWAR tur) region; area
- moderately (MOD uh rut lee) fairly well

"You're not Jimmy Wells," he snapped. "Twenty years is a long time, but not long enough to change a man's nose from a Roman to a pug."

"It sometimes changes a good man into a bad one," said the tall man. "You've been under arrest for 10 minutes, 'Silky' Bob. Chicago thinks you may have dropped over our way and wires us it wants to have a chat with you. Going quietly, are you? That's sensible. Now, before we go to the station here's a note I was asked to hand to you. You may read it here at the window. It's from Patrolman Wells."

The man from the West unfolded the little piece of paper handed him. His hand was steady when he began to read, but it trembled a little by the time he had finished. The note was rather short.

Bob: I was at the appointed place on time. When you struck the match to light your cigar I saw it was the face of the man wanted in Chicago. Somehow I couldn't do it myself, so I went around and got a plainclothesman to do the job.

JIMMY

ALL THINGS CONSIDERED _____

1. The story begins with the actions of a police officer (a) in plain clothes. (b) named "Silky" Bob. (c) named Jimmy Wells.
2. "After Twenty Years" there is supposed to be (a) a meeting of two old friends. (b) a new restaurant on the street. (c) a criminal arrest.

- **pug (nose)** (PUG) short; stubby
- **plainclothesman** (PLAYN KLOHZ man) police officer in ordinary clothes

3. When the third character in the story appears, he is at first (a) recognized as a police officer. (b) greeted as Jimmy Wells. (c) greeted as "Silky" Bob.

4. "Silky" Bob approaches the truth through clues involving the other man's (a) voice. (b) failure to know a password. (c) size and nose.

5. It is reasonable to think that the "one of the city departments" referred to on page 370 is (a) the Sanitation Department. (b) the Department of Education. (c) the Police Department.

THINKING IT THROUGH

1. The profile of O. Henry on page 367 refers to "one thing you will find in nearly all of his stories . . . ." Did you find it in "After Twenty Years"? Explain.

2. Although O. Henry appeals to many modern readers, he is sometimes criticized for using stereotyped, "cardboard-cutout" characters, as well as plots too fantastic for any reasonable person to believe. Do you think this criticism applies to "After Twenty Years"? The following questions will help you decide. There are no "right" or "wrong" answers. What you say will depend on your own experience.

a) Does it seem reasonable that a well-dressed man standing in a doorway at ten o'clock at night would feel it necessary to explain his presence to a passing officer? If you saw this happen, would it seem reasonable?

b) Does it seem reasonable for Bob, the waiting man, to immediately tell the police officer the whole story about himself and Jimmy Wells?

c) Does it seem reasonable that Bob, who describes himself and Jimmy Wells as having grown up "just like two brothers," would fail to recognize his old friend?

d) Does it seem reasonable that for 10 whole minutes Bob would accept the plainclothesman as his old friend?

e) Does it seem reasonable that Jimmy Wells would have his old friend arrested for a crime committed about a thousand miles away?

f) If you answered *no* to any of the above, do you think that O. Henry's surprise ending justifies the unreasonable aspect(s) of the story?

Literary Skills: Review

If you wish to review the meaning of any term in *italics* in this exercise, refer to the Glossary of Terms.

1. What detail in the *setting* (concerning the time of day) is absolutely essential to the story? In other words, what detail, if omitted, would make the events in "After Twenty Years" unlikely or impossible? If two details occur to you, list both of them.
2. Do you consider "Silky" Bob a *flat* character or a *rounded* one? Explain your answer.
3. In your opinion, which of the four kinds of *conflict* is the main one in the story? Might another kind of conflict be involved as well? If so, explain.
4. Does "After Twenty Years" end with a *climax* or with a *resolution* that follows a climax?
5. Explain the *figurative language* in the following sentences and identify it as *simile* or *metaphor*: "'A man gets in a groove in New York. It takes the West to put a razor-edge on him.'"
6. (a) From what *point of view* is the story told? (b) Would it have been difficult to tell the story in the *first person*, from Jimmy Wells's point of view? Explain.
7. In your opinion, did O. Henry attempt to use *foreshadowing* so that the ending would not come as a complete surprise? If so, explain.
8. What kind of *connotation* is suggested by the following terms considered together: "friend," "best chum," "finest chap," "truest, staunchest old chap," "my old partner"? What terms can you think of with similar connotations?

Composition

1. Suppose Jimmy Wells had not become a police officer, but had still met "Silky" Bob at the appointed time. Write five questions you think he might have asked of his old friend Bob.

2. In a paragraph, analyze one of the principal characters in the story.

Your analysis might focus on how believable the character's actions may seem to the reader. For instance, if you write about Jimmy Wells, you might explain whether or not you think the character would have actually shown up for a meeting with his friend 20 years after they last saw one another.

▶ There's "more than meets the eye" in this short poem from Japan—but the reader may not be sure exactly what. How do *you* interpret it?

BEAR

by Shigeji Tsuboi

Although it is the middle of March
this morning there is an unusual heavy snowfall.
With high boots
walking in the snow, crunch, crunch,
goodness how huge my own footprints!
Right in Tokyo I turned into a bear.
Aren't there any human beings!
Isn't there a creature called a human being?

WAYS OF KNOWING

1. How do the words "Right in Tokyo" (line 6) add to the surprise in the poem?
2. (a) Where do you see the speaker, on a crowded street or alone? (b) Does he see other people? (c) Does he see other bears?
3. In your own words, state why the speaker feels he has turned into a bear.

Anne Frank (1929-1945)

On Friday, June 12, 1942, Anne Frank celebrated her 13th birthday. One gift she received was a diary. In it, she began to record her thoughts and feelings. Several years later, her diary would become not only a best-selling book but also an important document of World War II.

The first few pages of Anne Frank's diary are just what the reader might expect from a sharp and lively teenager: She writes about her girl friends, her triumphs and tragedies in the classroom, her difficulty communicating with people on a serious level, her love of chatter, ice cream and Ping Pong, and her growing interest in boys. Then, little by little, the diary reveals Anne's past

life. Born in Germany, Anne Frank had moved with her family to Amsterdam, the Netherlands, in 1933. The family had not wanted to move, but there was really no other choice. The Franks were Jewish, and Jewish people were unwelcome in the Germany of Adolph Hitler and the Nazis.

Mr. Frank was a successful businessman in the Netherlands; in 1942 he was the managing director of one company and a partner in another. But as Anne's diary continues—in June and July of 1942—the reader sees that for the Franks, all was far from well. The Nazis have invaded the Netherlands, making life difficult for the Dutch people and next to impossible for Jewish people. At the time, Anne attended a Jewish school because regular schools were closed to her. She and her family were deprived of other basic rights as well. Finally the day came when the Frank family realized that they would have to go into hiding in order to survive.

The Diary of a Young Girl was written under trying conditions—with the family in hiding during the worst of World War II—yet Anne Frank manages to write sensitively about her growing understanding of herself and others, as well as about her hopes for living in a world free from war and prejudice. Her story is one of courage in the face of danger. Few readers will forget her bright spirit and her enthusiasm for a better world.

from THE DIARY OF A YOUNG GIRL

by Anne Frank

▶ Anne Frank's diary, which covers a period of about two years, is a story of the suffering of people forced to live in a world of whispers and distrust. But it is more than that. It is also the story of the hopes, joys, and despair of a teenager growing up in wartime.

Saturday, June 20, 1942

There is a saying that "paper is more patient than man"; it came back to me on one of my slightly melancholy days, while I sat chin in hand, feeling too bored and limp even to make up my mind whether to go out or stay at home. Yes, there is no doubt that paper is patient and as I don't intend to show this cardboard-covered notebook bearing the proud name of "diary" to anyone, unless I find a real friend, boy or girl, probably nobody cares. And now I come to the root of the matter, the reason for starting a diary; it is that I have no such real friend. . . .

I want this diary itself to be my friend, and I shall call my friend Kitty. No one will grasp what I'm talking about if I begin my letters to Kitty just out of the blue. So I will start by sketching in brief the story of my life.

My father was 36 when he married my mother, who was then 25. My sister Margot was born in 1926 in Frankfort-on-Main.* I followed on June 12, 1929, and, as we are Jewish, we emigrated to Holland in 1933. . . .

The rest of our family, however, felt the full impact of Hitler's anti-Jewish laws, so life was filled with anxiety. In 1938, after the pogroms, my two uncles (my mother's brothers) escaped to the U.S.A. My old grandmother came to us; she was then 73. After May 1940 good times rapidly fled: first the war, then the

---

- melancholy (MEL un kol ee) sad; depressing
- impact (IM pakt) force; effect
- pogrom (puh GRUM) organized massacre of a racial group

*A city in West Germany.

capitulation, followed by the arrival of the Germans, which is when the sufferings of us Jews really began. Anti-Jewish decrees followed each other in quick succession. Jews must wear a yellow star,* Jews must hand in their bicycles, Jews are banned from trains· and are forbidden to drive. Jews are only allowed to do their shopping between three and five o'clock and then only in shops which bear the placard "Jewish shop." Jews must be indoors by eight o'clock and cannot even sit in their own gardens after that hour.

Jews are forbidden to visit theaters, cinemas, and other places of entertainment. Jews may not take part in public sports. Swimming baths, tennis courts, hockey fields, and other sports grounds are all prohibited to them. Jews may not visit Christians. Jews must go to Jewish schools, and many more restrictions of a similar kind.

So we could not do this and were forbidden to do that. But life went on in spite of it all. . . .

Wednesday, July 8, 1942

Dear Kitty,

Years seem to have passed between Sunday and now. So much has happened, it is just as if the whole world had turned upside down. But I am still alive, Kitty, and that is the main thing, Daddy says.

Yes, I'm still alive, indeed, but don't ask where or how. You wouldn't understand a word, so I will begin by telling you what happened on Sunday afternoon.

At three o'clock someone rang the front doorbell. I was lying lazily reading a book on the veranda in the sunshine, so I didn't hear it. A bit later, Margot appeared at the kitchen door looking very excited. "The S.S.** have sent a call-up notice for Daddy," she whispered. "Mummy has gone to see Mr. Van Daan already." (Van Daan is a friend who works with Daddy.) It was a great shock to me, a call-up; everyone knows what that means. I picture

---

- capitulation (kuh pi chuh LAY shun) surrender
- **decree** (duh KREE) order or law
- **succession** (suk SESH un) one following another
- placard (PLAK ard) poster; notice
- veranda (vuh RAN da) porch

*The star was used as an identification tag for Jews.
**German secret police.

concentration camps and lonely cells—should we allow him to be doomed to this? "Of course he won't go," declared Margot, while we waited together. "Mummy has gone to the Van Daans to discuss whether we should move into our hiding place tomorrow. The Van Daans are going with us, so we shall be seven in all." Silence. We couldn't talk anymore, thinking about Daddy, who, little knowing what was going on, was visiting some old people in the hospital. . . .

When we were alone together in our bedroom, Margot told me that the call-up was not for Daddy, but for her. I was more frightened than ever and began to cry. Margot is 16; would they really take girls of that age away alone? But thank goodness she won't go, Mummy said so herself; that must be what Daddy meant when he talked about us going into hiding.

Into hiding—where would we go, in a town or the country, in a house or a cottage, when, how, where . . . ?

These were questions I was not allowed to ask, but I couldn't get them out of my mind. Margot and I began to pack some of our most vital belongings into a school satchel. The first thing I put in was this diary, then hair curlers, handkerchiefs, schoolbooks, a comb, old letters; I put in the craziest things with the idea that we were going into hiding. But I'm not sorry, memories mean more to me than dresses.

At five o'clock Daddy finally arrived, and Mr. Van Daan went and fetched Miep. Miep has been in the business with Daddy since 1933 and has become a close friend, likewise her brand-new husband, Henk. Miep came and took some shoes, dresses, coats, underwear, and stockings away in her bag, promising to return in the evening. Then silence fell on the house; not one of us felt like eating anything, it was hot and everything was very strange.

At 11 o'clock Miep and Henk Van Santen arrived. Once again, shoes, stockings, books, and underclothes disappeared into Miep's bag and Henk's deep pockets, and at 11:30 they too disappeared. I was dog-tired and although I knew that it would be my last night in my own bed, I fell asleep immediately and didn't wake up until Mummy called me at 5:30 the next morning. Luckily it was not so hot as Sunday; warm rain fell steadily all day. We put on heaps of clothes as if we were going to the North Pole, the sole reason being to take clothes with us. No Jew in our situation

---

- concentration (camp) (kon sun TRAY shun) prison for political enemies
- **vital** (VY tul) necessary

would have dreamed of going out with a suitcase full of clothing. I had on two vests, three pairs of pants, a dress, on top of that a skirt, jacket, summer coat, two pairs of stockings, lace-up shoes, woolly cap, scarf, and still more; I was nearly stifled before we started, but no one inquired about that.

Margot filled her satchel with schoolbooks, fetched her bicycle, and rode off behind Miep into the unknown, as far as I was concerned. You see, I still didn't know where our secret hiding place was to be. At 7:30 the door closed behind us. Moortje, my little cat, was the only creature to whom I said farewell. She would have a good home with the neighbors. . . .

There was one pound of meat in the kitchen for the cat, breakfast things lying on the table, stripped beds, all giving the impression that we had left helter-skelter. But we didn't care about impressions, we only wanted to get away, only escape and arrive safely, nothing else. . . .

Only when we were on the road did Mummy and Daddy begin to tell me bits and pieces about the plan. For months as many of our goods and necessities of life as possible had been sent away and they were sufficiently ready for us to have gone into hiding of our own accord on July 16. The plan had had to be speeded up 10 days because of the call-up, so our quarters would not be so well organized, but we had to make the best of it. The hiding place itself would be in the building where Daddy has his office. . . .

Friday, October 9, 1942

Dear Kitty,

I've only got dismal and depressing news for you today. Our many Jewish friends are being taken away by the dozen. These people are treated by the Gestapo* without a shred of decency, being loaded into cattle trucks and sent to Westerbork, the big Jewish camp in Drente. Westerbork sounds terrible: only one washing cubicle for a hundred people and not nearly enough lavatories. There are no separate accommodations. . . .

It is impossible to escape; most of the people in the camp are branded as inmates by their shaven heads. . . .

- stifled (STY fuld) smothered
- cubicle (KYOO bi kul) very small room
- accommodations (uh kom uh DAY shunz) rest rooms
- **inmate** (IN mayt) one forced to live in a prison or other institution

*Special secret police in Germany at the time of the Nazis.

If it is as bad as this in Holland whatever will it be like in the distant and barbarous regions they are sent to? We assume that most of them are murdered. The English radio speaks of their being gassed. . . .

The Dutch people are anxious too, their sons are being sent to Germany. Everyone is afraid.

And every night hundreds of planes fly over Holland and go to German towns, where the earth is so plowed up by their bombs, and every hour hundreds and thousands of people are killed in Russia and Africa. No one is able to keep out of it, the whole globe is waging war and although it is going better for the Allies,* the end is not yet in sight.

And as for us, we are fortunate. Yes, we are luckier than millions of people. It is quiet and safe here, and we are, so to speak, living on capital. We are even so selfish as to talk about "after the war," brighten up at the thought of having new clothes and new shoes, whereas we really ought to save every penny, to help other people, and save what is left from the wreckage after the war.

The children here run about in just a thin blouse and clogs; no coat, no hat, no stockings, and no one helps them. Their tummies are empty, they chew an old carrot to stay the pangs, go from their cold homes out into the cold street and, when they get to school, find themselves in an even colder classroom. Yes, it has even got so bad in Holland that countless children stop the passers-by and beg for a piece of bread. I could go on for hours about all the suffering the war has brought, but then I would only make myself more dejected. There is nothing we can do but wait as calmly as we can till the misery comes to an end. Jews and Christians wait, the whole earth waits; and there are many who wait for death.

Yours, Anne

- **barbarous** (BAR bur us) savage; uncivilized
- **capital** (KAP i tul) money carefully saved up and invested
- clog (KLOG) wooden shoe
- stay (STAY) stop; put off
- pangs (PANGZ) sharp pains
- **dejected** (di JEK tud) sad; gloomy

*Russia, the United States, Canada, and other countries that opposed the Nazis.

Sunday, January 2, 1944

Dear Kitty,

This morning when I had nothing to do I turned over some of the pages of my diary and several times I came across letters dealing with the subject "Mummy" in such a hotheaded way that I was quite shocked, and asked myself: "Anne, is it really you who mentioned hate? Oh, Anne, how could you!" I remained sitting with the open page in my hand, and thought about it and how it came about that I should have been so really filled with hate that I had to confide it all in you. . . .

I suffer now from moods which kept my head underwater (so to speak) and only allowed me to see the things subjectively without enabling me to consider quietly the words of the other side. . . .

I hid myself within myself, I only considered myself and quietly wrote down all my joys, sorrows, and contempt in my diary. This diary is of great value to me, but on a good many pages I could certainly put "past and done with."

I used to be furious with Mummy, and still am sometimes. It's true that she doesn't understand me, but I don't understand her either. She did love me very much and she was tender, but as she landed in so many unpleasant situations through me, and was nervous and irritable because of other worries and difficulties, it is certainly understandable that she snapped at me.

I took it much too seriously, was offended, and was rude and aggravating to Mummy, which, in turn, made her unhappy. So it was really a matter of unpleasantness and misery rebounding all the time. It wasn't nice for either of us, but it is passing.

I just didn't want to see all this, and pitied myself very much; but that, too, is understandable. Those violent outbursts on paper were only giving vent to anger which in a normal life could have been worked off by stamping my feet a couple of times in a locked room, or calling Mummy names behind her back.

The period when I caused Mummy to shed tears is over. I have grown wiser and Mummy's nerves are not so much on edge.

- **confide** (kun FYD) tell as a secret
- subjectively (sub JEK tuv lee) personally; from the private side
- **enable** (en AY bul) allow or help
- contempt (kun TEMPT) angry scorn
- **aggravating** (ag ruh VAYT ing) annoying; irritating
- vent (VENT) release; escape

I usually keep my mouth shut if I get annoyed, and so does she, so we appear to get on much better together. I can't really love Mummy in a dependent, childlike way—I just don't have that feeling.

I soothe my conscience now with the thought that it is better for hard words to be on paper than that Mummy should carry them in her heart.

Yours, Anne

Friday, April 4, 1944

Dear Kitty,

First I said a long prayer very earnestly, then I cried with my head on my arms, my knees bent up, on the bare floor, completely folded up. One large sob brought me back to earth again, and I quelled my tears because I didn't want them to hear anything in the next room. Then I began trying to talk some courage into myself. I could only say: "I must, I must, I must. . . ."

And now it's all over. I must work, so as not to be a fool, to get on, to become a journalist, because that's what I want! I know that I can write. . . .

I am the best and sharpest critic of my own work. I know myself what is and what is not well written. Anyone who doesn't write doesn't know how wonderful it is; I used to bemoan the fact that I couldn't draw at all, but now I am more than happy that I can at least write. And if I haven't any talent for writing books or newspaper articles, well, then I can always write for myself.

I want to get on; I can't imagine that I would have to lead the same sort of life as Mummy and Mrs. Van Daan and all the women who do their work and are then forgotten. I must have something besides a husband and children, something that I can devote myself to!

I want to go on living even after my death! And therefore I am grateful to God for giving me this gift, this possibility of developing myself and of writing, of expressing all that is in me.

I can shake off everything if I write; my sorrows disappear, my courage is reborn. But, and that is the great question, will I ever be able to write anything great, will I ever become a journalist or a writer? I hope so, oh, I hope so very much, for I am able to

---

- quell (KWEL) suppress; put down
- **bemoan** (bi MOHN) express sorrow over

recapture everything when I write, my thoughts, my ideals, and my fantasies. . . .

Yours, Anne

Monday, July 14, 1944

Dear Kitty,

"For in its innermost depths youth is lonelier than old age." I read this saying in some book and I've always remembered it, and found it to be true. It is true then that grown-ups have a more difficult time here than we do? No. I know it isn't. Older people have formed their opinions about everything, and don't waver before they act. It's twice as hard for us young ones to hold our ground, and maintain our opinions, in a time when all ideals are being shattered and destroyed, when people are showing their worst side, and do not know whether to believe in truth and right and God.

Anyone who claims that the older ones have a more difficult time here certainly doesn't realize to what extent our problems weigh down on us, problems for which we are probably much too young, but which thrust themselves upon us continually. Then, after a long time, we think we've found a solution, but the solution doesn't seem able to resist the facts which reduce it to nothing again. That's the difficulty in these times: ideals, dreams, and cherished hopes rise within us, only to meet the horrible truth and be shattered.

It's really a wonder that I haven't dropped all my ideals, because they seem so absurd and impossible to carry out. Yet I keep them, because in spite of everything I still believe that people are really good at heart. I simply can't build up my hopes on a foundation consisting of confusion, misery, and death. I see the world gradually being turned into a wilderness, I hear the ever approaching thunder, which will destroy us too. I can feel the sufferings of millions and yet, if I look up into the heavens, I think that it will all come right, that this cruelty too will end, and that peace and tranquility will return again.

In the meantime, I must uphold my ideals, for perhaps the time will come when I shall be able to carry them out.

Yours, Anne

- **fantasy** (FAN tuh see) imaginary happening; fancy
- **waver** (WAY vur) hesitate
- **tranquility** (tran KWIL i tee) quiet; calmness

On August 4, 1944, the German secret police discovered the hiding place of the Franks and the Van Daans. The families were arrested, and all were sent to concentration camps. Fortunately, the diary was overlooked by the Gestapo, and was later found by Miep, the family friend mentioned in the selection.

In March 1945, just two months before the liberation of the Netherlands, Anne Frank died in the concentration camp at Bergen-Belsen, Germany.

ALL THINGS CONSIDERED

1. The Franks go into hiding because of a call-up notice for (a) Mr. Frank. (b) Mrs. Frank. (c) Margot.

2. As Anne turns through earlier pages of her diary, she is surprised that she has written of her mother (a) very seldom. (b) with hatred. (c) as she would of a friend.

3. The person Anne believes to be "the best and sharpest critic" of her writing is (a) Kitty. (b) her mother. (c) she herself.

4. One reason Anne gives for wanting to write is (a) the chance it gives her to recapture her thoughts and fantasies. (b) the pleasure and comfort her words are sure to bring to others. (c) the glory of being a writer.

5. At the end of the selection, Anne struggles to uphold her (a) family name. (b) courage in dealing with her mother. (c) ideals.

THINKING IT THROUGH

1. Look back at the fourth and fifth paragraphs of the first diary entry (pages 376–377). List at least five hardships the Frank family was forced to bear. What do these restrictions indicate about the Nazis' regard for human rights?

2. Miep and Henk Van Santen, referred to on page 378, were not Jewish and did not have to go into hiding. (a) Why did they, rather than the Franks, carry bags containing the Franks' clothes to the hiding place? (b) What does this tell us about Miep and Henk?

3. In spite of her own difficulties, Anne finds herself writing with sympathy about others less "fortunate" than she. What diary entry makes this most clear?

Critical Thinking: Review

If you wish to review the meaning of any term in *italics* in this exercise, refer to the Glossary of Terms.

1. *The Diary of a Young Girl* is a written record of a normal teenage girl's feelings—Anne Frank didn't write for history, she wrote for herself. The most important thing about the diary is that it conveys a sense of normality amid horror. Look back at the selection. What *facts* can you find to support the view that Anne was very much a normal teenager?

2. In reading the selection, you may have noticed that Anne is sometimes angry with her mother. To Anne, her mother simply doesn't understand her. Do you support Anne's *opinion* of her mother? Why or why not?

3. How can Anne Frank's diary be considered both an *effect* of something and a *cause* of something else?

4. Anne Frank's diary is interesting because it contains many opinions that challenge the reader to *think critically*. Here are five of them.

Judge them in the light of your own experience. For each, first write a sentence explaining the extent of your agreement. Then think of one experience in your own life that leads you to think as you do.

a) [After writing that she packed the "craziest things" before "vital belongings"] "But I'm not sorry, memories mean more to me than dresses [or other things]."

b) ". . . it is better for hard words to be on paper than that Mummy [or another person] should carry them in her heart."

c) "'For in its innermost depths youth is lonelier than old age.'"

d) "That's the difficulty in these times: ideals, dreams, and cherished hopes rise within us, only to meet the horrible truth and be shattered."

e) ". . . in spite of everything I still believe that people are really good at heart."

Composition

1. *The Diary of a Young Girl* is read in many schools. Suppose you were a book salesperson. Tomorrow you have to speak before the English teachers in a certain school. Your job will be to sell *The Diary of a Young Girl*. Write a sales talk that can be presented in about two minutes. Don't forget to look at the profile of Anne Frank as well as at the excerpts from the book.

2. Do some critical thinking. Placed in Anne Frank's situation, how do you think most people would have reacted? If the typical behavior would have been different from Anne's, try to explain why.

Before completing the exercises that follow, you may wish to review the **bold-faced** words on pages 368 to 383.

I. On a separate sheet of paper, write the term in each line that means the same, or nearly the same, as the word in *italics.*

1. *well-nigh:* healthy, almost, forgotten, completely
2. *intricate:* expensive, careless, dishonest, complicated
3. *decree:* salad green, waste, order, loud sigh
4. *veranda:* large ship, open plain, attic, porch
5. *vital:* alive, dead, useless, necessary
6. *barbarous:* savage, poisonous, thoughtful, overly dressed
7. *dejected:* rejected, jealous, sad, satisfied
8. *aggravating:* thrilling, annoying, frightening, doubting
9. *waver:* offer, hesitate, act with greed, ruler
10. *tranquility:* wealth, good health, popularity, calmness

II. On a separate sheet of paper, mark each item *true* or *false.* If it is *false,* explain what is wrong with the sentence.

1. Most people hope destiny will favor them with life as an *inmate.*
2. People with enough *capital* can retire to a life of ease.
3. A very early retirement is a *fantasy* for most people.
4. Police detectives of either sex are sometimes called *plainclothesmen.*
5. Cyrano de Bergerac (pictured on page 289) was famous for his *pug* nose.
6. Pen pals sometimes *confide* in each other when they *correspond* from great distances.
7. The planned undersea tunnel from England to France is an enormous *proposition.*
8. A basketball team would probably *bemoan* a string of eight victories.
9. Modern tools *enable* people to work fewer hours for more money.
10. At most graduations, diplomas are given all at once, rather than in *succession.*

IF NOT STILL HIGHER

by Isaac Loeb Peretz

▶ Isaac Loeb Peretz was a Polish writer who lived in the second half of the last century. In his poems, novels, and short stories about the European Jews of his day, he shows that money isn't everything—or anything—to a people who are spiritually rich.

And the Rabbi of Nemirov,* early every Friday morning, disappears. He melts into thin air! He is not to be found anywhere, either in the synagogue or worshiping somewhere. And he most certainly is not at home. His door stands open. People go in and out as they please; no one ever steals anything from the rabbi. But there is not a soul in the house.

Where can the rabbi be?

Where should he be, if not in heaven? Yes, the townsfolk decide, surely the rabbi takes weekly trips to heaven. In heaven, that's where he is.

Is it likely that a rabbi should have no affairs on hand with the Holy Days so near?

The rabbi's followers need a livelihood, peace, health, successful matchmakings. They wish to be good and pious, and their sins are great. Satan with his thousand eyes spies out the world from one end to the other. He sees and accuses and tells tales. Who shall help if not the rabbi? So think the people of Nemirov.

Once, however, there comes a Lithuanian.** And he laughs at the idea of the rabbi's going to heaven. He points out a special bit of the Gemara*** and hopes it is plain enough. It says that even

- synagogue (SIN un gog) Jewish house of worship
- livelihood (LYV lee hood) support; way of making a living
- matchmaking (MACH mayk ing) arranging of marriages
- pious (PY us) holy; very religious

*A small town in Poland.
**A person from the country of Lithuania.
***Part of the Talmud, a book of Jewish law and custom.

Moses could not ascend into heaven, but remained suspended 30 inches below it. And who, I ask you, is going to argue with a Lithuanian?

What becomes of the rabbi?

"I don't know, and I don't care," says the Lithuanian one Thursday night. And all the while he is determined to find out.

That very same evening, soon after prayers, the Lithuanian steals into the rabbi's room, lays himself down under the rabbi's bed and lies low.

He intends to stay there all night to find out where the rabbi goes and what he does.

Another in his place would have dozed and slept the time away. Not so the Lithuanian.

Day has not broken when he hears the call to prayer.

The rabbi has been awake for some time. The Lithuanian has heard him sighing and groaning for a whole hour. Whoever has heard the groaning of the Rabbi of Nemirov knows what sorrow, what distress of mind, was in every groan. The soul that heard would be dissolved in grief. But the heart of a Lithuanian is of cast iron. The Lithuanian hears and lies still. The rabbi lies still too. The rabbi—long life to him!—lies *upon* the bed, and the Lithuanian *under* the bed.

He confesses afterwards, the Lithuanian, that when he was alone with the rabbi, terror took hold of him. He grew cold all over. An excellent joke, to be left alone with the rabbi before dawn!

But the Lithuanian is dogged. He quivers and shakes like a fish, but he does not budge.

At last the rabbi—long life to him!—rises.

First he does what is proper for a Jew. Then he goes to the wardrobe and takes out a bundle. This contains the dress of a peasant. There are linen trousers, high boots, a long coat, a wide felt hat, and a long, broad leather belt studded with brass nails. The rabbi puts them on.

Out of the pocket of the coat dangles the end of a thick cord, a peasant's cord.

On his way out the rabbi steps into the kitchen, stoops, takes a hatchet, puts it into his belt, and leaves the house. The Lithuanian, who has been watching all this, trembles. But he follows the rabbi out.

- dogged (DOG ud) determined
- studded (STUD ud) ornamented; decorated

A fearful Holy-Day hush broods over the dark streets. It is broken frequently by a cry of supplication or the moan of some sick person behind a window.

The rabbi keeps to the street side and walks in the shadow of the houses.

He glides from one house to the other, the Lithuanian after him. And the Lithuanian hears the sound of his own heartbeat mingle with the heavy footfall of the rabbi. But he follows on, and together they emerge from the town.

Behind the town stands a little wood. The rabbi—long life to him!—enters it. He walks on 30 or 40 paces, and then he stops beside a small tree. And the Lithuanian, with amazement, sees the rabbi take his hatchet and strike the tree. He sees the rabbi strike blow after blow. He hears the tree creak and snap. Then the little tree falls, and the rabbi splits it up into small logs. Then he makes a bundle, binds it round with the cord, throws it on his shoulder, replaces the hatchet in his belt, leaves the wood, and goes back into the town.

In one of the back streets he stops beside a poor, tumble-down little house and taps at the window.

"Who is there?" cries a frightened voice from within.

"I," answers the rabbi in a peasant accent.

"Who is 'I'?" inquires the voice further. And the rabbi answers again in a peasant speech.

"This is Vassil* speaking."

"Which Vassil? And what do you want, Vassil?"

"I have wood to sell," says the sham peasant. "Very cheap. Next to nothing."

And without further ado he goes in. The Lithuanian steals in behind him, and sees, in the gray light, a poor room with poor, broken furniture.

In the bed lies a sick woman huddled up in rags, who says bitterly, "Wood to sell. And where am I, a poor widow, to get the money to buy it? Even God does not send such gifts."

"I will give you six groschen** worth on credit."

"And how am I ever to repay you?" groans the poor woman.

- brood (BROOD) hang over like a dark cloud
- supplication (sup luh KAY shun) prayerful and humble request
- sham (SHAM) fake

*A common first name for a man in Poland.
**A small Polish coin.

"Foolish creature!" The rabbi scolds her. "See here. You are a poor sick woman, and I am willing to trust you with the little bundle of wood. I believe that in time you will repay. And you, you have such a great, mighty God, and you do not trust Him! Not even to the amount of a miserable six groschen for a little bundle of wood!"

"And who is to light the stove?" moans the widow. "Do I look like getting up to do it? And my son away at work!"

"I will also light the stove for you," says the rabbi.

And he lays the wood in the stove. Then he waits and watches the wood crackle merrily. Finally, when the fire is burning perfectly, he closes the stove door.

The Lithuanian, who sees all of this, remains with the rabbi as one of his most devoted followers.

And later, when anyone tells how the rabbi, early on Friday mornings, raises himself and flies up to heaven, the Lithuanian, instead of laughing, adds quietly, "If not still higher."

ALL THINGS CONSIDERED

1. The townspeople of Nemirov believe that the rabbi, when he disappears every Friday morning, goes to (a) the synagogue. (b) heaven. (c) the post office.
2. One Thursday evening, the curious Lithuanian (a) steals the rabbi's book. (b) leaves a book for the rabbi. (c) hides under the rabbi's bed.
3. After the rabbi has risen from bed, he (a) puts on the clothes of a peasant. (b) asks the Lithuanian to meet him at the synagogue. (c) groans with sorrow for an hour.
4. When the character who calls himself Vassil arrives at the woman's home, he is carrying (a) a bundle of wood. (b) the rabbi's books. (c) the Lithuanian's hat.
5. Before he leaves the old woman's house, Vassil (a) leaves money where she can find it. (b) lights her stove. (c) reveals to her where the rabbi goes on Fridays.

THINKING IT THROUGH

1. Explain the title in your own words: "If Not Still Higher." Higher than what?
2. Explain how the story is both humorous and serious.
3. In your own words, state the important theme of the story.

UNIT REVIEW

I. Match the terms in Column A with their definitions in Column B.

A

1. theme
2. conflict
3. climax
4. dramatic irony
5. simile
6. imagery
7. cause
8. stereotype
9. point of view
10. first person

B

(a) the exciting high point of a story, at or near the end

(b) a figurative comparison made with a special word such as *like* or *as*

(c) language that appeals to the five senses

(d) the meaning or lesson of a work of literature

(e) a case of the reader's knowing more than a character knows

(f) the "picture in our heads" that a certain word brings to mind

(g) the position from which a story is told

(h) the meeting of two opposing forces

(i) told from the viewpoint of a character in the story

(j) the reason something happens

II. In this unit you have read five major selections: "Three Letters . . . and a Footnote"; "You Can't Take It with You"; "The Highwayman"; "After Twenty Years", and "The Diary of a Young Girl". Which did you like best? Which did you like least? Explain.

On a separate sheet of paper, start by writing the number **1** and the title of the selection you liked the most. Then write at least two thoughtful sentences explaining your reaction. Proceed with your second choice, and continue down the list. Be sure to base your opinions on specific *reasons*. Use details and facts from the selections to support your judgments. Here is an example using the bonus selection, "If Not Still Higher":

"If Not Still Higher." I liked the story because it both made me laugh and helped me learn. The scene with the curious Lithuanian hiding under the groaning rabbi's bed made me chuckle. The story also introduced me to a new culture, a community of poor Jewish people in Poland about 100 years ago.

SPEAKING UP

Picture yourself back in ancient Greece about 2,400 years ago. You are in Athens (ATH inz), the city-state remembered as the cradle of democracy. In ancient Athens, all citizens participated in making the laws. Unemployment was rare, and few citizens were either very rich or very poor.

Right now imagine yourself as a voting Athenian (uh THEE nee un) citizen. You stand with hundreds of other young people in a huge stadium. Together, you are about to recite a pledge of allegiance to thousands of people who have gathered for the occasion:

THE OATH OF ATHENIAN YOUTH

We will never bring disgrace to this, our community, by any act of dishonesty or cowardice.

We will fight for the ideals and sacred things of the community, both alone and with many.

We will revere and obey the community's laws, and will do our best to incite a like reverence and respect in those above us who might try to annul them or set them at naught. We will try always to improve the public's sense of civic duty.

Thus, in all these ways, we will transmit this community, not only not less, but greater, better, and more beautiful than it was transmitted to us.

These words have been kept alive for over 2,400 years because they express an ideal that will never die in the hearts of free people. Practice reading them in a tone of reverence and respect.

- revere (ri VEER) treat with great respect
- incite (in SYT) encourage; bring about
- reverence (REV ur uns) feeling of deep respect, even worship
- annul (uh NUL) cancel; abolish
- civic (SIV ik) having to do with citizenship or government

WRITING A REPORT

Assignment: Write a one-page (or approximately 200-word) report on one of the longer selections in this book. The excerpt from *The Diary of a Young Girl* in this unit is suggested, although you may choose another selection if you prefer. Keep in mind the same *do's* and *don'ts* of writing a good book report:

DO'S

1. *Do* give a general idea of what the selection is about. Is it fiction or nonfiction? Who is the main character, and what problems does he or she face?
2. *Do* say something about the way the author has presented the material. You may want to comment on the author's style, including the use of figurative language and imagery. What has the author done to create the right mood and hold the reader's attention?
3. *Do* explain what the author made you think about. In other words, why might the selection be *important* as well as *interesting*?
4. *Do* tell what kind of readers would probably like the selection and what kind would not.

DON'TS

1. *Don't* begin with a meaningless sentence such as "I liked *The Diary of a Young Girl* because it was interesting." If you "liked" something, of course you found it "interesting!" Explain *why!*
2. *Don't* use words like "exciting" or "boring" without explaining the reasons for your opinions.
3. *Don't* devote more than half the report to a summary of the plot. Admittedly, you have to say something about the characters and their problems, but a good report is also a *review* of the selection.
4. *Don't* reveal the ending if it should come as a surprise to other readers.

To prepare your report, use the three-step process outlined in other exercises in this book: **prewriting, writing,** and finally **revising.** First make notes and organize your material into paragraphs. Then write the paragraphs out in complete sentences and revise carefully before making your final neat copy.

Glossary of Terms

This glossary defines terms that you have studied. The page references shown with the terms indicate where the terms are first defined and discussed. Turn to those pages if you need to review the lessons.

Analogy p. 61 An *analogy* is a statement that the relationship between one pair of terms is in some way similar to the relationship between another pair.

Aphorism p. 138 An *aphorism* is a memorable proverb or saying that expresses some general truth.

Autobiography p. 214 An *autobiography* is the story of a person's own life, written by that person.

Cause and Effect p. 166 A *cause* is an event that leads to a certain result, called an *effect*.

Character Clues p. 250 The clues an author supplies to help a reader understand a character are called *character clues*. Such clues are usually in the form of a character's speech, thoughts, or actions.

Characterization p. 151 The word *characterization* refers to the methods by which authors develop their characters. There are four main methods of characterization:

A. Direct statements by the author
B. Thoughts and words of the character
C. Actions of the character
D. Reactions of other characters to the character

Choral Reading p. 363 A *choral reading* is an oral presentation of a work of literature. It is usually performed by a small group.

Chronological Order p. 240 Within most stories, events are arranged in a normal time sequence. This time sequence is known as *chronological order*.

Climax p. 11 The *climax* is the most exciting part of the story. It comes at or near the end, and acts as a turning point in the story. At the climax, the final major conflict is resolved.

Comparison and Contrast p. 221 A *comparison* shows how two or more things, ideas, or feelings are alike. A *contrast* shows how they are different. (Note: the word *comparison* is sometimes used to establish both similarities and dissimilarities.)

Conclusion p. 81 In reaching a *conclusion*, a reader makes a decision or forms an opinion based on reasoning or inference. (See also *Inference*.)

Conflict p. 10 The plot of most stories depends on *conflict*, the meeting of two opposing forces. There are four main kinds of conflict:

A. Conflict between people
B. Conflict within a single person
C. Conflict between people and things
D. Conflict between people and nature

Connotation p. 324 Many words have two kinds of meanings. A word's *connotation* includes all the feelings and ideas the word brings to the mind of the reader or listener. (See also *Denotation*.)

Denotation p. 324 Many words have two kinds of meanings. The *denotation* of a word is its literal, dictionary meaning. (See also *Connotation*.)

Dialogue p. 20 *Dialogue* is the conversation between two or more characters in a work of literature. In fiction, quotation marks are used to indicate dialogue.

Fact p. 276 A *fact* is something known to be true. Most facts can be checked by direct observation or by studying reports of reliable witnesses. (See also *Opinion*.)

Fiction p. 28 *Fiction* is a literary selection about imaginary characters and events. Short stories and novels are two common forms of fiction. (See also *Nonfiction*.)

394

Figurative Language p. 118 In *figurative language,* one meaning is stated but another is suggested. For instance, when you say "Hold your horses!" you are simply telling someone to slow down. Some common forms of figurative language are *metaphor* and *simile.* (See also *Literal Language.*)

Figures of Speech p. 135 *Figures of speech* are specific forms of figurative language in which two or more things are compared. *Metaphor* and *simile* are two kinds of figures of speech. (See also *Figurative Language.*)

Flashback p. 9 In a *flashback,* an author interrupts the natural time sequence of a story to relate an episode or scene that occurred before the opening situation.

Foreshadowing p. 240 *Foreshadowing* occurs when an author provides hints or clues as to what might happen in a story. An author's skillful use of *foreshadowing* prepares the reader to accept an event that will happen in the future.

Haiku p. 178 *Haiku* is a form of poetry that is popular in Japan. Each haiku has three lines: The first line has five syllables; the second, seven syllables; the third, five syllables. In haiku, the poet paints a picture in the fewest possible words.

Homonyms p. 230 *Homonyms* are two or more words that are pronounced the same, but have different meanings.

Imagery p. 92 *Imagery* refers to the way an author uses words that appeal to any or all of the five senses. Writers use *images* to help readers experience the look, touch, sound, taste, and smell of what is being described.

Inference p. 81 An *inference* is a reader's understanding of something not directly stated in a selection. (See also *Conclusion.*)

Irony p. 29 *Irony* is the use of words to say something quite different from what is actually meant or appears to be true. **Irony of situation** (p. 39) occurs when there is a striking difference between what a character expects to happen and what actually does happen. **Dramatic irony** goes further than irony of situation by involving the reader's understanding of the story. Dramatic irony occurs when a reader knows something important that a character doesn't know.

Literal Language p. 118 *Literal language* is language that means exactly what it says. (See also *Figurative Language.*)

Main Idea p. 103 The *main idea* of a paragraph is the central thought, which is often stated in a single sentence. (See also *Supporting Details.*)

Metaphor p. 118 A *metaphor* is a figure of speech in which there is a suggested or implied comparison between two things. In a metaphor, one thing is said to be another. "Susan is a tower of strength" is a metaphor. (See also *Simile.*)

Narrative Poem p. 357 A *narrative poem* is a poem that tells a story.

Narrator p. 269 The *narrator* is the person who tells the story. Sometimes the narrator is involved as a character in the story.

Nonfiction p. 28 *Nonfiction* is literature that tells us about real characters and events. (See also *Fiction.*)

Opinion p. 276 An *opinion* is what a person thinks, believes, judges, or infers to be true. Opinions are usually based on a combination of emotions and facts. (See also *Fact.*)

Oral Interpretation p. 61 *Oral interpretation* means reading aloud with expression. Good oral interpretation adds to an audience's enjoyment of a poem or play.

Personification p. 120 *Personification* is a figure of speech in which a nonhuman subject is given human qualities.

Plot p. 10 The *plot* is the series of events in a story. It concerns not only what happens but also the way things happen—the way different scenes work together so that the reader is satisfied when the story is concluded. A well-written plot has a careful sequence of events and actions that progress through *conflict* and *rising action* to *climax.* A *resolution* or a *surprise ending* may follow the climax.

Plot Question p. 11 A *plot question* is a question raised in a work of literature by an action in the plot. The action that answers this question can either end the story or lead to still other questions. (See also *Plot*.)

Point of View p. 269 The *point of view* is the position from which a story is told. The two most common points of view are the *first person* and the *third person*.

In the *first-person point of view*, the narrator is a character in the story. Everything that happens in the story is presented through the eyes of this character. In some stories told in the first person, the narrator is the main character. In others, the narrator is not the main character but another character who is present when any important action takes place.

In the *third-person point of view*, the narrator, or storyteller, is not a character in the story. Sometimes the narrator presents the feelings and thoughts of a single character. This is called *third-person limited point of view*. At other times, the narrator skips around and enters the mind of one character and then another at will. The reader learns what each character thinks and feels. This is called *third-person omniscient point of view*.

Predictions p. 240 *Predictions* are judgments about what will happen in the future. (See also *Foreshadowing*.)

Resolution p. 38 The resolution is the part of a story (also called the *falling action*) that comes after the *climax* and gives the story a rounded-out, finished feeling.

Rising Action p. 11 A writer creates excitement, or *rising action*, by making each plot problem or conflict more interesting than the one before it.

Romantic Literature p. 281 *Romantic literature* is a type of writing in which the characters are highly emotional, unrestrained, and larger than life.

Rounded Characters p. 10 *Rounded characters* are distinct individuals rather than types. The reader hasn't met them before in literature, and can't predict exactly what they'll do when faced with certain problems. (See also *Stereotypes*.)

Setting p. 10 The *setting* of a story includes the place, the time, and certain natural events or conditions, such as the weather.

Simile p. 135 A *simile* is a *figure of speech* in which two things are compared directly, using the words *like, as,* or *than*. "Gentle as a lamb" is an example of a simile. (See also *Metaphor*.)

Stereotypes p. 10 In literature, *stereotypes* (sometimes called *flat characters*) are one-dimensional characters the reader has met before in literature. The thoughts and actions of stereotypes are easily predictable. The kind old grandmother and the football hero who always manages the last-minute touchdown are examples of stereotypes. (See also *Rounded Characters*.)

Supporting Details p. 103 The *supporting details* in a paragraph are the examples or reasons a writer uses to develop the main idea. (See also *Main Idea*.)

Symbols p. 177 A *symbol* is something that stands for something else. Although a symbol is usually something one can see and touch, what it most often stands for is an idea, a feeling, or a quality. For example, a heart is often considered a symbol of love or affection.

Theme p. 11 A *theme* is the meaning or message of a literary selection. Some stories and poems have more than one theme, and others have a theme of only minor importance.

Tragicomedy p. 281 A *tragicomedy* is a work of literature that contains elements of both tragedy and comedy. *Cyrano de Bergerac* is an example of tragicomedy.

Index of Authors and Titles

Page numbers in **bold-faced** type indicate profiles (short biographies).

ACKNOWLEDGMENTS

We thank the following authors, agents, and publishers for their permission to reprint copyrighted material:

T. K. ATHERTON, SATURDAY REVIEW—for cartoon by T. K. Atherton. Reprinted from *Saturday Review*. Copyright © 1978 by T. K. Atherton, Saturday Review.

CLAUS BREMER—for "Rendering the Legible Illegible" as in *Anthology of Concrete Poetry*, Emmett Williams, ed., 1967 by Something Else Press.

CLARENCE BROWN, SATURDAY REVIEW—for two cartoons by Clarence Brown. Reprinted from *Saturday Review*. Copyright © 1978 by Clarence Brown, Saturday Review.

CROWN PUBLISHERS, INC.—for "Three Letters . . . and a Footnote" by Horacio Quiroga, adapted from *A World of Great Short Stories*, edited by Hiram Haydn and John Coumos. Copyright 1947, 1975 by Crown Publishers, Inc.

REINHARD DOHL—for "Apfel" as in *Anthology of Concrete Poetry*, Emmett Williams, ed., 1967 by Something Else Press.

DODD, MEAD & COMPANY, INC.—for "My Financial Career." Reprinted by permission of Dodd, Mead & Company, Inc. from "Laugh With Leacock" by Stephen Leacock. Copyright 1930 by Dodd, Mead & Company, Inc. Copyright renewed by George Leacock.

DOUBLEDAY & COMPANY, INC.—for "After Twenty Years" from *The Four Million* in *The Complete Works of O. Henry*. Copyright © 1953 by Doubleday & Company, Inc.—for permission to adapt excerpts from *Anne Frank: The Diary of a Young Girl* by Anne Frank. Copyright 1952 by Otto H. Frank. (Permission for Canadian rights granted by Vallentine, Mitchell & Co. Ltd., London.)

ELSEVIER-DUTTON PUBLISHING CO., INC. and J. M. DENT AND SONS, LTD., PUBLISHERS—for "August Heat" from *The Beast with Five Fingers* by W. F. Harvey. Copyright 1947 by E. P. Dutton & Co., Inc.

FARRAR, STRAUS & GIROUX, INC.—for permission to adapt "After You, My Dear Alphonse" from *The Lottery* by Shirley Jackson. Copyright 1943 by Shirley Jackson. Copyright © renewed by [Lawrence Hyman, Barry Hyman, Mrs. Joann Schnurer, and Sarah Webster]. Originally published in *The New Yorker*.

ELLIS J. FREEDMAN—for "Beware: Do Not Read This Poem" by Ishmael Reed. Copyright © 1972 by Ishmael Reed.

EUGEN GOMRINGER—for "Silencio" as in *Anthology of Concrete Poetry*, Emmett Williams, ed., 1967 by Something Else Press.

HARPER & ROW PUBLISHERS, INC.—for "Mirror" from *Crossing the Water* by Sylvia Plath. Copyright © 1963 by Ted Hughes, originally appeared in *The New Yorker*.

W. F. HARVEY and J. M. DENT & SONS LTD. PUBLISHERS—for permission to adapt "August Heat" from *The Beast with Five Fingers* by W. F. Harvey. Copyright 1947 by E. P. Dutton & Co., Inc.

HOLT, RINEHART AND WINSTON,

PUBLISHERS—for "The Golf Links Lie So Near The Mill" from *Portraits and Protests* by Sarah N. Cleghorn.

HOUGHTON MIFFLIN COMPANY—for untitled poem by Lady Horikawa from *Japanese Poetry* by Curtis Hidden Page. Copyright 1923 by Houghton Mifflin Company.

OLWYN HUGHES—for "Mirror" from *Crossing the Water* by Sylvia Plath, published by Faber and Faber. Copyright © 1971 by Ted Hughes.

INDIANA UNIVERSITY PRESS—for "Africa's Plea" by Roland Tombekai Dempster and "Where The Rainbow Ends" by Richard Rive, from Langston Hughes, ed., POEMS OF BLACK AFRICA, Indiana University Press, 1963.

THE JEWISH PUBLICATION SOCIETY OF AMERICA—for "An Old Song" by Yehoash (Solomon Bloomgarden), reprinted from *The Menorah Treasury*, edited by Leo W. Schwartz. Copyright © 1964 by The Jewish Publication Society of America. Originally published in *The Menorah Journal*, Vol. X, no. 3.

ROBERT KIRCHER, SATURDAY REVIEW—for cartoon by Robert Kircher. Reprinted from *Saturday Review*. Copyright © 1977 by Robert Kircher, Saturday Review.

ALFRED A. KNOPF, INC.—for "The Hitchhiker" from *The Wonderful Story of Henry Sugar and Six More* by Roald Dahl. Copyright 1977 by Roald Dahl.

MACMILLAN PUBLISHING CO., INC.—for permission to adapt "My Lord, The Baby" from *The Hungry Stones and Other Stories* by Rabindranath Tagore. Copyright 1916 by Macmillan Publishing Co., Inc., renewed 1944 by Rabindranath Tagore.

(Permission for world reprint rights granted by Macmillan, London and Basingstoke.)—for "Cat" from *Menagerie* by Mary Britton Miller. Copyright 1928 by The Macmillan Company, Inc.

HENRY R. MARTIN, SATURDAY REVIEW—for cartoon by Henry R. Martin. Reprinted from *Saturday Review*. Copyright © 1977 by Henry R. Martin, Saturday Review.

HAROLD MATSON COMPANY, INC.—for "The Face Is Familiar But—" from *The Many Loves of Dobie Gillis* by Max Shulman. Copyright © 1945 by Hearst Magazine, Inc., © renewed 1963.

THE NEW YORKER, INC.—for drawing by Chas. Addams. Copyright © 1940, 1960 by The New Yorker Magazine, Inc.; copyright © 1946, 1974 by The New Yorker Magazine, Inc.; copyright © 1956 by The New Yorker Magazine, Inc.—for drawing by Alain. Copyright © 1953, 1981 by The New Yorker Magazine, Inc.

OPEN COURT PUBLISHING COMPANY—for "The Shepherd-Boy and the Wolf," translated from the Greek by William Ellery Leonard from *Aesop and Hyssop*, published by Open Court Publishing Company, La Salle, Illinois.

OPTIMUM PUBLISHING INTERNATIONAL INC.—for "The Bully" from *A Bar'l of Apples* by Gregory Clark. Copyright © 1971 by Optimum Publishing International, Inc.

OXFORD UNIVERSITY PRESS—for untitled poem from *Japanese Poetry*, translated by Arthur Waley. Copyright 1919 by Oxford University Press.

PLAYS INC., PUBLISHERS—for "Sherlock Holmes and The Second Stain" adapted by Olive J. Morley from the short story by A. Conan Doyle. Reprinted from *Plays, the Drama Magazine for Young People.* Copyright © 1971 by Plays, Inc. This play is for reading purposes only. For permission to produce the play, write Plays, Inc., 8 Arlington Street, Boston, MA 02116.

PETER PAUPER PRESS—for six haiku by Basho and Issa from: *Japanese Haiku,* copyright © 1955, 1956 by Peter Pauper Press; *The Four Seasons,* copyright © 1958 by Peter Pauper Press; *Cherry Blossoms,* copyright © 1960 by Peter Pauper Press.

S. RAJARATNAM—for permission to adapt "The Tiger" by S. Rajaratnam.

RANDOM HOUSE, INC./ALFRED A. KNOPF, INC.—for "Alone" from *Oh Pray My Wings Are Gonna Fit Me Well,* by Maya Angelou. Copyright 1975 by Maya Angelou.—for "If there is right in the soul. . . ." From *Tales from Old China,* by Isabelle C. Chang. Copyright © 1969 by Isabelle C. Chang. Reprinted by permission of Random House, Inc.

RUSSELL & VOLKENING, INC.—for "Go Free or Die" [Globe title] from *Harriet Tubman: Conductor of the Underground Railway* by Ann Petry, published by Thomas Y. Crowell Company. Copyright © 1955 by Ann Petry.

SCHOLASTIC, INC.—for "How I Write Minimysteries" by Julia R. Piggin. From *Voice.* Copyright © 1974 by Scholastic Inc. Reprinted by permission of Scholastic Inc.

CHARLES E. TUTTLE COMPANY, INC.—for "Bear" by Shigeji Tsuboi. From *Anthology of Modern Japanese Poetry,* translated and compiled by Edith Marcombe Shiffert and Yūki Sawa. Copyright in Japan 1972 by Charles E. Tuttle Co., Inc. of Rutland, Vermont and Tokyo, Japan. Reprinted by permission of the publisher.

VIKING PENGUIN INC.—for "You Can't Take It With You" by Eva-Lis Wuorio. From *Escape If You Can,* by Eva-Lis Wuorio. Copyright © Eva-Lis Wuorio, 1977. Reprinted by permission of Viking Penguin, Inc.

HALLIE BURNETT (ZEISEL)—for "Polar Night" by Norah Burke, from *Story.* Copyright © 1953 by Whit and Hallie Burnett.

DR. ADAM ZWEIG and THE ESTATE OF ARNOLD ZWEIG—for permission to adapt "Kong at the Seaside" from *Playthings of Time* by Arnold Zweig. Copyright © 1935, 1962 by The Viking Press, Inc.

Every effort has been made to locate Miloš Macourek to obtain permission to reprint his poem "The Punching Clock", and Leon Hugo to obtain permission to reprint his story "My Father and the Hippopotamus." If either the authors or heirs are located subsequent to publication, they are hereby entitled to due compensation.

The following selections are in the public domain. Some have been slightly adapted for the modern reader by Globe Book Company. "Abu the Wag," from *The Arabian Nights;* "The Athenian Oath"; Giovanni Boccaccio, "The Falcon"; Elizabeth Barrett Browning, "How Do I Love Thee?"; Lewis Carroll, "Jabberwocky"; Anton Chekhov, "The Bet"; Samuel Taylor Coleridge, "The Rime of the Ancient Mariner"; Ellen T. Fowler, "Laugh, and the world laughs with you . . . " Guy de Maupassant, "The Necklace"; Thomas Hardy, "The Man He Killed"; Nathaniel Hawthorne, "Dr. Heidegger's Experiment"; Hierocles, "Jests"; Oliver Wendell Holmes, "The Height of the Ridiculous"; W. W. Jacobs, "The Monkey's Paw"; Alfred Noyes, "The Highwayman"; Arthur O'Shaughnessy, "We are the music makers ... "; Isaac Loeb Peretz, "If Not Still Higher"; Po Chü-i, untitled poem; Edgar Allan Poe, "The Pit and the Pendulum"; Edmond Rostand, "Cyrano de Bergerac"; John Godfrey Saxe, "The Blind Men and the Elephant"; Algernon Charles Swinburne, "The Garden of Proserpine"; the *Talmud;* Leo Tolstoy, "Where Love Is, There God Is Also"; Mark Twain, "The History of a Campaign That Failed"; Ella Wheeler Wilcox, untitled poem.

Photo Acknowledgments

Photo Researchers/Will McIntyre Photography: xii; The Bettmann Archive: 2 (left); Culver Pictures, Inc.: 2 (right); The National Tourist Office of Spain: 70; Library of Congress: 82 (left); The Bettmann Archive: 82 (right); H. Armstrong Roberts: 142; The Bettmann Archive: 170; Brown Brothers: 180 (left); Historical Pictures Service, Inc., Chicago: 180 (right); The Bettmann Archive: 191; Comstock: 212; The Bettmann Archive: 242 (left); Wide World Photos: 242 (right); © Four By Five Inc.: 262; Black Star/Joe Rodriguez: 342; Culver Pictures, Inc.: 367; Springer/The Bettmann Archive: 375. **Cover:** The Bettmann Archive (Elizabeth Barrett Browning, Sir Arthur Conan Doyle, Anne Frank, Nathaniel Hawthorne, Rabindranath Tagore, Leo Tolstoy); Culver Pictures, Inc.: (Samuel Taylor Coleridge); Harper & Row/Mollie McKenna (Sylvia Plath); Heinemann Educational Books, London/ Trygve Andersen (Richard Rive).

Illustrators

Linda Benson: 265; Ted Burwell: 32, 33, 34, 224, 358, 361; Peter Catalanotto: 21, 27; Jeff Fischer: 67, 84, 87; Joseph Forté: 43, 49, 52, 57; Mary Lopez: 97, 101; Glee LoScalzo: 243, 248; Eileen McKeating: 14, 16, 119, 145; Neal McPheeters: 122, 125, 129, 131, 133; Linda Miyamoto: 110, 115; Charles Molina: 154, 157, 164, 172, 370; Steve Moore: 272, 273; Karen Pritchett: 234, 238; Bob Sabin: 255; Don Schlegel: 5, 8, 76, 77, 183, 185, 187, 215; Robert Shore: 282, 289, 297, 299, 306, 316, 320; Gerald Smith: 192, 351, 353; Marvin Stein: 31; Marsha Tidy: 41, 178; Kimanne Uhler: 344; Lynda West: 328, 330, 334.

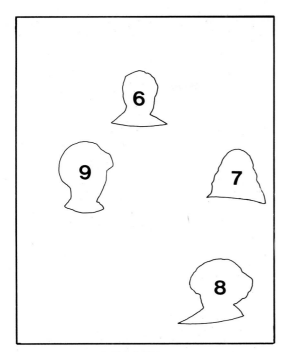

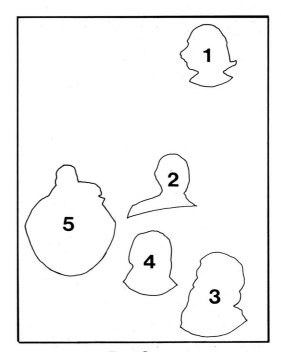

Back Cover   Front Cover

Authors on the Cover:

1. Anne Frank   6. Richard Rive
2. Sir Arthur Conan Doyle   7. Elizabeth Barrett Browning
3. Rabindranath Tagore   8. Nathaniel Hawthorne
4. Samuel Taylor Coleridge   9. Sylvia Plath
5. Leo Tolstoy